Underwater Minerals

OCEAN SCIENCE, RESOURCES AND TECHNOLOGY
An International Series

EDITORS

H. HERMAN
State University of
New York at Stony Brook,
New York, USA

D. S. CRONAN
Imperial College of
Science and Technology,
London, England

D. S. Cronan, Underwater Minerals, 1980

Underwater Minerals

D. S. Cronan

*Applied Geochemistry Research Group,
Department of Geology, Imperial College
of Science and Technology, London, England*

1980

ACADEMIC PRESS

A Subsidiary of Harcourt Brace Jovanovich, Publishers

London · New York · Toronto · Sydney · San Francisco

ACADEMIC PRESS INC. (LONDON) LTD
24–28 Oval Road,
London NW1

U.S. Edition published by
ACADEMIC PRESS INC.
111 Fifth Avenue,
New York, New York 10003

British Library Cataloguing in Publication Data
Cronan, David S
 Underwater minerals.
 1. Marine mineral resources
 2. Mineral resources in submerged lands
 I. Title
 553'.09162   TN264   80–49966
 ISBN 0–12–197480–4

Filmset by Northumberland Press Ltd,
Gateshead, Tyne and Wear
Printed in Great Britain by
Fletcher and Son Ltd, Norwich

Preface

During the past few years there has been an increasing interest, academic, governmental and commercial, in underwater mineral deposits. This has been accompanied by an explosion of literature on the subject, scattered in a large number of diverse journals, theses and reports. However, the subject as a whole has not been treated in one place since John Mero's book fifteen years ago. A few books have appeared since then, mostly compilations of papers dealing with one or other aspect of the subject, the largest single group being exploitation orientated. The present book attempts to satisfy the need for an up-to-date textbook and pull together the diverse literature on the subject. It has been written to be of interest to a wide audience including undergraduate and postgraduate students, civil servants concerned with marine affairs, and people generally interested in the marine environment. The subject matter has been developed from first principles, and no prior knowledge of underwater minerals has been assumed. Throughout, the emphasis is on synthesizing available knowledge, but where desirable the conventions of the authors referred to have been kept.

In structuring the book, an attempt has been made to separate the subject material into chapters in such a way that each chapter can stand on its own, and serve as a foundation to which future knowledge can be welded as it becomes available. However, a certain amount of cross-referencing has been inevitable. Chapter 1 introduces the subject by placing underwater minerals in their geological framework and describing some of the influences on them. Chapters 2 to 7 deal with the nature, distribution and origin of the deposits themselves. Chapter 8 is an attempt to view marine minerals as a whole in terms of recent ideas on plate tectonics and ocean evolution, and is a development of a lecture I gave at a recent Inter-University Geological Congress at Cambridge University. Chapter 9 is a review of exploration methods for underwater minerals, much of it based on personal experience gained during sixteen years of going to sea largely to further the aims of marine mineral programmes in the Applied Geochemistry Research Group at Imperial College. Finally, Chapter 10 is an attempt to review, in an elementary

manner, some of the factors of consequence in the exploitation of underwater minerals. This area has probably undergone the most extensive
development of any in the field during the past few years, and it is the one
changing most rapidly. It is hoped that Chapter 10 will serve as a basic
introduction to the many more advanced texts on the exploitation of underwater minerals.

This preface would not be complete without thanking all those people
who have influenced my thoughts and helped in the preparation of the book.
My thanks go to Sir Kingsley Dunham and Dr D. M. Hirst of the University
of Durham who first introduced me to the subjects of economic geology
and marine geochemistry which I have attempted to marry in this book;
to Professor J. S. Webb of Imperial College whose foresight in the early
1960s enabled the subject of underwater minerals to be taken up at Imperial
College at a time when the deposits were regarded by most people simply
as interesting curiosities; to Dr J. S. Tooms with whom I took my first steps
in research on underwater minerals sixteen years ago; and, more recently,
to all my friends, colleagues and students both in the Applied Geochemistry
Research Group at Imperial College, and elsewhere, who have influenced
my thinking on the subject. I would also like to thank the Natural Environment Research Council who financed much of the original work referred
to in this book. More specifically in regard to the preparation of the book,
I would like to thank the following people for reviews: Chapters 2 and 10,
Mr Alan Archer of the Institute of Geological Sciences, London; Chapter
3, Dr Roy Chester and Ms Joan Petzing of Oceanography Department,
Liverpool University; Chapter 4, Dr Frank Manheim of the U.S.G.S., Woods
Hole Oceanographic Institute, and Dr John McArthur of the Geology
Department, University College, London; Chapter 5, Dr Tony Moorby of
Imperial College; Chapter 6, Ms Sarah Shearme of the A.G.R.G. Imperial
College; Chapter 7, Professor Joe Cann of the Geology Department,
University of Newcastle upon Tyne; part of Chapter 9, Dr Tim Francis of
the Institute of Oceanographic Sciences, Wormley. Their comments were
most helpful. In a subject which is moving so fast, I benefited greatly from
preprints by various workers, thus enabling me to incorporate their most
recent work into the book. These are too numerous to mention them all,
but special thanks go to Mr Alan Archer for providing me with several
manuscripts long in advance of their publication, Dr Miriam Kastner for
a copy of Kastner and Stonecipher (1978) two years in advance of publication, Dr Frank Manheim for an advance copy of Manheim et al. (1978),
Dr Steve Calvert for an advance copy of Calvert (1978), Dr Geoff Glasby
for an unceasing flow of manuscripts over the years, Dr Claude Lalou
for advance copies of several papers, and to the contributors to the
International Monograph on the Geology and Geochemistry of Manganese,

on the editorial board of which I served, whose papers I had the privilege of reading in advance of their publication. My thanks also go to those of my ex-postgraduate students in the Applied Geochemistry Research Group whose unpublished Ph.D theses I have referred to in the text. Naturally, thanks also go to all those authors and publishers acknowledged in the text, who have given me permission to reproduce diagrams, and to the Academic Press, especially Arthur Bourne, for their patience and help. Finally, greatest thanks go to my wife, the dedicatee of this book, who helped in so many different ways to bring the work to fruition.

April, 1980   D. S. CRONAN
London

Contents

3
Miscellaneous Authigenic Minerals

4
Phosphorites

7
Sub-surface Deposits

8
Interrelation between Sub-sea Mineral Deposits and their Relationship to Ocean Evolution

9
Exploration Methods

To my wife, Jill Ann, for her understanding, encouragement and help in the preparation of this book

1

General Introduction

Mankind is using up the Earth's natural resources at an ever increasing rate. This is particularly true of non-renewable resources such as minerals upon which much of our industry and commerce depends. Many mineral deposits on land have been worked out or are nearing exhaustion, and alternative deposits of the metals that they contain will have to be found in the future.

Within the past twenty years, more and more attention has been paid to the possibility of retrieval of minerals from the sea. Of course, this is not a new idea. Salt has been derived from the ocean since ancient times and more recently bromine and magnesium have been extracted from sea water in commercial quantities. Placer minerals such as cassiterite have been mined from near-shore sediments in various parts of the world. In addition coal and oil deposits sometimes extend from land under the sea in continental shelf areas, or occur in isolated basins, and are being extracted in great quantities at the present time. Nevertheless, it is only recently that major surface marine mineral deposits such as manganese nodules and metalliferous sediments have received serious consideration as future ore deposits. As time goes on it is inevitable that these and other mineral deposits will be mined in increasing quantities from under the sea.

This book seeks to review the nature, occurrence, origin and exploitability of marine mineral deposits and, where appropriate, related deposits in lakes and rivers. The minerals to be considered can be divided into six groups: (a) minerals occurring in the bedrock below the sea floor; (b) aggregates and placer minerals on the sea floor, which are detrital deposits found generally in near-shore areas and which usually have been supplied from the adjacent land mass; (c) phosphorites, which are chemical precipitates containing phosphates mixed with other phases and which also generally occur on the sea floor in relatively shallow environments; (d) ferromanganese oxide deposits, which are chemical precipitates of iron and manganese oxides in the form of nodules and encrustations, sometimes containing high concentrations of metals such as nickel, copper and cobalt, and which form predominantly on the deep-sea floor but which also occur in some lakes; (e) metalliferous sediments, which are chemical precipitates of a variety of elements formed as a result of volcanic activity in underwater volcanic areas; and (f) minor authigenic minerals. Interrelationships between the deposits will also be considered.

1.1 Physiographic Regions of the Sea Floor and their Mineral Potential

As a result of the great advances which have been made in underwater geology and geophysics in the last few decades, we now have a fairly good knowledge of the major physiographic features of the sea floor (Fig. 1). Furthermore, theories of sea floor spreading and plate tectonics as propounded by various authors (e.g. Vine and Matthews, 1963; Vine and Hess, 1970) have provided a key to our understanding of the origin of these features.

Continents are usually surrounded by a continental shelf of variable width which is the submerged portion of the continental land mass. Its depth rarely exceeds 200 m and on it can occur aggregates, placer minerals and phosphorites. Under it can occur the same mineral deposits that are found on land. Seawards of the continental shelf occurs the continental slope at the foot of which is the continental rise which represents the margin of the continental land mass. Somewhere near the foot of the continental slope occurs the transition between continental crust and oceanic crust; the former is relatively light and the latter is denser and composed of basaltic rocks. No mineral deposits of consequence have been found on the continental slope but it is thought to have great potential for oil and natural gas.

Seawards of the continental slope and rise is the deep-sea floor. This represents the ocean basin proper and has a rather variable physiography. Seawards of the continental slope and rise at seismically inactive continental margins flat abyssal plains often occur floored by continentally derived sediments which, as for example in the Atlantic, can extend out almost to the middle of the ocean basin. Few, if any, mineral deposits of consequence occur on such abyssal plains. At seismically active continental margins there is a trench, down which, on the basis of plate tectonic theory, oceanic crust is thought to be consumed. To date trenches have not been found to contain significant mineral deposits. Much of the deep-sea floor seawards of abyssal plains and trenches is thinly covered with sediment above the oceanic crust and is composed of a rolling abyssal hill topography broken by isolated seamounts or seamount ranges. Some of these seamounts are sites of phosphorite

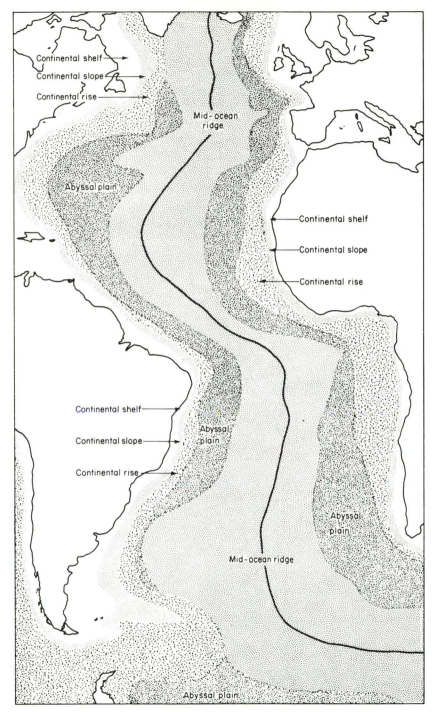

Fig. 1. Physiographic features of the sea floor (from Open University Oceanography Course).

deposition and most are encrusted with low grade ferromanganese oxide deposits, while the deep-sea floor itself is the major site of manganese nodule formation.

Towards the centres of the ocean basins there is usually, but not always, a volcanically active mid-ocean ridge. This is often the site of metalliferous sediment formation. Mid-ocean ridges are frequently cut by transform faults which expose the oceanic crust to considerable depth in fracture zones. These may be the most favourable sites for metalliferous sediment formation on the deep ocean floor. However, submarine volcanic activity is not restricted to mid-ocean ridges. Chains of volcanic islands occur in various parts of the ocean, and island arcs behind oceanic trenches can be sites of intense submarine volcanic activity. Metalliferous sediments have been reported in the latter environment too.

The theory of plate tectonics enunciated in the late 1960s provides a key to our understanding of ocean basin physiography. Under this hypothesis, in its simplest form, the ocean floor is split apart at mid-ocean ridges and new oceanic crust in the form of basaltic rock is being created by the upwelling of lava. This new crust moves away from these spreading centres, and as it does so it cools, becomes denser and therefore subsides. This would help to explain the increasing depth of the ocean floor with increasing age of the oceanic crust and distance from the spreading centre. Eventually the oceanic crust disappears down a trench to be consumed. The whole area of the sea floor between the mid-ocean ridge and the trench is called a plate, and the Earth's surface is envisaged as consisting of several plates in motion. The continents float on the oceanic crust and take little part either in the generation of new sea floor at constructive plate boundaries, i.e. mid-ocean ridges, or its consumption at destructive plate boundaries, i.e. ocean trenches. The relationships of undersea mineral deposits to plate tectonics and ocean evolution are described in Chapter 8.

1.2 Lakes

Lake basins can be very variable in their morphology. Many lakes are shallow while others have a shallow peripheral area surrounding a deeper basin. Most mineral deposits in lakes occur in the peripheral areas. Placers and aggregates are found there because such minerals usually travel only short distances after discharge into the lake, and processes operating in shallow areas can lead to their concentration. Ferromanganese oxides also occur in the peripheral areas of lakes, as it is there that the oxidizing conditions required for manganese oxide precipitation occur. The centres of lake basins are sometimes stagnant and reducing, and under these conditions ferromanganese oxide precipitation will not take place. Such areas are generally floored with fine-grained organic rich sediments and contain no mineral deposits of consequence.

1.3   Sources of Materials to the Oceans

Deposits accumulating on the ocean floor receive contributions from various sources which include the continents, submarine volcanic activity, outer space and biological activity. Some minerals can be supplied from just one of these sources, placer minerals being solely derived from runoff from the continents, for example, and some metalliferous sediments being wholly or almost wholly formed as a result of submarine volcanic activity. Other mineral deposits receive their constituents from more than one source, marine manganese nodules for example receiving metals from the continents via sea water and sometimes organisms, and from submarine volcanic activity. Sources of elements to individual types of mineral deposits will be considered in detail in the chapters dealing with those deposits, but general supply paths to the oceans will be considered here.

Continental sources of elements to the oceans are of considerable importance. Materials enter the sea either as detrital, colloidal or solution phases.

Most detrital phases entering the marine environment precipitate in ocean margin areas, leaving only very fine-grained material to remain longer in suspension and to precipitate elsewhere. However, there are variations on this general pattern. Some near-shore areas receive only fine-grained detrital sediments, or no sediment at all, either as a result of limited continental runoff or sediment entrapment near the shore. Likewise, relatively coarse detrital sediments can be carried far out into the deep ocean basins by turbidity currents, as for example in the north-eastern Atlantic. As mentioned, placer minerals together with aggregates such as sand and gravel are almost wholly detrital in origin.

Continentally-derived materials entering the oceans in colloidal or solution phases rapidly become indistinguishable from such phases entering from other sources. They contribute to the total mass of materials in sea water and thus to phases precipitated from sea water. Such phases are to be found in manganese nodules, phosphorites and probably also in some metalliferous sediments.

Volcanic sources of elements to the oceans are also of importance. Volcanism can supply elements to the sea in at least three ways: in the form of solid volcanic detritus such as volcanic glass and pyroclastics; in the form of hydrothermal solutions; or by the underwater alteration of volcanic rocks (halmyrolysis). The relative importance of these three mechanisms in contributing to marine mineral deposits differs considerably. Elements supplied in volcanic detritus are probably of minimal importance in this regard and may even serve to dilute other phases containing the elements in higher concentrations, as do volcanic nuclei in manganese nodules for example. A hydrothermal supply of metals is important in the formation of metalliferous sediments in submarine volcanic areas but its role in contributing elements to sea water at large is less clear. On oceanic mixing, hydrothermally derived elements in sea water will be indistinguishable from those derived from the continents and thus their importance is difficult to evaluate. The slow alteration of volcanic rocks on the sea floor is probably quantitatively the most important volcanic supply of elements to sea water and sediments, and thence to marine mineral deposits. Its role in the formation of some manganese nodules may be particularly important, as is discussed in Chapter 5.

Biological supply of constituents to the sea floor is mainly brought about by the sinking from the surface waters of the bodies of dead organisms, or of the products of their life processes such as excrement (faeces). When alive, such organisms extract elements from sea water which they utilize in their growth processes, and thus their constituents, like others in sea water, are probably ultimately derived from more than one source. Therefore, biological supply of elements cannot be considered to be a primary source of elements to the sea floor, but a mechanism whereby elements in sea water are concentrated prior to their removal from the oceans.

Cosmic sources of elements to the oceans are of relatively minor importance. Cosmic spherules are found in small quantities in slowly accumulating deep-sea sediments and manganese nodules but do not contribute appreciably to any underwater mineral deposits.

1.4   Sediment Distribution on the Ocean Floor

The nature of sediments on the ocean floor (Fig. 2) reflects both their differing sources, as outlined in the previous section, and the processes influencing their redistribution and removal.

The distribution of detrital sediments on the sea floor is largely a function of supply. The continental margins are generally floored by detrital sediments derived from the adjacent land masses, although relict sediments, biogenic debris and authigenic minerals, are common in some continental shelf areas where detrital input is limited for some reason or other. Detrital sediments also cover much of the continental slope and, as mentioned, in some cases extend seawards of it for considerable distances in areas of turbidite deposition. The deep ocean floor is largely covered with the fine-grained products of continental runoff such as clay minerals, but as will be described, biogenic

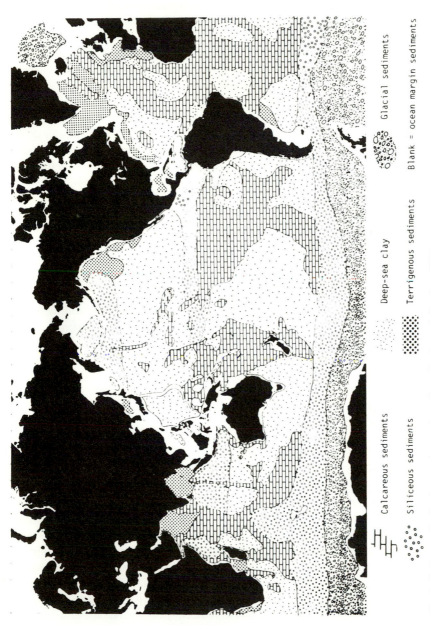

Calcareous sediments

Siliceous sediments

Deep-sea clay

Terrigenous sediments

Glacial sediments

Blank = ocean margin sediments

Fig. 2. Sediment distribution on the sea floor (from Davies and Gorsline, 1976).

debris, authigenic minerals, and the products of *in situ* alteration of the basaltic rocks of the ocean crust are also of importance. Most often, mixtures
of these constituents are present in deep-sea sediments.

The distribution of biogenic constituents is largely a function of biological
activity in the surface waters of the oceans and the depth of the ocean floor
itself. High biological productivity can occur in parts of the equatorial and
polar regions and in certain marginal areas of the oceans. This results in
a flux of organisms and their life products sinking to the sea floor which
can accumulate as biogenic remains. However, the solubility of some biogenic
material changes with depth, such that it may dissolve without reaching the
sea floor or dissolve on the sea floor itself. This phenomenon is particularly
important in controlling the distribution of calcium carbonate rich sediments
on the ocean floor because calcium carbonate increases in solubility with
depth and dissolves either on or before reaching the sea floor in the deepest
parts of the oceans. The depth at which a significant increase in the rate
of dissolution of calcium carbonate occurs is known as the lysocline, and
the depth below which all calcium carbonate has dissolved is known as the
calcium carbonate compensation depth (CCD). The depth of the lysocline
and the CCD vary in different parts of the oceans, and particularly from
ocean to ocean, depending on a number of factors (see Berger, 1976, for
a review), but the former generally occurs around 3500–4000 m and the latter
somewhat deeper. Thus, calcium carbonate is an important sediment type
on the deep-sea floor above about 4000 m, but is absent from many areas
below about 4500–5000 m. Biogenic silica from radiolarians and diatoms
does not undergo the same dissolution effect with depth as calcium carbonate,
and thus siliceous ooze is often a principal sediment type on the sea floor
underlying areas of high productivity but which are too deep to allow the
accumulation of calcium carbonate.

The distribution of the remaining marine sediments is a function of a variety
of factors. The absolute abundance of non-detrital and non-biogenic
sediments such as those composed chiefly of authigenic minerals (zeolites,
manganese micronodules, etc.) in the oceans is largely a function of depth
and distance from the continents. Authigenic minerals are precipitated very
slowly from solution in sea water and thus any other material precipitated
serves to dilute them. They are most abundant therefore in those parts of
the ocean which are below the CCD, away from areas of high productivity
and where sedimentation of continentally derived material is minimal. Much
of the South Pacific fulfils these criteria. The distribution of sediments formed
by halmyrolysis is restricted to those areas of extensive outcrop of submarine
volcanic rock, where sedimentation rates of other materials are low. Again,
parts of the South Pacific fulfil these criteria but such sediments also occur
in other submarine volcanic areas.

1.5 Metal Concentration Processes in the Aqueous Environment

Elements introduced into oceans and lakes are usually present initially in low concentrations. Only rarely, for example in some hydrothermal solutions, are elements introduced into the aqueous environment in concentrations sufficient to form a mineral deposit of potential ore grade directly on precipitation. Some selective concentration process is therefore required to form most other underwater mineral deposits. This can be either the selective sorting and winnowing of detrital particulates, selective leaching, the extraction and concentration of elements from solution, or diagenetic processes.

1.5.1 Selective sorting

Selective sorting by mechanical action is the principal mode of enrichment of minerals in detrital mineral deposits such as placers and aggregates introduced into the aqueous environment in a solid state. However, it can also serve to concentrate minerals precipitated from solution such as phosphorites. The minerals are selectively concentrated by the sifting and winnowing away of associated fine-grained constituents or by gravity settling in the case of large particles or minerals of high specific gravity. In this way, minerals which were initially widely dispersed throughout the sediment can become concentrated into ore grade deposits.

Mechanical sorting of detrital minerals is most effective on beaches as a result of surf action and in the near-shore zone where wave action is important. As water depth increases, the energy level of the depositional environment generally decreases as a result of decreased wave action, and the opportunity for selective concentration of minerals diminishes. Naturally, however, variations in the configuration of the continental shelf and sources of energy such as tidal currents can modify this general trend. Furthermore, owing to changes in sea level during the recent geological past as a result of successive glaciations, much of the present day continental shelf has been subjected to marine transgressions and regressions, coastlines have varied, and thus conditions conducive to placer deposition could have occurred almost anywhere on continental shelves in the past. Relict placers and aggregates are therefore often found under conditions which would not lead to their formation at the present day.

1.5.2 Selective leaching

The leaching of some elements from rocks or sediments to form a residue enriched in certain other elements is a common process on land. Laterites represent a good example of an ore deposit formed by such a process. Its importance in subaqueous environments is much more limited. It can be of importance in selectively removing the volatiles associated with phosphorite formation, thus enriching the residues in P_2O_5. It may also be of importance in the slow dissolution of the volcanic nuclei of manganese nodules, allowing them to be replaced by manganese oxide minerals and thus upgrading the metal content of the deposits as a whole.

1.5.3 Concentration from aqueous solution

The bulk of elements in underwater minerals deposits, other than those forming detrital minerals such as placers and aggregates have passed through an aqueous solution phase at some stage in their history. Other than in submarine hydrothermal solutions, their abundances in such solutions are very low and thus considerable concentration is required for them to form subaqueous mineral deposits.

Adsorption is one of the principal mechanisms by which elements are selectively extracted from solution into authigenic mineral deposits in both lakes and the oceans. Possibly the most important illustration of the importance of adsorption in the formation of underwater mineral deposits of potential economic value is the uptake of nickel, copper and cobalt on manganese nodules, although adsorption is not solely responsible for the high concentrations of these elements found in some nodules (see Chapter 5). The adsorption of metals from sea water by some metalliferous sediments may also be of importance in enhancing their concentration in the deposits, as discussed in Chapter 6. Manganese and iron oxides are particularly good scavengers of metals from both fresh water and sea water, while phosphorites and some silicate minerals can also be of importance in this regard.

As mentioned, biological concentration is another important process by which elements are selectively extracted from solution prior to their incorporation into underwater mineral deposits. Aquatic organisms have the capacity to selectively concentrate many elements in their body tissues to several orders of magnitude over their normal concentrations in solution (Vinogradov, 1953). Such concentration normally takes place in the upper waters of lakes and the oceans by plankton. The organisms sink after death and undergo partial or complete dissolution resulting in the liberation of the elements that they contain into the water column or into the interstitial waters of the underlying sediments. When the latter occurs, high concentrations of elements can build up in solution which can lead to the precipitation of new mineral phases and the enhanced uptake of metals on to mineral phases already present in the sediments. Such processes are important in the formation of both phosphorites and manganese nodules as will be described later.

1.5.4 Diagenesis

Diagenesis is the name given to those processes by which sediments and mineral deposits undergo chemical and physical changes after deposition. It can lead to considerable increases in the concentration of certain elements in minerals and thus is of considerable importance in the formation of some underwater mineral deposits. For example, the diagenetic remobilization of elements in near surface sediments in certain areas is important in enriching those elements in manganese nodules (Chapter 5). The post-depositional increase in the P_2O_5 content of phosphorites is another example of diagenetic enrichment (Chapter 4). However, diagenetic reactions can also serve to degrade some mineral deposits. On burial in near-shore areas underlain by reducing sediments, for example, manganese nodules dissolve. Manganese can then migrate back to the surface to become more concentrated than before, but other elements such as nickel, copper and iron remain behind in the sediment as sulphide phases or organic complexes and are thus lost to the nodules (Chapter 5).

Although in many instances diagenetic enrichment of elements in underwater mineral deposits takes place during and immediately after their deposition, later diagenetic modification to the deposits can also occur. For example, the post-depositional recrystallization and reorganization of manganese nodule interiors may lead to the formation of layers containing considerably higher concentrations of valuable metals than in the nodules as a whole. Similarly, as mentioned, the progressive dissolution and replacement of nodule nuclei by ferromanganese oxides can result in an upgrading of the deposits. Compaction and recrystallization of metalliferous sediments on burial can lead to the expulsion of interstitial dissolved materials, and increase in the grade of the deposits as a consequence. Likewise post-depositional alteration of phosphorites can lead to elimination of volatiles and a concomitant increase in the grade of the deposits.

1.5.5 Post-diagenetic concentration processes

After the formation of underwater mineral deposits, further concentration processes can still take place. Deposits on continental shelves, for example, have been subject to transgression and regression of the sea during glacial periods and in some cases uplift and erosion also. Such processes can lead to a physical redistribution of mineral deposits and occasionally in their further mechanical concentration. Phosphorites and placers are good examples of minerals that have sometimes undergone such processes. Furthermore, after an uplift and erosion cycle the re-establishment of chemical conditions suitable for further deposition of authigenic minerals may lead to the upgrading of an existing mineral deposit rather than the formation of a new one. Re-phosphatization of existing phosphorites is an example of this process, and appears to have taken place in the Cretaceous and Tertiary phosphorites off north-west Africa. Similarly, metal rich hydrothermal solutions ascending through sediments previously deposited by hydrothermal activity can deposit a proportion of their metals thereby enhancing the concentration of such metals in the deposits as a whole. Examples of this have been found in the Atlantis II Deep of the Red Sea.

2

Placers and Aggregates

Placers and aggregates are detrital minerals which have been transported to their sites of deposition in a particulate form. Placers are metallic minerals, while aggregates include sands and gravels consisting principally of quartz but which also contain other minerals, polymineralic rock fragments and shells.

2.1 Placers

Placers are mineral deposits that have been formed by the mechanical concentration of detrital mineral particles in subaqueous environments, and can occur in rivers, lakes and on the sea floor. They usually originate from primary igneous or vein minerals which have been liberated on breakdown of their parent rock. Most placers are of high specific gravity and are resistant to chemical breakdown, otherwise they would not have survived the erosional, transportational and depositional processes that took place prior to their concentration.

Important examples of placer minerals include elements in their native state such as gold, platinum and diamond, and resistant minerals such as cassiterite, ilmenite, rutile, zircon, monazite, garnet, magnetite and corundum (Dunham, 1969). Emery and Noakes (1968) have classified placer minerals into heavy heavy minerals with specific gravities of 6·8 to 21, light heavy minerals with specific gravities of 4·2 to 5·3 and gems with specific gravities from 2·9 to 4·1. Gold, platinum and cassiterite are important heavy heavy minerals; ilmenite, rutile, zircon and monazite are important light heavy minerals, and diamonds are the most important gem placer mineral. Examples of placer minerals are given in Table 1.

Most placer minerals occur within a few kilometres of their source, and

Table 1. Examples of placers, aggregates and other minerals.

Commodity	Ore mineral	Specific gravity
Non-metallic		
Silica	quartz sand	2·65
Lime	shells and shell sands	2·7
Sand and gravel	various	3·0
Topaz	topaz	3·4–3·6
Spinel	spinel	3·5–4·0
Corundum	corundum	3·9–4·1
Heavy mineral sands		
Beryllium	beryl	2·75–2·8
Titanium	rutile	4·18–4·25
Titanium	ilmenite	4·7
Chromium	chromite	4·6
Zirconium	zircon	4·68
Manganese	hausmannite	4·72–4·84
Manganese	braunite	4·72–4·83
Iron	magnetite	5·18
Thorium	monazite	5·0–5·3
Nb, Ta	columbite, tantalite	5·2–7·9
Rare-Earths	group of 15 REE oxides	
Tin	cassiterite	6·8–7·1
Mercury	cinnabar	8·10
Precious and rare		
Diamond	diamond	3·5
Copper	native metal	8·9
Silver	native metal	10·5
Gold	native metal	15–19·3
Platinum	native metal	14–19

thus marine placers are virtually confined to the near-shore zone. However, ancient placers occur on fossil submerged beaches or in drowned valleys far out on the continental shelf and on raised beaches on land. Their locations can be explained in terms of rises and falls in sea level during the glacial period and are illustrated schematically in Fig. 3. Moore (1976) has classified environments of marine placer mineral deposition into high energy and low energy types. High energy environments are those where waves and currents are very active leading to the concentration of deposits of coarse-grained noble metals and tin, chromium, titanium and tungsten bearing minerals associated with coarse sands and gravels, all from nearby source areas. Low energy environments are those of quiet depositional conditions such as protected coastal bays and estuaries, and principally contain grains of wider provenance comprising noble metals with mean sizes between 5 and 50 μm.

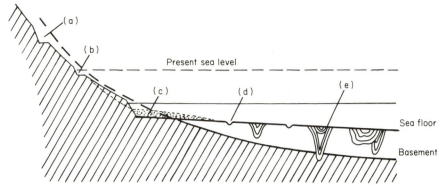

Fig. 3. Environments of possible placer mineral occurrence: (a) placers on raised beaches; (b) placers on modern beaches; (c) placers on submerged beaches; (d) placers trapped in surface depressions on the sea floor; (e) placers in buried river valleys. Modified from Aleva (1973).

2.1.1   Requirements for placer formation

The formation of placer mineral deposits requires a primary source and involves processes of erosion, transport and concentration.

(i) *Primary source.* Primary sources for placer mineral formation are usually igneous rocks. For example, cassiterite, one of the most important placer minerals, occurs in granite both in south-east Asia and south-west England, two areas where placer cassiterite occurs, and in hydrothermal veins in sedimentary country rocks, for example on Belitung Island, Indonesia (Aleva, 1973). Light heavy minerals usually comprise the resistant accessory minerals of plutonic rocks.

(ii) *Weathering.* Weathering of the placer mineral source has to take place in order to release the minerals concerned for transport to their site of deposition. Chemical weathering is most conducive to the liberation of placer minerals from source rocks, as through this process the less chemically resistant minerals in the rocks undergo selective dissolution leading to breakdown of the rock as a whole. Chemical weathering of cassiterite source rocks in Indonesia has released cassiterite without the grains undergoing any damage (Aleva, 1973).

(iii) *Transport.* Transport of placer minerals is predominantly by running water. The unstable products of chemical weathering such as clay minerals and other alteration products of primary rocks are selectively removed from the heavier and more resistant placer minerals by aqueous processes. The former are transported in suspension down streams and rivers to the sea, while the latter are often concentrated in traps within the river system itself because of their size and density. Where the source of the placer minerals is close to the sea, transport processes will normally move the placers at least to the beach zone and may transport them to the offshore environment. Fine-grained cassiterite which has been selectively washed out of old mine dumps near the coast in the tin mining area of Cornwall, for example, has been washed into the river systems and deposited in estuaries and on beaches around the Cornish peninsular (Yim, 1974). Once in the offshore environment, shallow marine sedimentological processes control placer mineral distribution. According to Emery and Noakes (1968), most economic deposits of heavy heavy placer minerals are not transported more than about 15 km from their source, owing to their high specific gravity and, in the case of cassiterite, its tendency to fracture easily.

(iv) *Concentration.* Placer minerals are usually concentrated in traps because of their high specific gravity. During transport down rivers or offshore, a decrease in the energy level of the environment can lead to their deposition. Once this has happened, a much higher energy level is required to pick them up again. In this way lighter and smaller minerals are separated from the placer minerals, which can be concentrated in sink holes, depressions on beaches, in areas of sluggish currents or in other sediment traps.

2.1.2   Environments of placer mineral deposition

The main environments of placer mineral deposition are rivers, beaches and the offshore area. Each will be considered separately.

2.1.2.1   *Rivers*

As described, concentration of placer minerals occurs locally in rivers draining suitable source areas where the energy level in the river drops sufficiently to allow the placers to settle. Stream gold, for example, has been worked in a number of areas in North America and elsewhere, as have several other alluvial placer deposits. Alluvial cassiterite in south-east Asia is an important example of this type of deposit (Aleva, 1973). Emery and Noakes (1968) have concluded that streams and rivers are the most favourable environment for heavy heavy minerals, near to primary sources of the minerals concerned.

Many offshore placer mineral deposits are alluvial in origin. As a result of a period of lowered sea level during the glacial epochs, many rivers drained out across what is now the continental shelf. Some of those draining mineralized areas, either on land or now submerged, deposited placer minerals in their valleys, just as some rivers on land do today. These have subsequently been covered over with more recent sediments and now constitute offshore buried alluvial deposits (Fig. 3). They are not marine in origin but require marine exploration techniques to find them (see Chapter 9).

2.1.2.2 *Beaches*

The formation of placer mineral deposits on beaches results essentially from the selective sorting of the beach deposits in the intertidal zone by wave and current action, with the velocity of the backwash being sufficient only to remove light minerals thus leaving the heavy minerals behind (Dunham, 1969). Beaches are the preferred location for the light heavy minerals of Emery and Noakes (1968). Light heavy minerals are only slightly denser than the quartz and feldspar with which they are initially associated, and a high energy environment of wide extent as is found on a beach is required to concentrate them into deposits rich and large enough to be worth mining.

According to Emery and Noakes (1968) modern beaches probably represent the optimum conditions for the concentration of light heavy minerals. A recent slow change of sea level of only a few metres over the past 5000 years or so has resulted in relatively stable conditions and the concentration of light heavy minerals supplied by rivers and coastal erosion over wide areas on beaches. However, seasonal and latitudinal effects can influence beach placer mineral processes. Beaches narrow during the winter months due to high waves, which results in increased concentration of gravel and heavy minerals because of the more energetic removal of the lighter minerals. High waves also tend to occur at high latitudes owing to the greater frequency and intensity of storms at sea. Emery and Noakes (1968) consider that even where provenance is favourable, light heavy minerals are likely to be absent or rare in glaciated areas at high latitudes, and in very low energy environments in low latitudes. In both situations, potential placer deposits can be diluted with large amounts of worthless material. This would indicate that mid-latitude and high energy tropical beaches are likely to be the most favourable environments for light heavy placer mineral concentration to take place.

2.1.2.3 *The offshore area*

Placer minerals can occur in several situations in the offshore area (Fig. 3) and for a variety of reasons.

As mentioned, drowned river valleys containing fossil alluvial placer minerals occur on some continental shelves (Fig. 3). For example, trial drilling for cassiterite off Cornwall in the late 1960s revealed its presence near bedrock and within the sediment column in several filled ancient river valleys.

A second occurrence of offshore placer deposits comprises those formed in the past on ancient beaches now submerged (Fig. 3). Most continental shelves contain several submerged terraces which were once beaches (Emery and Noakes, 1968; Bee, 1974) and which are usually parallel to the present coastline. However, modern beaches generally contain higher concentrations of placer minerals than submerged beaches. This is because as sea level rose the placer minerals either tended to follow the landward moving surf zone or to become dispersed seawards. In some instances glacial or marine sediments covered over the deposits. Thus, in general, submerged beaches are unlikely to be as attractive as modern beaches for placer mineral occurrence.

It is possible that small concentrations of placer minerals can occur as a result of the submarine erosion of outcrops of mineralized bedrock on the sea floor. Tooms (1969) has reported enhanced tin values near the supposed offshore extension of tin lodes in Mounts Bay, Cornwall, and W. W. S. Yim (personal communication 1974) has reported similar enrichments off north Cornwall. However, because of the probable localized extent of most outcrops of mineralized bedrock on the sea floor, and the relative inefficiency of offshore processes in eroding them, placer deposits formed by submarine erosion are likely to be limited in both extent and importance.

As mentioned, transport of placer minerals from the land and their deposition in the offshore area is a mechanism that can lead to the formation of offshore placer deposits. For example, Yim (1974) has found high tin concentrations in surface sediments off parts of north Cornwall which he attributes to selective transport of detrital cassiterite offshore. Similarly cassiterite brought into St Ives Bay, Cornwall, by the Red River has been trapped in the bay and the tin locally reaches concentrations of a few tenths of a percent (Dunham and Sheppard, 1969). Moore and Welkie (1976) have drawn attention to the occurrence of low energy placer deposits of noble metals off Alaska. These are extremely fine-grained deposits of platinum and gold which are being deposited in quiet bays and protected estuaries. Their distribution was reported as being related to circulation gyres of slackening currents within the bays (Moore, 1976).

2.1.3   World-wide distribution of placer mineral deposits

Some of the more important placer minerals are shown in Fig. 4, which illustrates the widespread occurrence and diverse nature of these deposits. They will be considered geographically.

2.1.3.1   *North America*

Placer minerals have been most commonly reported off North America in the Pacific North West, particularly Alaska, and have been reviewed by Moore and Welkie (1976). Platinum has been found to occur in the Goodnews-Chagvan area of Alaska in the form of fine-grained particles. The source is probably the nearby Red Mountain ultramafic body. Particulate

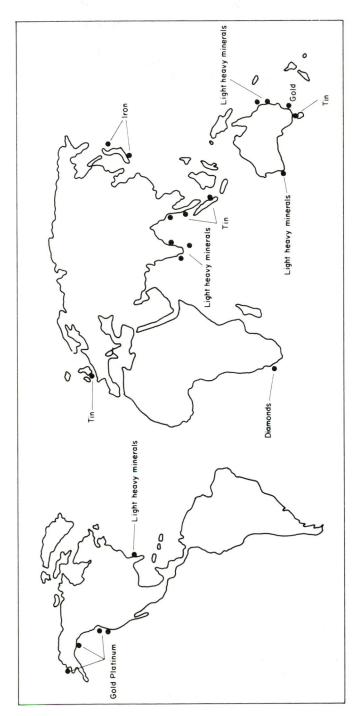

Fig. 4. Locations of certain placer mineral deposits (from Emery and Noakes, 1968).

gold has been reported in the near-shore area off the Seaward Peninsular, Alaska (Nelson and Hopkins, 1972) and off Nome. Light heavy minerals have been mined off Florida and South Carolina (Wang and McKelvey, 1976).

2.1.3.2 Africa

Diamonds in raised beach sands were first discovered along the coast of south-west Africa in 1908 (Murray, 1969) and as the diamond bearing beds extend down the coast, it was thought that they might also occur on the sea floor. In 1961 the Marine Diamond Corporation commenced offshore operations and located several areas of diamond concentration. Mining was subsequently undertaken in three of these areas but was discontinued in 1972 because the operation was uneconomic (Archer, 1973a). However, it has recently started again (Prentice, personal communication, 1979). Ilmenite and associated minerals have been reported off both west Africa and east Africa (Bell, 1977).

2.1.3.3 South-east Asia

South-east Asia contains some of the world's most important placer mineral deposits. The cassiterite deposits off Indonesia, Malaysia and Thailand have been well reviewed in the literature (Overeem, 1960; Aleva, 1973) and need not be considered in detail here. They are essentially alluvial placers that occur in stream deposits now submerged below sea level (Emery and Noakes, 1968). Placer minerals are also known to occur off India and Sri Lanka (Mero, 1965). Rutile and zircon have been produced from the beaches of Sri Lanka, and monazite and ilmenite from off Kerala, south India. Other light heavy minerals occur off both the eastern and western coasts of peninsular India (Siddique and Rajamanickam, 1979).

2.1.3.4 Australasia

Placer mineral mining has been of considerable importance in Australia for some time. Rutile, zircon and monazite sands occur on beaches in Queensland and New South Wales (Dunham, 1969). The deposits lie at present beach levels or on storm beaches up to 3 m above this (Gardner, 1955). They vary from a few cm to several dm in thickness. Around Banbury in western Australia, heavy mineral beds up to 8 m thick and dominated by ilmenite occur at present sea levels and higher (Dunham, 1969). The ilmenite is heavily altered to leucoxene. Rutile and zircon bearing sands have also been found off east Australia. Gold and tin deposits have been reported on beaches and in the offshore area of south-east Australia and Tasmania (Emery and Noakes, 1968; Jones and Davies, 1979).

Summerhayes (1967b) has extensively reviewed the occurrences of placer minerals around New Zealand. Raised beaches on the west coast of the North Island contain several million tonnes of titanomagnetite. Also of economic interest are ilmenite beach deposits near Auckland. Beaches of the west coast of South Island New Zealand contain ilmenite while smaller deposits of gold, magnetite, rutile, monazite and zircon also occur. Garnet occurs on beaches of Fiordland, cassiterite occurs on Campbell Island and also sporadically on west coast South Island beaches. Offshore iron sand concentrations have been found in 27 m water depth off North Island.

2.1.3.5 *North-west Europe*

There has been little mining of placer minerals off north-west Europe. Much of the sea floor is covered by glacial debris. The cassiterite deposits off Cornwall have already been mentioned and have been mined for a short period in the past. Proposals have been made to mine the deposits off north Cornwall using a mobile platform (Chapter 10). The deposits are both superficial and buried. Superficial deposits consist largely of fine-grained tin eroded from spoil heaps in the old mining areas on land, although erosion of coastal lodes may also have supplied some of the cassiterite. Buried deposits consist of stream tin in buried river channels up to at least 12 m below the sea floor. Light heavy mineral sands have been observed as streaks of limited extent on beaches around the United Kingdom.

2.2 Aggregates

Aggregates are deposits of sands, gravels or shells which have a use in the construction industry and for some other purposes. They occur on beaches, in rivers, lakes, and in the offshore area. Like placer deposits, underwater aggregates have been concentrated by normal hydrodynamic processes and in many cases their origin is similar to that of placers. Quantitatively they are the most important offshore mineral deposit being extracted at the present time other than oil. Examples of aggregates are given in Table 1.

2.2.1 Sand and gravel

2.2.1.1 *Composition*

Underwater gravels generally consist of fragments of stable rocks such as quartzite, flint and chert which can be transported for considerable distances without breaking down. However, less stable rock fragments also occur in some instances. For example, minor amounts of diabase occur in gravels off the eastern United States (Schlee, 1964), and a complex assemblage of chert, volcanic rocks, sandstones, and quartz diorites occur in gravels from off the state of Washington (Venkatarathnam and McManus, 1973).

Sands also generally consist of stable minerals with quartz usually being predominant. However, non-quartzose sand deposits do occur, as for example in the case of the black volcanic sand beaches of Hawaii. Mixed sand assemblages containing quartz, feldspar and other minerals occur in some areas where the source rock is a granite or some other polymineralic rock.

2.2.1.2 *Sources*

Most sand and gravel deposits in rivers and lakes are glacial in origin or derived from the erosion of rocks in the local vicinity. Likewise, on modern beaches, much of the aggregate material is derived from the erosion of local sources such as cliffs. However, some beach deposits also accrue material from offshore as a result of onshore transport of sand and gravel by wave and current action. Aggregate deposits in the offshore area can also be derived from transport of material from the adjacent land area, but many modern aggregate deposits are the reworked products of relict deposits formed during periods of lowered sea level.

Many of the offshore sand and gravel deposits in middle and high latitudes such as off north-western Europe and North America result from the reworking of glacial or fluvioglacial debris deposited during the recent ice ages. When the ice sheets, which covered large areas of the northern hemisphere, melted several thousand years ago, they deposited a complex ill-assorted assemblage of minerals and rock fragments in the form of boulder clay, or, near the glacier's margins, as outwash deposits discharged in streams of glacial melt water. The subsequent reworking of this material first in beach zones during transgressive sea level rises, and then by wave and tidal current action after submergence, has given rise to many of the commercially exploitable aggregate deposits on northern continental shelves at the present time. For example, sand deposits on the British continental shelf are thought to have been derived mainly from Pleistocene deposits. Baak (1936) has suggested that those in the North Sea were left behind by ice sheets and the River Rhine during periods of lowered sea level. Stride (1963) considers a similar origin to be probable for much of the sand in the Bristol Channel, the Irish Sea, and the north-eastern portion of the Celtic Sea, all of which were glaciated at the same time. By contrast, he pointed out that the floor of the English Channel was unglaciated, but that melt waters would have carried sand into the eastern end of the Channel and icebergs may have distributed material throughout it.

Some sand and gravel deposits of complex lithology may have more than one source. The lithology of pebbles in gravels off Washington State, for example, points to their being derived from a number of sources (Venkatarathnam and McManus, 1973). Pebbles can be traced to the Olympic Peninsular, the Cascade Mountains, the Western Canadian Cordillera, and the Columbia River drainage basin. Some of the deposits were thought to have been transported by ice to the southern end of Puget Sound and then by glacial outwash on to the continental shelf during periods of lowered sea level, where they were then reworked by marine processes as sea level rose.

2.2.1.3 *Offshore transport*

The transport of sands and gravels on the continental shelf is brought about largely by wave action and tidal current action. Little was known about the transport paths of offshore sediments until the work of van Veen (1936, 1938) and more recently that of Stride (1963). These workers have shown the presence of a variety of morphological features on the sea floor such as sand waves and ribbons which can be related to sediment transport processes, largely by tidal currents. Stride (1963) pointed out that the amount of material transported is a non-linear function of the strength of the current. Peak tidal currents are thus a principal transport mechanism. In such a situation only slight differences between ebb and flood tide velocities can determine the direction of sediment movement. Furthermore, where the strength of a tidal current is enhanced by wind induced currents, large amounts of sediment can be moved in short periods. Sediment transport on the open continental shelf is at its greatest when high tides are augmented by storm-generated currents.

Stride (1963) has used two morphological features on the sea floor to infer the direction of sea floor sand movement; ribbons of sand and sand waves. Sand ribbons are markedly elongated thin patches of sand which have their long axes in the direction of the set of the strongest tidal currents (Fig. 5). They can vary considerably in morphology. Some formed under weak tidal currents, have rather diffuse edges. Currents of about 2 knots increase the length to breadth ratio of the ribbons. Furthermore while some ribbons are well defined, others are broken up into a series of bands. Sand waves are current ripples with a steep lee slope in the direction of sand advance, determined by the set of the strongest tidal currents (Fig. 6). Their height can be up to 20 m with distances between wave crests up to about 1000 m and crest lengths up to 40 times greater than the distance between crests. However,

Fig. 5. Sand ribbons (from Stride, 1963).

most sand waves are much smaller than this. A difference in speed of only 0·1 knot between the peak speeds of ebb and flood tides seems to be enough to drive sand waves forward. Stride (1963) has also suggested that the general direction of sand transport on the continental shelf can be inferred from the direction of decrease in grain size of the deposits. In support of this, he pointed to a decrease in grain size along four inferred sediment transport paths on the British continental shelf (Fig. 7).

2.2.1.4 *Concentration processes*

Processes leading to the concentration of sand and gravel deposits include river action, wave action and tidal current action.

River gravels tend to occur in those rivers with strong currents. Rock fragments can be transported by torrents and those not susceptible to fracture become more and more rounded with distance from their source (Sneed and Folk, 1958). The gravels can be deposited where the current slackens for some reason such as, for example, due to a change in gradient. Where rivers debouch on to a plain, an alluvial fan may form containing coarse-grained gravels at its apex and becoming finer with increasing distance away. Some offshore gravels are thought to be submerged examples of river deposits

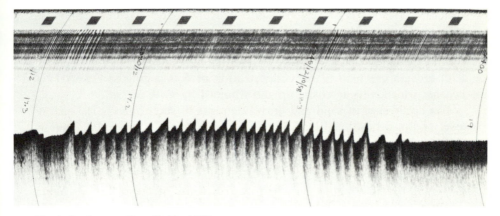

Fig. 6. Sand waves (from Stride, 1963).

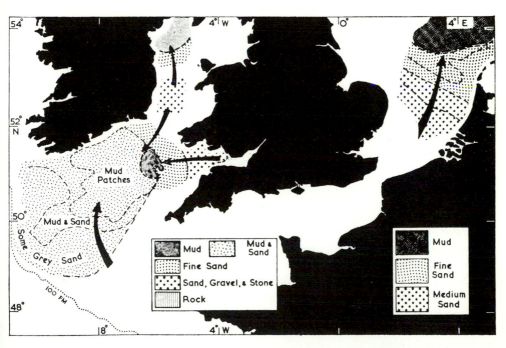

Fig. 7. Sediment transport paths and sediment distribution on parts of the north-west European continental shelf (from Stride, 1963). Arrows show the direction of decrease in grain-size for the uppermost loose sediments. Grade boundaries are shown as pecked lines.

(Schlee, 1964). Rivers rarely transport gravels to the sea unless they are torrents draining an uplifted coastal area.

Waves can concentrate either sands or gravels in the surf zone, depending on their strength and the nature of the material supplied to the beaches. Cliff erosion can lead to the concentration of coarse-grained material on beaches which is then broken up and rounded by wave action.

The occurrence of sand and gravel deposits offshore reflects the energy level of the depositional environment. For example, where tidal scour is sufficiently strong to erode a mixed deposit such as boulder clay or other debris of mixed grain sizes, fine material can be removed to leave gravels behind as lag deposits. Cronan (1969b) considered this to be the origin of gravels in part of the northern Irish Sea. Because offshore currents alone are rarely strong enough to transport gravel sized material an appreciable distance, except perhaps during storms, many other gravel deposits on middle and high latitude continental shelves may also originate in this way.

Some offshore sands may be relict in origin, but many are probably in dynamic equilibrium with the prevailing current regime on the sea floor. The presence of sand waves and ribbons on continental shelves would support this. If the sands are transported by slackening tidal currents, successively finer grain sizes will be deposited in a down current direction leading to good sorting of the deposits as a whole and an effective separation of the various grain size classes. Clean well sorted sands in the central north-east Irish Sea are thought to have been formed by this process (Cronan, 1969b). Tidal currents entering the basin to the south of the Isle of Man (Fig. 8) slacken in strength towards the English coast and the load that they can carry thus diminishes. This results in the deposition of zones of successively finer sediment (Fig. 8) culminating in the deposition of muds off the Cumberland coast.

2.2.2   Shells

Offshore calcareous sediments are of use in the manufacture of cement and lime. The deposits are formed by the break up of marine shells and their concentration into shell banks, etc. by hydrodynamic processes. Oyster shells occur in San Francisco Bay, and have been used in cement manufacture. Shells from the Gulf of Mexico have been used in the manufacture of lime (Mero, 1965). Lithothamnion shells occur off Scotland (Dunham and Sheppard, 1969) and large well sorted shell banks containing up to 80% calcium carbonate have been found in the Irish Sea off the Isle of Man (Cronan, 1970).

One of the largest operations to recover offshore shell for the cement industry has been off Iceland. The deposits are located in Faxa Bay on the

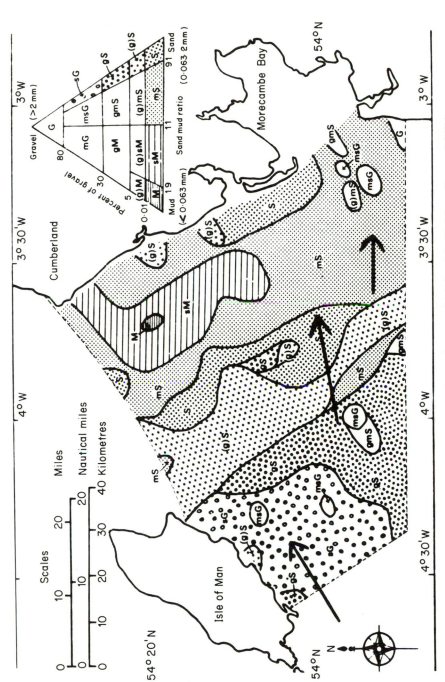

Fig. 8. Sediment distribution and inferred transport paths in the north-eastern Irish Sea. Modified from Cronan (1969b).

south-west of the island and contain about 80% calcium carbonate. The deposit is in a maximum depth of about 40 m of water and it is about 1–4 m thick (Mero, 1965).

The factors giving rise to concentration of shell sand and gravel are variable in nature. Naturally a source of shell debris is required. Because of their differing sizes and shapes to those of detrital sands and gravels, shell deposits respond differently to wave and current action on the sea floor. Such differences can lead to their separation from detrital sediments and their concentration into deposits containing high concentrations of calcium carbonate.

3

Miscellaneous Authigenic Minerals

Authigenic minerals in subaqueous environments either form directly from reactions between dissolved species in sea water or fresh water, or from the alteration of pre-existing phases in subaqueous sediments. They are of considerable importance because of their influence on the marine geochemistry of several elements (Kastner and Stonecipher, 1978). They are also of interest because they are formed *in situ* and thus they can be used to elucidate chemical processes operating on the ocean floor, or which have operated in the past (Cronan, 1974). Zeolites, barite, feldspar and garnet will be dealt with in this chapter. The more abundant and potentially valuable authigenic deposits such as phosphorites, manganese nodules and metalliferous sediments will be discussed in separate chapters.

3.1 Zeolites

Zeolites are a minor constituent of marine and lacustrine sediments as a whole (Deer *et al.*, 1963). Commonly occurring varieties are phillipsite ($KCa[Al_3Si_5O_{16}] \cdot 6H_2O$; Strunz, 1970) and clinoptilolite ($(Na,K)_4CaAl_6Si_{30}O_{72} \cdot 24H_2O$; Kastner and Stonecipher, 1978), the latter being a high silica member of the heulandite group (Mumpton, 1960). Other zeolites which occur more rarely in subaqueous environments include harmotome which is a barium rich phillipsite with the ideal composition $Ba[Al_2Si_6O_{16}] \cdot 6H_2O$ (Strunz, 1970), and analcime ($NaAlSi_2O_6 \cdot H_2O$; Kastner and Stonecipher, 1978), and a number of minor phases including chabazite, erionite, gmelinite, laumontite, mordenite, thaumasite, and thomsonite (Kastner and Stonecipher, 1978; Surdam and Sheppard, 1978; Iijima, 1978).

(a)

(b)

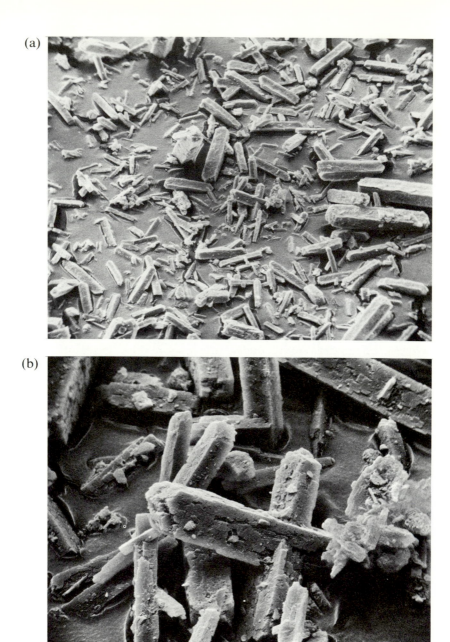

Fig. 9. Crystals of marine phillipsite: (a) composite of phillipsite crystals, × 600; (b) phillipsite twins, × 2400; (c) phillipsite multi-twin, × 4000; (d) phillipsite twin, × 5000. (a), (b) and (c) were taken from samples prepared by T. Church and M. Bernat with a CAMECA Inc. scanning electron microscope under support from the Centre National de la Recherche Scientifique, France. (d) was kindly supplied by W. S Ferguson of Colorado State University (from Cronan, 1974).

(c)

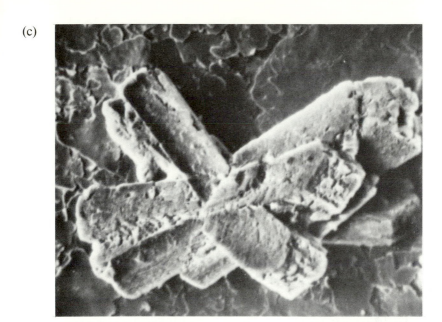

(d)

3.1.1   Phillipsite

3.1.1.1   *Nature and occurrences*

Phillipsite is a common zeolite in marine sediments and also occurs in some saline lakes. It was first described in deep-sea deposits by Murray and Renard (1891) who recognized it in sediments associated with volcanic material in the Pacific and Indian Oceans. Its first reported occurrence in the Atlantic Ocean was more recent (Young, 1939), but it has now been recognized at a large number of stations from throughout the Oceans (Bonatti, 1963; Kolla and Biscaye, 1973; Stonecipher, 1976; Petzing and Chester, 1979).

Phillipsite forms elongated prismatic crystals from as small as 8 μm to as large as 5 mm in length (Sheppard *et al.*, 1970; Steinfink, 1962) and also exists as ball shaped and complex sector twinned crystals (Sheppard *et al.*, 1970; Kastner and Stonecipher, 1978). However, most phillipsites are between 10 and 120 μm in length (Fig. 9). They are generally colourless to yellow-brown and sometimes contain inclusions, particularly of iron oxides. Structural and optical data on phillipsite have been reviewed by Cronan (1974) and Kastner and Stonecipher (1978), among others.

Compositionally, deep-sea phillipsites are intermediate in their Si/Al ratio between those associated with basic igneous rocks and those associated with silicic tuffs in saline lacustrine deposits (Table 2). The ratio ranges between 2·3 and 2·8 and the mineral is rich in alkalis with K in excess of Na and Ca. The elements Si, Al and K, together with H_2O show little overall variation between different phillipsite samples. Minor element determinations in phillipsite are rare but Ra has been identified by Revelle *et al.*

Table 2. Average composition of marine phillipsites (in weight %) (from Cronan, 1974).

	Maximum[a]	Minimum[a]	Average[a]	Goldberg[b]	Rex[c]
SiO_2	55·92	52·05	54·06	53·47	53·20
Al_2O_3	18·50	16·95	17·71	16·62	16·80
MgO	1·28	0·02	0·49	0·06	0·30
CaO	5·41	0·02	1·29	0·29	0·30
BaO	0·73	0·07	0·24		
Na_2O	5·60	1·11	3·82	7·41	7·40
K_2O	7·54	4·79	6·77	6·14	6·0
H_2O	17·55	14·19	15·58		15·70

[a] Data of Sheppard *et al.* (1970).
[b] Data of Goldberg (1961).
[c] Data of Rex (1967).

(1955), Ti has been found in concentrations of up to 0.02% and P in concentrations of up to 0.09% by Goldberg (1961), and small concentrations of U and Th have been found by Bernat and Goldberg (1969) and Bernat *et al.* (1970). More recently Bernat and Church (1978) have determined that a selection of phillipsites that they analysed contained 61–80 p.p.m. Rb, 66–191 p.p.m. Sr, which was quite uniform with sediment depth, and 8–24 p.p.m. La, 8–29 p.p.m. Ce, 10–34 p.p.m. Nd, 2–7.7 p.p.m. Sm, 1–2 p.p.m. Eu, 3–9.7 p.p.m. Gd, 2.7–9.1 p.p.m. Dy, 1.2–5.2 p.p.m. Er, 1.3–5.1 p.p.m. Tb and 0.27–1 p.p.m. Lu. These authors also noted a regular decrease in the concentration of Ba from 1200 to 220 p.p.m. and of Th from 3.0 to 0.6 p.p.m. in the minerals with depth, suggesting their continued growth after burial from solutions containing decreasing concentrations of these elements, as will be mentioned shortly.

3.1.1.2 *Distribution and associations*

The distribution of phillipsite in surface marine sediments has been described by Goldberg (1961) and Bonatti (1963) among others. More recently large amounts of data on its distribution have become available as a result of deep ocean drilling during the Deep Sea Drilling Project, and these have been reviewed by Stonecipher (1976), Kastner and Stonecipher (1978), Petzing and Chester (1979), Hay (1978) and Iijima (1978) among others.

Phillipsite reaches its greatest abundance in marine sediments in areas of low sedimentation rates far from land and below the calcium carbonate compensation depth. Bonatti (1963) has reported more than 50% phillipsite on a carbonate free basis in sediments from the central, south and south-eastern Pacific, while Petzing and Chester (1979) have found high concentrations in a number of other areas in the Pacific (Fig. 10). It is less abundant in the Indian and Atlantic Ocean, in that order, than in the Pacific (Kolla and Biscaye, 1973; Kastner and Stonecipher, 1978; Petzing and Chester, 1979). In the Indian Ocean it occurs principally in the Central Indian and Wharton Basins, on parts of the mid-Indian Ocean Ridge and the 90°E Ridge, and in a smaller area associated with the Carlsberg Ridge (Fig. 11). Less data are available on phillipsite occurrences in the Atlantic Ocean but those collected (Fig. 12) indicate its presence generally in low concentrations.

In its sediment associations phillipsite shows a fair degree of variability. Murray and Renard (1891) found phillipsite to be most common in red clays and less common in calcareous and siliceous sediments, but Goldberg (1961) has reported high phillipsite concentrations associated with calcareous sediments in the south-eastern Pacific. Stonecipher (1976) and Iijima (1978) have found from statistical analysis of phillipsite distribution in a large number of sediments that it occurs primarily in clays, carbonates and volcanogenic

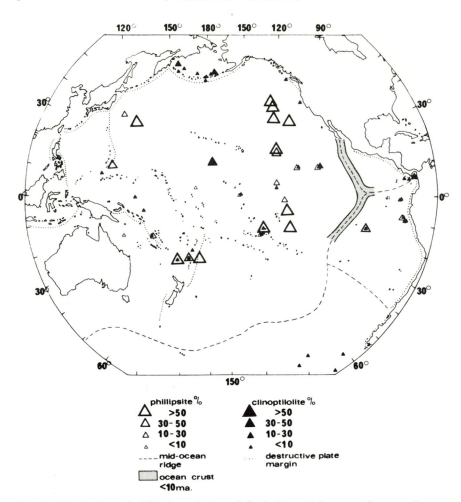

Fig. 10. Distributions of phillipsite and clinoptilolite in Upper Miocene to Recent sediments of DSDP drilling sites in the Pacific Ocean, as percentage of the total sediment (from Petzing and Chester, 1979).

sediments, but is also present in some siliceous oozes and terrigenous muds. Similar associations have been reported by Petzing and Chester (1979) but, by and large, were not considered by them to be of genetic significance. The association of phillipsite with volcanic material is common, even in calcareous and siliceous sediments. Quartz and plagioclase are other minerals commonly co-existing with phillipsite. Barite and ferromanganese oxides are also common, and the clay mineral assemblage associated with phillipsite is rich in smectite, particularly so in the Indian Ocean (Kolla and Biscaye, 1973).

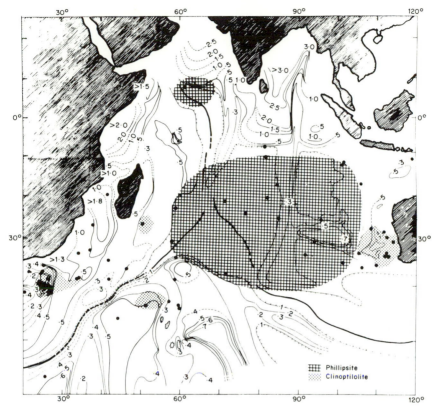

Fig. 11. Distributions of phillipsite and clinoptilolite in sediments of the Indian Ocean. The dots are sediment core locations, and the shaded areas enclose cores with more than 10% zeolites at any horizon. The isopachs are numbered in kilometres and the Mid-Indian Ocean Ridge is accentuated with bold lines. Phillipsite occurs in cores within the cross-hatched patterns and clinoptilolite is restricted to cores within the stippled areas (from Kolla and Biscaye, 1973).

Phillipsite in saline, alkaline lake deposits has been reviewed by Surdam and Sheppard (1978).

3.1.1.3 *Origin*

The common association of phillipsite with volcanic glass and its alteration products has led most workers to consider marine phillipsite to be derived from the breakdown of submarine volcanic material (Murray and Renard, 1891; Bonatti, 1963; Sheppard *et al.*, 1970; Czyscinski, 1973; Kolla and Biscaye, 1973; Kastner and Stonecipher, 1978; Iijima, 1978; Honnorez, 1978 and others).

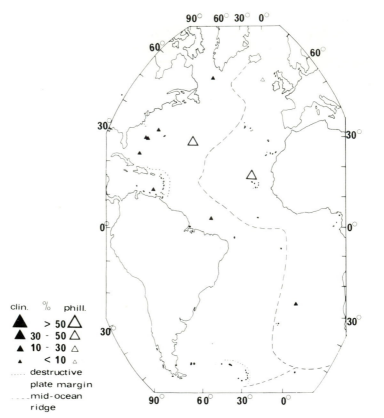

Fig. 12. Distributions of phillipsite and clinoptilolite in Middle Miocene to Recent sediments of DSDP drilling sites in the Atlantic Ocean, as percentage of the total sediment (from Petzing and Chester, 1979).

Most commonly suggested as the immediate precursor of marine phillipsite is palagonite, itself an alteration product of submarine basaltic glass. However, smectite, another basaltic alteration product, has also been considered to be important in this regard (Arrhenius and Bonatti, 1965). By contrast, in alkaline, saline lacustrine environments, rhyolitic glass is the most common precursor of phillipsite (Kastner and Stonecipher, 1978). This may be because the solubility of rhyolitic glass increases with increasing alkalinity (Mariner and Surdam, 1970). Petzing and Chester (1979) considered the ultimate precursor of phillipsite not to be *submarine* volcanic rocks but glass shards introduced into the ocean largely from terrestrial volcanoes. They drew a correlation between the distribution patterns of phillipsite in the Pacific Ocean and the present day pattern of global volcanicity.

In some instances, phillipsite has been observed to continue growing within sediments after burial. Bernat *et al.* (1970) found that the Th and U content of phillipsite they studied decreased while the absolute concentrations of the mineral increased with increasing depth of burial indicating continued phillipsite growth within the sediments. Furthermore, Czyscinski (1973) observed an increase in phillipsite concentration and siliceous organism dissolution with depth in some sediments suggesting that silica from organic remains can promote phillipsite formation at depth. Observations such as these are very important as they indicate that authigenic minerals do not just precipitate in the water column or form at the sediment water interface but may continue to grow from chemical reactions taking place within the sediments after burial.

3.1.2 Harmotome

According to Rinaldi *et al.* (1974) harmotome has the same structure as phillipsite with Ba as the principle cation. It has been found mainly in areas of the Pacific where sedimentation rates are low, often in association with phillipsite (Kastner and Stonecipher, 1978). Arrhenius and Bonatti (1965) have reported that harmotome can occur in a microcrystalline state dispersed through aggregates of the hydration products of volcanic glass, possibly representing an early stage of reaction between the glass and sea water. Harmotome has also been reported as a cementing material in tuffaceous deposits near the Society Islands by Morgenstein (1967) who considered it to be an alteration product of palagonite. However, on the whole harmotome seems to be a relatively uncommon mineral in deep sea sediments.

3.1.3 Clinoptilolite

3.1.3.1 *Nature and occurrence*

Clinoptilolite occurs throughout the World Ocean, and in saline lakes (Biscaye, 1965; Turekian, 1965; Kolla and Biscaye, 1973; Stonecipher, 1976; Iijima, 1978; Surdam and Sheppard, 1978; Boles and Wise, 1978). As mentioned, according to Mumpton (1960) it is a high silica member of the heulandite structural group. However, according to Kastner and Stonecipher (1978), the distinction between clinoptilolite and heulandite in marine sediments is not entirely clear, and some reported clinoptilolite occurrences in deep-sea sediments may have to be reclassified as heulandites. It forms fine-grained euhedral crystals (Fig. 13) often less than 45 μm long and thus is often difficult to identify under the microscope. It also occurs as radiolarian casts (Berger and von Rad, 1972). Kastner and Stonecipher (1978) report that the Si/Al ratio of clinoptilolite can vary between 4 and 5·25, and they review optical and structural data on the mineral.

Fig. 13. Crystals of marine clinoptilolite (from Lancelot *et al.*, 1972). × 1300.

3.1.3.2 *Distribution and associations*

The distribution and associations of marine clinoptilolite have been well described (Biscaye, 1965; Kolla and Biscaye, 1973; Cronan, 1974; Kastner and Stonecipher, 1978; Stonecipher, 1976; Petzing and Chester, 1979 and others). In contrast to phillipsite, the mineral appears to be preferentially associated with older sediments showing a steadily increasing abundance in sediments of Miocene to Cretaceous age (Stonecipher, 1976; Boles and Wise, 1978). It is therefore least common in surface and shallow buried sediments but is abundant between 700 and 1200 m depth (Kastner and Stonecipher, 1978).

    In its geographic distribution, clinoptilolite in surface sediments tends to favour more marginal areas of the oceans than phillipsite (Figs 10, 11, 12), but also occurs in the equatorial region of the Pacific (Stonecipher, 1976). In the Indian Ocean, clinoptilolite is most abundant in surface sediments off Australia and South Africa (Fig. 11). In the Atlantic where it is the most abundant zeolite (Iijima, 1978), clinoptilolite occurs principally off south-eastern North America and off South America where some of it may have been derived from erosion of the adjacent land mass (Biscaye, 1965).

In its associations clinoptilolite occurs principally in calcareous oozes, or calcareous/siliceous sediments, and is lower in abundance in pelagic clay sediments. It also occurs in association with terrigenous and volcanoclastic sediments (Iijima, 1978). In its mineralogical associations clinoptilolite has been found with chert, palygorskite, calcite, K feldspar, opal, pyrite, siderite and sepiolite (Stonecipher, 1978; Iijima, 1978). In sediments of Pliocene to Eocene age it is associated with kaolinite, illite and smectite, while in older sediments it occurs principally with palygorskite and illite, especially when also associated with cherts (Stonecipher, 1976). Clinoptilolite in saline lake deposits has been reviewed by Surdam and Sheppard (1978).

3.1.3.3 *Origin*

Most workers on the subject consider that clinoptilolite is derived from the alteration of silicic volcanic glass (Hathaway and Sachs, 1965; Hay, 1966; Sheppard and Gude, 1968; Iijima, 1971) in contrast to phillipsite which is thought to form from basaltic glass. However, Stonecipher (1978) considers that it can also form in non-volcanic siliceous terrigenous sediments. Petzing and Chester (1979) have suggested that in the marine environment it is the Si/Al ratio of the parent glass that is the main factor in determining whether clinoptilolite or phillipsite will occur, clinoptilolite formation being favoured by a high Si/Al ratio. This might partly explain the general occurrence of clinoptilolite in older sediments than phillipsite because acid glasses break down more slowly than basic glasses and thus clinoptilolite will take longer to form than phillipsite. However, volcanic precursors are not the only source of elements for clinoptilolite formation. Goodell (1965) considered that clinoptilolite in Southern Ocean sediments derived its silica from soluble opaline diatom and radiolarian remains, and Berger and von Rad (1972) considered that the dissolution of siliceous microfossils was at least in part responsible for the formation of the clinoptilolite that they examined. Boles and Wise (1978) suggested that clinoptilolite may form from the alteration of phillipsite with increasing age.

3.1.4 Analcime

Murray and Renard (1891) first reported analcime in deep-sea sediments, where it is much less abundant than phillipsite and clinoptilolite (Kastner and Stonecipher, 1978). It is normally associated with basaltic material in the marine environment, in contrast to lake sediments where in the absence of fresh glass it appears to form from other zeolites such as clinoptilolite,

(a)

(b)

(c)

(d)

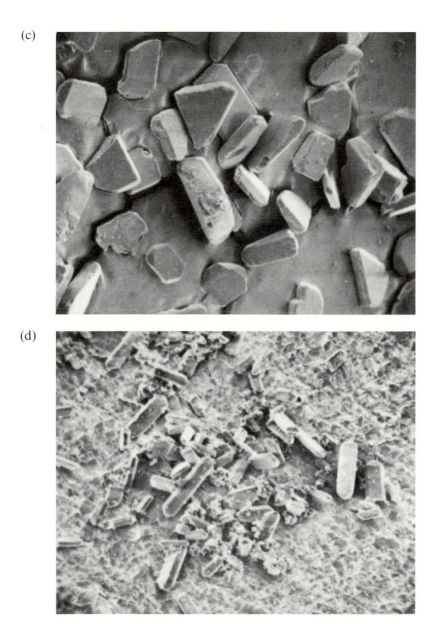

Fig. 14. Crystals of marine barite: (a) barite twin, × 2400; (b) barite microcrystal, × 2400; (c) barite crystals, × 1200 (d) barite euhedra and common microcrystals, × 480. Photographs were taken on samples prepared by T. Church and M. Bernat with a CAMECA Inc. scanning electron microscope under support from the Centre National de la Recherche Scientifique, France (from Cronan, 1974).

erionite and phillipsite (Hay, 1966; Sheppard and Gude, 1968, 1969). Hay (1966) and Kastner and Stonecipher (1978) have noted that analcime tends to increase in abundance with increasing age of sediments. In its associations, analcime occurs with smectite, chlorite and celadonite, as well as with the two more abundant zeolites, phillipsite and clinoptilolite. According to Kastner and Stonecipher (1978), conditions for analcime formation probably become more favourable within the sedimentary column rather than at the sediment surface, as the activity of silica in the interstitial waters increases.

3.1.5   Other zeolites

Many other zeolites including some more calcic varieties than those described above, have been reported from subaqueous environments. In the deep sea, they occur mostly in association with basaltic material. Some of these zeolites are evidently alteration products. For example, Bass *et al.* (1973) found the calcic zeolites chabazite, gmelinite and thomsonite replacing plagioclase. Others may be low temperature primary minerals. For example, thaumasite was reported by Walker (1972) in a cement of tuffaceous biocalcarenite and tuff breccia in the North Atlantic, and authigenic laumontite has been reported in the Southern Ocean by Sands and Drever (1978). Others may have formed at higher temperatures from hydrothermal solutions (Kastner and Stonecipher, 1978). More work is needed to resolve the interrelationships between these zeolites.

3.2   Barite

3.2.1   Nature and occurrence

Barite ($BaSO_4$) is widespread in marine sediments, mostly in association with biogenous remains. It was first described in deep-sea sediments by Murray and Renard (1891) and has subsequently been reported in the form of nodules, faecal pellets, euhedral crystals, and microcrystalline aggregates and assemblages with individual grains a few micrometres in size (Fig. 14) (Jones, 1887; Revelle and Emery, 1951; Vinogradov, 1953; Goldberg and Arrhenius, 1958; Arrhenius and Bonatti, 1965; Church, 1970; Dean and Schreiber, 1977). While it only averages about 1% by weight, or less, in deep-sediments as a whole, Arrhenius and Bonatti (1965) have reported concentrations of as much as 10% in the calcium carbonate free fraction of some Pacific deep sea sediments (Fig. 15).

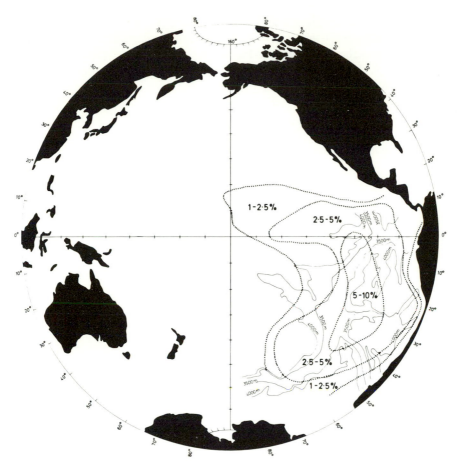

Fig. 15. Barite concentrations in some Pacific pelagic sediments (from Cronan 1974, after Arrhenius and Bonatti, 1965).

3.2.2 Distribution and associations

Barite distribution in marine sediments has been discussed by a number of authors. Chesselet (1975) has reported particulate barite in ocean waters which is probably authigenic in origin and which on settling may contribute appreciably to the concentration of barite in marine sediments. Localized surface occurrences of barite concretions containing over 75% of $BaSO_4$ were reported off Sri Lanka by Jones (1887), and Sverdrup *et al.* (1942) have reported similar concretions off Indonesia and southern California ranging in weight from several grams to about a kilogram (Mero, 1965). In the deep sea, Turekian and Imbrie (1966) found higher than average barium concentrations in surface sediments on the mid-Atlantic Ridge, and Arrhenius and Bonatti (1965) found the highest concentrations of barium in Pacific sediments to be in the south-eastern Pacific in the vicinity of the East Pacific Rise (Fig. 15). However, Church (1970) has found the distribution of barite in the south-eastern Pacific to be rather irregular, with highest concentrations occurring in the equatorial and south-eastern parts of the basin rather than at the crest of the East Pacific Rise itself. Cronan (1974) and Dean and Schreiber (1977) have reviewed the occurrences of barite in buried deep-sea sediments cored during the Deep Sea Drilling Project. Dean and Schreiber conclude:

(a) that barite is more abundant in cores from the tropical eastern Pacific than from anywhere else cored, confirming that its geographic distribution in buried sediments is similar to its distribution in surface sediments;
(b) that it is more abundant in older sediments in the Atlantic and Indian Oceans than in the Pacific, although it occurs in sediments of all ages in all oceans;
(c) that it tends to increase in abundance with depth of burial at any given site;
(d) that while it is most commonly associated with calcareous sediments, it can be found in association with a wide variety of sediment types.

3.2.3   Origin

There has been some controversy over the origin of barite in marine sediments. Some workers such as Emery (1960) have suggested that it may be of hydrothermal origin, while others such as Church (1970) consider organic factors to be more important in its origin. Yet other workers such as Arrhenius and Bonatti (1965) have suggested that both hydrothermal and organic controls may be of importance in influencing barite occurrence and distribution in marine sediments.

A hydrothermal source of barium occurring in barite nodules off southern California was proposed by Revelle and Emery (1951) who considered that interstitial waters rich in sulphate ions had reacted with ascending barium rich magmatic solutions. However, more recent work has indicated that although these concretions may be hydrothermal in origin they might have been formed in restricted lagoons, and in any event are not in situ but could have been transported from the adjacent land mass (Goldberg et al., 1969).

The importance of biological activity in the formation of marine barite has been emphasized by Church (1970). There are many data on barium enrichment in the soft parts of marine organisms. For example, Bowen (1956) has reported barium concentrations many times greater than that in sea water in a variety of marine creatures. Similar data have been reported by Arrhenius (1963), Goldberg (1965) and Thompson and Bowen (1969). Church (1970) considered that the barium extracted from sea water by marine organisms is released at depth on the dissolution of their remains. This leads to an enrichment of barium in the bottom waters and interstitial waters of the underlying sediments, which in turn can lead to barium saturation and barite precipitation. However, according to Goldberg and Arrhenius (1958) barite granules may form in the protoplasts of some marine organisms and could remain behind on the sea floor when the organisms dissolve after death. Processes such as these could account for the high concentrations of barite found in sediments underlying the equatorial zone of high productivity (Arrhenius and Bonatti, 1965; Church, 1970; Chesselet et al., 1976).

A combination of volcanic and organic activity has been proposed by Arrhenius and Bonatti (1965) to account for barite enrichment in East Pacific Rise and equatorial Pacific sediments. Barium entering sea water from volcanic sources near the Rise crest was thought to react with dissolved sulphate to form barite soon after discharge. However, it was also thought that waters containing residual barium were moving north and north-west away from the East Pacific Rise and that barium they contained was extracted by organisms in the equatorial zone of high productivity to accumulate as barite in the organic rich sediments typical of the area. This dual origin for marine barite has an advantage over single theories of origin for the mineral in that it can explain most of its observed associations. Much of the barite in marine sediments is probably non-volcanic in origin being precipitated from normal sea water or interstitial waters, its formation probably influenced in part by organic agencies. However, where a local hydrothermal source of barium may be present, as would be expected on mid-ocean ridges or in other volcanic areas, local barium enrichments in sea water could lead directly to barite precipitation or to an additional supply of barium to organisms to be sedimented as barite later when the organisms die.

Recently, increasing amounts of evidence have indicated that barite formation is not necessarily restricted to the water column or the sediment surface, but that it can continue within marine sediments after their burial (Church and Bernat, 1972; Church and Wolgemuth, 1972; Cronan, 1974; Dean and Schreiber, 1977). This would account for the increasing barite concentrations with depth reported in many sediment cores mentioned already.

3.3 Feldspars

According to Elderfield (1976a) authigenic feldspar formation is not quantitatively important on the sea floor. Authigenic feldspars have been described from both the Atlantic and Pacific Oceans usually in association with the products of submarine volcanism (Mellis, 1952; Matthews, 1962, 1971;

Kastner and Stonecipher, 1978 and others). Often they replace igneous calcic plagioclase or volcanic glass, or sometimes occur as euhedral crystals in volcanic sediments, in foram chambers, and in porcelanite (Kastner and Stonecipher, 1978). Feldspar varieties reported include microcline (Kelts and McKenzie, 1976), orthoclase replacing plagioclase (Mellis, 1952; Matthews, 1962, 1971), and sanidine replacing volcanic glass (Lancelot *et al.*, 1972). Kastner and Stonecipher (1978) have reported that authigenic feldspars occur at all depths in marine sediments, but are most common in Upper Cretaceous sediments of the Pacific Ocean. Illite and smectite are commonly associated with them, but, unlike their associations in saline lakes, occurrences of zeolites with them are rare. Authigenic albite has been reported as an overgrowth around detrital albite by Kastner and Siever (1972) but is rare. Most sea floor authigenic feldspars are thought to form at low temperatures, but some may have formed at slightly more elevated temperatures, although not higher than 200°C (Matthews, 1962). Potassium feldspar was thought by Surdam and Sheppard (1978) to form from zeolite precursors in saline alkaline environments, but may not necessarily form during initial deposition stages.

3.4   Garnet

Kemp and Easton (1974), Cook *et al.* (1974) and Easton *et al.* (1977) have described a rare occurrence of a metasomatic andraditic hydrogrossular garnet ($Gros_{52}And_{40}Py_6Alm_{1.5}Sp_{0.5}$) in sediments cored during the Deep Sea Drilling Project. The occurrence was in recrystallized calcium carbonate rich sediments overlying the basement basalt at DSDP site 251 on the south-western branch of the mid-Indian Ocean Ridge System. Oxygen isotope evidence reported by Easton *et al.* (1977) indicated that the garnets formed at about 170°C from heated circulating sea water which had passed through the underlying basalts. In this respect, the garnets may have genetic features in common with the metalliferous sediments described in Chapter 6. A comprehensive search of DSDP cores collected more recently by the discoverers of this mineral revealed no further occurrences. However, similar occurrences in the stratigraphic column were reported.

4

Phosphorites

4.1 Introduction

Phosphorite has been described as a sedimentary deposit composed mainly of phosphate minerals (Pettijohn, 1957). Its principal mineral is a variety of apatite called carbonate fluorapatite or francolite. Collophane is the term used to describe optically isotropic fine-grained phosphorite under the microscope. Apatite can occur in a variety of forms in the marine environment including fish debris, reptile and mammal bones, shells, coprolites, microcrystalline aggregates in nodular, pelletal, oolitic or laminar forms, and carbonate and wood replacements (Gulbrandsen, 1969). In shallow marine environments, apatite is most commonly present as pellets or nodules. Reworking, concentration and uplift of these deposits can give rise to the large bedded phosphorites common on land. The resource potential of these deposits lies principally in their use in the manufacture of fertilizers and elemental P and phosphoric acid but there is the possibility that vanadium, uranium, fluorine and the REE may also be obtained from them as by-products (Tooms et al., 1969).

Submarine phosphorites were first recovered from the Agulhas Bank, off South Africa, during the Challenger Expedition (1873–1876) (Murray and Renard, 1891), although apatite had been known for some considerable time to occur in the stratigraphic record (Buckland, 1829). Murray and Renard (1891) considered the formation of the Agulhas Bank samples they examined to be related to organic processes resulting from mass fatalities of marine organisms, a hypothesis which has recently been re-evaluated in relation to phosphorite genesis elsewhere (Manheim et al., 1975). Subsequent discoveries of marine phosphorite, in addition to the many reports of phosphorites of marine origin now on land (Gulbrandsen, 1969), have been reviewed by Tooms et al. (1969), Baturin and Bezrukov (1979) and Cook (1977) and will

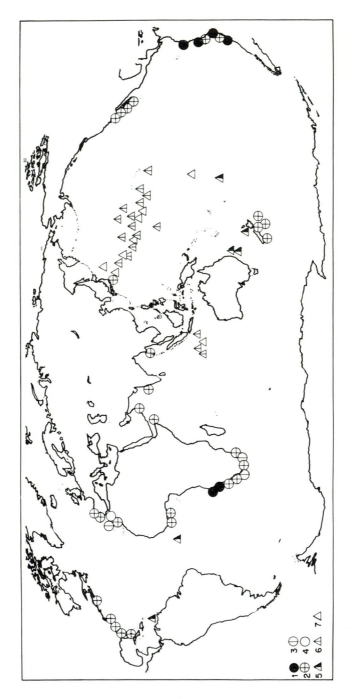

Fig. 16. Phosphorite location on the sea floor. 1–4 = phosphorites on continental margins; 5–7 = phosphorites on submerged mountains. Geological age: 1 = Holocene; 2–5 = Neogene; 3–6 = Paleogene; 4, 7 = Cretaceous (from Bezrukov and Baturin, 1979).

not be discussed in detail here. In the present chapter phosphorites will largely be reviewed in general terms, but specific reference will be made to recent work on north-west African phosphorites in order to illustrate certain facets of their nature.

4.2   Occurrence and Associations

Submarine phosphorites generally occur in water depths of less than 1000 m on continental shelves, offshore banks or marginal plateaux. They reach their greatest abundance off the western margins of the continents (Fig. 16) but also occur off some eastern continental margins, such as on the Blake Plateau off south-eastern North America (Manheim *et al.*, 1978) and on the plateaux east and south-east of New Zealand (Pasho, 1976). Phosphorites also occur on some oceanic seamounts in association with calcareous and volcanic rocks (Baturin and Bezrukov, 1979).

One of the most common associations of phosphorites is with areas of upwelling and high biological productivity. Upwelling brings to the surface large quantities of cold nutrient and phosphate-rich waters from intermediate depths which support abundant organisms, mostly diatoms, which give rise to a rapid flux of organic material to deeper waters when they die.

The cause of upwelling off western continental margins can probably be ascribed to oceanic and atmospheric circulation patterns, giving rise to current divergence. However, although there is an association between areas of upwelling and the occurrence of sea floor phosphorite, most of the phosphorites which occur in these areas are not geologically recent. Summerhayes (1967b, 1969) has suggested that the physicochemical and biochemical conditions in areas where phosphorites are found were more conducive to phosphorite formation in the Tertiary than at present.

Sediments usually associated with continental margin phosphorites include siliceous deposits in the form of chert, porcellanite and diatomite, carbonates, glauconite and occasionally volcanic rocks in the form of bentonite and tuffs (Gulbrandsen, 1969). Depositional features in areas of phosphorite occurrence include condensed sequences indicating slow deposition and minimal input of detrital sediment, conglomerates indicating reworking, and sometimes evaporites indicating a warm arid climate.

4.3   Nature

4.3.1   Form

Phosphorite nodules (Fig. 17) and pellets are usually structureless, but may

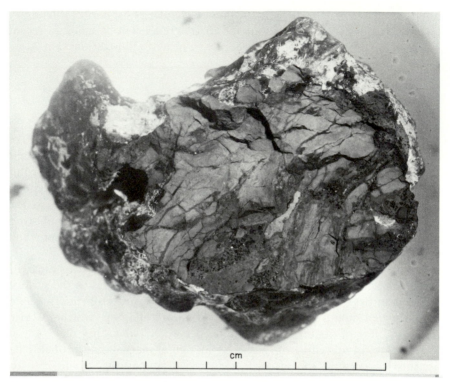

Fig. 17. Phosphorite concretion from off north-west Africa (photograph kindly supplied by J. McArthur).

have a layered, conglomeratic or oolitic internal structure, the last of these possibly caused by haloes of included organic matter (D'Anglejan, 1967). Pelletal phosphorites generally have a pellet grain size of 0·1–0·3 mm, which is often similar to that of their associated detritus. Phosphorites are normally pale brown, but can be considerably darker, or even black, if the content of impurities such as carbonaceous matter and pyrite is high. Glazing of pelletal phosphorites is not uncommon and may result from abrasion. Other physical properties of phosphorite include a hardness of about 5 on the Moh scale, and a specific gravity of 2·7–2·8.

Phosphorites are usually very impure. Impurities include various proportions of clay minerals, detrital mineral grains, rock fragments, glauconite, silica, carbonaceous matter, calcite, dolomite, iron oxides and siliceous skeletal material. Authigenic pyrite and fluorite are also sometimes present.

Cretaceous and Tertiary phosphorites outcrop on the Moroccan continental shelf in the form of pelletal, conglomeratic and massive phosphorite (Fig. 18) and have been studied petrographically by Summerhayes (1970)

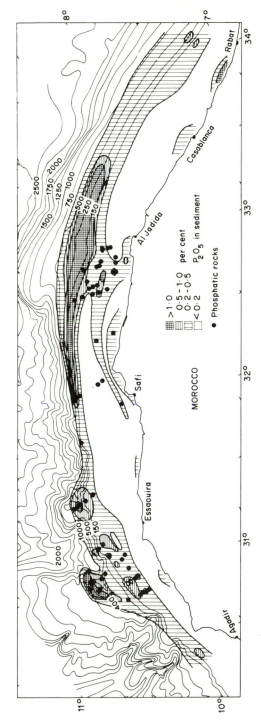

Fig. 18. Distribution of phosphate (as per cent P_2O_5) in sediments off Morocco, and location of sites at which phosphatic rocks were dredged (from Summerhayes *et al.*, 1972).

and McArthur (1974). The deposits have been divided into four groups. These are, first, a group consisting of glauconitic conglomerates, secondly, phosphatized limestones, thirdly, pelletal phosphorite, and, lastly, phosphatic ferruginous limestone. Some of the samples showed evidence of extensive reworking and contained many impurities.

4.3.2 Mineralogy

As mentioned, the principal mineral in phosphorites is largely carbonate fluorapatite which contains more than 1% F and substantial amounts of CO_2 (McConnell, 1973). It is usually present in a cryptocrystalline or isotropic form. The structure of the fluorapatite consists of columnar arrangements of CaO groups, which are linked by PO_4^{3-} groups and at any one level each F^- ion is surrounded by three Ca^{2+} ions.

4.3.3 Geochemistry

The composition of carbonate fluorapatite approximates to $Ca_{10}(PO_4 \cdot CO_3)_6$ F_{2-3} (Altschuler et al., 1958), the CO_3^{2-} groups being able to substitute for PO_4^{3-} groups (McConnell, 1952; Altschuler et al., 1958; Ames, 1959; Le Geros, 1965) probably on a one to one basis (Price and Calvert, 1978). Usually, CO_3^{2-} comprises 2–3% by weight of carbonate fluorapatite (Silverman et al., 1952; Altschuler et al., 1958; Simpson, 1964), but may constitute up to 5–6% in sea floor samples (J. McArthur, personal communication 1978). The imbalance of charge consequent on CO_3^{2-} substitution for PO_4^{3-} is compensated for by the introduction of F (Gulbrandsen et al., 1966) and possibly OH^- (Altschuler et al., 1958; Price and Calvert, 1978). Other possible substitutions are Na^+ for Ca^{2+} and SO_4^{2-} for PO_4^{3-} (Altschuler et al., 1958; Gulbrandsen, 1966). The average P_2O_5 values in submarine phosphorites are between 20 and 30% (Mero, 1965) and the major element compositions of some offshore phosphorites are listed in Table 3.

The minor and trace element composition of phosphorites is very variable (Table 4) and depends to a large extent on the nature of the contaminating phases present. Controls on the composition of marine phosphorites have been reviewed by Tooms et al. (1969), Price and Calvert (1978), McArthur (1978), Baturin and Bezrukov (1979), Manheim et al. (1978) and others. Adsorption processes have been postulated as a control on phosphorite composition and could be of considerable importance in governing trace element uptake on them from sea water. In addition, organic matter may be important in concentrating some metals. Observed correlations between the amount of organic matter in phosphorites and elements such as Ni, Cu, Zn, Ag, Mo, V, Cr, Se and Cd may be partially due to their having

Table 3. Composition of phosphorites from various submarine localities.

	1	2	3	4	5	6	7	8
SiO_2	6·20	3·45	15·30	13·79		1·8[a]	2·0[a]	3·1[a]
TiO_2	0·06	0·04	0·10	0·11		0·019	0·016	0·074
Al_2O_3	1·13	0·92	2·14	2·12		0·37	0·36	1·95
Fe_2O_3	1·40	25·80	5·58	7·34		0·54	0·77	8·6
MnO	0·01	0·06	0·01	0·02		0·01	0·09	0·017
MgO	0·97	1·49	1·34	1·45				
CaO	47·02	33·42	37·04	36·54	47·4	26·2[b]	8·0[b]	9·0[b]
Na_2O	0·62	0·34	0·78	0·73		1·99	2·79	1·96
K_2O	0·43	0·39	1·57	1·51		0·15	0·13	2·10
P_2O_5	14·82	10·26	17·89	16·82	29·6	18·3	26·2	16·5
S	0·31	0·21	0·46	0·45		0·44[c]	0·56[c]	<0·1[c]
F	2·12	1·42	2·21	2·04	3·3			
LOF	25·52	23·24	16·15	16·89				
Organic C						0·61	0·76	0·32

	9	10	11	12	13	14	15
SiO_2	1·6[a]	4·6[a]	22·13	8·93	0·95	0·20	
TiO_2	0·053	0·087					
Al_2O_3	1·12	2·00	5·15	1·38		0·51	
Fe_2O_3	10·7	8·7	2·85	1·00	1·83	2·80	1·14
MnO	0·025	0·016					
MgO			1·07	0·71	0·50	1·02	1·83
CaO	7·9[b]	6·7[b]	33·93	44·48	52·29	51·33	50·73
Na_2O	1·82	1·61	0·85	0·83	0·55	0·58	0·46
K_2O	0·41	1·75	1·30	0·60	0·64	0·45	0·15
P_2O_5	18·3	16·2	22·61	30·63	19·97	25·80	14·62
S	<0·1[c]	<0·1[c]	0·16	0·35	0·35	0·61	0·30
F			2·22	3·45	2·47	3·25	1·38
LOF			8·78[d]	9·34[d]	20·8[d]	15·2[d]	30·10[d]
Organic C	0·21	0·34					

1–4 = Agulhas Bank phosphorites, South Africa, from Parker (1971), Parker and Siesser (1972), Dingle (1975).
  5 = Forty Mile Bank Phosphorite, Baja, California, from Mero (1965).
6–10 = North-west African Continental Margin Phosphorites, from McArthur (1974).
  11 = Peru–Chile Continental Margin, average from Burnett (1974).
  12 = sea off California, average of two samples from Burnett (1974).
  13 = Chatham Rise off New Zealand, average of two samples, from Burnett (1974).
  14 = Blake Plateau Phosphorite, from Burnett (1974).
  15 = Necker Bank Phosphorite, from Burnett (1974).
[a] Quartz only.
[b] Calcite only.
[c] Pyrite sulphur only.
[d] Loss on fusion (loss on ignition at 1000 C in 11–15).

Table 4. Trace element abundance data in phosphorites, apatites and the earth's crust in p.p.m. (modified after Tooms *et al.*, 1969).

	1	2	3	4	5	6	7
Ag	0·07	3		1–50			
As	1·8	40	20·5	0·4–188	40		
B	10·0		16·0	3–33			
Ba	425·0	100		1–1000	27		
Be	2·8			1–10			
Cd	0·2			1–10			
Ce	60·0					120	1545
Co	25·0		3·3	0·6–11·8			
Cr	100·0	1000	28	7–1600	50		
Cu	55·0	100	21·7	0·6–394	16		120*
I	0·5		24·1	0·15–280	28		
La	30·0	300				150	769
Li	20·0			1–10			
Mn	950·0	30	428·0	0–10000	126		570
Mo	1·5	30	18·7	1–138			
Ni	75·0	100	12·5	1·9–30	27		63*
Pb	12·5			0–100	11		
Rb	90·0			0–100	26		
Sb	0·2	7		1–10			
Sc	22·0	10		10–50		3	
Se	0·05	10	2·7	1–9·8			
Sn	2·0			10–15			
Sr	375·0	1000	1900	1800–2000	1284		2106
Ti	5700		476	100–3000	300		
U	2·7	90	190	8–1300	144		
V	135·0	300	167	20–500	79		807*
Y	33·0	300		0–50	48	110	696
Zn	70·0	300	90	4–345	49		
Zr	165·0	30		10–500			1000*

1 = Crustal abundance (Taylor, 1964).
2 = Phosphoria formation averages (Gulbrandsen, 1966).
3 = World-wide phosphorite averages from data of Swaine (1962).
4 = Range of data in Swaine (1962).
5 = Trace element averages of north-west African phosphorites (McArthur, 1974).
6 = REE determinations on carbonate apatite (Altschuler *et al.*, 1967).
7 = Average element abundances in igneous and metamorphic fluorapatites: figures marked with an asterisk are maximum determinations used where averages are not given (Cruft, 1966).

an organic association. The environment of deposition is also of importance in determining the minor and trace element composition of phosphorites; for example, certain elements such as Mo, Se and V tend to be concentrated under reducing conditions. Sulphides form under reducing conditions and could be partly responsible for concentrating portions of elements such as Ag, Pb, Cu, Zn, Cd, Mo and Se into the deposits. Detrital matter also supplies a proportion of some elements such as Si, Al, Ti, Na and K. Uptake into the carbonate fluorapatite lattice is responsible for the presence of fractions of several elements such as Ba, Mo, Sr, Y, Ni, Zn, U and the rare earths (Price and Calvert, 1978). It is evident therefore, that no one factor controls the composition of phosphorites. Carbonate fluorapatite lattice characteristics, adsorption phenomena, organic matter, sulphides and detrital matter all play a variable role in this regard.

4.4   Environments of Modern Phosphorite Deposition

There are at least two areas of the world where phosphorites are thought to be forming at the present day. These are off south-west Africa and off Peru–Chile (Fig. 16), both areas of upwelling and high biological productivity. Consideration of how these deposits are forming will help to elucidate the mode of formation of older, more economically valuable phosphorites.

4.4.1   South-west Africa

Phosphorus-rich deposits between 18°S and 24°S off south-west Africa have been described by Baturin (1969), Baturin et al. (1970) and Price and Calvert (1978) among others. The area is one of high biological productivity and is floored by sands, silts, calcareous remains and diatomaceous mud. The deposits are more or less confined to the diatomaceous mud which is rich in amorphous silica, organic matter (up to 14% organic carbon) and contains up to 1% phosphorus. It is restricted to the inner shelf at depths of between 50 and 130 m. However, pelletal phosphorites are found in calcareous sands on the middle shelf (Price and Calvert, 1978). The bulk of the deposits consist of phosphatized clots of mud, nodules and phosphatized lumps of excrement, comprising not more than a few percent by weight of the diatomaceous mud. Only the unconsolidated phosphorite is thought to be modern (Veeh et al., 1974). The P_2O_5 content reaches 8% or more in the lumps of phosphatized mud, 25% in unconsolidated nodules, 27–29% in brittle fine-grained nodules and 31–33% in compact concretions, illustrating increasing P with degree of lithification. Increase in P_2O_5 is accompanied by increases in CaO, CO_2 and F, but by a decrease in H_2O, organic carbon, SiO_2 and Fe.

The authigenic nature of these deposits is demonstrated by the unconsolidated clots and lenses being similar in consistency to the surrounding sediments, by their gradation into lithified concretions and by the fact that the local currents are too weak to transport the more lithified varieties. Furthermore, an apparent young age of the concretions is indicated by their low U content and their being associated with relatively young fish debris.

The gradation from loose poorly lithified deposits to compact concretions suggests that they are all the products of one diagenetic process. Baturin (1969) considered that the P in the deposits has been derived from the breakdown of the surrounding P-rich diatomaceous mud and from fish debris. Baturin (1971) proposed three stages of phosphorite formation off south-west Africa. First, a biogenic-depositional stage, during which phosphorite deposition is initiated; secondly, a diagenetic stage, during which P_2O_5 increases in the deposits, together with their degree of lithification; and thirdly, a dynamic stage, during which the deposits are concentrated by reworking. He considered there to be at least two generations of phosphorite off south-west Africa, a conclusion supported by the U isotope data of Veeh *et al.* (1974).

4.4.2   Peru and Chile

Phosphorus-rich deposits were discovered off Peru by Baturin and co-workers and have been described by Veeh *et al.* (1973) and Burnett (1974, 1977). The deposits occur in depths shallower than 1000 m and are confined chiefly to two narrow bands at about 100 m and 400 m respectively, which coincide with the upper and lower limits of where the oxygen minimum zone impinges on the bottom. Between these two zones occur laminated organic-rich diatomaceous oozes, evidence of the high organic productivity of the region. The area is one of strong upwelling.

The deposits are irregular in form, with protruberances and burrows. Their colour varies from dark to light grey to pale green and their surfaces are mostly dull. Concretions generally range in diameter from 5 to 10 cm, and phosphate-rich pellets ranging in size from a few millimetres to a few centimetres occur within the anaerobic sediments associated with them.

Chemically, the deposits are characterized by high P_2O_5 values, ranging from about 12–28% P_2O_5. Other major constituents are SiO_2 and CaO (Burnett, 1977). The deposits are mineralogically complex, containing apatite as their major mineral phase, together with varying amounts of detrital quartz, mica, kaolinite, feldspar and tremolite. Small quantities of calcite, dolomite, glauconite and pyrite are also present.

The authigenic nature of the Peruvian and Chilean phosphorite is evidenced by their lumpiness and friability, which rules out significant transport (Burnett, 1974). Furthermore, scanning electron micrographs of the deposits showed that the apatite commonly grows in rosettes and clusters within the pores and other openings of biological material, which would suggest that it was formed by direct precipitation. A euhedral crystal form, coupled with element ratios close to that of pure apatite, would support this contention.

Uranium series isotope studies in the deposits have indicated that they have a recent origin (Burnett and Veeh, 1977). Corrected ^{234}U ages range from greater than 150 000 years B.P. to Holocene, and ^{230}Th ages give similar results. However, the ages of the samples are not randomly distributed, over 90% falling into one of four age groups: 0–10 000, 40 000–50 000, 100 000–105 000, and 130 000–140 000 years B.P. All these ages appear to coincide with high stands of sea level, probably resulting from ice melting during inter-glacial periods of the ice age.

Other investigations of phosphorite collected off Peru have been described by Manheim *et al.* (1975). In their samples, the phosphorite was not con-sidered to be a direct precipitate, but to be localized in apatite replacement of Holocene benthonic foraminifera. A continuous transition from fresh unphosphatized forams to infilled phosphorite grains was observed at several sites. Manheim *et al.* (1975) thought that, rather than being supplied continu-ously, the benthonic foram tests might remain from mass mortalities during short pauses in the upwelling. The carbonate was thought to be phosphatized on resumption of normal conditions of upwelling and breakdown of organic matter.

4.5 Controls on Phosphorite Formation

According to Gulbrandsen (1969), a basic requirement for the formation of phosphorite is a supply of phosphorus to the sea floor in excess of normal. The most likely source for the excess phosphorus is that held by marine organisms, particularly diatoms, which have been shown to be adequate in areas of high organic productivity to supply all the P required to form phos-phorites (Cressman and Swanson, 1964; Gulbrandsen, 1969). The organic matter must be continuously oxidized and destroyed in order to liberate the P required.

Another requirement for phosphorite precipitation is a suitable pH. Krumbein and Garrels (1952), Robertson (1966) and Pytowicz and Kester (1967) have shown that apatite solubility decreases with increase in pH and thus a high pH in the marine environment should favour phosphorite formation. The decay of organisms which supply the phosphorus could lead to a pH suitable for phosphorus precipitation, as Berner (1969) has shown that organic decomposition can lead to an increase in the pH of the local environment.

A third factor which may influence the formation of phosphorite is the concentration of Mg in the solution from which phosphorus precipitates. It has been shown that Mg^{2+} ions inhibit the precipitation of apatite, probably because Mg^{2+} competes with Ca^{2+} for sites in the apatite structure (Bachra *et al.*, 1965; Martens and Harriss, 1970). It would appear necessary therefore, that Mg be removed from solution in order for apatite to precipitate. This can occur in several ways, including diagenetic reactions within interstitial waters (Drever, 1971), ion exchange, dolomitization and the authigenic formation of Mg-rich silicates (Burnett, 1974).

A fourth factor which might influence the precipitation of phosphorite is the nature of the surface offering a nucleation site for apatite growth. Many workers consider that calcite offers the most suitable surface for apatite precipitation (Stumm and Morgan, 1970; Stumm and Leckie, 1970), but Burnett (1974) considers, on the basis of SEM work, that siliceous skeletal material, feldspar crystals and fish bone apatite are suitable surfaces for the initiation of authigenic apatite precipitation when calcite is not present.

Finally, Gulbrandsen (1969) stresses that a low rate of supply of terrigenous detritus to the depositional environment is an important factor in allowing phosphorite to form in abundance. This would be favoured by low continental runoff, ideally under arid conditions. Such conditions are fulfilled in the case of the phosphorite deposits thought to be forming at present off south-west Africa, Peru and Chile.

4.6 Formation of Phosphorites

The two main theories proposed for phosphorite formation involve (i) direct inorganic precipitation of phosphorus and (ii) the replacement of CO_3 by PO_4 in calcium carbonate to form a replacement deposit. Available evidence indicates that both modes of formation are feasible.

Kazakov (1937) proposed a model of phosphorite formation whereby ascending phosphorus-rich waters in areas of upwelling become supersaturated with phosphorus which results in its precipitation. Evidence for direct precipitation of apatite is forthcoming from various sources. As mentioned, Burnett (1974) found apatite growing on biological material. In addition, the occurrence of apatite in loose friable pellets showing no evidence of replacement structures would favour an origin by direct precipitation. Furthermore, apatite has been synthesized from solution in the laboratory by various workers (Simpson, 1964; Le Geros, 1965), thus providing additional evidence of its direct inorganic precipitation.

Baturin and his co-workers have provided a detailed model for the inorganic precipitation of phosphorite off south-west Africa and Chile. On the basis of dissolved P values, Baturin *et al.* (1970) considered that the precipitation of phosphorus within the water column is unlikely, in contrast to the model of Kazakov (1937), but that it could occur in the interstitial waters of the sediments. The oversaturation of phosphorus in the interstitial waters leads to its precipitation in areas of the sediment where the pH is high. This results in the formation of soft gel-like lenses, laminae and pellets containing 5–10% P_2O_5. Diagenetic processes within the sediments result in the lithification of the deposits and increase in their P content, as mentioned previously. The deposits increase in CaO, CO_2 and F as well as P_2O_5, incorporated organic matter loses N and H more rapidly than C, diatom frustules dissolve and gradually the deposits take on a crystalline structure (Baturin, 1971).

A similar model to account for the direct precipitation of phosphorites off Peru and Chile has been advanced by Burnett (1974, 1977). He proposed that phosphorus precipitation took place in the anoxic pore waters of the organic-rich sediments, the concentration of the deposits at the edges of where the oxygen minimum zone impinges on the bottom possibly being due to pH fluctuations associated with oxygen variations. Interfering Mg^{2+} ions were thought to be removed from the interstitial waters by diagenetic reactions. Apatite precipitation occurs initially on nucleation sites such as the surfaces of siliceous skeletal debris, after which it may be self-perpetuating.

By contrast, evidence for apatite replacing $CaCO_3$ is forthcoming from the many reports of apatite pseudomorphing calcareous organic remains on the sea floor. It is apparent, therefore, that phosphorus-rich solutions are capable of converting calcium carbonate to carbonate fluorapatite. Replacement most probably occurs through the medium of the interstitial waters of the sediments by P derived from the decay of organisms, rather than at the surface. This is because the phosphorus content of interstitial waters is generally much higher than in the overlying sea water. The observations of Burnett (1974) and Manheim *et al.* (1975) on the direct precipitation and replacement origin, respectively, of phosphorites off Peru, indicates that the two processes are not mutually exclusive in any particular environment.

The conversion of disseminated phosphorites to large bedded phosphorites of the type found off north-west Africa, for example, is probably the result of geological processes operating over a prolonged period of time. The initial lithification of the deposits may be followed by reworking and concentration due to winnowing away of enclosing sediment, possibly as a result of current variations related to changes in sea level. The shallow portions of continental shelves, where phosphorites are most abundant, are particularly prone to reworking and sediment erosion as a result of changes in sea level. In this way, several generations of phosphorite concretions could become concentrated into a single deposit. Furthermore, in addition to reworking, further phosphatization could occur. Actual uplift and complete lithification of the phosphorite is also possible, followed by erosion and redeposition as a phosphorite conglomerate which might, in turn, be further phosphatized if the physicochemical conditions leading to phosphorus precipitation were re-established. At least part of such a cyclical series of events has been recognized in the bedded phosphorites off north-west Africa.

The origin of phosphorites on oceanic seamounts is not clear (Baturin and Bezrukov, 1979). Some may have formed as guano deposits in a sub-areal environment, but not those older than the Tertiary. Others may have formed as a result of phosphatization of carbonate rock.

5

Manganese Nodules and Encrustations

5.1 Introduction

It is popularly believed that marine manganese nodules were first discovered during the Challenger Expedition, 1873–1876. However, as pointed out by Manheim (1978), they were found shortly before that in the Kara Sea. By contrast lacustrine manganese nodules have been known for many centuries. They were mined intermittently in Sweden during medieval times and as recently as the late nineteenth century in Quebec. In some cases, regeneration of the ore took place in as little as ten to fifty years, attesting to the rapid rate of growth of the deposits in certain lakes.

It was during the Challenger Expedition that deep-sea manganese nodules were first studied in detail. They were found in all the oceans of the world, in varying abundances. Characteristically the deposits consisted of concretionary oxides of iron and manganese with high concentrations of certain trace elements, and of variable admixture of silicate material. Biogenous material was also sometimes present in them.

Since the Challenger period, studies of manganese nodules have, for the most part, been conducted at an ever increasing rate. Other major early nodule collecting expeditions were those of the "Valdivia" in the 1890s, and the "Albatross" in the early 1900s. Between the two World Wars little work was done on nodules, although samples were collected on a number of oceanographic cruises. Since the Second World War studies on nodules have rapidly expanded, in part no doubt as a result of the realization that they may be of economic value (Mero, 1959). We now have a reasonably good idea of the world-wide distribution and nature of the deposits, and are beginning to understand their origin.

5.2   Origin of Manganese Nodules

The origin of manganese nodules involves not one problem but at least three. First, the sources of the elements in the nodules have to be accounted for, part of the more general problem of the supply of elements to the marine environment at large, which has already been reviewed in Chapter 1. Secondly, it is necessary to understand the mechanisms by which these elements are brought to the reaction site, i.e. the sediment–water interface or specific locations within the sediment column. Thirdly, no real appreciation of nodule origin can be acquired without an understanding of the precipitation and growth mechanisms involved in their formation. The first two of these problems will be discussed in this section, while the third is best considered after a discussion of nodule structures and growth rates.

5.2.1   Sources of elements

For many years there was a controversy between the followers of J. Murray (Murray and Renard, 1891) who considered that elements in nodules and encrustations were principally derived from the products of submarine volcanism, and those of A. Renard (Murray and Renard, 1891), who considered that they were largely derived from continental runoff. However, in the 1950s and 1960s, opinion began to move towards the idea that nodules could accrue metals from both volcanic and continental sources (Skornyakova et al., 1962; Arrhenius et al., 1964; Cronan, 1967), as well as possibly from cosmic sources (Pettersson, 1959) and by diagenetic recycling of elements through the sediment column (Lynn and Bonatti, 1965). This led Cronan (1967) to conclude that elements from any source are a potential constituent of manganese nodules and therefore the problem is not to establish a single source for the elements in nodules but to differentiate between nodules containing elements from different sources.

Bonatti et al. (1972b) attempted a qualitative classification of ferromanganese oxide deposits on the basis of different potential sources of elements, dividing them into hydrogenous, hydrothermal, halmyrolytic and diagenetic varieties. Hydrogenous deposits are defined as those which derive their constituents by slow precipitation of elements from normal sea water (sedimentary Fe and Mn), Renard's preferred mechanism of nodule formation. Hydrothermal deposits are defined as those in which the elements are supplied to the sea floor by hydrothermal activity in areas of high heat flow associated with volcanism, a mechanism first proposed by Gumbel (1878). Halmyrolytic deposits are defined as those in which the elements are at least in part derived from the submarine alteration (halmyrolysis) of basaltic material on the sea floor. Murray's preferred mechanism of nodule formation. Diagenetic deposits are defined as those in which the elements are supplied partly by their post-depositional redistribution within the sediment column, a mechanism first proposed by Murray and Irvine (1894).

The classification of Bonatti et al. (1972b), while useful in focusing attention on "end member" varieties of nodules and encrustations, should not be applied too rigidly as most of the deposits derive their metals from more than one of the possible sources, and deposits formed in different ways, e.g. hydrothermal and diagenetic, can have similar compositions. Furthermore, it is not possible in many cases to distinguish between elements derived by, for example, halmyrolysis or continental weathering, as elements from each are cycled through normal sea water. The relative importance of different sources of elements to nodules and encrustations is likely to vary depending upon the location of the deposits relative to these sources, and thus examination of the deposits in relation to their environment of formation is important if their genesis is to be understood.

Elements dispersed in normal sea water, after supply in both solution and particulate phases from the continents (Tooms et al., 1969) and the more widespread submarine volcanic processes such as halmyrolysis (Varentsov, 1970) are probably the most important sources of elements to forming manganese nodules and encrustations. The residence times in sea water of most of the important elements in the concretions are sufficiently long (Goldberg and Arrhenius, 1958; Murray and Brewer, 1977) that they become well mixed in the oceans thus ensuring their relatively uniform supply (extractive mechanisms permitting) to the sea floor by the various processes to be outlined in the next section. However, some elements which are supplied in abundance from the continents and which have relatively short residence times in sea water such as iron, for example, may be enriched in deposits formed near the continent margins (Mero, 1965; Cronan, 1967) or in areas where there is a large inflow of terrigenous detritus (Cronan, 1975b).

Cosmic sources of elements, particularly nickel, although generally considered to be insignificant (Smales and Wiseman, 1955), will be relatively uniformly supplied to nodules over the ocean floor because of the relatively constant flux of cosmic material to the oceans.

Diagenetic sources of metals, which are really metals supplied to the sea floor from various sources and diagenetically remobilized within the sediment column, are likely to be most important where there are strong chemical gradients within the sediments. One of the best examples of this process is the diagenetic remobilization of manganese (Lynn and Bonatti, 1965; Li et al., 1969 and others). It is well known that in areas where reducing conditions prevail below the sediment–water interface, Mn^{4+} in manganese dioxide minerals is reduced on burial to divalent manganese which passes into solution in the interstitial waters of the sediments. It then migrates upwards to become reoxidized in the oxidizing upper sediments and reprecipitates as manganese dioxide. This is a cyclical process leading to the continual enrichment of manganese in the uppermost parts of the sediment column in many lakes and continental margin areas where reducing conditions are encountered at shallow depths. However, Elderfield (1976b) has calculated on the basis of vertical advection-diffusion-reaction models that diagenetic remobilization of manganese from buried reducing sediments is only likely to be important in supplying manganese to the surface if the reducing sediments are overlain by less than 20–30 cm of oxidizing sediments. Furthermore, Bender (1971) has calculated on the basis of a diffusion model that manganese cannot migrate through the thickness of oxidized sediment found in deep-sea areas to contribute appreciably to the manganese accumulation at the sediment–water interface. Thus the upward diffusion of manganese from deeply buried sediments would not appear to be an important supply path for this element in deep-sea nodules, but is likely to be of considerable importance in supplying manganese to concretions forming in continental margin, near-shore, and lacustrine areas.

It is the role of volcanic activity in supplying metals to nodules and encrustations that is still surrounded by most controversy. As mentioned in Chapter 1, in this there are not one but at least three possible sources. First, there is direct hydrothermal supply of elements to the sea floor by submarine hot springs, the elements either being derived from magmatic sources or from the high temperature interaction between sea water and newly consolidated lava (Bostrom et al., 1969; Corliss, 1971). Secondly, there is the low temperature alteration of basalt (halmyrolysis), on the sea floor (Varentsov, 1970) which has already been considered. Naturally, there are all gradations between these two processes with likely variations in the rate and nature of element supply to the sea floor. Thirdly, there is the direct occlusion of detrital volcanic fragments by forming nodules, most prevalent in areas of submarine volcanoclastic deposition and of significance in enriching some metals such as chromium and silica in the deposits (Cronan and Tooms, 1967b). Determination of what proportions of the elements supplied to the deposits that accrue from these different volcanic sources is very difficult indeed.

Low temperature alteration of submarine basalt might be expected anywhere that volcanic rocks outcrop on the sea floor, although this possibility conflicts with the finding sometimes of fresh submarine basalts of considerable age. The quantitative importance of halmyrolysis in supplying metals to nodules and encrustations cannot be fully evaluated although Varentsov (1970) has estimated on the basis of leaching experiments of volcanic material that it is not less important than continental runoff in this regard.

Rather less difficult to quantify is the role of submarine hydrothermal activity in supplying elements to forming nodules and encrustations. Evidence accumulated to date suggests that its role may be rather limited, other than possibly in contributing to the manganese content of sea water in general (Lyle, 1976). Data reviewed in Chapter 6 indicate that iron and manganese of hydrothermal origin are the end precipitates in a selective hydrothermal fractionation process, most of the other elements in which have already been precipitated. Under the oxidizing conditions in which ferromanganese oxide concretions form, the bulk of such iron and manganese would be expected to precipitate close to their point of discharge on the sea floor. Furthermore they would be strongly fractionated from each other over short distances, and fractionated from minor metals, quite the opposite of what is found in most large nodule fields. For example, the manganese oxides of hydrothermal origin in the TAG hydrothermal field on the Mid-Atlantic Ridge, are closely related to the hydrothermal vents and poor in minor metals (Rona, 1976). Similarly, Hoffert *et al.* (1978) have found hydrothermal iron and manganese oxides closely associated with other hydrothermal deposits near vents in the FAMOUS area on the Mid-Atlantic Ridge in which the iron and manganese are fractionated from each other and the deposits are low in metals normally enriched in nodules. They are very different in composition from more normal ferromanganese oxide encrustations on nearby basalt outcrops.

5.2.2 Transport and extraction mechanisms

Whatever the source of the potential constituents of nodules and encrustations, some mechanism is required to transport them to reaction sites where they can be extracted into the forming ferromanganese oxides. As with the sources of the elements, this is part of the more general problem of element supply to the sea floor which has already been considered in general terms in Chapter 1. However, some specific mechanisms have been proposed for bringing elements to forming ferromanganese oxide deposits and these will be considered here.

The most obvious mechanism by which manganese and associated elements can be transported to the sediment–water interface is by the normal processes of oceanic circulation and mixing. It has become increasingly evident in recent years that different sea water masses have distinctive properties. These may influence the composition of nodules and encrustations precipitated from them. Ferromanganese oxides forming in areas swept clear of bottom sediments by strong currents, such as the tops of some seamounts for example, are amongst the deposits most likely to receive their constituents principally by simple chemical removal from sea water.

According to Murray and Brewer (1977), the removal of iron and manganese from sea water is dependent on the forms in which the metals exist. Both elements can occur as colloids or associated with fine-grained clay minerals, or as various solution species.

The small size of the colloidal and particulate phases ensures that they remain in suspension for long periods unless they agglomerate into larger particles or take part in biological processes such as fecal pellet formation. Adsorption of organic matter can influence the stability of colloidal varieties of iron and manganese. Iron in oxygenated sea water is in the 3^+ oxidation state which is very insoluble. However, more iron appears to be present in the oceans than would be expected on the basis of solubility considerations alone, suggesting that much of it is in a very fine particulate form indistinguishable from soluble iron by conventional filter techniques. Murray and Brewer also note that thermodynamic considerations lead to the prediction that manganese should exist in sea water in the 4^+ oxidation state, and, as MnO_2, would be very insoluble. However, they report that most experimental work has tended to suggest that manganese is predominantly in sea water in the Mn^{2+} state, the upper limit of the solubility of which may be controlled by the formation of $MnCO_3$.

Adsorption is a mechanism often proposed for extracting minor elements from sea water into forming ferromanganese oxides (Crerar and Barnes, 1974; Glasby, 1974) often on the basis of correlations between certain elements, or groups of elements, and either manganese or iron. Goldberg (1954) suggested that elements were adsorbed either on to particulate iron or manganese phases, depending on the relationship between the charge density of the adsorbing surface and that of the adsorbed ion. Opposite charges attract, so negatively charged MnO_2 would attract positively charged ions and vice versa for positively charged Fe oxides. Murray and Brewer (1977) report experimental data which suggest that manganese and iron oxides can remove considerable amounts of minor metals from sea water, MnO_2 being about two to three times more effective than iron oxides in this regard. However, recent considerations on the charges on manganese and iron oxides in the marine environment by Calvert and Price (1977b), among others, have indicated that the charges vary according to the nature of the depositional environment, and that this can markedly affect the adsorption capacities of the oxides. This will be discussed more fully when the chemistry of the deposits is considered in section 5.7.

Another mechanism for extracting metals from sea water and transporting them to the sea floor is that of biological removal (Chapter 1). Correns (1941) suggested that manganese could be extracted from sea water by foraminifera, transported to deep waters when the organisms die, and liberated to the bottom waters on dissolution of their tests. Many other metals are known to be enriched in plankton assemblages (Vinogradov, 1953) and could also be supplied to the sea floor when the organisms die. This mechanism is thought to be especially important in enriching certain metals in nodules under areas of high biological productivity, and will be reviewed in more detail in section 5.9.1.2. Some workers have suggested that bacteria play a role in the formation of nodules (Ehrlich, 1972), which will be discussed when the growth mechanisms of the nodules and encrustations are considered (section 5.6).

5.3   General Appearance

Ferromanganese oxide concretions from oceans, seas, and lakes exhibit a great variety of shapes and sizes, which in some cases can vary quite considerably over relatively short distances. Sometimes more than one morphological population can occur at the same site (Cronan and Tooms, 1967b; Raab and Meylan, 1977). Characteristically, the deposits contain a nucleus consisting of a foreign body of some sort or another, encrusted by ferromanganese oxides of variable thickness. Raab and Meylan (1977) have divided ferromanganese concretions into four categories on the basis of their depositional nature. These are stains, agglutinations, nodules, and crusts. Stains are very thin deposits on rocks and other materials. Agglutinations are clusters of nuclei covered by a thin encrustation of oxides, nodules have thicker oxide accumulations around their nuclei, and crusts are more or less continuous accumulations of ferromanganese oxides on rock outcrops or large boulders. These various depositional types grade into one another and there are no clear cut boundaries between the different forms defined.

   Almost all ferromanganese oxide deposits contain a nucleus of one sort or another, which determines the shape of the early formed concretion. Almost any object will serve as a nucleus for concretionary ferromanganese oxide growth but quantitatively most important, at least on the deep sea floor, is volcanic debris of various types. In general, the more altered it is, the thicker is the oxide coating. Sometimes relatively fresh and altered volcanics are found at the same locality, the latter being much more heavily encrusted than the former. This may in some way be related to the alteration of the volcanics catalysing the precipitation of iron and manganese oxides (Cronan, 1976c). Other nuclei commonly found in deep sea nodules are various organic remains such as sharks' teeth, foram tests, etc., while phosphorite and other inorganic deposits may also serve in this regard. Often, however, the nucleus is a fragment of a pre-existing nodule which has been fractured. Some nodules appear to have no nucleus at all. When this occurs sometimes there is a void at the centre but more frequently the nucleus has simply been replaced by accreting ferromanganese oxides. Most lacustrine and near shore concretions form around pebbles or sand grains, but lumps of glacial clay, organic remains and even beer cans sometimes serve as suitable nuclei (Sozanski and Cronan, 1976).

Various authors have devised terminologies to describe the morphology of manganese nodules, as distinct from the other varieties of ferromanganese oxide deposits (Murray and Renard, 1891; Manheim, 1965; Goodell *et al.*, 1971; Heezen and Hollister, 1971; Raab, 1972; Meylan, 1974). Such obvious terms as spherical, ellipsoidal, tabular, flattened, polygonal and tubercular have been used, together with some colourful, but geometrically less explicit, terms such as potato, saucer, grape or hamburger shaped. According to Raab and Meylan (1977), the shapes of most mononucleate nodules would fit into the four main classes of pebble shapes described by Zingg (1935), i.e. oblate, equant, bladed and prolate. However, the morphology of polynucleate nodules formed by the coalescence of several smaller nodules cannot be classified so easily, nor can some formed around odd-shaped nuclei such as various artifacts or organic remains.

In their surface texture, ferromanganese oxide concretions commonly exhibit a mamillated appearance (hemispherical protrusions) on which small tubercles or "goose bumps" are sometimes superimposed (Raab, 1972). The size of the mamillae vary greatly in proportion to the overall size of the concretion, as does their relief. Other concretions exhibit smooth surfaces while in other cases cracks and pits are common. In extreme cases, the surface of the nodule has almost a vesicular appearance like that of some lava flows, but this is rare and the resemblance should not be considered to be of genetic significance.

Microscopic studies on nodule surfaces have revealed a wealth of organic structures not visible to the naked eye. Greenslate (1974, 1975) has reported the presence of several shelter building organisms on nodule surfaces, that benthic foraminifera of the genus *Saccorhiza* agglutinate manganese micro-nodules to the nodule surface as part of their tube building activities, and that other organisms build structures containing iron and manganese compounds in abundance. No data were available to indicate what proportion of the structures were occupied at the time of the sample collection. Most of the structures were found to be less than 0·5 mm in diameter and were generally tubular or dome shaped. The larger tubes were made up of agglutinated mineral grains, radiolarian fragments and sponge spicules, as well as micronodules. Dugolinsky (1976a, b) has also reported a number of organic structures on nodules, considering that they are most abundant on specimens collected in the north-east equatorial Pacific. However, he reported that the ·areas of the nodules covered were often highly variable. Interestingly he found the remains to be most abundant on those surfaces of nodules exposed to sea water, with the greatest abundances occurring on or near the "equatorial bulge" of *in situ* nodules where growth is probably faster than elsewhere.

Organic structures are not confined to marine concretions. Sozanski (1974) has reported the presence of biological structures on concretions collected in Shebandowan Lakes, Ontario. Particularly common were colonies of the fungus *aposphaeria* whose diameters were very similar to those of iron and manganese botryoids common on the concretion surface, and which may have served as structures in which the botryoids could grow. The possible genetic significance of organic structures on nodule surfaces will be discussed subsequently (section 5.6.2).

5.3.1 Deep-sea concretions

There have been several attempts to classify deep-sea concretions on the basis of their shape, surface textures and other morphological characteristics. Grant (1967) and Goodell *et al.* (1971) defined "nodules" which have a single nucleus and a relatively thick oxide coating, "botryoidals" which are oval or flattened concretions with several nuclei which resemble grape-like clusters, "crusts" which have a single nucleus and relatively thin oxide coating and "agglomerates" which consist of irregular masses composed of pebbles, or similar objects, encrusted by a thin ferromanganese oxide coating. Meyer (1973) has described six facies of manganese nodules in the North Pacific

Table 5. Field classification of manganese nodules (from Meylan, 1974).

Prefix:	s = small = <3 cm m = medium = 3–6 cm l = large = >6 cm	nodule size (Maximum diameter)
Primary morphology:	[S] = Spheroidal [E] = Ellipsoidal [D] = Discoidal (or tabular-discoidal form) [P] = "Poly" (coalespheroidal or botryoidal form) [B] = Biological (shape determined by tooth, vertebra, or bone nucleus) [T] = Tabular [F] = Faceted (polygonal form due to angular nucleus or fracturing)	
Suffix:	s = smooth (smooth or microgranular) r = rough (granular or microbotryoidal) b = botryoidal	surface texture
Examples:	l[D]b	= large discoidal nodule with botryoidal surface
	$m - l[E]_{r-b}^{s}$	= medium to large ellipsoidal nodules with smooth tops, rough to botryoidal bottoms

on the basis of a combination of characteristics. He recognized discoidal types, ellipsoidal or spheroidal types with a smooth surface, spheroidal types which tend to be elongated and with a rough gritty surface, spheroidal types with intergrowths, very spheroidal types with smooth surfaces and no intergrowths and irregular spheroidal types with differences between the upper and lower surfaces. Perhaps the most comprehensive classification of nodule morphology compiled to date is that of Meylan and Craig (Meylan, 1974) devised to describe nodule morphology in the North Pacific "ore zone". The deposits were classified on the basis of size, shape and surface texture and the scheme is given in Table 5.

An important difficulty in attempting to devise a uniformly applicable morphological classification for all deep-sea manganese nodules, let alone encrustations and other forms, is their tremendous diversity. Most of the classification schemes published to date have tended to be compiled for nodules from specific regions, i.e. the Antarctic (Goodell et al., 1971) or the north-eastern equatorial Pacific (Meyer, 1973; Meylan, 1974). However, common morphological features in any one area rarely persist unchanged into other areas. In order to be universally valid, a morphological classification has to be so general as to be of limited value in describing nodules from individual regions. Descriptive classifications are of considerable use in characterizing nodules within individual deposit regions, particularly for exploration purposes, but on a world-wide scale genetic classifications are probably more useful.

A good description of the variability of nodules on an ocean wide basis has been provided by Moorby (1978). Working on Indian Ocean nodules, Moorby described a wide range of morphologies based on size, shape and surface texture which illustrates some of the features of nodule appearance discussed in the previous pages. Moorby's samples exhibited a wide range of diameters varying from less than 1 cm to more than 25 cm with the largest samples being from the African continental margin. However, most samples had a diameter of between 3 and 6 cm. In their shape, the nodules were also very variable, ranging from spheroidal, through ellipsoidal to flattened and irregular (Fig. 19). Some nodules showed slight surface irregularities (Fig. 20) probably due to small secondary growths. Irregularities could sometimes be due to irregularities in the shape of the nucleus of the nodule (Fig. 21), but these tend to become smoothed out with increasing growth. Further irregularities observed were caused by individual nodules adhering together (Fig. 22) particularly common in the Madagascar Basin. From one station off Madagascar, Moorby observed highly elongated nodules (Fig. 23) which were associated with small fairly regular shaped nodules in the same haul. The former are thought to have formed around iron nails which have become completely oxidized and in some cases partially dissolved. The area in which

Fig. 19. Shapes of manganese nodules from the Indian and Atlantic Oceans: (a) spherical nodule; (b) irregular to elongated nodule; (c) flattened nodule. Scales on Figs 19–26, 28 are in centimetres (from Moorby, 1978).

Fig. 20. Surface irregularities on a manganese nodule from the Indian Ocean (from Moorby, 1978).

Fig. 21. Influence of the shape of the nucleus on internal banding in a manganese nodule from the Indian Ocean (from Moorby, 1978).

Fig. 22. Polynucleate nodules from the Indian Ocean (from Moorby, 1978).

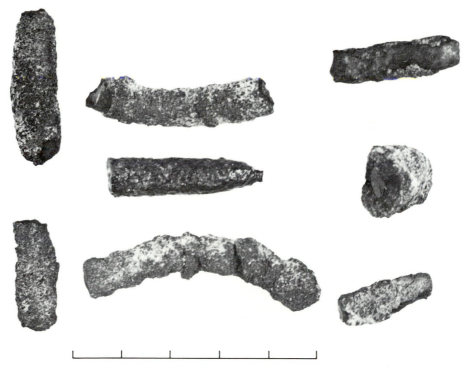

Fig. 23. Elongate nodules from off Madagascar (from Moorby, 1978).

Fig. 24. Surface textures of manganese nodules from the Indian ocean: (a) smooth, (b) granular (from Moorby, 1978).

the deposits were found has been one of shipping ever since the early Portuguese excursions into the Indian Ocean, and the occurrence of normal shape nodules at the same site indicates that the shape of the elongated deposits is not conditioned by the depositional environment. These curious deposits add to the list of artifacts around which ferromanganese concretions accumulate, others including naval shells, spark plugs and beer cans. The surface textures of the samples described by Moorby varied from smooth and polished to coarsely granular with transitional varieties between the two (Fig. 24). Often the most polished specimens were those from areas of strong bottom scour. The surface shapes of the deposits varied from regular to highly botryoidal or cavernous. Nobby lumps were common in many samples (Fig. 25) which if large gave the whole sample an irregular appearance. Some nodules, especially those from the Central Indian Basin, had a very cavernous surface, a structure which was also common on many encrustation fragments (Fig. 26). Moorby was not able to discern any distinct regional trends in the shapes or surface textures of the samples he examined, but many areas were so sparsely sampled that rigorous inter-regional comparisons were not possible. Despite this, some general trends were observable. For example, nodules from the south-western Indian Ocean generally had smoother surfaces, were less friable and were browner in colour than those from the central and eastern basins. The latter tended to be blacker in colour and to exhibit cavernous surfaces. The colour of the deposits is probably a reflection of their composition, the browner deposits being richer in iron than the black ones, while the differences between the surface features may be ascribed to environmental differences between their respective depositional regions.

Individual deep-sea nodules do not always have a uniform morphology on every side (Murray and Renard, 1891; Hubred, 1970; Raab, 1972). In general, the larger the concretion, the greater is the likelihood of differences between one side and another, particularly between top and bottom. The latter feature is well illustrated by the so-called "hamburger"-shaped nodules (Fig. 27) from the North Pacific ore zone described by Raab (1972). The surfaces of these nodules often have a smooth texture where they are exposed to sea water. By contrast the buried undersides exhibit a coarse gritty texture in which underlying sediment is often trapped. These nodules are also characterized by a pisolitic or knobby band near the equatorial rim which marks the position at which the nodule rested in the sediment, and which is often rich in organic debris (Greenslate, 1975). The characteristic shape of these nodules implies that they have not been overturned on the sea floor in recent times, and, while not common throughout the World Ocean, has a very important genetic implication with regard to the sources of their elements (see section 5.9.1.2).

5.3.2   Near-shore and lacustrine concretions

Shallow marine and lacustrine concretions often have appearances different from those in the deep ocean. A wide range of shapes occur in such environments, often very variable on a local scale, but there is a marked tendency for flattened, saucer, and especially disc-like concretions to be more abundant than on the deep ocean floor (Fig. 28).

Winterhalter (1980) has reviewed the extensive work done on ferromanganese oxide concretions in the Baltic Sea, one of the best studied environments of near-shore ferromanganese oxide deposition. He defined

Fig. 25. Nobby lumps on a manganese nodule from the Indian Ocean (from Moorby, 1978).

Fig. 26. Cavernous surface on an encrustation fragment from the Indian Ocean (from Moorby, 1978).

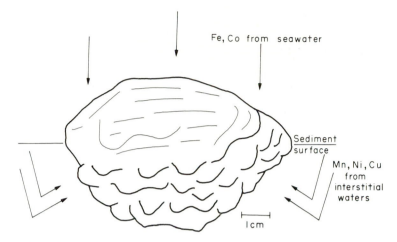

Fig. 27. Morphological and compositional differences between the top and bottom of a "hamburger"-shaped nodule from the north-eastern equatorial Pacific "ore zone" (from Cronan, 1978b).

three distinctly different types of concretions. First, there are spheroidal (oolitic or pisolitic) concretions ranging in size from microscopic up to 3 cm in diameter. Secondly, there are discoidal "penny ore" concretions with a marked lateral growth around a mineral fragment or pebble which acts as a nucleus. Thirdly, there are crust-like accretions of iron and manganese oxides on various substrates such as erosion surfaces or areas where no sedimentation is taking place at the present time. The spheroidal concretions are the most abundant and generally occur at the sediment–water interface. However, they may be partly covered by a thin mobile layer of sediment, or, more rarely, can be completely buried to a depth of a few centimetres. Very occasionally, the concretions have been observed buried at a depth of more than 10 cm, where they are undergoing dissolution. The discoidal concretions generally have a convex upper side and a concave lower side, with the top surface showing botryoidal growth features, but with the main growth occurring laterally around the concretion rim. The crusts can be divided into encrustations on the sea floor itself or around various objects. The latter are the most common and occur everywhere that objects available for encrustation protrude above the sediment surface. Often the crusts comprise no more than a thin film of oxide coating (stains), especially on pebbles and boulders, but sometimes reach thicknesses of several millimetres on indurated lumps of glacial clay. In some instances, evidence was observed of crusts having been broken and later re-cemented to form larger aggregates. Some fragments of crusts were also observed to have changed their style of growth

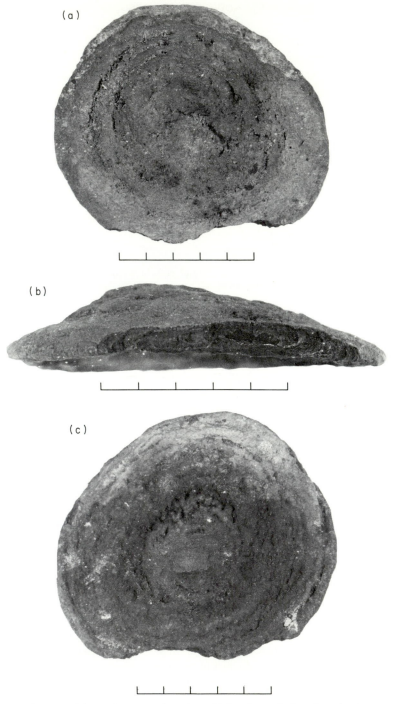

Fig. 28. Disc-shaped lacustrine concretions from Shebandowan Lakes, Ontario: (a) top view; (b) side view; (c) bottom view.

to that of discoidal concretions, suggesting a change in depositional conditions during the growth history of the deposits.

Lacustrine concretions are best developed in north temperate latitudes, often having been reported in Russia, Northern Europe, the United States and Canada. Dean and Ghosh (1980) have reviewed data on concretions from North American lakes, illustrating the variability of these deposits. Great Lakes' concretions tend to consist largely of oxide coatings on an unconsolidated substrate, often sand grains, and usually have thinner ferromanganese oxide accumulations than are found in smaller lakes (Rossmann and Callender, 1968; Cronan and Thomas, 1970); however, spherical concretions also occur. Schottle and Friedman (1971) have described three types of concretion morphology in the smaller Lake George, New York. Most samples are spherical, ranging in diameter from less than 1 mm to about 1 cm. Rarer discoidal concretions range up to 6 cm in size and are between 2 mm and 1 cm thick. Irregular lumps of ferromanganese oxides also occur. Like shallow marine concretions, discoidal lacustrine concretions form convex side up, a feature which when observed in Oneida Lake, New York, gave rise to the term "Oneida pancakes" for the deposits (Gillette, 1961). These deposits range in size up to 15 cm across, and more (Dean and Ghosh, 1980). Several varieties of concretion morphology have been observed in the small Shebandowan Lakes system, Ontario (Sozanski and Cronan, 1976), all but one approximating to the discoidal type which develops just above and parallel to the sediment–water interface (Fig. 28). Examples of the morphologies found are given in Figs 29 and 30. Differences between morphologies were thought to reflect differences between the environments in which the concretions were formed. "Mushroom" and "top ring" concretions developed well away from the sediments around the apices of large pebbles

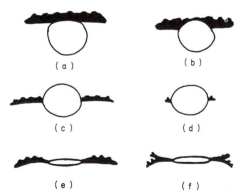

Fig. 29. Schematic vertical cross-sections of common morphological variants of concentric concretions in Shebandowan Lakes, Ontario: (a) mushroom; (b) top ring; (c) saturnine; (d) equatorial skirt; (e) disc with downcurl; (f) pulley (from Sozanski and Cronan, 1976).

1a

1b

2

3

4

5

6

7

8

0 Cm 1 2 3 4 5 6 7 8 9 10

or cobbles, and populated the shallowest most oxygenated portions of the lakes. By contrast, "equatorial" and "bottom ring" varieties accumulated at or near the sediment–water interface. Surface textures on these concretions indicated growth on active surfaces at the concretion rims with possible dissolution of the inner rims on aging.

5.3.3 Factors influencing the morphology of ferromanganese oxide concretions

The morphological characteristics of manganese nodules and encrustations can be related to a number of factors, among which the source of their elements, the nature and age of their nuclei, their depositional environment, and diagenetic processes are particularly important. Probably the main factor in determining the major morphological features of ferromanganese oxide concretions, particularly their shape, is the principal supply path through which they receive their constituents. Notwithstanding the general considerations regarding element sources to ferromanganese oxides already discussed, elements will be supplied to concretions either from overlying sea water or underlying interstitial waters. In oxidizing deep-sea environments with little sediment accumulation, encrustations are a common depositional feature on exposed rock outcrops. These must receive the bulk of their constituents from sea water as they rest on a substrate through which interstitial waters cannot pass. Nodules formed in many current-swept deep-sea areas probably also receive the bulk of their metals from sea water, and approach equal dimensionality as a result of being moved around on the sea floor (Fig. 31a). By contrast, in lakes and shallow water near-shore areas, where there is a reducing substrate, diagenetic recycling of elements through the sediments and their upward migration from below are important factors influencing nodule

---

Fig. 30. Concretions from Shebandowan Lakes. 1a, b, Bottom and side views of a saturnine concretion. Unusually deep down-concavity and height are probably due to progressive emergence of granitic nucleus in sand. 2, Side view of a pulley showing angle, between active upper side ridge and downcurl edges, peppered with oxide globuli. 3, Polygonal fracturing of nucleus, an old concretion fragment. Bottom view. 4, Fracturing and healing by oxide material along radial and concentric directions. Veins stand out in relief by as much as 1 mm, possibly suggesting partial dissolution of the concretion, evidently more soluble than injected material. Veins do not penetrate active edge (fracturing does), implying outward concretion growth subsequent to veining. This bottom side view is very similar to upper side of the specimen. 5, Large hatlike concretion, with upper side ridge located well inward relative to downcurl (cf. 2 and 6). Presence of globuli throughout upper surface is not common and possibly suggests a reactivation of central portion. 6, Top view of a pulley with inactive centre. 7, Top view of a mushroom. 8, Slaglike concretion resulting from intergranular penetration by Fe-Mn oxides of *in situ* eroded hunks of hardpan sand. Presence of rounded holes and arcuate sculpturing of surface testifies to powerful or prolonged bottom current action at a depth of about 6 m below lake surface (from Sozanski and Cronan, 1976).

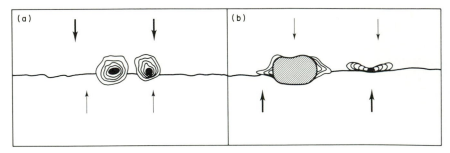

Fig. 31. Morphology of ferromanganese oxide concretions as a function of metal supply: (a) dominant supply from sea water; (b) dominant supply from interstitial water (from Manheim, 1965).

morphology (Fig. 31b). For example, Mn migrating from below through interstitial waters will be deflected to the margins of potential nuclei and precipitates at or near the boundary between oxidizing and reducing sediments. In this way, the discoidal concretions so common in shallow water areas can be formed. Thin oxide coatings sometimes found on the tops of nuclei and ridges developed atop oxide rings probably represent the fraction of the elements precipitated from overlying waters, and the latter in conjunction with supply from below is thought to give rise to the pulley-like structures at the leading margins of the discoidal lacustrine concretions described by Sozanski and Cronan (1976). The common absence of an oxide coating on the underside of nuclei of lacustrine concretions is probably due to their burial in a reducing substrate.

Some deep sea nodules exhibit evidence of element supply from both above and below. As mentioned, the characteristic morphology of the "hamburger"-shaped nodules from the North Pacific "ore zone" indicates that they have not been turned over in the sediments, at least during the latter part of their growth histories. Raab (1972) attributed compositional differences between the tops and bottoms of some of the nodules he examined to accretion of elements on their undersides and dissolution from their tops. By contrast, several authors (Greenslate, 1975; Fewkes, 1975; Calvert and Price, 1977a) suggest that a better explanation of this feature, which would also explain morphological differences between the tops and bottoms of the nodules, is accretion of elements from sea water on the upper sides of the nodules and from interstitial waters on their undersides (Fig. 27). However, when these nodules were sectioned it was found that the interior layers were relatively uniform in composition all round, in strong contrast to the surface layers (Raab and Meylan, 1977). This would appear to conflict with supply of elements from above and below unless the most recent phase of growth is atypical or the differences between the interior and surface layers are caused by post-depositional reorganization of material within the nodules (section 5.6.1) as has been postulated in other circumstances by Cronan and Tooms (1968), Sorem and Foster (1972b) and Murray and Brewer (1977) among others. The abundance of organic structures on the surfaces of the equatorial bulges of these nodules has already been mentioned and suggests that the organisms themselves may at least be partially responsible for the bulges by agglutinating more material than normal from the sediments.

Source considerations aside, other important factors affecting the shape of manganese nodules are the shapes, ages and natures of their nuclei. As illustrated in Fig. 21, the nucleus of the nodule is very important in determining the shape of the early formed concretionary layers and, because irregularities are smoothed out with time, young nodules with large nuclei are likely to be more irregular than more mature varieties. Nevertheless, the shape of the nucleus can influence nodule morphology throughout its growth history. Cylindrical nodules accreting around nails have already been mentioned. Similarly elliptical nodules tend to have elliptical nuclei, and the morphology of polynucleate nodules is largely determined by the shapes, sizes and relative positions of their several nuclei.

The energy level of the depositional environment is also important in influencing nodule morphology. In areas of strong bottom currents, for example, sediment accumulation may be minimal and nodules can coalesce. In some areas such as the Blake Plateau, sedimentation is absent over large areas and ferromanganese oxide pavements form rather than nodules.

The role of fracturing as a control on nodule morphology has been discussed by Heye (1975), Sozanski and Cronan (1976) and Raab and Meylan (1977), among others. Heye (1975) has argued that fracturing in nodules is an aging feature. This would set a limit to nodule size, and the fractured portion could serve as a nucleus for new ferromanganese oxide growth. This is commonly observed in the Pacific "ore zone" where relatively small near equidimensional nodules often contain as their nuclei fragments of pre-existing nodules. Fracturing and subsequent veining by oxide material is a common feature in discoidal Shebandowan Lakes concretions (Sozanski and Cronan, 1976). The fractures are usually hairline and, if radial, often extend near to the edge of the concretion. Veining usually stands out in relief above the concretion surface, but does not extend to the active "fronts" at the concretion margin. This would suggest that post-depositional dissolution of the inner concentric rings has occurred, and, together with fracturing, may be a factor limiting the size of the concretions and causing their eventual destruction.

Surface textures of nodules and encrustations may also be influenced by a number of factors, including some of those determining concretion shape. For example, source considerations have been invoked to explain the textural differences between the tops and bottoms of nodules. Granular or botryoidal surface textures are usually found in contact with sediments on the bottom of many nodules, while the upper portions in contact with sea water tend to be smooth (Murray and Renard, 1891; Raab, 1972; Craig, 1975). However, the relationship between texture and way up in nodules may not be this straightforward. Moorby (1978) has reported smooth nodules from areas where diagenetic supply of elements from the underlying sediments might be expected, and irregular granular surface textures on encrustation surfaces which must have received elements from the overlying sea water. The matter is complicated by the possibility of post-depositional erosion of nodules under changed environmental conditions. Moorby (1978) described nodules on which the prominent areas had become smoothed while granular textures were preserved in depressions. Furthermore, in areas of strong bottom currents where sediment may be transported in suspension, highly polished nodules quite different in appearance from normal have been found. Similar features have been reported by Heye (1975) on a nodule, the radiometric dating of which indicated that the surface was in the order of 300 000 years old. Biological agencies may also influence the surface texture of nodules as has been described, but a greater understanding of this problem must await further work.

5.4   Distribution

The distribution of manganese nodules and encrustations is very variable on an ocean-wide basis, and can also be highly variable on a scale of a kilometre or less. Nevertheless there are certain regional regularities in average nodule abundance that permit broad areas of the oceans to be categorized as containing abundant nodules or otherwise, although it should always be borne in mind that within these regions large variations in nodule abundance can occur. Understanding the distribution of encrustations poses less of a problem as they occur mainly on rock outcrops and thus their distribution is related to that of exposed rock surfaces. In this section the factors determining nodule abundance on both regional and local scales are reviewed, and the regional distribution of nodules in the World Ocean is described.

5.4.1   Factors determining nodule distribution

The distribution of nodules and encrustations in marine and lacustrine environments is a function of a variety of factors which include the degree of oxidation of the depositional environment, the presence of nucleating agents and/or the nature and age of the substrate, the proximity of sources of elements, sedimentation rates largely influenced by proximity to sources of sediment supply or bottom current activity, and the influence of organisms. Both local and regional variations in nodule distribution result from complex interplay of these and possibly other factors, in a way that is not yet fully understood.

An important prerequisite for any underwater concretionary ferromanganese oxide accumulation is a high degree of oxidation of the depositional environment. Unless the redox potential of the environment is significantly positive, oxidation of Mn^{2+} to Mn^{4+} and the formation of MnO_2 will not take place. This important fact restricts the occurrence of manganese nodules and encrustations to oxidizing environments. Ferromanganese oxides are not found in stagnant areas of seas or lakes, nor on areas of the sea floor where reducing conditions prevail at the sediment surface. Under poorly oxidizing conditions manganese carbonate may occur rather than manganese oxide, and has been reported in both lake and near-shore environments (Callender, 1973; Calvert and Price, 1970). The degree of oxidation of the depositional environment is thus of prime importance not only in determining the presence or absence of ferromanganese oxide concretions but also in influencing where and to what extent other manganese minerals occur on the floors of oceans and lakes.

Even if environmental conditions are suitable for ferromanganese oxide deposition, concretion accumulation will not take place unless a suitable nucleus is present on which the oxides can accrete. In the absence of such nuclei, manganese micronodules dispersed throughout the sediments may occur in preference to manganese nodules. The abundance of potential nuclei on the sea floor is thus of prime importance in determining nodule distribution. As most nodule nuclei are volcanic in origin (section 5.3) patterns of volcanic activity and the subsequent dispersal of volcanoclastics have an important influence on where and in what amounts nodules occur. Pumice fragments from terrestial volcanic eruptions can travel long distances before sinking to the sea floor and thus volcanic nuclei are not restricted to submarine volcanic areas. However, within such areas submarine eruptions and subsequent brecciation of the lava flows can provide abundant nuclei around which nodules can accrete. Glasby et al. (1974) have noted for example that the distribution of nodules in a small area on the Carlsberg Ridge is largely governed by the distribution of tuffaceous nuclei. In addition, Craig (1979) has suggested that different volcanic events can lead to several generations of nuclei in areas of submarine volcanic activity, and this can give rise to varying nodule distributions and morphologies. As mentioned earlier, materials other than volcanoclastics can also be important as nodule nuclei. Biogenic debris such as sharks' teeth, etc. can be locally abundant in areas of slow sedimentation, and their distribution will influence the abundance of nodules in such areas. Glacial erratics can serve as nodule nuclei in high latitudes, and thus nodule distribution in these areas will be partly a function of the dispersal patterns of icebergs which in turn are related to surface ocean currents and high latitude wind patterns.

In addition to the presence of potential nuclei on the sea floor influencing the distribution of manganese nodules, the age of the nuclei is also important in this regard. In areas where the nuclei have only recently formed, insufficient time may have elapsed to enable significant concretionary ferromanganese oxide accumulation to have taken place. By contrast, where the nuclei are older, not only are thicker oxide accumulations likely to occur leading to the nodules occupying a greater area of the sea floor, but in areas of closely spaced nuclei coalescence of nodules may occur leading to ferromanganese oxide pavement formation. As most nuclei are subject to replacement with time, old nodules have sometimes completely replaced their nuclei and have fractured in the manner described in the previous section, thus providing abundant nodule fragments to serve as fresh nuclei for ferromanganese oxide deposition. In this way, given sufficient time, areas which initially contained only limited nuclei may become covered with nodules. Such appears to be the case in parts of the North Pacific "ore zone".

Another important factor in determining the distribution of nodules and the thickness of encrustations, is the proximity of sources of metals. Nodules may occur in abundance in lakes and near-shore environments in the vicinity of river inflow where iron and manganese are being precipitated on mixing of two water masses. High biological productivity in surface waters of the equatorial regions of the oceans may assist in leading to widespread nodule accumulation on the underlying sea floor, because of biological fluxing of metals to the bottom waters (section 5.2.2). Piper and Williamson (1977), among others, have suggested that manganese accumulates faster than normal under such circumstances. Proximity of a local diagenetic source of manganese just below the sediment–water interface may lead to locally abundant nodules on the sea floor as was noted by Cronan (1976c) in the Mexican continental borderland. Andrews (1976) has suggested that higher than average abundances of nodules in Pacific fracture zones may be related to local volcanic sources of elements, and/or nuclei, and the rapid accumulation of manganese crusts on ridge crests in association with submarine hydrothermal activity is well documented (Rona, 1980; Moore and Vogt, 1976; Burnett and Piper, 1977).

One of the most important environmental conditions affecting nodule abundance on the sea floor is the rate of accumulation of their associated sediments, low sedimentation rates favouring nodule development. Sedimentation rates are determined either by the rate of sediment supply or bottom conditions affecting sediment accumulation. Areas of the sea floor where sedimentation is rapid are generally poorly covered with nodules, most likely because potential nodule nuclei or even embryonic nodules are buried before appreciable ferromanganese oxide accumulation can take place. Furthermore, rapid sedimentation of organic material can result in its preservation in the sediments which may lead to insufficiently oxidizing conditions at the sediment–water interface to permit ferromanganese oxide formation. Most continental margin areas have sedimentation rates too rapid for appreciable nodule development, as do turbidite-floored deep-sea basins and large portions of many lakes. Low rates of sedimentation can result either from a minimal sediment supply or bottom conditions, particularly currents, inhibiting sediment deposition. Large areas in the centres of ocean basins receive minimal terrigenous input and are either under poorly productive waters resulting in little accumulation of biogenous sediment, or are below the carbonate compensation depth and thus receive no carbonate debris. Under these conditions, sedimentation rates as low as a few millimetres per thousand years can occur, as, for example, in parts of the North Pacific (Hayes *et al.*, 1969; Opdyke and Foster, 1970), favouring substantial accumulation of nodules at the sediment surface. Bottom current activity can be very important in inhibiting sediment accumulation on a local scale and thus influencing local distribution patterns of nodules (Pautot and Melguen, 1976), but if sufficiently extensive can also influence nodule distribution on a regional scale, as for example under the Antarctic Circumpolar Current between Antarctica and Australia where sedimentation is limited and nodules are abundant (Watkins and Kennett, 1971, 1972; Payne and Connolly, 1972).

A good illustration of the importance of sedimentation rates in influencing the distribution and abundance of nodules at the sediment surface has been provided by Mizuno and Moritani (1976). During exploration for ore grade nodules in the Central Pacific, they noted a relationship between nodule abundance on the sea floor and the thickness of the upper transparent sediments which appeared on 3·5 kHz PDR (precision depth recorder) records. With rare exceptions the thinner the transparent layer the greater was the abundance of nodules at the sediment surface, the two being generally correlated over a large area. The age of the transparent layer was not closely defined in the region studied, but was considered to represent Quaternary or Upper Tertiary sediments, and its thickness is obviously largely a function of the sedimentation rates. The greatest abundance of nodules therefore occurs on the slowest accumulating sediments. Mizuno and Moritanis' work has an exploration significance in that by looking for the transparent layer at its thinnest, the chances of finding abundant nodules increase.

The role of benthic organisms in influencing nodule distribution is not very clear. On a local scale, bottom dwellers can move nodules, or cover them with sediments, or maintain nodules at the surface which would otherwise become buried (Mero, 1965; Andrews and Meylan, 1972; Glasby and Read, 1976). Glasby (1977b) has estimated that the energy required to keep nodules at the surface by bottom dwellers is very small.

5.4.2   Local variability in nodule distribution and morphology

The factors affecting nodule distribution and morphology outlined in previous sections interact to cause local variability in nodule distribution and morphology over small areas. For example, Cronan and Tooms (1967b) noted the occurrence of two morphological populations of nodules in a single dredge haul on the Carlsberg Ridge which could have been because the dredge had sampled two separate populations during the course of its traverse, or because two separate populations of nodules were present on the sea floor together. Craig (1975) has even reported different types and sizes of nodules occurring within a single free-fall grab sampler in the Pacific. Craig (1979) has noted in the North Pacific that areas of rugged bathymetric relief along structural trends have the most irregularly distributed nodule populations and this generalization can be extended to other high relief areas. Flat areas tend to have more evenly distributed nodule populations, but sometimes with a lower overall density of coverage than on nearby hills.

Most of the work that has been done to date on small-scale variability in nodule abundance and distribution on the sea floor has been done in the North Pacific. The variability can be largely accounted for by small-scale variations in topography, nodules preferentially occupying certain parts of hills or valleys depending upon the local circumstances. For example, Andrews and Friedrich (1980) have recorded considerable variability in the abundance of nodules on an abyssal hill 250 m high. Near the top of the hill the nodule population was sparse and lava outcrops were common. On the slopes of the hill, basalt outcrops were also found, and dense nodule fields occurred between the flows. Near the bottom of the hill the nodules were sparse at the sediment surface and partially buried nodules were sometimes recognized. On part of the hill slope, two distinct nodule populations were found. In another area these authors found nodule distribution following topographic trends. The lowest nodule abundances were found in the centre of a valley and on the crest of a hill, whereas the highest densities were found near the sides of the valley and on slopes. In addition to nodule abundance varying with topography in the North Pacific, Andrews and Friedrich found that nodule morphology also varied with topography. Polynucleate nodules predominated on the slopes of high relief features, whereas larger mononucleate nodules occur elsewhere, especially on plains. It may be that the mononucleate nodules are *in situ*, especially when "hamburger"-shaped, whereas the polynucleate nodules are mobile and in the process of moving down the sides of hills. Such movement could lead to the inter-mingling of two morphological populations of nodules near the base of the slope, which might account for the occurrence of two nodule populations at some of the sites investigated.

The control of topography on localized nodule distribution in the North Pacific is most probably through its influence on bottom currents, sedimenta-tion rates and sediment redistribution. Craig (1979) has pointed out that sediment thickness and thus presumably sedimentation rates are very variable in the North Pacific abyssal hill region at large, and are strongly influenced by bathymetric relief. Sorem *et al.* (1979) have noted that at least in parts of the North Pacific "ore zone" the uppermost sediment boundary layer with sea water consists of a soft mud with a probable density between that of the underlying more consolidated sediment and the overlying sea water. Small nodules appear to be buoyed up in this layer and grow largely surrounded by it. Thus, it would not require much energy to move them, especially on slopes. According to Craig (1979), the mass movement of sediments is probably enhanced by tectonic activity accompanied by seismic shocks, but because of their watery nature the uppermost sediments could also probably be redistributed by vigorous bottom currents. Downslope sediment redistribution could expose partially buried nodules on hills, bury those on plains and aid in the downslope movement of nodules on high relief features. Complex interplay between such processes in the benthic boundary layer, and others mentioned in previous paragraphs, could lead to the highly variable nodule distribution found on a local scale in areas of bathymetric contrasts. By contrast, more uniform sedimentation in low-relief areas would lead to the more uniform nodule distribution often found in such areas. A further possibility in dense nodule fields is that bottom water turbulence at the sediment–water interface, caused by the unevenness of the sea floor due to the presence of the nodules, might inhibit sedimentation and thus preserve the field from being buried.

The role of bottom current activity in influencing the localized distribution of manganese nodules in the South Pacific has been well illustrated by Pautot and Melguen (1976). In the Tuamoto Archipelago region the ocean floor situated at depths shallower than 4000 m is relatively poor in nodules. Below the lysocline, however, which more or less marks the upper limit of the Antarc-tic Bottom Water, manganese nodules are much more abundant. Similar observations were noted in the South Atlantic where, in the Vema Channel, indurated beds rich in manganese nodules were found to be associated with the passage of the Antarctic Bottom Water. It is evident therefore that this current, by either inhibiting sedimentation or eroding pre-existing sediment, can exert an important influence upon manganese nodule distribution patterns.

More detailed investigations of nodule distribution within individual basins in the South Pacific by Pautot and Melguen (1979) have shown that the nodules are often preferentially concentrated in a limited depth interval. This interval can be as little as 300–500 m. Similar observations have been made in part of the North Atlantic by Addy (1978). In each of these reports, the depth of maximum nodule abundance coincided with the known or inferred upper boundary of the Antarctic Bottom Water. As mentioned, this boundary often coincides with the lysocline, and the supply of metals from the dissolution of the remains of carbonate organisms may be promoting the formation of abundant nodules in the depth interval concerned. These observations have an obvious exploration significance which will be discussed in Chapter 9.

5.4.3 World-wide ferromanganese oxide concretion distribution patterns

In spite of the localized nodule variability discussed in the previous section, generalized nodule distribution patterns can be outlined throughout the World Ocean (Fig. 32). However, as mentioned, within areas of generally abundant nodules, surface concentrations can vary considerably over small distances.

5.4.3.1 *Pacific Ocean*

On average, nodules are most abundant in the Pacific Ocean in a broad band of gently rolling abyssal hills between about 6°N and 20°N extending from approximately 120°W to 160°E (Skornyakova and Andrushchenko, 1970; Ewing *et al.*, 1971; Horn *et al.*, 1972), part of which is the so-called "ore zone" (Fig. 33). The limits of the area are largely determined by sedimentation rates. Towards the equator, rapid biogenic sedimentation associated with the equatorial zone of high productivity limits nodule growth, and concretions are isolated and rare. Similarly, towards the margin of the North Pacific, increasing terrigenous sedimentation, some of it in the form of turbidites, likewise limits nodule growth partly by burial of potential nuclei and partly by promoting an environment not conducive to manganese oxidation. Sediments in the northern part of the area of abundant nodules are red clays with accumulation rates of around 1 mm per thousand years (Opdyke and Foster, 1970) while in the south they are siliceous oozes with rates nearer 3 mm per thousand years or more (Hayes *et al.*, 1969). Interestingly, the highest nodule concentrations appear to occur on the siliceous oozes even though their average sedimentation rate is marginally higher than that of the red clays. This would indicate that factors possibly related to

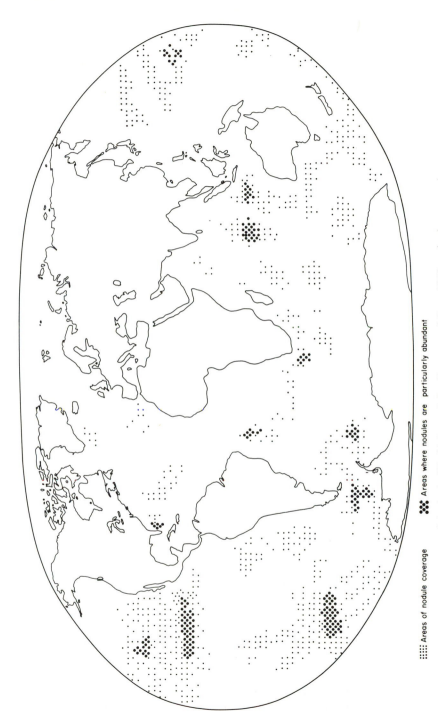

::::: Areas of nodule coverage   ❖❖ Areas where nodules are particularly abundant

Fig. 32. Distribution of manganese nodules in the World Ocean (after Rawson and Ryan 1978, and other sources).

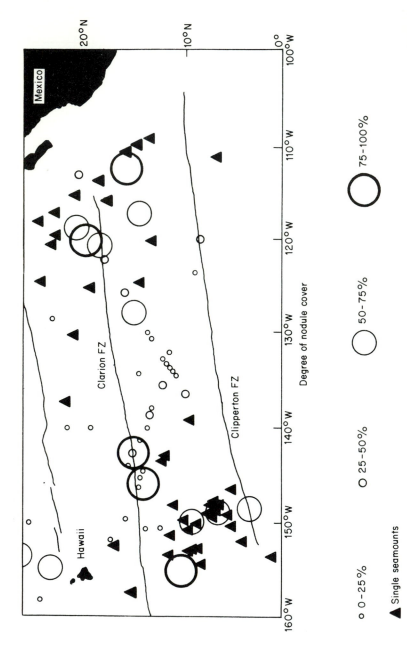

20°N

Mexico

10°N

0°

Clarion FZ

Clipperton FZ

Hawaii

160°W 150°W 140°W 130°W 120°W 110°W 100°W

Degree of nodule cover

○ 0-25%   ○ 25-50%   ◯ 50-75%   ◯ 75-100%

▲ Single seamounts

Fig. 33. Zone of high grade manganese nodules in the north-eastern Pacific Ocean (from Cronan, 1978b, after Horn and co-workers).

a biological source of the metals in the equatorial zone (section 5.2.2) or the environment of deposition (section 5.4.1) are more important in determining average nodule abundance in this area than small differences in sedimentation rates. Nodule distribution becomes more patchy towards the western margin of the North Pacific as the sea floor topography becomes increasingly dissected, and also towards the topographically rugged Clarion and Clipperton fracture zones (Rawson and Ryan, 1978).

In addition to manganese nodules, encrustations coat exposed rock surfaces throughout the ocean, even in continental margin areas. Thick encrustations have been recovered on seamounts off Baja California, and in the vicinity of the Mendocino Fracture Zone. The Mid-Pacific Mountains are also heavily manganese encrusted. Encrustations thicken along the Hawaiian chain from near zero thickness off Hawaii to several centimetres thickness off Midway Island and the Emperor Seamounts as the sea floor ages (Glasby and Andrews, 1977).

Nodule distribution appears to be more irregular in the South Pacific than in the North Pacific, possibly as a result of the greater topographic and sedimentological diversity of the South Pacific. Glasby and Lawrence (1974) have compiled a large amount of data on the distribution of South Pacific nodules, on the basis of which Glasby (1976) has divided environments of manganese nodule formation in the South Pacific into three major categories: basin type environments such as the south-western Pacific Basin, Peru Basin, Chile Basin, South Tasman Basin and the basin north of Tahiti; the circumpolar belt; and mountainous regions. The basins are largely floored with red clay, the circumpolar area with siliceous ooze and the mountainous areas with calcium carbonate. As in the North Pacific, sedimentation rates are the main factor determining large-scale regional variations in nodule distribution in the South Pacific. Nodules are most abundant where sedimentation is limited, such as in the south-western Pacific basin and the region around Antarctica influenced by the circumpolar current. Shallower basins receiving terrigenous detritus, like the Tasman Basin, contain fewer nodules, as do elevated areas and those of highly dissected topography. Two areas in the South Pacific which have received particular attention are the south-western Pacific basin and the circumpolar region. Glasby et al. (1980) have concluded that the southern basin of the south-western Pacific has a coverage of nodules in the range 75–100%, with similar values occurring in the eastern sector of the northern basin. In the circumpolar region, a broad belt of nodules occurs under the circumpolar current. Its presence is largely determined by the current inhibiting sedimentation, but also by the presence of abundant volcanoclastics and glacial erratics which can serve as nuclei (Glasby, 1976).

5.4.3.2 Indian Ocean

Data on the distribution of nodules in the Indian Ocean are far fewer than in the Pacific, reflecting the limited amount of work done in this ocean to date. However, the information available indicates that regional nodule distribution in the Indian Ocean is largely controlled by the same factors as in the Pacific, namely sedimentation rates, bottom current activity, etc.

Udintsev et al. (1975) have shown that the most extensive areas of nodule coverage in the Indian Ocean are predominantly to the south of the equator. Few nodules have been recorded in continental margin areas, the Arabian Sea or the Bay of Bengal, most probably because of the high rates of sediment input in these regions. The equatorial zone is also largely devoid of nodules because of rapid carbonate sedimentation. Sporadic occurrences of nodules have been reported in the Somali Basin and in the southern Arabian Sea (Cronan and Tooms, 1967b; Wiseman, 1937; Fisher et al., 1974) and encrustations occur extensively on the Carlsberg Ridge (Cronan and Tooms, 1967b; Glasby et al., 1974) and other areas of rock exposure. High nodule concentrations have been recorded by bottom photography in parts of the Crozet Basin and the Central Indian Basin, and deposits have also been reported in the other major southern Indian Ocean basins (Moorby, 1978) and off Australia (Frakes and O'Brien, 1980). As in the Pacific, locally high nodule concentrations occur in association with high current velocities under the circumpolar current and a patchy nodule distribution has been recorded in the Mozambique Channel (Vincent, 1976) where bottom currents are also active.

5.4.3.3 Atlantic Ocean

Nodule abundance in the Atlantic Ocean appears to be more limited than in the Pacific or Indian Oceans, probably as a result of its relatively high sedimentation rates. The Atlantic receives a greater amount of terrigenous sediment relative to its size than either of the other two major oceans, and the accumulation rate of this sediment is probably too high to permit extensive nodule development over much of the ocean. Another feature which inhibits nodule development in the Atlantic relative to the other two oceans is that much of the sea floor is above the calcium carbonate compensation depth, particularly on the Mid-Atlantic Ridge which occupies a large part of the ocean.

As in the other two oceans, the areas of the Atlantic where nodules occur in appreciable amounts are those where sedimentation is inhibited for some reason. The deep water basins on either side of the Mid-Atlantic Ridge which are below the calcium carbonate compensation depth and far enough from land to receive only limited input of terrigenous sediment contain nodules in reasonable abundance, particularly in the western Atlantic (Horn *et al.*, 1972). Similarly, there is a widespread occurrence of nodules and encrustations in the Drake Passage-Scotia Sea area (Cronan, 1975b) probably due to the strong bottom currents in this region. Bottom current activity has also been invoked to account for greater abundances of nodules in the western South Atlantic than in the east, the Walvis Ridge acting as a barrier to the northward flow of bottom water in the east. Abundant nodule deposits on the Blake Plateau can also be related to high bottom currents (Manheim, 1972).

Partly because the Mid-Atlantic Ridge occupies such a large proportion of the Atlantic Ocean, encrustations have been recovered with greater frequency than in the other oceans. These thicken away from the ridge axis (Aumento *et al.*, 1968; Cronan, 1975b) indicating time-dependent deposition of ferromanganese oxides from sea water and are extensively developed on seamounts and other topographic elevations in the marginal areas of the ocean.

5.4.3.4 *Marginal seas and lakes*

Unlike the deep oceans which, for the most part, are highly oxidizing at the sediment–water interface, marginal seas and lakes contain extensive bottom areas which are either reducing or only poorly oxidizing. Under these conditions ferromanganese oxides will not form.

Basin geometry is an important factor in determining the degree of oxidation of waters in lakes and semi-enclosed seas. Shallow basins such as Oneida Lake, New York, for example, contain waters that are well mixed by wind action thus preventing thermal stratification which would result in utilization of available oxygen and stagnation in the bottom waters. Under these conditions ferromanganese oxides are abundant over much of the basin floor (Dean and Ghosh, 1980). By contrast, deep basins such as in the Black Sea and many lakes are stratified and develop reducing conditions either within the water column or on the basin floor. Under these circumstances, iron and manganese will not precipitate as oxides in the deeper portions of the basins, and ferromanganese oxide concretions are restricted to their margins.

Even within the oxidizing portions of lakes and shallow marine basins, the distribution of ferromanganese oxide concretions is by no means uniform. Important factors determining nodule type and abundance are the nature of the substrate and the amount and nature of any sedimentation. Shallow marine concretions occur under a variety of environmental conditions and on a variety of substrates, including muds, sands and gravels. In the Baltic Sea, for example, the three main types of concretion, spheroidal, discoidal and crust-like, are differentiated on the basis of their depositional environment, but all occur in areas where no sediment is accumulating (Winterhalter, 1980). Spheroidal concretions are generally associated with areas being by-passed by sediment at the present time, whereas discoidal concretions and crusts appear to be related to areas of active erosion. Lacustrine concretions appear to be more restricted in the type of bottom on which they occur (Calvert and Price, 1977b), being more or less confined to gravels, coarse-grained sands or hard glacial clays. In Shebandowan Lakes, Ontario, for example, concretions are restricted to shallow littoral areas along the sides and point extensions of islands or in isolated shoals, where the substrate consists either of sand interspersed with coarser material, or shingle-like aggregates of gravel to cobble-sized debris. Nowhere does organic-rich silt form the surface on which the concretions are developed, but, significantly, several deposits were observed to end at the sand/silt boundary (Sozanski and Cronan, 1976). On the basis of an extensive review of North American lake concretions, Dean and Ghosh (1980) have concluded that the two principal requirements for fresh water nodule formation are a firm substrate and a rate of sedimentation which is either low, zero or negative.

5.4.4   Buried nodules, and the paradox of nodules being preferentially concentrated at the sediment surface

As well as occurring in abundance at the sediment surface, manganese nodules are widely distributed in buried sediments (Menard, 1964; Mero, 1965; Cronan and Tooms, 1967a; Goodell *et al.*, 1971; Horn *et al.*, 1972; Cronan, 1973; Menard, 1976; Glasby, 1978). They have been found in all the oceans of the world, but most of the information available on them is from the Pacific.

Menard (1964) was the first to attempt to estimate the relative proportions of nodules within sediments and at the sediment surface. He found in gravity cores from the Pacific that the concentration of nodules in the first metre of sediment was approximately half of that found at the surface. Similarly, Bender *èt al.* (1966) found the ratio of nodules at the surface to those within the sediments in the first metre of 48 gravity cores to be 1·7. The surface to depth ratio of nodules in the upper metre of cores examined by Cronan and Tooms (1967a) was 1·8. By contrast, the distribution of nodules in about 50 gravity cores from the Pacific and Atlantic Oceans collected by the Lamont Doherty Geological Observatory was found to be rather different to that found in Pacific cores alone. Horn *et al.* (1972) reported that the top 3 m of sediment contained about one-third as many nodules as at the surface, a proportion considerably lower than that found in Pacific cores. The reason for this is not altogether clear but might be related to higher sedimentation rates in the Atlantic than in the Pacific, and probably reflects the lower abundance of nodules in the Atlantic compared to the Pacific mentioned previously.

The possibility that the distribution of buried nodules may not be entirely random has been proposed by Skornyakova and Andrushchenko (1970). These authors reported buried concretions in large diameter cores being concentrated into distinct horizons. Menard (1976) also reported the occurrence of nodules in distinct horizons in sediment cores. These horizons may represent ancient erosion surfaces or surfaces of non-deposition upon which manganese nodules were concentrated in the past. Alternatively, there may have been periods of extensive ferromanganese oxide deposition in the past separated by periods of little or no deposition. The possible exposure of buried nodules at the sediment surface as a result of sediment erosion by bottom currents, and the possibility that such erosion might lead to the mixing of populations at different horizons in the sediments, might partly account for some of the local variability in nodule distribution described in section 5.4.2.

Data obtained during the course of the Deep Sea Drilling Project (DSDP) have indicated that nodules occur deeply buried in sediments as well as in the uppermost part of the sediment column. However, many of the buried nodules in DSDP cores may have fallen from the surface as a result of the drilling process and are therefore not *in situ* (McManus *et al.*, 1970). This possibility complicates an assessment of the importance of buried nodules in DSDP cores but such an assessment is possible if those nodules from the tops of the core intervals are excluded. Menard (1976) has used this approach in an evaluation of nodules in DSDP cores, mainly those collected in the Pacific Ocean. Even if consideration of buried nodules in DSDP cores is restricted to those that appear to be *in situ*, it is not clear whether they were formed at the surface at the same time as their surrounding sediment and subsequently buried, or were formed within the sediment after burial. Both possibilities must be admitted. For example, a nodule recovered at a depth of 131 m in DSDP 162 from the Pacific was enclosed in an undisturbed mottle of bleached sediment which contained the same microfauna as the surrounding darker sediment, and is therefore likely to have been formed in place.

Glasby (1978) has also examined the distribution of buried nodules in DSDP cores using data collected from sites 1 to 370 of the DSDP. He found that the majority of cores containing buried nodules were from the equatorial North Pacific although a considerable percentage came from the Atlantic. Most nodules were associated with pelagic clays, and to a lesser extent with siliceous and calcareous sediments. In relation to age, most nodules were found in Pleistocene or Pliocene sediments, with lesser amounts in older sediments. These data led Glasby to conclude that the formation of manganese nodules had been more prevalent during the recent geological past than in earlier epochs, particularly since the Pliocene. He attributed this to the onset of strong bottom currents associated with the flow of water around the Antarctic region about 3·5 million years ago, presumably enhancing the flow of the Antarctic Bottom Water over much of the deep ocean floor. Craig (1975) has also noted the importance of the inception of the Antarctic Bottom Water flow in promoting nodule development in the Pacific, by reducing overall sedimentation rates.

Although nodules are not exclusively present on the sediment surface, as has been described, the bulk of them are concentrated there, sometimes in areas where the average sedimentation rate is more rapid than nodule growth. Why then do these nodules not become buried? Various suggested mechanisms for keeping nodules at the sediment surface, at least until they reach a certain critical size (Bender *et al.*, 1966; Glasby, 1977b), include the activity of bottom organisms, earthquake shock waves, and sediment winnowing and erosion by bottom currents. Glasby (1977b) has calculated that the energy in ocean bottom currents expended by marine organisms is more than sufficient to keep growing manganese nodules at the sediment–water interface. He considered that nodules, especially small nodules, are probably rolled about on the sea floor over long time periods thus keeping them free of accumulating sediment. Similarly, periodic nudging by bottom organisms coupled with their burrowing around nodules could help to keep the nodules at the surface. An alternative mechanism proposed by Sorem *et al.* (1979) is related to their observation of the watery sediment–water interface boundary mentioned in section 5.4.2. They propose that this boundary layer has special physical properties which permit the "floating" of nodules as large as 3 or 4 cm. These nodules would remain at the surface because they are buoyant and could be moved with a minimum of force.

Both the hypotheses of Glasby and Sorem *et al.* for maintaining nodules at the surface assume that sediment is accumulating faster than the nodules. This is probably so on average over large areas of the sea floor, but may not be so everywhere within these areas. Craig (1979) has drawn attention to the wide variations in sedimentation rate over short distances found in the North pacific "ore zone" and it is possible to envisage situations where no sediment is accumulating at all. This is likely to be the case on the slopes of abyssal hills where nodules tend to be most abundant, especially in view of the possible watery nature of the sediment–water interface boundary layer (Sorem *et al.*, 1979) which would be prone to flow away on anything but the most gentle slope. If sediment had not accumulated at a particular site for some time, a high abundance of nodules on the sea floor could readily be accounted for. Furthermore, pulsations in the bottom water flow in the geological past, and perhaps other factors, have lead to the erosion of large amounts of sediments leading to hiatuses in the stratigraphic column. During these periods of erosion not only would newly formed nodules remain at the sediment surface, but previously buried nodules could be exposed on erosion surfaces. Van Andel *et al.* (1975) have outlined the distribution of hiatuses in the Pacific during the past few million years and according to Glasby (1978) they correspond closely to the present day distribution of manganese nodules. Thus in many instances, high concentrations of nodules at the sediment surface may be a result of erosion or non-deposition, and recourse to extraneous mechanisms for keeping these nodules from being buried is not necessary.

5.5   Mineralogy

Manganese nodules and encrustations contain a variety of authigenic iron and manganese minerals, often very fine-grained and intergrown, as well as amorphous material and a host of minor and accessory phases of both authigenic and non-authigenic origin.

5.5.1   Descriptive mineralogy

The principal method that has been used to characterize the mineralogy of nodules and encrustations is X-ray diffraction. Two approaches have been, first, to grind bulk samples followed by analysis by diffractometer and, secondly, to pluck out small specimens from sections for mounting in a powder camera. Each method has its advantages. The analysis of bulk samples allows the dominant minerals in a large number of specimens to be determined fairly rapidly, but provides little or no information on the minor or accessory constituents, if there are any, due to their dilution by amorphous or cryptocrystalline material. Plucking out small specimens under the microscope facilitates detailed assessments of the mineralogical variability within individual nodules, but is too laborious and time-consuming to enable a characterization of the major mineralogical variations in nodules throughout the oceans to be made. Sorem and Fewkes (1977) have questioned mineralogical identifications made on the basis of analysis of bulk samples of nodules, first because the powders used almost certainly consist of mixtures of minerals, and secondly because the minerals may have suffered deleterious effects due to the grinding. However, the identification of the main minerals in mixtures should pose no serious problems as long as sufficient principal reflections are available, and while prolonged grinding may degrade the structure of some minerals, the little grinding required to crush most manganese nodules is very unlikely to lead to the occurrence of minerals that would not otherwise be present. Comparative mineralogical studies using both techniques on nodules from the same area have given similar results (section 5.5.3).

The first identifications of manganese minerals in nodules were by Buser and Grütter (1956) who reported three phases which they termed 7 Å manganite, 10 Å manganite and δ MnO_2 on the basis of comparison with synthetic manganese oxides. Other workers adopted a different approach and compared the X-ray powder patterns of manganese nodules to those of known manganese minerals (e.g. Manheim, 1965; Cronan and Tooms, 1969) and concluded that the most commonly occurring reflections could be assigned to todorokite (Yoshimura, 1934), birnessite (Jones and Milne, 1956) and δ MnO_2, and that these were the equivalent of the minerals of Buser and Grütter (1956). In a comprehensive review of the mineralogy of manganese nodules, Burns and Burns (1977) have recommended that the terminology todorokite, birnessite and δ MnO_2 should be retained for the three most commonly occurring manganese minerals in nodules, a recommendation that is followed throughout this book. Selected powder patterns of these minerals are given in Table 6. Less common manganese minerals present in nodules include pyrolusite, ramsdellite, nsutite, cryptomelane and psilomelane (Burns and Burns, 1977).

Information about the crystal structures of the manganese minerals in ferromanganese oxide concretions is incomplete. The structure of todorokite has not been completely determined, but Burns and Burns (1977, 1979) have reviewed evidence that suggests it may be related to the psilomelane structure (Wadsley, 1953). Both minerals have structural sites which specifically accommodate Mn^{2+} in octahedral coordination with oxygen, and the divalent cations are necessary to stabilize the mineral's structure. Giovanoli et al. (1970) believe that the structure of birnessite is similar to that of chalcophanite, which has a layer structure composed of a $Mn^{4+}-O$ octahedral sheet alternating with a sheet of Zn ions coordinated to oxygen and water (Glover, 1977). Some Mn may be present as Mn^{2+}. The δ MnO_2 is a poorly crystalline disordered phase, which yields only a few weak diffuse X-ray reflections. In general, the degree of crystallinity of these three minerals in nodules decreases from todorokite through birnessite to δ MnO_2 (Glover, 1977).

The mineralogy of the iron phases in nodules has not been as closely studied as that of the manganese phases. Buser (1959), Arrhenius (1967), Andrushchenko and Skornyakova (1969), Glasby (1972) and Cronan and Moorby (in preparation) among others have reported goethite as being an important iron phase in nodules. Additionally, Burns and Burns (1977) have noted reported occurrences of lepidocrocite, maghemite, hematite and akaganeite in some nodule samples. Johnson and Glasby (1969) have shown by Moss-

Table 6. X-ray powder patterns of selected manganese minerals and nodules (from Cronan, 1967).

	1 Todorokite		2 Birnessite		3 Challenger Sta. 297		4 MV-65-1-41		5 Loch Fyne		6 MP 43 a		7 10 Å manganite	8 δ MnO$_2$
	d Å	I	d Å	I	d Å	I	d Å	I	d Å	I	d Å	I	d Å	d Å
	9·56–9·65	100			9·56	100			9·66	100			9·7	
	6·98–7·20	15	7·27	S	7·10	55	7·18	100						
	4·76–4·81	80			4·81	45			4·81	75			4·8	
	4·42–4·45	10							4·48	5				
			3·60	W			3·57	30						
	3·40	5							3·34	5				
	3·19–3·20	30			3·19	40							3·25	
	3·10–3·11	10			3·11	10								
	2·45–2·46	25	2·44	M	2·44	40	2·44	20	2·45	15	2·43	b	2·46	2·43
	2·39–2·40	45			2·39	30			2·40	20			2·39	
	2·33–2·36	15			2·35	20			2·35	10				
	2·21–2·23	30							2·23	20				
	2·13–2·16	10							2·13	15			2·18	
	1·98–2·00	10			1·97	10			1·97	25				
	1·92–1·93	10							1·916	5				
	1·83	5												
	1·78	10												
	1·73–1·75	10												
	1·68	5			1·67	20								
	1·53–1·56	10			1·53	15			1·53	5				
	1·49	30												
	1·419–1·43	30	1·412	M	1·42	40	1·41	15	1·41	25	1·41	b	1·42	1·41
	1·38–1·40	15			1·40	30			1·40	25				
	1·33	5												

1 = Todorokite: range of d spacings from Straczek *et al.* (1960), Frondel *et al.* (1960) and Levinson (1960).
2 = Birnessite: data from Jones and Milne (1956).
3 = Challenger 297 (37 29′S, 83 07′W) containing both todorokite and birnessite.
4 = MV-65-1-41 (24 34′N, 113 28′W) containing birnessite.
5 = Loch Fyne nodule, containing todorokite.
6 = MP 43 a (13°00′N, 165°00′E), containing δ MnO$_2$.
7 = 10 Å manganite: data from Buser and Grütter (1956).
8 = δ MnO$_2$: data from Buser and Grütter (1956).

bauer Spectroscopy that iron is principally present in nodules in the form of Fe^{3+} compounds and concluded that the spectra they observed were probably those of iron phases consisting of a mixture of goethite and lepidocrocite. However, much of the iron oxide in manganese nodules appears to be amorphous (Glasby, 1972; Crerar and Barnes, 1974). Burns and Burns (1977) suggest that a hydrated ferric oxyhydroxide polymer is the dominant iron phase in many nodules.

The minor and accessory minerals in nodules are both many and diverse. Burns and Burns (1977) list the following: quartz, feldspar, mica, olivine, stilpnomelane, pyroxene, amphibole, prehnite, clay minerals, zeolites, apatite, calcite, aragonite, rutile, anatase, barite and spinels. The most common of these is quartz. Several of the accessory minerals listed are alteration products of submarine volcanic rocks, most importantly zeolites such as phillipsite (Chapter 3) and clay minerals such as montmorillonite and nontronite. Biological materials such as calcite tests and apatite fish debris are not uncommon in nodules, and cosmic spherules represent a distinctive but minor accessory component. Some of these minerals may take part in, or be formed by, chemical reactions during nodule diagenesis, and thus may be considered to be authigenic.

5.5.2 Manganese mineral interrelationships and paragenesis

Buser and Grütter (1956) first proposed that there was a relationship between the manganese minerals in nodules in that the degree of disorder and oxidation increased from 10 Å manganite to 7 Å manganite to δ MnO_2. Similarly there is good evidence for oxidation differences between naturally occurring todorokite and δ MnO_2. The O : Mn ratios of terrestrial todorokite vary from 1·74 to 1·87 (Straczek et al., 1960; Frondel et al., 1960) in contrast to a ratio of up to 1·99 for δ MnO_2 (Bricker, 1965). Thus independent of whether synthetic or naturally occurring manganese oxides are considered, there does appear to be an important oxidation difference between the two major manganese minerals in manganese nodules.

In view of the oxidation difference between todorokite and δ MnO_2, it is likely that their occurrence in nodules will at least partly be determined by the degree of oxidation (redox potential) of the environment of deposition (Cronan, 1967; Cronan and Tooms, 1969; Glasby, 1972; Calvert, 1978 and others). Nodules, or more commonly encrustations, from highly oxidizing open ocean environments largely swept clear of sediment accumulation by bottom currents, such as the tops of seamounts and on mid-ocean ridges, usually contain the more highly oxidized mineral δ MnO_2 as their principal manganese phase. By contrast, those nodules from areas where sediments containing organic remains are accumulating and which are more poorly oxidizing in consequence, or from continental margins where redox potentials are generally lower than in the open ocean, are usually more rich in todorokite. This will be illustrated when the regional mineralogy of nodules and encrustations is discussed shortly. Birnessite appears to occupy an intermediate position between the other two minerals, occurring in minor amounts in nodules from both highly oxidizing and not so highly oxidizing environments (Cronan, 1975b; Moorby, 1978). However, as pointed out by Glasby and Read (1976), the boundary conditions for the transition between the different manganese minerals in nodules is not at all clear. Blake Plateau nodules, for example, often contain todorokite (Cronan, 1975b) even though their environment of deposition must be rather similar to that on some oceanic seamounts where δMnO_2 normally occurs. It is evident therefore that a simple environmental differentiation of redox potential is not the only factor determining mineralogical differences between nodules.

Other factors which may affect the mineralogy of manganese nodules are the bottom-water characteristics in the region in which they are formed. Addy (1978) has reported that nodules in a small area of the North Atlantic contain todorokite where the sea floor is overlain by the Antarctic Bottom Water, but δMnO_2 at shallower depths where it is overlain by the North Atlantic Deep Water. Reported differences in Eh between the water masses may be responsible for the mineralogical differences between the nodules, but other bottom-water characteristics may also be of importance in this regard.

Lyle *et al.* (1977) have recently drawn attention to the chemistry of ferromanganese oxide formation in determining the mineralogy of the precipitates found in nodules and encrustations. They have suggested that the formation of ferromanganese oxides in the presence of reactive silica, as for example in an area of siliceous ooze deposition, could lead to reactions between iron and silica to give iron rich smectites, leaving the incompatible manganese to crystallize as todorokite. This process was thought to be analogous to that suggested as occurring between hydrothermal Fe/Mn oxyhydroxide precipitates formed at the crest of the East Pacific Rise and biogenic silica (Heath and Dymond, 1977). It is difficult to evaluate this proposed reaction in the absence of experimental evidence. However, that it alone cannot account for all occurrences of todorokite in nodules is evinced by the widespread occurrence of the mineral in areas where biogenic silica is low or absent. However, it could well be operative where silica is available for reaction, or where some other species is reacting with the iron. Burns and Burns (1977) have suggested that where both iron and manganese are available for incorporation into forming ferromanganese oxides, epitaxial intergrowth of δMnO_2 with $FeOOH \cdot H_2O$ may occur which would inhibit the formation of other manganese minerals. By contrast where iron is removed from the system by reaction with something else, silica for example, such epitaxial intergrowth would not occur and other manganese minerals such as todorokite and birnessite would be able to form.

5.5.3 Regional and environmental differentiation of nodule mineralogy

Investigation of mineralogical variations in nodules and encrustations throughout the World Ocean goes beyond academic interest. Ore grade nodules rich in nickel and copper almost invariably contain todorokite as their principal mineral phase. Indeed, the presence of this mineral is thought by many to be necessary for nickel and copper enrichment in nodules to take place. Investigation then of the regional variability of nodule mineralogy throughout the oceans, and particularly its environmental differentiation, can lead to the rejection, as prospective areas for nodule exploration, of large regions of the oceans which contain depositional environments unfavourable for todorokite formation. Conversely, those environments in which todorokite is likely to occur, while not necessarily containing ore grade nodules, would, if certain other conditions to be described later were fulfilled, warrant further exploration for such deposits.

Regional variations in nodule mineralogy and mineralogical variations with depth were first noted in the Pacific Ocean by Barnes (1967a) and Cronan (1967). These variations were generally considered to result from regional and depth related changes in the environment, although the influence of increasing pressure with depth on nodule mineralogy as advocated by Barnes is untenable in view of the occurrence of todorokite in some shallow water and lake concretions.

A number of workers have provided regional mineralogical data on Pacific nodules, both from the ocean as a whole and in more detail from the north-eastern equatorial Pacific ore zone (Barnes, 1967a, b; Cronan, 1967; Cronan and Tooms, 1969; Calvert and Price, 1977a; Meylan, 1976; Sorem and Banning, 1976). Calvert (1978) has summarized available data (Fig. 34) showing that todorokite occurs mainly in the eastern marginal part of the ocean and in two deep water east-west zones in the north-eastern and south-eastern tropical areas. δ MnO_2 occurs principally in the western Pacific and is particularly abundant on seamounts, although it also occurs in some abundance in deep water in the south-western Pacific (Meylan, 1976; Glasby, 1976).

Continental margin nodules from the eastern Pacific have been found to contain todorokite and birnessite (Cronan and Tooms, 1969), possibly as a result of the lower redox potential relative to that in the open ocean to be expected in such an environment (reducing conditions occur at shallow depths beneath the deposits), or as a result of the reaction of iron with sulphur ions in the reducing conditions below to form iron sulphide, thus liberating

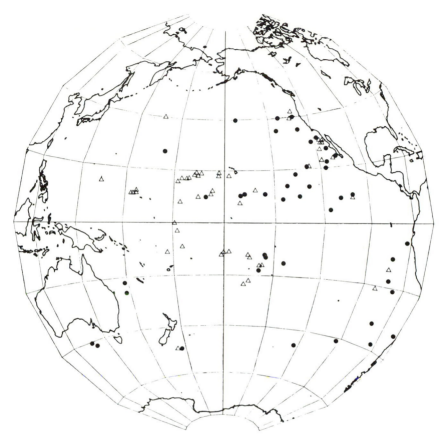

Fig. 34. Distribution of todorokite and δ MnO₂ in manganese nodules from the Pacific Ocean. Samples labelled ● contain todorokite and δ MnO₂; samples labelled △ contain only δ MnO₂ (from Calvert, 1978).

manganese to form todorokite in the manner discussed in section 5.5.2.

That todorokite is the principal manganese mineral in nodules from the ore zone in the north-eastern Pacific has been confirmed by a number of workers on the basis of both bulk analyses of ground nodules and on individual sub-samples of nodules picked out from polished sections under a microscope (see for example Friedrich and Roonwal, 1975; Meylan, 1976; Sorem and Banning, 1976). This is one of the few areas in which sufficient data are available to compare the two approaches to the study of nodule mineralogy described in section 5.5.1. Although detailed study of individual north-eastern Pacific nodules indicates the presence of minerals other than just todorokite (Sorem and Banning, 1976), it confirms the results of bulk

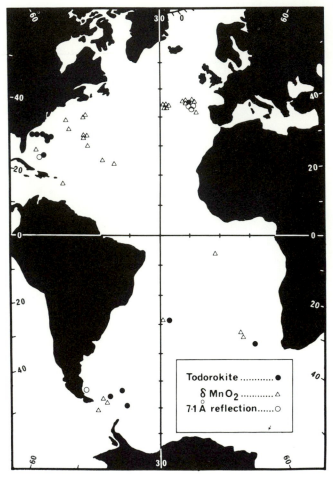

Fig. 35. Distribution of todorokite, δ MnO$_2$, and a 7·1 Å reflection in Atlantic ferromanganese oxide deposits (from Cronan, 1975b).

analyses that todorokite is the principal phase in these deposits thus demonstrating that the latter approach is a simple and viable way of determining the predominant mineralogical constituents of nodules.

The mineralogy of Atlantic nodules and encrustations is similar to that of deposits in the Pacific (Fig. 35). Cronan (1975b) reported that δ MnO$_2$ was the most common mineral encountered in a large suite of Atlantic concretions, with over 75% of its occurrences being in encrustations on exposed rock surfaces in elevated areas. By contrast todorokite was found to have a more limited distribution, with over 50% of its occurrences in nodules rather than encrustations. Apart from the Blake Plateau, todorokite was generally found to occur in deep water areas such as the Cape Basin and the Scotia Sea. The Mn/Fe ratio in Blake Plateau nodules is generally greater than one, in contrast to Atlantic nodules as a whole, and this enrichment in manganese may be promoting the formation of todorokite in these deposits. It is evident therefore that there is a differentiation of the mineralogy of Atlantic ferromanganese oxide deposts, just as in the Pacific, δ MnO_2 occurring principally on elevated areas of little or no sedimentation and todorokite occurring mainly in sediment covered basins. These differences, together with the concentration of δ MnO_2 in encrustations and todorokite in nodules, can probably be explained, as in the Pacific, largely on the basis of the nature of the environment of deposition. Encrustations receive their constituents predominantly from the overlying sea water, generally in a highly oxidizing environment. By contrast, nodules receive some of their constituents from sea water and some, including manganese, from interstitial waters of the underlying sediments under probably less oxidizing conditions, at least partially brought about by reactions resulting from the decay of organic material.

The regional variability of nodule mineralogy in the Indian Ocean provides abundant confirmation that the nature of the depositional environment is of paramount importance in influencing the mineralogy of ferromanganese oxide concretions. Of a total of 95 Indian Ocean nodules and encrustations subjected to X-ray diffraction analysis by Cronan and Moorby (in preparation), todorokite was identified in 20 samples, todorokite and birnessite together in 13 samples, birnessite alone in 3 samples, δ MnO_2 in 27 samples and todorokite and δ MnO_2 in 12 samples, with a considerable differentiation of mineralogy between nodules from basins and other features. Todorokite was found in samples from all the basins from which material was obtained (Fig. 36), showing a more widespread distribution than had been noted in the other two major oceans. It was also found in continental margin areas, as in the Pacific. Those samples showing the strongest development of todorokite were from the Central Indian Basin, an area of potential ore grade nodules, where siliceous ooze is accumulating below the CCD as a result of high biological productivity in the overlying waters. Their enrichment in todorokite could be due to a number of factors or combinations of them. According to Wyrtki (1971), dissolved oxygen levels in the bottom waters of the Central Indian Ocean Basin are lower than in the other major basins of this ocean, and, while not being the sole influence on redox potential, may be leading to a potential in the bottom waters low enough to promote abundant todorokite formation. Alternatively, the presence of "available silica" in the siliceous ooze may be promoting todorokite formation by reacting with iron in the manner suggested by Lyle *et al.* (1977). Yet again, decay of organic material in the sediments underlying the nodules could be

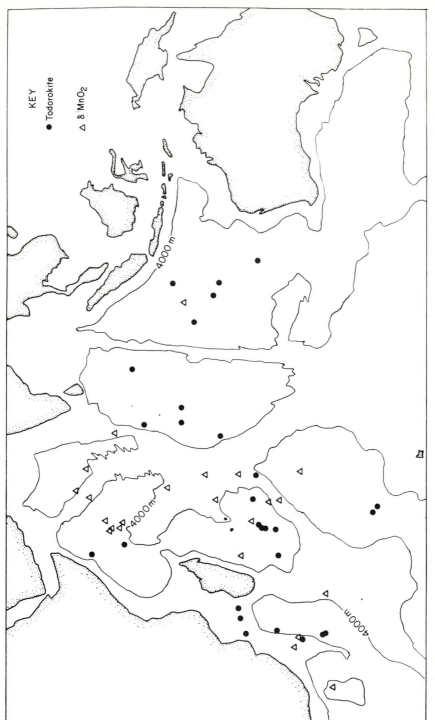

Fig. 36. Distribution of minerals in Indian Ocean manganese nodules and encrustations (after Cronan and Moorby, in preparation).

reducing the Eh and thereby leading to manganese reduction in the interstitial waters and the formation of todorokite. These possibilities will be discussed when the chemistry of ore grade nodules is evaluated (section 5.9).

As in the other two oceans, δ MnO_2 occurs mainly in samples from elevated areas in the Indian Ocean, particularly on the Central Indian Ocean Ridge System and on seamounts. The samples in which it occurs are mainly encrustations. However, δ MnO_2 also occurs in some abundance in deep water samples from the Madagascar Basin. Strong bottom currents are a feature of this basin, and Wyrtki (1971) has shown that the dissolved oxygen contents of its bottom waters are relatively high. This feature may be leading to a high redox potential at the sediment–water interface thus promoting δ MnO_2 formation. The location of the basin well away from areas of high productivity, and thus the accumulation of abundant organic remains which would utilize dissolved oxygen and favour todorokite formation, may also be leading to δ MnO_2 formation in its nodules in an analogous manner to δ MnO_2 formation in the south-western Pacific.

Local variations in the mineralogy of ferromanganese oxide concretions have been documented by a number of workers. Cronan and Tooms (1967b) found that encrustations from elevated features on the flanks of the Carlsberg Ridge contained δ MnO_2, whereas nodules from a deeper sediment covered location in the same vicinity contained todorokite. Differences between the redox conditions of the depositional environment in these two locations may have caused these mineralogical differences. More recently, Halbach and Ozkara (1979) have described mineralogical variations in nodules from a small area in the north-eastern equatorial Pacific "ore zone" which could be associated with topographic variations. Nodules occurring on the slopes of seamounts contained δ MnO_2 as their principal mineral phase, whereas those in basins away from elevations were richer in todorokite. Intermediate varieties were also found. The todorokite-rich nodules were considered to have grown largely within the sediments, whereas those rich in δ MnO_2 were thought to have grown on the sediment surface. Differences in the redox potential between the surface and the uppermost few centimetres of the sediments may be responsible for the mineralogical differences between the nodules found in these two situations.

It is evident from the above that the mineralogy of the manganese phases in nodules and encrustations is relatively sensitive to a number of factors among which may be included the redox potential of the depositional environment as influenced by organic productivity, sedimentation rates, bottom water characteristics, etc., and possibly by the nature of the associated sediments and reactions they may enter into with the ferromanganese oxides. Encrustations from elevated areas tend to be most enriched in δ MnO_2, whereas nodules from basins tend to be more enriched in todorokite. However, there is a more or less continuous gradation between these two end members, with mixtures of minerals occurring in some deposits from all environments.

5.6 Growth Characteristics

Understanding of the growth characteristics of manganese nodules and encrustations involves consideration of several separate but related topics. Of prime importance in any assessment of how nodules grow is an appreciation of their internal structures, as textural and structural evidence of the complexities of nodule growth are preserved in their interiors. Secondly, no appreciation of the growth characteristics of nodules can be attained without some knowledge of the actual precipitation mechanisms involved in their formation. Finally, the rate at which nodules and encrustations grow is also an important if somewhat controversial topic. In this section, therefore, internal structure, precipitation mechanisms and growth rates will be considered in that order.

5.6.1 Internal structure

The main features of the internal structure of nodules and encrustations were first recognized by Murray and Renard (1891). Characteristic is the concentric banding which is developed to a greater or lesser extent in most nodules (Fig. 37). The bands represent thin layers of varying reflectivity in polished section, the more highly reflective layers being generally richer in manganese than the more poorly reflective ones.

An important but often neglected major structural feature of manganese nodules is the non-ferromanganese oxide framework in which the oxides reside. This framework was first noted by Murray and Renard (1891) after leaching cut sections of nodules with HCl and in it the characteristic concentric banding of nodules was found to persist. Lalou and Brichet (1976) have recently drawn attention again to the presence of this framework in a number of nodules, and have discussed its genetic significance. These workers leached cut surfaces of several nodules with dilute H_2SO_3 followed by a mixture of oxalic acid and ammonium oxalate. This process dissolved the ferromanganese oxides and revealed a honeycomb structure able to support itself (Fig. 38) which comprised about 30% of the total mass of the nodules and consisted, for the most part, of about 90% SiO_2 and 10% Al_2O_3, containing crystals of quartz, plagioclase, pyroxene, kaolinite, and "amorphous silica or silicate". This framework is undoubtedly that which previous

Fig. 37. Cross-section of a manganese nodule from the Pacific showing characteristic concentric banding (reproduced by kind permission of CNEXO, France).

workers had recognized under the microscope as "interstitial material" (Fig. 39) and which has been confirmed by electron probe analysis to be rich in Si, Al and Fe (Cronan and Tooms, 1968; Dunham and Glasby, 1974; Cronan, 1974). Interestingly, in some nodules the composition of the framework is similar to that of the nodule nuclei. Furthermore, in it are sometimes preserved the remains of planktonic and benthonic organisms (Harada, 1978).

On a microscopic scale, a great variety of structures and textures are apparent in nodules and encrustations. Under low power, Sorem (1967) has recognized irregularities in nodule growth, with cross cutting layers indicating not only periods of non-deposition, but actual erosion too. This is good evidence that nodule growth can be discontinuous, an important fact in the interpretation of the radiometric dating of nodules to be reviewed in section 5.6.3. With increasing magnification, finer and finer structures become apparent within concretions, down to the limits of resolution possible with existing microscopic techniques. One of the most commonly observed and most easily recognizable structures is that of collomorphic globular segregations of ferromanganese oxides (Fig. 40) on a scale of tenths of a millimetre or less, which often persist throughout much of the nodule interior (Arrhenius, 1963; Mero, 1965; Cronan and Tooms, 1968; Friedrich *et al.*, 1969; Dunham and Glasby, 1974; Heye, 1975; Sorem and Fewkes, 1977). Often the segregations become linked into polygons or cusps (Fig. 41) elongated radially in the direction of growth of the nodules (Cronan and Tooms, 1968; Dunham

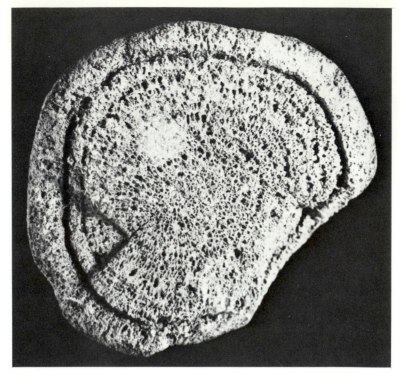

Fig. 38. Cross-section of a leached manganese nodule (photograph reproduced by kind permission of Dr C. Lalou).

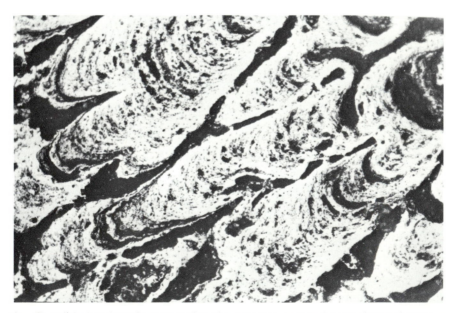

Fig. 39. Polished surface of a cross-section of a manganese nodule showing elongated segregations of ferromanganese oxides (light) in an interstitial silicate framework (dark) (from Cronan, 1967). × 130.

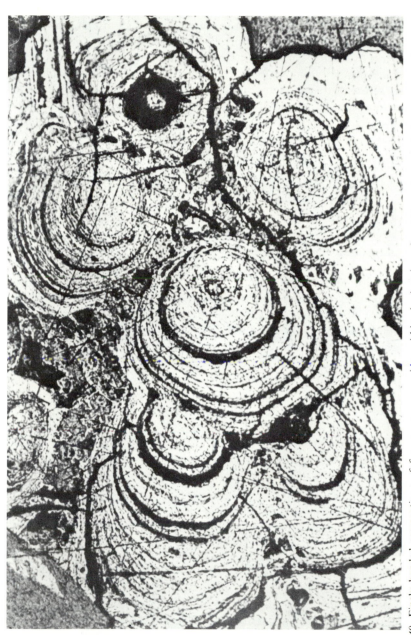

Fig. 40. Finely banded segregations of ferromanganese oxides within the interior of a manganese nodule from the Indian Ocean (from Cronan, 1967). × 190.

and Glasby, 1974). In a suite of nodules from the Carlsberg Ridge, Cronan and Tooms (1968) found the segregations to be better developed in the interiors of the nodule crusts than in the surface layer, although they became more isolated as the cores were approached probably because of the increasing content of detrital core material present. The latter observation, among others, was thought to indicate progressive replacement of the nodule nuclei by the ferromanganese oxides. In the outer layers of the nodules where segregations were absent, a more or less crenellated layer of manganese oxides was observed, the crenellations possibly representing the development of embryonic segregations. Foster (1970) and Sorem and Fewkes (1977) reported the occurrence of well developed broadly concentric outer layers in many other nodules. This variation in segregation development with increasing distance from the nodule surface was considered by Cronan and Tooms (1968) to be strongly indicative of post-depositional rearrangement of the ferromanganese oxides, as will be discussed shortly.

Many other structures have been recorded in the interiors of ferromanganese oxide concretions. Andrushchenko and Skornyakova (1969) have described what they consider to be several distinct structures in Pacific concretions. Not only were the globular segregations present, but concentrically banded, parallel and shelly laminar structures were also noted. Sorem and Foster (1972a) recognized what they termed massive, mottled, compact, columnar and laminated structures in a suite of nodules from off Baja California, noting that the columnar and mottled structures were the most abundant. Heye (1975) has described in detail the internal structures of a suite of Pacific nodules on which growth rates were also determined, thus enabling some assessment of the influence of growth rates on nodule structure to be made. He recognized the presence of both straight layers and cusps, in keeping with the observations of previous workers, and concluded that the straight layers grew more slowly and under less favourable conditions than the cusps. Straight layers were found at the initiation of growth, as for example near the nucleus, followed by a changeover to cuspate growth. More recently, Heye (1978) has proposed that certain non-directional structures in the centres of some manganese nodules represent aggregates of micronodules which coalesced in the sediments prior to the precipitation of concentric layers of ferromanganese oxides. Using scanning electron microscopy, Margolis and Glasby (1973) have found that microfine laminae on a scale of $0·25–10$ μm were a characteristic growth feature of the nodules they examined, indicating that the banding characteristics of these deposits persist down to the finest sizes resolvable with existing techniques.

Several workers have recognized organic structures within manganese nodules, largely those surface structures which were reported by Greenslate and Dugolinsky (section 5.3) which have become buried. Greenslate (1974)

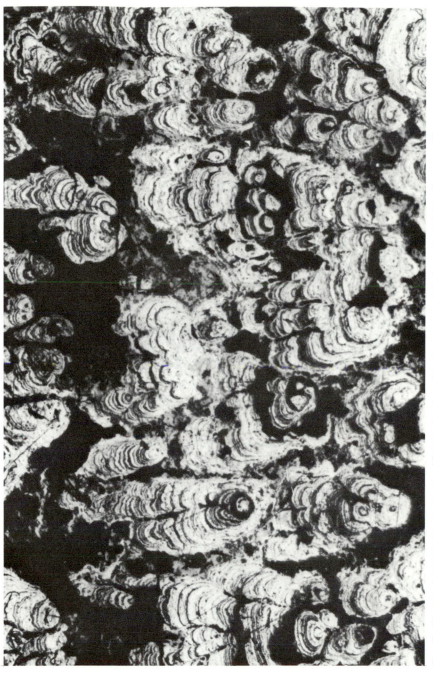

Fig. 41. Elongated segregation structures within the interior of a manganese nodule from the Atlantic Ocean. × 60.

has found preserved *Saccorhiza* tubes in the silicate framework of nodules leached with hydroxylamine hydrochloride, and Sorem and Fewkes (1977) have reported what are probably similar structures. However, other common surface structures on nodules could not be found within nodule interiors by Greenslate (1975), suggesting that they may have been destroyed by redistribution of material during nodule growth. Dugolinsky (1976a, b) has reported that the near-surface internal zones of many nodules contain the partially replaced tests of encrusting protozoans. The tests are composed of siliceous mineral grains and biogenic detritus, which are partially covered or replaced by ferromanganese oxides. Agglutinated tests located deeper in the nodule are more completely replaced. Test voids are often filled with microlaminated ferromanganese oxides suggesting that some of the segregations or cusps described may be due to infilling.

Cracks and fissures of various sorts are a common feature of nodule interiors (Manheim, 1965; Raab, 1972; Heye, 1975; Raab and Meylan, 1977). Raab and Meylan (1977) have described two types of internal fractures in Pacific nodules, radial or random fractures, and concentric or tangential fractures. Both types are generally filled with extraneous material. Many fractures vary in width throughout the nodules, and often do not penetrate to the nodule surface. Heye (1975) noted the same types of cracks as described by Raab and Meylan (1977) and concluded that they resulted from internal self-fracturing on aging of the nodules. Fracturing of nodules is evidently therefore a process which can lead to their break up on the sea floor, either unaided, assisted by benthic organisms, or by the activity of bottom currents. It is thus an important process both in providing nodule fragments to serve as nuclei for new nodule growth, and in limiting the overall size of nodules growing under any particular set of conditions.

As mentioned, some of the textural and structural features of nodules and encrustations can be taken to indicate post-depositional reorganization of material within nodule interiors, together with progressive replacement of nodule nuclei. For example, Sorem and Fewkes (1977) have found recrystallized dendrites in some nodules, and Dugolinsky (1976b), Dudley (1979), Margolis *et al.* (1979) and Burns and Burns (1979) have reported the progressive replacement of organic structures in several nodule interiors. Glasby and Andrews (1977) have noted progressive replacement of volcanic substrates in old encrustations from the Hawaiian chain, and diffusion of metals across physical boundaries. The observation of Cronan and Tooms (1968) that the segregation structures in nodules become more regular towards the nodule interiors, coupled with electron probe data, led them to suggest that the structures were formed by the post-depositional migration of manganese and other elements to centres of nucleation and crystallization within the interiors of the nodules. The observation of Burns and Burns that the outer layers of nodules they examined were either amorphous or contained poorly crystal-line δ MnO_2 while the inner layers contained todorokite would support this suggestion, as the re-crystallization would provide a mechanism for re-distribution of material in nodule interiors. Some evidence to support the internal reorganization of nodule interiors has been provided by Burns and Burns (1978). The interiors of manganese nodules from the Pacific siliceous ooze region were examined by scanning electron microscopy (SEM) and an electron microprobe, and were found to exhibit post-depositional recrystal-lization textures and oxide bands containing as much as 40% manganese, 5% nickel and 3% copper. Siliceous biogenic material was seen in all stages of degradation and dissolution within the nodule interiors. Authigenic phillip-site was found to be forming in vugs and was coated with clusters of ferromanganese oxides.

Lalou and Brichet (1976) have suggested an alternative mechanism involv-ing hydrothermal activity to explain the origin of the silicate framework of nodules. They considered that hot acidic solutions could arrive on basaltic debris or volcanic glasses giving rise to a micro-environment supersaturated in silica, which on cooling precipitates silica as well as oxides. The two phases were thought to separate into framework and oxide segregations respectively. This hypothesis may have some validity in ferromanganese oxides in which the constituents can be shown to be hydrothermal in origin. However, even in such situations, evidence to be reviewed in Chapter 6 on hydrothermal deposits suggests that hydrothermal silica becomes separated from ferro-manganese oxides prior to deposition of the latter (see also Seyfried and Bischoff, 1977).

In the writer's opinion, an explanation of the origin of the silicate frame-work and internal segregations of ferromanganese oxides in nodules and encrustations which fits most of the available observations, involves the re-crystallization and segregation of the initially precipitated ferromanganese oxides and the expulsion to the interstices between the segregations of excess ferruginous material, insoluble admixed silicates, organic fragments and other non-ferromanganese oxide phases deposited from sea water. On this basis, the framework would be a diagenetic feature and not an original depositional feature. Likewise, progressive replacement of volcanic core material would also result in the insoluble fraction being expelled from the forming ferro-manganese oxide minerals and this too could contribute to the silicate frame-work. In this instance it would be a replacement phenomenon. That the silicate framework in some instances is similar in composition to the nodule nuclei (Cronan and Tooms, 1968; Lalou and Brichet, 1976) would further support its diagenetic/replacement origin, as would the presence in it of plagioclase and pyroxenes, minerals unlikely to have been deposited by hydrothermal solutions or transported in abundance as detrital phases from the continents. The observation of Lalou and Brichet (1976) that only the inner oxide layers of some of the nodules they examined contained material similar in composition to that of the nucleus, provides an indication of the extent of the replacement in these nodules. Their outer layers probably represent normal precipitation of ferromanganese oxides and other phases from sea water, and their structures could be interpreted simply in terms of reorganization of the precipitates on aging. It is likely that during any diagenetic/replacement post-depositional reorganization of nodule interiors, chemical reactions will take place between the different phases present. In this context it is significant that in Carlsberg Ridge nodules, Cronan and Tooms (1968) and Cronan (1974) observed that manganese and many minor elements were concentrated into the segregation structures, iron was more evenly distributed between these and the interstitial framework, whilst silica and aluminium were almost entirely concentrated in the latter. As mentioned in section 5.5.2, Lyle *et al.* (1977) have proposed that reactions between ferromanganese oxides and silica in the Bauer Deep can lead to the precipitation of an iron-rich smectite in the sediments, while the incompatible manganese is incorporated into nodules together with minor elements. Some such process may explain the observed distribution of elements in relation to the segregation structures within individual nodules. During reorganization of the ferromanganese oxides and admixed non-ferromanganese oxide material, reactions between the two, and between the ferromanganese oxides and the nucleus, could lead to the formation of iron-rich silicates and iron-poor ferromanganese oxide phases, the latter being segregated within a recrystallized framework composed of the former and insoluble phases that are either left over or have not taken part in the reactions. This process would explain the rigidity of the silicate framework of nodules by the cementing action of the newly formed iron silicates, a feature difficult to explain on the basis of simple reorganization of material within nodules without chemical reactions having taken place.

In summary, therefore, a combination of progressive replacement of nodule nuclei by ferromanganese oxides and deposition of a mixture of ferromanganese oxides, silicate debris and organic remains from sea water, with, on recrystallization, the diagenetic expulsion of the non-ferromanganese oxide material to the interstices between the oxides in each case, can account for much of the internal structure characteristic of manganese nodules. It must be emphasized, however, that this conclusion does not preclude other growth forms either primary or secondary occurring in nodules and encrustations.

5.6.2   Precipitation mechanisms

A detailed review of precipitation mechanisms in manganese nodules is beyond the scope of this book, and discussion here will be limited to the catalytic oxidation and precipitation of the major elements iron and manganese, and the possible role of organisms in nodule development.

The chemistry involved in the oxidation and precipitation of iron and manganese in natural waters has been described by Stumm and Morgan (1970). The oxidation of Mn^{2+} to MnO_2 is catalysed by a reaction surface. This MnO_2 can then adsorb additional Mn^{2+} which in turn becomes oxidized. That the oxidation and precipitation of manganese to form ferromanganese oxides requires a surface has been recognized by many workers. It was suggested by Goldberg and Arrhenius (1958) that ferric oxide could provide such a surface on which manganese would be oxidized according to the equation

$$2OH^- + Mn^{2+} + \tfrac{1}{2}O_2 = MnO_2 + H_2O.$$

Electron probe studies by Burns and Brown (1972) have provided some support for this view. These authors found that iron oxides had been deposited around the nuclei of some nodules prior to the deposition of the manganese oxides, which could catalyse manganese oxidation and precipitation. It has been suggested by Morgenstein and Felsher (1971) that in nodules with volcanic nuclei, the iron for the initial reaction surface might be provided by the decomposition of the volcanic material. The derivation of iron in this way might help to explain why some highly weathered volcanics have thick manganese encrustations while others which are less weathered are more thinly encrusted. However, Greenslate (1975) has noted that ferromanganese oxides can accumulate in and around the tests of organisms in the absence of an initial precipitation of iron oxides, and Glasby and Andrews (1977) have found the lack of an iron oxide substrate to ferromanganese oxide deposition in some crusts from the Hawaiian Archipelago, indicating that surfaces other than iron oxide do no inhibit the precipitation of ferromanganese oxides.

Once ferromanganese oxide accumulation is initiated the concretions can continue to grow so long as there is an adequate supply of iron and manganese to the reaction surface. As mentioned in section 5.5.2, Burns and Burns (1977) have discussed a mechanism by which this process may proceed. These authors note that certain pairs of iron and manganese minerals have either identical crystal structures or layers of atoms in common in certain crystallographic planes. They suggest therefore that in manganese nodules the possibility exists for epitaxial intergrowths of one phase on the other. For example, ramsdellite (MnO_2) crystallites have been observed to grow in crystallographic continuity with goethite because the mismatch in their cell parameters is less than 10%. Burns and Burns (1977) point out that although δ MnO$_2$ and FeOOH, two of the phases present in nodules (section 5.5.1), consist of small disordered crystallites, they too are capable of epitaxial intergrowth, which could sustain concretion growth.

The role of organic agencies in contributing to ferromanganese oxide growth has been the subject of much discussion and speculation. That organisms live on nodules and encrustations has been noted by many authors (Murray and Renard, 1891; Graham and Cooper, 1959; Greenslate, 1975; and others) but their role in contributing to nodule growth is not clear.

According to Greenslate (1974) and others, the abundance of biological structures in and on nodules strongly suggests that their growth is aided by microorganisms in that the latter provide a superstructure on which the oxides can accrete, and which they can replace. However, there is little evidence that the organisms themselves secrete iron and manganese as part of their life processes. As described, many of the species of organisms found on manganese nodules construct their tests from biogenic or other debris that were already present in the sediments. In this respect, they are simply incorporating existing sedimentary material into the nodules rather than creating new phases. However, Dugolinsky (1976b) has pointed out that some species do reveal evidence of organically precipitating trace metals, but their importance in this regard is likely to be small in relation to the physical incorporation of material by organisms into the growing nodules.

The role of bacteria in influencing nodule growth has been the subject of considerable controversy. Several authors have pointed out that manganese nodule growth can be explained in terms of purely physicochemical mechanisms. This does not mean, however, that bacteria do not play a role in nodule formation. According to Calvert and Price (1977b), experimental work by Ehrlich (1963, 1968) led to the suggestion that *arthobacter* enhanced the adsorption of Mn^{2+} from culture media and promoted its oxidation to Mn^{4+}. However, the experiments were not conducted under natural conditions, and their applicability to natural environments is therefore not clear. Nevertheless, what are considered to be fossil bacterial colonies have been reported in nodules by Harada (1978), and thus bacteria probably do influence nodule growth. Krauskopf (1967) has pointed out that bacteria serve to speed up reactions that are thermodynamically feasible and which would thus take place anyway given enough time. In other words their role may be essentially catalytic. He suggested that the rapid precipitation of manganese oxides in bogs and lakes relative to the deep sea may be influenced by bacteria.

5.6.3 Growth rates

It is possible to assess the rate of growth of nodules and encrustations either by dating their nuclei, which gives a minimum rate of growth, or by measuring age differences between their different layers. Early radiometric dating techniques indicated a slow growth for nodules, although inaccuracies in the methods used may have led to considerable errors in the values obtained. Existing radiometric and other techniques for nodule dating have been reviewed by Ku (1977) and include uranium series disequilibrium methods utilizing ^{230}Th ^{231}Pa, the ^{10}Be method, K-Ar, fission track dating of nodule nuclei, and hydration rind dating.

Uranium series disequilibrium methods rely on the principle that newly formed manganese nodules will show deviations from the equilibrium parent to daughter isotopic ratio within the series. If the system remains closed with no gain or loss of the isotopes concerned, the departure from equilibrium will disappear at a rate depending on the half lives of the isotopes involved. Using this method, ages can be determined at points measured, and generally indicate low rates of accumulation for most deep-sea nodules analysed (Table 7). The ^{10}Be method of nodule dating assumes that ^{10}Be concentrations or the specific activity of ^{10}Be/^{9}Be in nodules has remained constant with time at any point on the ocean floor, and that ^{10}Be does not migrate within the deposits (Ku, 1977). Nodule growth rates obtained using this method

Table 7. Published growth rates of pelagic nodules based on radiometric methods (from Ku, 1977).

Sample	Latitude	Longitude	Depth (m)	Growth rate (mm/10^6 yr)	Method
North Atlantic:					
C58–100	30°57′N	65°47′W	4800	4	^{230}Th,^{231}Pa
A266–41	30°59′N	78°15′W	830	<2	^{230}Th,^{231}Pa
G74–2374	30°31′N	79°01′W	876	<2	^{230}Th,^{231}Pa
G74–2384	30°53·5′N	78°44′W	843	<2	^{230}Th,^{231}Pa
Lusiad AD4	6°03′N	32°22′W	1020	8–10	^{230}Th,K-Ar
BP1	—	—	—	∼0	^{230}Th
South Atlantic:					
V16–T3	13°04′S	24°41′W	4415	3	^{230}Th,^{231}Pa
North Pacific:					
FanBd–20	40°15′N	128°27′W	4500	3	K-Ar
Horizon	40°14′N	155°05′W	5500	2·5	K-Ar,^{230}Th

cont.

Table 7—cont.

Sample	Latitude	Longitude	Depth (m)	Growth rate (mm/10⁶ yr)	Method
V21–D2	35°54′N	160°19′W	5400	4	^{230}Th,^{231}Pa ^{234}U
V21–71a	27°54′N	162°31′E	5870	2·5	^{230}Th
V21–D4b	14°25′N	145°52′W	4618	3	^{230}Th,^{231}Pa
6A	19°39′N	113°44′W	4000	4	^{230}Th,^{231}Pa
Carr 5	9°26·5′N	113°16·5′W	3700	17–24	^{230}Th,^{234}U
MP 26	19°N	171°W	1464	10	^{230}Th
Zetes–3D	40°16′N	171°20′E	3000	0·8–2·3	^{10}Be,^{230}Th Fission track
Tripod–2D	20°45′N	112°47′W	3000	4	^{10}Be,^{230}Th
Dodo–9D	18°16′N	161°50′W	5500	2·1	^{230}Th, Fission track
Dodo–15–1	19°23′N	162°20′W	4160	1·8	^{10}Be
Wah 24F–8	8°18′N	153°03′W	5143	10(3 nods.)	^{230}Th
V21–116	19°34′N	134°30′E	5826	28	Fission track
2P–52	9°57′N	137°47′W	4930	7·3	^{230}Th
Sta. 3996	4°56′N	135°29′E	—	33	^{230}Th
Sta. 3782	23°55′N	173°39·9′E	—	40	^{230}Th
South Pacific:					
V18–D32	14°18′S	149°32′W	2000	3·1	^{230}Th
V18–T119a	12°27′S	159°25′W	5000	6	^{230}Th,^{231}Pa
V18–T119b	12°27′S	159°25′W	5000	3	^{230}Th,^{231}Pa
DWHD–47	41°51′S	102°01′W	4240	1–6	K-Ar,^{230}Th
DW72	21°31′S	85°14′W	920	18	^{230}Th
2P–50	13°53′S	150°35′W	3695	1	^{230}Th
TF–1, TF–2	13°52′S	150°35′W	3623	1(2 nods.)	^{230}Th
E24–15	36°48′S	134°50′W	4696	6·4	^{230}Th
D023G	near Taumoto 1.		1600	3·5	^{230}Th
Pacific:					
J1	—	—	—	10·7–15·1	^{230}Th
H1d	—	—	—	6·8	^{230}Th
G1d	—	—	—	3·6–10·3	^{230}Th
Indian Ocean:					
V16–T19a	29°52′S	62°36′E	4500	2·8	^{230}Th
V16–T19b	29°52′S	62°36′E	4500	2·9	^{230}Th
V16–T19c	29°52′S	62°36′E	4500	2·3	^{230}Th
M1	east of Madagascar		—	~0	^{230}Th
Dodo–66a	19°56′S	100°E	—	5·5	^{230}Th(^{226}Ra)
Antarctic:					
E17–36	55°S	95°W	4700	3	^{230}Th,^{231}Pa
E5–4	60°02′S	67°15′W	3475	4–19	^{230}Th

(Krishnaswami *et al.*, 1972; Guichard *et al.*, 1978) give values similar to those obtained by ^{230}Th dating and have been confirmed by ^{26}Al dating also (Guichard *et al.*, 1978). Potassium-argon dating (Dymond, 1966; Barnes and Dymond, 1967) and fission track dating (Shima and Okada, 1968) of nodule nuclei yield average growth rates of 1–4 mm per million years and 28 mm per million years respectively on certain samples analysed (Ku, 1977). These rates are lower limits, for they assume that growth was initiated immediately after deposition of the nucleus and has been continuous ever since. In general, growth rates derived by these two techniques are similar to those using uranium series disequilibrium methods and ^{10}Be (Table 7). Hydration rind dating assumes that given constant temperature, water availability and glass composition, volcanic glasses will hydrate to palagonite at a constant rate which is linear with time (Glasby and Read, 1976). This technique gives growth rates comparable with those obtained by radioactive age dating methods.

A different approach to the determination of nodule growth rates is by the use of microfossils. Harada and Nishida (1976) and Harada (1978) have found what they consider to be *in situ* calcareous nannofossils in a nodule from the western Pacific. From these, they calculated the growth rate in the outer layers of one nodule was 1·0–6·7 mm per million years, similar to nodule growth rates determined by radiometric techniques (Table 7). Furthermore, thermoluminescence has been used to date an Atlantic nodule and has indicated a faster growth rate than normally obtained by radiometric techniques (Schvoerer *et al.*, 1980).

In spite of the overwhelming radiometric evidence for slow growth, data have been accumulating from a number of sources which indicate that the growth rates described above may be misleading and that nodule growth is not continuous, periods of possibly rapid accumulation being separated by periods of little or no growth. Changes in the growth rates of nodules have been demonstrated by Heye (1975) using nuclear emulsion techniques to determine the activity of ionium (^{230}Th) and its daughter products. While Heye found average growth rates of 4–9 mm per million years in a suite of North Pacific nodules, resolution of his measurements was fine enough for him to distinguish zones of growth greater than 50 mm per million years, and also interruptions in growth. Similarly Harada and Nishida (1976) noted that whereas the outer layers of a nodule they analysed grew slowly, microfossil evidence in the innermost layer of the nodule suggested an overall growth rate of 39 mm per million years, indicating at least one change in growth rate during the nodule's history. Variations in nodule growth rate have also been suggested by structural and morphological studies on nodules. As mentioned earlier, Sorem (1967) noted unconformities in nodules where not only had there been no growth, but erosion had actually taken place.

Morphological differences between the tops, bottoms and sides of *in situ* nodules in the North Pacific (section 5.3.1) may be partly related to growth rate differences. Dugolinsky (1976a) has suggested that the presence of encrusting organisms on nodules serves to increase the rate of nodule growth by providing an increased surface area for oxide precipitation. It was noted by Dugolinsky (1976b) that the equatorial bulges at the sediment–water interface on some nodules had a greater abundance of life forms on them than elsewhere on the nodule surface, suggesting that the bulges may be due to rapid growth promoted by the organisms. Harada (1978) supports these findings by noting layers of nodules containing abundant organic remains which appear to have grown faster than more laminated layers. It is evident therefore from these investigations that nodule growth cannot be regarded as being continuous, or regular. Nodules may accrete material at different rates at different times and on different surfaces. They may also be completely buried for periods of time (Krishnaswami and Lal, 1972; Halbach and Ozkara, 1979) during which it is possible that they may grow from interstitial waters at rates different from those while on the surface, or possibly not grow at all for some periods. Such changes in growth rate due to burial or other factors may explain some of the variations in internal structure in nodules noted previously.

Growth rate data of Heye (1975) and Heye and Marchig (1977) suggest that manganese-rich layers in nodules grow faster than those rich in iron, and Piper and Williamson (1977) have concluded that nodules with a high bulk Mn/Fe ratio grow faster than those with lower bulk Mn/Fe ratios. On this basis, Calvert (1978) has proposed that nodules with high Mn/Fe ratios represent precipitates that have received metals via diagenetic processes in addition to those received by precipitation from sea water (section 5.9.1).

Recently the whole concept of slow growth in nodules, either regular or intermittent, has been criticized by several workers. Lalou (1980) has questioned the interpretation of published radioactive decay patterns in nodules in terms of slow growth, suggesting that they could equally well be interpreted in terms of rapid growth. Furthermore, Cherdyntsev et al. (1971), Lalou and Brichet (1972) and Lalou et al. (1973) have reported excess ^{230}Th in the cores of several nodules which led them to suggest that the nodules accreted rapidly around the nuclei. Of critical importance in the interpretation of radioactive decay patterns in nodules is the isolation of the system from sea water or sediments. Ku et al. (1975) have suggested that excess ^{230}Th may be associated with clay which can penetrate into nodules along cracks. Such a process may account for excess ^{230}Th in nodule nuclei. Unless it can be proved that nodules truly represent a closed system, radiometric decay techniques cannot be successfully applied to them. Available evidence indicates that near-shore continental margin and lacustrine nodules and encrustations grow at rates much faster than their deep-sea counterparts. In many cases, an upper limit can be placed on the age of the concretions by the age of their substrate.

Many concretions in northern seas and lakes, including those in northern Europe, Russia and America, are in areas known to have been glaciated and thus their formation must date from after the retreat of the glaciers (Manheim, 1965; Glasby, 1970; Cronan and Thomas, 1970, 1972; Winterhalter, 1980). In other cases, rapid growth rates in near-shore nodules over relatively short time periods have been obtained by radiometric techniques (Ku and Glasby, 1972). Very rapid growth rates have been proposed for some lacustrine concretions. In a number of Swedish lakes where concretions were mined for iron in medieval times, regeneration of new ore crops within 50 years or so have been reported. In the Canadian Ore Lake, Lac LaTortue, Quebec, replenishment occurred in 5- to 10-year periods. In Baltic Sea concretions, Suess and Djafari (1977) find evidence for anthropogenic input of metals during the recent past.

Special cases of exceptionally rapid growth of nodules or encrustations around artifacts have been reported from both marine and lacustrine environments. Goldberg and Arrhenius (1958) reported thick coatings of ferromanganese oxides around naval shells found in a Pacific firing range, and concretionary coatings have been found also around spark plugs. Ferromanganese oxide coatings have been found around nails in the south-western Indian Ocean (section 5.3.1) and the writer has dredged a beer can in Shebandowan Lakes, Ontario, which was thickly encrusted with ferromanganese oxides. In these instances, the metallic nature of the nucleus may be catalysing a much more rapid oxidation and precipitation of ferromanganese oxides than normal.

Nodules and encrustations formed in association with submarine volcanism also show evidence of rapid growth. Zelenov (1964) reported the observation of precipitation of ferromanganese oxides around hydrothermal vents on the submarine Banu Wuhu volcano, Indonesia. Radiometric techniques and considerations related to the age of the sea floor have indicated that manganese encrustations in the TAG hydrothermal area on the Mid-Atlantic Ridge are growing rapidly (Scott et al., 1974). Similarly ^{230}Th dating has indicated a minimum growth rate in the order of 50 mm per million years for ferromanganese deposits in the Hess Deep on the volcanically active Galapagos Spreading Axis (Burnett and Piper, 1977). However, other techniques including hydration rind dating have indicated that the deposits actually grow much faster than this, demonstrating that ferromanganese oxide deposits formed in association with submarine volcanic activity can grow much faster than normal, and casting doubt on the validity of the ^{230}Th method of nodule dating in this instance.

It is evident from the preceding paragraphs that there are considerable variations in the growth rates of nodules and encrustations from different environments, and differences of opinion as to how growth rate data should be interpreted. In general, the most important factor influencing nodule growth rate is likely to be the rate at which elements are supplied to the deposits, which in turn will depend on, among other factors, the nearness of the deposits to the sources of the elements. Concretions forming in volcanic areas where hydrothermally derived metals are introduced into sea water and which may be available for precipitation, or in lakes and near-shore areas where there are abundant dissolved constituents in river runoff, probably do form rapidly. By contrast, nodules in the deep sea far from local volcanic sources of metals probably accumulate slowly. All gradations between the two are possible. It is evident therefore that one should not think of nodule and encrustation formation in terms of slow growth or fast growth but in terms of a variable growth dependent upon the rate of supply of their constituents.

5.7   Bulk Geochemistry

The composition of ferromanganese oxide deposits can probably be ascribed to a combination of factors which include the availability and chemical behaviour of elements in marine and freshwater environments, the adsorptive and crystallo-chemical properties of the authigenic phases of the concretions, their rate of accumulation and hence the time available for elements to be incorporated into them, and the physicochemical nature of the environment of deposition. The deposits are often chemically heterogeneous, both within individual nodules and over small distances on the sea floor, as well as on a world-wide scale. Study of their chemistry is of considerable importance not only from the scientific point of view, but also because metals such as Ni, Cu and Co can be enriched in some deposits to ore grade. An understanding of the processes by which these enrichments occur will simplify the task of locating such deposits elsewhere on the sea floor.

   A review of the geochemistry of manganese nodules and encrustations such as this poses a problem of data selection. The literature on nodule geochemistry is very diverse and the data available of variable quality. In view of the heterogeneity of individual nodules described earlier (section 5.6) and often reported in the literature (Willis and Ahrens, 1962; Cronan and Tooms, 1967b; 1968; Burns and Fuerstenau, 1966; Raab, 1972, Glasby and Read, 1976) the representativeness of some published analyses of nodules is questionable. This problem was highlighted by Horn *et al.* (1973) in their compilation of all available data on Pacific nodules, when they showed large compositional variations between some nodule samples taken from the same hauls. Many such reported discrepancies can be attributed to whether or not whole nodules or possibly unrepresentative fragments were analysed, and whether or not the water loss on drying (sometimes up to 30% by weight) and the aluminosilicate impurity in the nodules were taken into account in presenting the data. Frazer (1979) has presented a thorough review of such problems regarding the representativeness of manganese nodule analyses and has pointed out many of the difficulties in the interpretation of the data. In order to minimize these problems, the data reviewed here are mostly drawn from a limited number of large groups of analyses of either whole nodules or representative sections of them, the analytical methods by which the data were obtained having been well described. Nevertheless the problem of representativeness of nodule and encrustation analyses should always be borne in mind when using data from more than one source, and especially when they have been derived from small sections of nodules which are not likely to be wholly representative. Fortunately, however, the problem is not so serious as to obscure the major features of nodule geochemistry.

5.7.1 Element abundances

Data on the composition of manganese nodules and encrustations are summarized in Table 8 where the average composition of deposits from each of the three major oceans and selected shallow marine and lacustrine environments are presented. However, average abundance data obscure the large compositional variations found in ferromanganese oxide deposits. For example, the maximum and minimum concentrations of, among others, Mn, Fe, Ni, Co and Cu in deep-sea nodules, five of the economically most important elements, vary considerably on a world-wide basis and vary even more if lacustrine and shallow marine concretions are included in the compilations. It should be emphasized, however, that the averages for shallow water and lacustrine concretions are based on relatively few groups of analyses (Calvert and Price, 1977b) and may not be representative of these deposits as a whole. They serve only to illustrate gross differences between the deposits and deep-sea concretions. Other elements which vary considerably in deep-sea nodules include K, Si, Ti, Ga, Zr, Mo and Pb (Mero, 1965), Zn (Cronan, 1975c), V (Cronan and Tooms, 1969) and a host of rare metals.

One of the most striking features shown by chemical data on nodules and encrustations are enrichments of many elements in deep-sea ferromanganese oxides over and above their concentrations in other concretions and their normal crustal abundances. Some elements such as Mn, Co, Mo and Tl, are concentrated about 100-fold or more in deep-sea nodules and encrustations relative to their normal crustal abundances, Ni, Ag, Ir and Pb, from about 50- to 100-fold, B, Cu, Zn, Cd, Yb, W and Bi, from about 10- to 50-fold and

Table 8. Average abundances of elements in ferromanganese oxide deposits from each of the major oceans, shallow marine environments and lakes (in wt.%), together with the world oceanic average, crustal abundance (in wt.%), and enrichment factor for each element in oceanic deposits.[a]

	Pacific Ocean	Atlantic Ocean	Indian Ocean	Southern Ocean[b]	World Ocean average	Crustal abundance[c]	Enrichment factor	Shallow marine	Lakes
B	0·0277	—	—	—	—	0·0010	27·7	—	—
Na	2·054	1·88	—	—	1·9409	2·36	0·822	0·81	0·22
Mg	1·710	1·89	—	—	1·8234	2·33	0·782	0·55	0·26
Al	3·060	3·27	2·49	—	2·82	8·23	0·342	1·80	1·16
Si	8·320	9·58	11·40	—	8·624	28·15	0·306	8·76	5·38
P	0·235	0·098	—	—	0·2244	0·105	2·13	0·91	0·15
K	0·753	0·567	—	—	0·6427	2·09	0·307	1·30	0·40
Ca	1·960	2·96	2·37	—	2·47	4·15	0·595	2·40	1·14
Sc	0·00097	—	—	—	—	0·0022	0·441	—	—
Ti	0·674	0·421	0·662	0·640	0·647	0·570	1·14	0·212	0·338
V	0·053	0·053	0·044	0·060	0·0558	0·0135	4·13	0·012	0·001
Cr	0·0013	0·007	0·0029	—	0·0035	0·01	0·35	0·002	0·006
Mn	19·78	15·78	15·10	11·69	16·02	0·095	168·6	11·88	12·61
Fe	11·96	20·78	14·74	15·78	15·55	5·63	2·76	21·67	21·59
Co	0·335	0·318	0·230	0·240	0·284	0·0025	113·6	0·008	0·013
Ni	0·634	0·328	0·464	0·450	0·480	0·0075	64·0	0·014	0·022
Cu	0·392	0·116	0·294	0·210	0·259	0·0055	47·01	0·002	0·003
Zn	0·068	0·084	0·069	0·060	0·078	0·007	11·15	0·011	0·051
Ga	0·001	—	—	—	—	0·0015	0·666	—	—
Sr	0·085	0·093	0·086	0·080	0·0825	0·0375	2·20	—	—

Table 8.—cont.

	Pacific Ocean	Atlantic Ocean	Indian Ocean	Southern Ocean[b]	World Ocean average	Crustal abundance[c]	Enrichment factor	Shallow marine	Lakes
Y	0·031	—	—	—	—	0·0033	9·39	0·002	0·002
Zr	0·052	—	—	0·070	0·0648	0·0165	3·92	0·004	0·045
Mo	0·044	0·049	0·029	0·040	0·0412	0·00015	274·66	0·004	0·003
Pd	$0·602^{-6}$	$0·574^{-6}$	$0·391^{-6}$	—	$0·553^{-6}$	$0·665^{-6}$	0·832		
Ag	0·0006	—	—	—	—	0·000007	85·71		
Cd	0·0007	0·0011	—	—	0·00079	0·00002	39·50		
Sn	0·00027	—	—	—	—	0·00002	13·50		
Te	0·0050	—	—	—	—	—	—		
Ba	0·276	0·498	0·182	0·100	0·2012	0·0425	4·73	0·287	0·910
La	0·016					0·0030	5·33		0·027
Yb	0·0031					0·0003	10·33		
W	0·006					0·00015	40·00		
Ir	$0·939^{-6}$	$0·932^{-6}$	—	—	$0·935^{-6}$	$0·132^{-7}$	70·83		
Au	$0·266^{-6}$	$0·302^{-6}$	$0·811^{-7}$	—	$0·248^{-6}$	$0·400^{-6}$	0·62		
Hg	$0·82^{-4}$	$0·16^{-4}$	$0·15^{-6}$	.	$0·50^{-4}$	$0·80^{-5}$	6·25		
Tl	0·017	0·0077	0·010	—	0·0129	0·000045	286·66		
Pb	0·0846	0·127	0·093	—	0·090	0·00125	72·72	0·002	0·063
Bi	0·0006	0·0005	0·0014	—	0·0008	0·000017	47·05		

[a] Modified from Cronan (1976c) to include data in Appendix. Shallow marine and lake deposits from Calvert and Price (1977b).
[b] Data from Goodell et al. (1971).
[c] Data from Taylor (1964).

Note: Superscript numbers denote powers of ten, e.g. $^{-6} = \times 10^{-6}$.

P, V, Fe, Sr, Y, Zr, Ba, La and Hg up to about 10-fold. By contrast some elements including Na, Mg, Ca, Sn, Ti, Ga, Pd and Au show little or no enrichment in nodules and encrustations, while some such as Al, S, I, Sc and Cr, are actually somewhat depleted relative to their normal crustal abundance. No elements are very strongly depleted in nodules because the deposits always contain some detrital minerals which contain many of the elements which are present in low concentrations or absent from the authigenic phases.

The abundance patterns of elements in shallow marine and lacustrine concretions are rather different from those in deep-sea concretions (Table 8). In particular, several minor elements such as Ni, Co, Cu, Pb, Zn, etc., which are markedly enriched in deep-sea nodules are not so enriched in their shallow marine and freshwater counterparts. Caution has to be exercised in interpreting these differences, as many of the data available on shallow marine and lacustrine concretions are based on only a few samples or parts of samples and may be non-representative. However, the differences in the content of many elements between the different deposits is sufficiently large not to be significantly affected by this limitation and will be discussed in the next section.

5.7.2   Major element behaviour

Manganese is the principal metallic constituent of nodules and encrustations and attains its high concentration as a result of its fractionation and separation from the principal rock-forming elements in the natural environment during processes of weathering, transport, deposition, diagenesis and subduction. One of the most important chemical characteristics of nodules is their greater enrichment in manganese than in iron relative to the crustal abundances of these two elements. As described in Chapter 6, the separation of these elements in aqueous environments is largely a function of pH and Eh. Increase in either of these parameters leads to the precipitation of iron from solution before manganese. Manganese is thus more soluble than iron under most natural conditions. However, pH and Eh are not the only controls on the precipitation of iron and manganese. Other ions in solution such as phosphates, for example, or organic complexes can alter the stability fields of iron and manganese dependent upon pH and Eh alone (Stumm and Morgan, 1970).

Notwithstanding the influence of organic complexes and dissolved ionic species on the stability fields of iron and manganese in solution, redox potentials and pH do appear to exert the major influence on the selective precipitation of iron and manganese oxides in natural environments. Redox potentials and pH generally increase from lacustrine through near-shore environments to the deep sea, and iron is selectively removed in the former environment leaving manganese to be enriched in the latter. This process is well illustrated by the iron-rich nature and high Fe/Mn ratio of many nodules and encrustations in small lakes which receive their metal input from the immediate vicinity (Dean and Ghosh, 1980), the intermediate and rather variable Fe/Mn of concretions in large lakes such as the Great Lakes system and in near-shore environments (Manheim, 1965; Cronan and Thomas, 1970; Calvert and Price, 1977b), and the generally low Fe/Mn ratio of deep-sea nodules. However, manganese is not always enriched relative to iron in deep-sea nodules. Those forming in areas receiving a high iron-bearing detrital input or near potential submarine volcanic sources of iron often have Fe/Mn ratios greater than unity (Cronan, 1975b).

Available data indicate a fractionation of manganese and iron between the two major mineralogical types of nodules, manganese being enriched in todorokite-rich nodules and iron in δMnO_2-rich nodules (Table 9). The causes of this differentiation are not entirely clear. Manganese enrichment in todorokite-rich nodules may be due to chemical fractionation processes such as those suggested by Lyle et al. (1977) (section 5.5.2). Alternatively the

Table 9. Variations in the average composition of manganese nodules of differing mineralogy.

(a) Pacific Ocean (Cronan and Tooms, 1969)

	Mn	Fe	Ni	Co	Cu	Pb	Zn
Todorokite	19·53	9·07	0·985	0·172	0·562	0·033	
δMnO_2	15·30	13·78	0·390	0·790	0·107	0·115	

(b) Atlantic Ocean (Cronan, 1975b)

	Mn	Fe	Ni	Co	Cu	Pb	Zn
Todorokite	19·85	16·39	0·62	0·29	0·17		0·09
δMnO_2	17·35	21·45	0·26	0·47	0·078		0·073

(c) Indian Ocean (Cronan and Moorby, in preparation)

	Mn	Fe	Ni	Co	Cu	Pb	Zn
Todorokite	20·0	9·5	0·844	0·130	0·689	0·076	0·103
δMnO_2	14·7	19·3	0·250	0·360	0·079	0·142	0·054

greater diagenetic mobility of manganese than of iron under poorly oxidizing conditions might lead to its enrichment in todorokite, the formation of which, as mentioned, appears to be favoured by less oxidizing conditions than are required to form δ MnO_2.

The enrichment of iron in nodules rich in δ MnO_2 is difficult to explain since iron is not a constituent of this phase. It may be related to the possible need for epitaxial intergrowth between δ MnO_2 and $FeOOH \cdot H_2O$ to stabilize the former as discussed previously. δ MnO_2 reaches its greatest abundance in nodules and encrustations on rock outcrops such as seamounts and mid-ocean ridges which may receive iron from both volcanic sources and sea water, but which do not receive manganese from interstitial waters as do nodules.

5.7.3   Minor element behaviour

Of considerable importance in explaining minor element behaviour in nodules and encrustations is the nature of the major element phases with which the minor elements are associated, and the chemical behaviour of the minor elements themselves in marine and lacustrine environments. Variations in element behaviour between different classes of ferromanganese oxide deposits will be deferred until subsequent sections of this chapter. The general behaviour of minor elements in ferromanganese oxide concretions as a whole will be discussed here.

The mineralogical nature of the major element phases in deep-sea nodules and encrustations appears to exert a considerable influence on the minor element composition of the deposits. Independent investigations based on bulk chemical analyses in all three major oceans have shown nodules rich in todorokite to be enriched in nickel, copper and zinc, whereas those enriched in δ MnO_2 are enriched in cobalt and lead (Table 9). These findings have been supported by electron-probe studies on individual nodules (Burns and Fuerstenau, 1966; Sano and Matsubara, 1970).

The causes of the partition of elements between the two principal types of deep-sea nodules and encrustations are not entirely clear. Are they due to the incorporation of the elements concerned into the different mineralogical phases themselves, or are the conditions under which the different minerals in nodules are formed independently influencing the minor element composition of the deposits? Each of these alternatives may apply in the case of some elements.

As mentioned on p. 100, the structure of todorokite is not fully known, but the mineral does appear to contain Mn^{2+} ions for which, on the basis of ionic radii considerations, divalent cations such as Zn^{2+}, Ni^{2+} and Cu^{2+} could substitute. Indeed Burns and Burns (1978) have suggested that as much as 8% by weight of nickel and copper could be accommodated in todorokite-bearing deep-sea manganese nodules. This would obviously partly explain the enrichment of todorokite-rich deep-sea nodules in these elements, and their lower concentrations in those rich in δ MnO_2 which contains quadrivalent manganese for which they would be less likely to substitute. Moorby (1978) has shown from selective leaching with hydroxylamine hydrochloride that nodules rich in todorokite contain most of their nickel, copper and zinc in the reducible manganese phases, strongly supporting the concept that these elements are at least partly substituting in the todorokite lattice. A similar conclusion has been reached by Arrhenius et al. (1979). McKenzie (1971) has shown that synthetic preparations of todorokite can accept large concentrations of nickel and copper. However, some todorokite-rich nodules from continental margin environments are not enriched in nickel and copper, in contrast to the deep-sea varieties (Grill et al., 1968; Cronan and Tooms, 1969; Calvert and Price, 1970). This demonstrates that nodule mineralogy is not the only factor determining nodule composition. Nodules of this type have probably formed rapidly (section 5.6.3) by the precipitation of diagenetically remobilized manganese which has become separated from its normally associated elements leaving them to be contained in other phases. This factor, possibly coupled with insufficient time being available for significant minor element uptake to take place because of the rapid growth rate of these nodules, may partly account for their low nickel and copper content. Similar factors may partly account for the low nickel and copper content of some lake nodules which contain todorokite.

The enrichment of cobalt in nodules rich in δ MnO_2 may be due to the ability of this element in its higher oxidation state to substitute for Mn^{4+} (Goldberg, 1961b; Sillen, 1961; Burns and Burns, 1977), or as $Co^{3+}OOH$ for $Fe^{3+}OOH$ (Arrhenius, 1963; Burns, 1965; Arrhenius et al., 1979). If this is the case, a prerequisite for its enrichment in nodules would be its oxidation from normal Co^{2+} ions in sea water to Co^{3+} ions, which would be favoured under the highly oxidizing conditions which are thought to favour the formation of δ MnO_2. The enrichment of lead in δ MnO_2-rich nodules has been suggested as also being due to its substituting in its higher oxidation state (Pb^{4+}) for Mn^{4+} in δ MnO_2 (Burns and Burns, 1977). However, the considerable difference in ionic radii between these two species (0·775 and 0·540 respectively) would appear to limit this possibility, and adsorption of lead on to δ MnO_2 may be a more likely explanation. Such a conclusion has also been reached by van der Weijen and Kruissink (1977) on the basis of adsorption experiments.

The role of adsorption in enriching metals in nodules is not very well understood. It is well known that hydrous manganese and iron oxides are characterized by high specific surface areas, and are capable of strong interactions with cations in solution. Stumm and Morgan (1970) consider that adsorption of Cu, Ni, Zn and Pb on to these oxides can explain the initial fixation of the metals in nodules, and Krauskopf (1956) has reported experiments in which several elements were rapidly removed from sea water by adsorption on to manganese oxides. Murray and Brewer (1977) have thoroughly discussed the role of adsorption in removing metals from sea water on to ferromanganese oxide minerals. Selective leaching experiments on nodules described by Fuerstenau *et al.* (1973) and Fuerstenau and Han (1977) have indicated that it is possible to extract much of the nickel and copper in nodules and about half of their cobalt without appreciably taking the major constituents into solution. These data are important from the point of view of commercial processing of nodules and, in the present context, would suggest that nickel and copper and to a lesser extent cobalt are not present in the lattices of the minerals in the samples examined but are adsorbed on to their surfaces. Fuerstenau *et al.* (1973) particularly favoured this conclusion for nickel and copper in iron-rich nodules. However, in nodules at large, the greatest enrichments of nickel and copper occur not in iron-rich nodules but in manganese-rich iron-poor varieties which contain todorokite, and in such situations substitution within the mineral lattice as well as adsorption is likely.

It is evident from the above that available data do not allow us to categorize unequivocally minor element uptake by nodules and encrustations in terms of only lattice substitution or only adsorption, and it is likely that both processes are of importance. Adsorption can probably account for the low to intermediate concentrations of most minor elements found in those nodules categorized as "amorphous" and background values in crystalline samples, but the considerable enrichments of nickel and copper in some todorokite-rich nodules and of cobalt in some δ MnO_2-rich nodules probably does result from their substitution in the lattices of these minerals.

5.7.4   Rare element behaviour

As mentioned, one of the principal characteristics of deep-sea nodules and encrustations is their enrichment in a host of rare elements. Many of these elements have only been poorly investigated and thus the factors determining their concentrations in the deposits are not always clear. Data on the enrichment of many rare elements are given in Table 8. Data have also been provided in the literature on many elements including Sn (Smith and Burton, 1972), Te (Lakin *et al.*, 1963) the Rare Earths (Goldberg *et al.*, 1963; Ehrlich, 1968; Piper, 1972; Glasby 1974) Ga, Ge, Sr and Sn (Riley and Sinhaseni, 1958); Li, Be, S, Cl, Ge, As, Se, Br, Rb, Nb and I (Cronan and Thomas, 1972); As, Br, Rb, Nb, In, Sn, Sb, I, Cs, Hf, Os and Au (Glasby, 1974) and Hg (Harriss, 1968).

One group of elements that has received considerable attention are the

Rare Earths. Goldberg *et al.* (1963) thought that the enrichment of the Rare Earths in marine deposits relative to their crustal abundances could be the result of the increasing stability of the heavier Rare Earth complexes with ligands derived from sea water. In contrast, Ehrlich (1968) suggested that the principal source of the Rare Earths in nodules was partly from the incorporation of Rare Earth bearing detrital material, and partly from surface transfer. However, Glasby (1974) and Piper (1972) have provided additional data that suggest that the Rare Earths are provided by sea water, and Piper (1972) has further suggested that their distribution in nodules and encrustations is influenced by the mineralogy of the host phases.

The enrichment of mercury in some nodules from volcanic areas has been suggested as being due to supply of the element from volcanic sources (Harriss, 1968). Mercury enrichment in mid-ocean ridge sediments of hydrothermal origin is a common phenomenon (Bignell *et al.*, 1976b; Bostrom and Fisher, 1969). Another suggested example of the influence of source on the rare metal content of ferromanganese oxide concretions is that of meteoritic material. Several authors have suggested that cosmic spherules might supply an appreciable portion of the nickel in the deposits, but this is not generally considered to be true. Harriss *et al.* (1968) have suggested that some noble metals, because of their homogeneous distribution within nodules and lack of correlation with other elements, might be derived from extraterrestrial sources. Barium may occur in nodules in a variety of phases including their manganese minerals, and as barite or celestobarite (Arrhenius, 1963). It may be derived from either volcanic or biological sources, depending upon its situation (section 3.2.3) (Arrhenius and Bonatti, 1965; Church, 1970). Adsorption probably controls the initial uptake of a large number of rare elements from sea water on to forming ferromanganese oxide concretions, but their substitution in the lattice of the principal minerals present may also be of importance.

5.7.5   Element associations and relation to depth

Element associations in nodules and encrustations have sometimes been used to determine with which major element phases the different minor elements are associated. This is based on the philosophy that in a group of analyses of polymineralic deposits, the highest correlation coefficients will normally occur between elements present in the same mineral phases (Chave and Mackenzie, 1961). An exception to this rule occurs if one phase dominates the assemblage, in which case positive correlations will occur in mineralogically unrelated phases simply because they are negatively correlated with the major phase. However, this situation rarely applies in nodules and encrustations which usually consist of three phases, manganese minerals, iron minerals and silicate minerals, in not too strikingly different proportions.

Correlation coefficients have been calculated between various pairs of elements in nodules and encrustations by a number of workers. Goldberg (1954) found positive correlations of Fe with Ti, Co and Zr and of Mn with Ni and Cu in a small suite of Pacific nodules from a limited depth range; Cronan (1969a), in a large suite of Pacific and Indian Ocean nodules, confirmed the correlations between Mn, Ni and Cu and noted one between Mn and Mo, found no correlation between Fe and Co, but reported them between Fe and Ti and between Co and Pb; Glasby *et al.* (1974) reported correlations between Mn, Ni, Cu and Zn and between Fe, Ti, Co and Zr in nodules from the Carlsberg Ridge; Cronan (1975b) reported correlations of Ni, Cu, Zn and Co with Mn in a diverse suite of Atlantic nodules and encrustations; Moorby (1978) found Ni, Cu, Zn and Cd to correlate with Mn and Co, Pb and Ti to correlate with Fe in a large suite of Indian Ocean nodules, and Cronan (1977a) found a diverse set of inter-element correlations in nodules and encrustations collected world wide from a variety of environments.

It is evident from the above that inter-element correlations in deep-sea nodules and encrustations vary between the different sample populations chosen for analysis. Nodules from some regions or environments show differ-

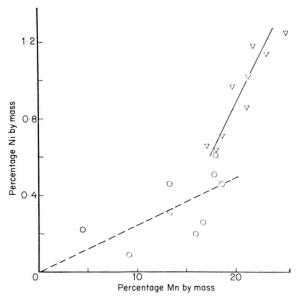

Fig. 42. Relation between the Mn and Ni contents of ferromanganese nodules from the abyssal Pacific, illustrating the mineralogical control on minor metal concentration; ▽, todorokite, ○, δ MnO$_2$ (from Calvert and Price, 1977a).

ent element associations to those from other regions or environments. These differences can be related to a number of factors. For example, as described below, where the samples have been collected from a wide range of depths, correlations of some elements with depth may obscure their correlations with other elements which are apparent when samples from more limited depth ranges are considered (Cronan, 1969a). In addition, inter-element associations in nodules and encrustations are likely to be different when different minerals are present in the deposits (Cronan and Tooms, 1968; Glasby, 1970). This has recently been demonstrated by Calvert and Price (1977a) who found different correlations between Ni and Mn for example in nodules containing δ MnO_2 and todorokite respectively (Fig. 42). It follows therefore that caution has to be exercised in interpreting correlation co-efficients in deep-sea nodules and encrustations.

Some elements in nodules and encrustations show considerable variation with depth. For example, in a large suite of open ocean nodules and encrustations from the Pacific and Indian Oceans, Cronan (1967) found Ni and Cu to increase with depth and Co and Pb to decrease. However, the relationship between these elements and depth were not linear, nor are such relationships linear in suites of samples from the Indian and Atlantic Oceans (Fig. 43) (Cronan, 1975b; Moorby, 1978).

The causes of variations in the composition of nodules and encrustations with depth has been the subject of considerable discussion. Barnes (1967b) and Cronan (1967) thought that they might be partly due to the enrichment of the elements concerned in one or other of the two principal mineral phases in nodules, themselves showing a relationship to depth as has already been described. It was also thought that depth related variations in environmental conditions might partly be responsible for the observed behaviour of the elements concerned. In this regard it is instructive to compare the plot of copper, for example, against depth in nodules with that of calcium carbonate against depth in sediments. It is well established that calcium carbonate abundance in sediments decreases with depth due to carbonate dissolution (Fig. 43). Comparison of its abundance in sediments with that of copper in nodules (Fig. 43) shows that around the depth of maximum calcium carbonate decrease, the maximum increase in copper takes place. As mentioned earlier, the ability of planktonic organisms to concentrate minor metals is well known (Vinogradov, 1953 and others) and Fig. 43 could be interpreted in terms of copper being released from carbonate organisms on dissolution and being taken up by forming nodules in the same depth interval. Such a mechanism would imply that copper enrichment in nodules will only occur on a large scale at depths at or greater than that required for carbonate dissolution. As will be described later, this appears to be the case. Furthermore, the lack of enrichment of copper in shallow water todorokite-rich nodules with struc-

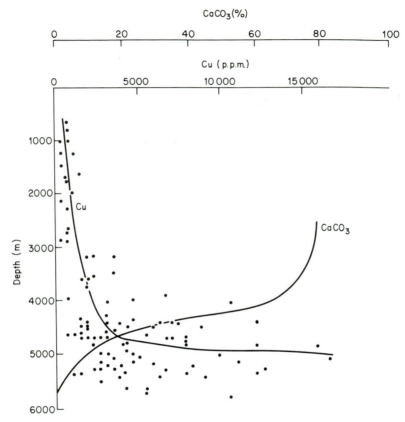

Fig. 43. Relationships of Cu in Pacific nodules and CaCO₃ in Pacific sediments to depth (after Arrhenius, 1963 and Cronan, 1967). (Note that distribution of Ni is similar to that of Cu.)

tures seemingly suitable for copper uptake could partly be explained on the basis that organisms would not release copper to be taken up by the todorokite at such shallow depths. Similar arguments apply to nickel.

Colley *et al.* (1979) have drawn attention to the selective role of organisms in influencing a variable uptake of nickel and copper in nodules and encrustations with depth in the Indian Ocean. Comparing suites of concretions from the Carlsberg Ridge (*c.* 3800 m) and from a range of equatorial seamounts (*c.* 2600 m) in the north-west Indian Ocean, these authors found that nickel and copper were positively correlated in the ridge samples but not in the seamount samples. In addition, the absolute concentration of copper was higher in the ridge samples than in the seamount samples. Furthermore, Moorby (1978) has found a linear correlation of the Cu/Ni ratio with depth

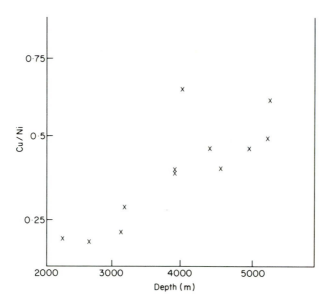

Fig. 44. Cu/Ni plotted against depth in Indian Ocean manganese nodules.

(Fig. 44) in Indian Ocean nodules and encrustations at large. The explanation offered to account for these observations was that copper was being selectively concentrated in organisms relative to nickel at shallow depths and was only being released on dissolution of the organisms at depths at or below the lysocline. This would be in accordance with the greater involvement of copper in the marine biogeochemical cycle than of nickel (Nicholls *et al.*, 1959; Greenslate *et al.*, 1973; Turekian, 1977). The very low concentrations of copper in ferromanganese oxide concretions from elevated areas and its marked enrichment in deeper water deposits relative to shallow water deposits compared to the relative enrichment of nickel in this regard has been recognized for a considerable time in other areas of the World Ocean (Cronan and Tooms, 1969; Cronan, 1975b). In these areas too, biological retention of copper in shallow waters and its release at or near the lysocline may be the explanation of the phenomenon.

Some idea of how metal enrichments might take place in nodules in the depth interval between the lysocline and the CCD where most carbonate dissolution takes place can be gleaned from studies on nodules from small areas by Addy (1978) and Pautot and Melguen (1979). In a detailed study of Atlantic nodules between 24°–29°N and 58°–63°W, Addy found that Ni, Cu and the Mn/Fe ratio were highest in the depth interval 5050–5300 m and lower both above and below this interval. As mentioned (section 5.4.2) the nodules were also most abundant in this depth interval, and the Ni and Cu-rich varieties contained todorokite. The depth at which the metal enrichments occurred marked the approximate boundary between the Antarctic Bottom Water and the overlying North Atlantic Deep Water. The top of the AABW has been found to coincide approximately with the lysocline at a number of locations (M. Melguen, personal communication) its "aggressive" character promoting carbonate dissolution. Thus, in the area studied by Addy, we may be seeing the results of the corrosive effect of the AABW liberating metals from calcareous organisms to give rise, in the same depth interval, to abundant nodules enriched in several metals contained in the organisms. In the South Pacific, Pautot and Melguen (1979) have found the preferential concentration of nodules in specific depth intervals in different basins (section 5.4.2) and in some cases a local concordance between nodule abundance and their Ni and Cu content. In many cases the maximum nodule abundance and grade was within the AABW, generally within the depth interval between the lysocline and the CCD. Here too therefore we may be seeing the result of metals being made available for nodule formation over a specific depth interval as a result of dissolution of calcareous organisms by "aggressive" bottom water.

In summary, therefore, in the areas studied by Addy (1978) and Pautot and Melguen (1979), and presumably elsewhere on the deep-sea floor, biogenic material is undergoing dissolution within the water column and on the sea floor over specific depth intervals below the lysocline which are determined by bottom water conditions and other local factors. Such dissolution will result in a reduction of the Eh in the sediments, thus promoting the formation of todorokite, and also in the liberation of metals from the organisms thereby making them available for uptake by the forming ferromanganese oxides.

5.8   Environmental Differentiation of Ferromanganese Oxide Concretion Compositions

Manganese nodules and encrustations from different depositional environments show considerable variations in chemical composition. Lacustrine and near-shore deposits generally have lower minor element concentrations and more variable Mn/Fe ratios than deep-sea varieties. Furthermore, there is a considerable degree of compositional variability within the deep-sea environment itself (Table 10). For example, nodules from seamounts are characterized by high Co values, continental borderland varieties by high Mn/Fe ratios and abyssal nodules by a high Cu and Ni content.

Table 10. Average abundances of Mn, Fe, Ni, Co and Cu in manganese nodules and encrustations from different environments (wt. %) (from Cronan, 1977a).

	Sea-mounts	Plateaux	Active ridges	Other ridges	Continental borderlands	Marginal seamounts and banks	Abyssal nodules
Mn	14·62	17·17	15·51	19·74	38·69	15·65	16·78
Fe	15·81	11·81	19·15	20·08	1·34	19·32	17·27
Ni	0·351	0·641	0·306	0·336	0·121	0·296	0·540
Co	1·15	0·347	0·400	0·570	0·011	0·419	0·256
Cu	0·058	0·087	0·081	0·052	0·082	0·078	0·370
Mn/Fe	0·92	1·53	0·80	0·98	28·8	0·81	0·97
Depth (m)	1872	945	2870	1678	3547	1694	4460

5.8.1   Deep-sea concretions

Deep-sea environments of ferromanganese oxide deposition have been divided into several classes (Table 10), including seamounts, elevated marginal areas, plateaux, active mid-ocean ridges, inactive ridges, deep water continental borderland areas and the deep ocean floor itself (Cronan, 1977a).

Oceanic seamount concretions contain higher than average cobalt and lead concentrations, but the topographic complexity of seamounts would preclude their concretions being mined for these elements in the foreseeable future. The main mineral phase in these concretions is δ MnO$_2$. The cause of the cobalt enrichment in seamount ferromanganese oxide concretions has been the subject of considerable discussion (section 5.7.3). One mechanism that has been proposed favours the oxidation of Co^{2+} to Co^{3+} under the highly oxidizing conditions in which seamount nodules are thought to form, which then substitutes for Mn^{4+} in δ MnO$_2$ or for Fe^{3+} in FeOOH. Another possibility is that cobalt is derived from the alteration of the basalts of which the seamounts are composed (Burns, 1965; Arrhenius *et al.*, 1979). Factors leading to lead enrichment in seamount nodules are less clear. Van der Weijen and Kruissink (1977) consider it to be due simply to the surface adsorption of lead on to δ MnO$_2$. Barium and titanium are sometimes enriched in Pacific seamount nodules (Cronan, 1967) perhaps in the case of barium, due to local volcanic supply of barium, or organic agencies, and in the case of titanium to the inclusion of volcanic debris.

Plateau nodules are known from only a few areas, and so it is difficult to obtain an overall picture of their geochemistry. The data reviewed by Cronan (1977a) suggested that plateau nodules are compositionally distinct from those on oceanic seamounts, especially in their lower cobalt content, even though they inhabit the same depth range. This reinforces the view that depth *per se* does not determine nodule composition and that it is the nature of the depositional environment and the sources of the metals which are of greater importance in this regard. Plateau nodules analysed to date tend to contain todorokite rather than δ MnO_2 as their principal mineral phases (Manheim, 1965; Glasby, 1972) and this factor may be partly responsible for their compositional distinctiveness from seamount concretions, including their lower cobalt content. Nodules from the Blake Plateau off Florida have a higher Mn/Fe ratio than the Atlantic Ocean average (Cronan, 1975b). The reasons for this are not entirely clear. Many other continental margin nodules with higher than average Mn/Fe ratios obtain their excess manganese by diagenetic remobilization from the underlying sediments (Lynn and Bonatti, 1965; Cronan and Tooms, 1969; Price and Calvert, 1970), but this mechanism would be unlikely to apply to the Blake Plateau deposits as the area is largely swept clear of sediment accumulation by strong bottom currents related to the Gulf Stream. This indicates that diagenetic remobilization of manganese is not the only way in which manganese can become enriched in nodules from near the continents. The high ratio, and the presence of todorokite, may be partly due to the lack of iron-bearing detritus on the Blake Plateau, unlike in the other marginal areas of the Atlantic where detrital sedimentation rates are probably higher (Cronan, 1975b).

Nodules and encrustations from active mid-ocean ridges generally exhibit Mn/Fe ratios less than unity, slightly higher than average cobalt contents, and, as a class, appear to contain δ MnO_2 in excess of todorokite (Cronan, 1977a). The low Mn/Fe ratio of the deposits could be related to a number of factors. Their common occurrence on outcrops of volcanic rock rather than on sediments would preclude their receiving mobile elements such as manganese by upward diffusion through interstitial waters and thus they must receive the bulk of their constituents from sea water, with perhaps some contribution from the *in situ* alteration of their volcanic substrate. Other deposits from exposed rock areas receiving the bulk of their constituents from sea water, such as on seamounts and abyssal hills for example, also have Mn/Fe ratios of about or less than unity, suggesting that when sea water is the dominant source of metals, Fe is normally supplied in excess of Mn. However, an important factor contributing to the Fe enrichment in mid-ocean ridge nodules and encrustations is likely to be volcanic sources of iron. Betzer *et al.* (1974) have reported that in the TAG area on the crest of the Mid-Atlantic Ridge at $26°N$ (section 6.4.1.3), particulate iron from hydrothermal sources is being flushed out of the hydrothermal vents to become enriched in the superjacent sea water. Such iron could disperse away from the ridge crest and together with iron from sea water be picked up by forming ferro-manganese oxide concretions on the ridge flanks.

Few ferromanganese oxide concretions have been obtained from inactive ridges and thus it is difficult to generalize on their geochemistry. One difference between inactive ridge and active ridge concretions appears to be in their Mn/Fe ratio which is higher on the inactive ridges (Cronan, 1977a). If the depositional environment is similar in these two situations, the difference in the Mn/Fe ratio would support a volcanic source for the additional iron on the active ridges.

Marginal seamount and bank nodules contain lower than average nickel and copper, higher than average cobalt and iron, and have a low Mn/Fe ratio (Cronan, 1977a). Two differences between marginal seamount and oceanic seamount concretions appear to be in the lower cobalt and higher iron contents of the former. Both features could be due to differences between the two environments of deposition. The lower cobalt values might reflect a lower degree of oxidation in marginal than in open ocean environments due to higher sedimentation rates and burial of organic matter to be expected in a continental margin situation. The higher iron values could result from proximity to sources of iron-bearing detritus from the continents. Manheim (1965) has suggested that iron increases relative to manganese in nodules as continental influences increase, due to the greater amount of releasable iron than of manganese present in most continental detritus. The similarity of the Mn/Fe ratio in these deposits to that in concretions from active mid-ocean ridges could thus be due to excess iron in each supplied from the continents on the one hand and from volcanic sources on the other.

Deep water continental borderland nodules tend to be very rich in manganese, poor in trace elements and to have a very high Mn/Fe ratio (Cronan and Tooms, 1969; Price and Calvert, 1970; Cronan, 1977a). Mineralogically, they consist principally of todorokite (Glasby, 1972). The distinctive composition of these deposits can largely be accounted for by their growth from diagenetically remobilized manganese. During the diagenetic process, manganese becomes separated from the elements with which it is usually associated which remain behind in the sediments, Fe, for example, in the form of iron sulphide (Cheney and Vredenburgh, 1968) and some minor metals complexed with organic compounds (Price, 1967). In addition, the rapid growth of the deposits (Ku and Glasby, 1972) probably precludes their taking up significant concentrations of these metals from the overlying sea water. In some respects, deep water continental borderland nodules are similar to those from shallow marine environments which will be discussed shortly.

Abyssal nodules are by far the most abundant class of ferromanganese oxide deposits on the ocean floor. Relative to other groups of nodules and encrustations, they are rich in nickel, copper and zinc among other elements, low in cobalt and lead and contain both todorokite and δMnO_2 as important mineral phases. They are thus the only class of nodules likely to be mined. Their enrichment in nickel and copper may partly be due to the presence of todorokite which can take up these metals, but as already discussed, other conditions have to be fulfilled before nickel and copper enrichment in abyssal nodules can take place. Although, as a class, abyssal nodules are enriched in nickel and copper, when deposits from different depth ranges are considered it is evident that these elements increase with increasing depth within the abyssal environment. This, coupled with other factors, leads to regional variations in the composition of the deposits which will be discussed in section 5.9.1.1.

5.8.2   Local compositional variations in deep-sea nodules

In addition to gradual variations in the depositional environment of nodules and encrustations over large areas giving rise to variations in the composition of the deposits, local variations in the bottom environment can produce similar effects on a much more local scale.

As one of the first found examples of local compositional variability in deep-sea ferromanganese oxide concretions, Cronan (1967) and Cronan and Tooms (1967b) noted quite large differences between two morphologically different populations of nodules at one site on the Carlsberg Ridge. A population of small nodules each approximately 0·5 cm in diameter was significantly enriched in Mn, Ni and Cu, whereas Fe and Ti were enriched in an associated population of larger nodules. Similar compositional variations were observed between morphologically similar nodules collected in different topographic settings from sites only a few km apart. Significant compositional variations between ferromanganese oxide concretions from different depths in another small area of rugged topography in the North Atlantic Ocean were also noted (Cronan, 1967). These observations led to the suggestion that where local sharp topographical variations occur, on the sea floor, local variations in the composition of associated ferromanganese oxides will also occur.

A more recent example of local compositional variability of ferromanganese oxide deposits in an area of strong topographic contrasts and possible submarine volcanic activity has been described by Bezrukov and Skornyakova (1976). In a small area in the south-western Pacific, these authors have reported irregularly distributed nodules in relation to a volcanic topography with almost a 2000 m relief. The Mn/Fe ratio of the deposits varied from 0·2 to 50, with variable contents of nickel and cobalt also. Other examples of local variations in nodule composition in relation to topographic variations have been reported by Hubred (1970) and Moorby (1978).

The causes of large-scale local variations in the composition of ferromanganese oxide deposits from areas of very strong topographic contrasts has been attributed to both submarine hydrothermal activity (Bezrukov and

Skornyakova, 1976) and to local changes in the nature of the environment of deposition (Cronan, 1967). Consideration of the likely fractionation behaviour of elements in sub-sea floor hydrothermal systems reviewed elsewhere in this book (section 6.7.2) suggests that local variations in Cu, Ni and Zn etc., in ferromanganese oxide deposits are not likely to be due to hydrothermal sources of these elements. In an oxidizing environment, these elements would be expected to precipitate from hydrothermal solutions below the sea floor, and thus would not be available to enter ferromanganese oxides. In support of this conclusion, those ferromanganese oxide deposits which have been observed during their formation to be of hydrothermal origin, such as those on the submarine Banu Wuhu volcano, Indonesia (Zelenov, 1964) and in the Galapagos region (Corliss et al., 1978), are low in Ni, Cu and most of the other minor elements normally enriched in oceanic ferromanganese oxide deposits as, at least in the Galapagos area, are the solutions from which they are formed (Corliss, 1979).

Thus, the variation in composition encountered in ferromanganese oxide deposits from topographically dissected areas is more likely to be due to local environmental variations than to submarine volcanic activity.

The nature of the environmental influence on the local compositional variability of manganese nodules and encrustations such as are recorded on the Carlsberg Ridge can be deduced from a consideration of the factors determining concretion variability reviewed already. Concretions from tops and upper slopes of topographic elevations are likely to be largely deposited from sea water and thus will be enriched in Fe and Co, whereas those from the sediment covered lower slopes and basins will probably receive manganese and other elements such as Ni and Cu as a result of diagenetic recycling through the topmost sediments. Furthermore, the deeper nodules are more likely to contain todorokite than $\delta\, MnO_2$, and this will enhance their uptake of Ni, Cu and Zn. Should the topographic variations traverse the lysocline or the CCD, an organic supply of metals to the concretions in the depth interval of maximum organic dissolution is probable. Similarly should they transect water mass boundaries, this too is likely to influence the compositional variability of the deposits (section 5.7.5). Local variations in concretion composition in topographically diverse areas can thus probably be accounted for in terms of the normal influences on ferromanganese oxide composition, but which are operating in a markedly variable manner on a local scale due to large variations in the environment of deposition conditioned by the topographic variability.

In addition to the large local variations in concretion composition such as those in highly topographically dissected areas, more subtle compositional variations in the composition of the deposits have been noted in some small areas of weaker topographic contrasts. Friedrich and Pluger (1974) described compositional variations in nodules from a small area in the "ore zone" in the Pacific. Nodules from the northern part of the area have high Mn/Fe ratios and are enriched in Ni and Cu, whereas those from the south have lower Mn/Fe ratios and lower concentrations of Cu and Ni. Furthermore, G. Friedrich (personal communication) and Halbach and Ozkara (1979) have reported that nodules containing δ MnO$_2$ resting on the upper slopes of abyssal hills within the region and which derive their constituents largely from sea water have lower Mn/Fe ratios and more cobalt than nodules which are resting on or in sediments on the lower slopes of abyssal hills or on abyssal plains. The latter could receive elements through interstitial waters as a result of diagenetic processes, are enriched in Mn, Ni and Cu and contain todorokite as their main mineral phase. Calvert *et al.* (1978) have also described variations in the Mn/Fe ratio and minor element content of nodules from part of the Pacific "ore zone", similar to those reported by Friedrich and Pluger (1974). The chemical variations found in these limited areas of relatively gentle topographic variations are much smaller than those described above from areas of comparable size containing strong topographic contrasts, but are probably caused by the same processes operating on a smaller scale.

Local variations in nodule and encrustation composition do not invalidate conclusions on the regional variability of these deposits described by many workers and reviewed in the next section. They are simply superimposed upon them when environmental conditions change locally.

5.8.3   Shallow marine concretions

Manganese nodules and encrustations from shallow marine environments are sufficiently different from deep-sea nodules to warrant separate consideration. They are characterized by highly variable Mn/Fe ratios, low contents of many elements normally enriched in deep-sea concretions, relatively high contents of organic matter, lower average O:Mn ratios than in deep-sea nodules, and an aluminosilicate component of variable composition (Manheim, 1965; Cronan, 1976c; Calvert and Price, 1977b).

The Mn/Fe ratio in shallow marine concretions varies from about 45 to less than 0·1, but individual geographic regions sometimes contain concretions with roughly similar Mn/Fe ratios (Calvert and Price, 1977b). However, superimposed on geographic differences are sometimes considerable variations in the Mn/Fe ratio within any one area. In the Baltic Sea, for example, the ratio ranges between about 0·007 to 1·37 and appears to vary with the morphology of the concretions and the nature of their substrate (Winterhalter, 1966; 1980). Both local and regional variations in the Mn/Fe ratio of shallow marine concretions can probably be ascribed to variations in their depositional environment. On average, iron is more abundant than manganese in the deposits. As already mentioned, iron is also more abundant in continental runoff products than is manganese, and this, coupled with the lesser mobility of Fe than of Mn in the marine environment, might partly account for the iron enrichment in these deposits. The very low manganese concentrations found in some shallow marine concretions might be due to their being deposited in an environment in which the redox potential is too low for manganese oxidation and precipitation. In such cases, the little Mn present may simply be adsorbed on to the Fe oxides (Stumm and Morgan, 1970; Collins and Buol, 1970). By contrast, shallow marine concretions containing high concentrations of manganese relative to iron are probably formed as a result of the diagenetic remobilization of manganese in the manner already described. Thus it is evident that in the shallow marine environment there occur ferromanganese concretions showing extreme fractionation of iron from manganese and vice versa, to a much greater degree than in the deep-sea environment. This probably reflects a greater degree of variability in those characteristics of the depositional environment affecting manganese and iron precipitation in near-shore areas than in the deep sea.

Enrichments of several elements including Si, K, Mg, Ti and P in shallow marine concretions over their probable contributions from aluminosilicate impurities have been reported by Calvert and Price (1977b). In Loch Fyne, K is associated with the Mn phase (Calvert and Price, 1970) as it also appears to be in some deep-sea concretions (Cronan and Tooms, 1968), while Si, Ti and P are associated with the iron phase. The P appears to be correlated with Fe, most probably as a result of its adsorption by iron oxides (Winterhalter and Siivola, 1967) or its entering into the formation of ferric phosphate (Sevast'yanov and Volkov, 1967; Glasby, 1970). The enrichment of Ti suggests that it may also enter into authigenic oxide formation (Calvert and Price, 1977b), while that of Si may be related to the activity of organisms. The lower O : Mn ratios and higher organic carbon contents of near-shore nodules relative to those in the deep sea probably reflect the less oxidizing conditions and greater abundance of organic material in near-shore than in deep-sea environments.

The low concentrations of many minor elements in near-shore ferromanganese oxide concretions relative to their concentration in deep-sea varieties has been noted by several authors (Manheim, 1965; Price, 1967; Glasby, 1970; Cronan, 1976c; Calvert and Price, 1977b and others). However, Calvert and Price (1977b) have also pointed out that some elements such as As and Ba are actually enriched in these concretions relative to in their deep-sea counterparts. In Loch Fyne concretions, for example, the order of enrichment is As, Mo, Ba, Sr, Pb, Ni, Y, Cu, Zn, Zr, and in the Black Sea

Mo, Ni, Co, As, V, Cu, Zr, Cr. Several of the most highly enriched elements probably occur in the marine environment in an anionic form.

The distinctive minor element composition of shallow marine concretions is probably the result of a number of factors. Of importance may be the pH of the depositional environment. Calvert and Price (1977b) have noted that the charges on hydrous Mn and Fe oxides vary with the pH of the medium in which they occur. Over a pH range of 1·5 to about 7·0 they can be both positively and negatively charged, being positive at low pH and decreasing to zero with increasing pH to become increasingly negative as pH increases further. The pH of zero point of charge is the pH at which the surfaces are uncharged. According to Calvert and Price (1977b), the manganese oxide component of nodules and encrustations is probably electronegative over the entire range of pH values encountered in sea water, having a zero point of charge in the low pH range. Iron oxides are probably also electronegative at normal oceanic pH values of about 8·1, but are much more weakly charged and some could be electropositive in shallow marine environments of lower than normal pH. It follows therefore that variations, due to pH changes, in the intensity of charge on the surfaces of Fe and Mn oxides in different marine environments may explain some of the compositional differences between shallow marine and deep-sea concretions by influencing their ability to adsorb charged minor element ions from sea water. In particular, the enrichment in shallow marine concretions of certain elements which occur in sea water in an anionic form may be due to their being adsorbed on to electropositive iron oxides.

A second factor influencing compositional variations between near-shore and deep-sea nodules and encrustations may be complexation of minor elements by organic compounds in near-shore environments, where organic material is much more abundant than in much of the deep sea (Calvert and Price, 1977b).

A third factor which has been proposed to explain the differences in composition between near-shore and deep-sea concretions is the rapid growth rate of the former. As a result of this, such concretions have less time during which to scavenge metals from sea water than their deep-sea counterparts. However, Calvert and Price (1977b) consider this could only be an important effect if the rate of minor element uptake was relatively constant in relation to the growth rate of the concretions, which it is probably not. Nevertheless, it may be of importance in explaining depletion of metals in some very rapidly precipitated concretions, especially in lakes.

5.8.4   Lacustrine concretions

It is evident from Table 8 that, on average, lacustrine concretions are compositionally distinct from most other groups of ferromanganese oxides, being much lower in many minor elements, even taking into account the great compositional variability of the deposits and the possible lack of representivity of the averages calculated (section 5.7.1).

Dean and Ghosh (1980) have illustrated the variability in the Mn/Fe ratio of lacustrine concretions in relation to those of other varieties. Phosphorus is enriched in the concretions over its likely detrital contribution, and is correlated with iron (Calvert and Price, 1977b). Barium shows some enrichment in concretions in Lake Michigan, probably due to the presence of psilomelane (Rossman, 1973). Lake Ontario concretions are higher in Ni, Co and Cu than the levels found in many concretions from other smaller North American lakes (Cronan and Thomas, 1970), but are still below normal deep-ocean values.

Inter-element correlations within different groups of lacustrine concretions have been reported by various authors. Rossman (1973) found correlations of Ba, Co, Cu, Ni, Mo, Sr, and Zn with Mn and of As and Cr with Fe in Green Bay concretions, Lake Michigan. Cronan and Thomas (1972) found correlations of Co, Ni and Zn with Mn in Lake Ontario concretions. Sozanski and Cronan (1979) found that K, Ca, Mg, Cu, Ni and Co are positively correlated with Mn in Shebandowan Lakes nodules. Recently Dean and Ghosh (1980) have reviewed the composition of various groups of lacustrine concretions in comparison with those from other environments, and their inter-element associations, confirming that most elements are positively correlated with Mn and negatively correlated with Fe.

The factors influencing the distinctive composition of lacustrine concretions may largely be similar to those determining the composition of nearshore shallow marine concretions. However, the pH range of lake waters is more variable than that in sea water, with a tendency towards lower pH values. This may be affecting trace metal uptake on to manganese oxides which generally decreases with decreasing pH (Dean and Ghosh, 1980), thus partly accounting for the generally low minor element content of the deposits. The role of metal complexation may be similar in importance in lakes as in shallow marine environments. The very rapid growth rates of some lacustrine concretions, occasionally in the order of millimetres per year (section 5.6.3) may also be responsible for their low minor element content. According to Goldberg (1954), the efficiency of the adsorption process is, among other things, a function of the length of time the solid phase is in contact with the ions to be adsorbed.

In considering the composition of lacustrine concretions in relation to other varieties, the lake to lake inhomogeneity of the deposits must always be taken into account. Many lakes receive input from relatively small catchment areas and thus the composition of their waters, sediments and concretions is likely to reflect the composition of rocks and soils in these areas, and the nature of any human activities giving rise to pollution around the lakes. This may account for some of the anomalous metal values found in some lake concretions. For example, Varentsov (1972) reported an average of 10 300 p.p.m. Cd in Enigi-Lampi Lake concretions in Karelia; Schoettle and Friedman (1971) reported an average of 1177 p.p.m. Zn in Lake George concretions; Gorham and Swaine (1965) reported averages of 2551 p.p.m. Pb and 1112 p.p.m. Zn in Lake Windermere concretions; and Cronan and Thomas (1972) reported higher than normal Pb and Zn concentrations in Lake Ontario concretions. Sozanski and Cronan (1979) noted an enrichment of Zn in concretions from part of the Shebandowan Lakes system in Ontario, thought to be due to zinc mineralization in the catchment area. Analysis of lacustrine ferromanganese oxide concretions may thus be a useful tool in geochemical reconnaissance exploration for mineral deposits in that it could outline catchment areas worthy of more detailed exploration.

5.9   Regional Geochemical Variations and the Formation of Ore Grade Deposits

It is evident from the preceding section that large-scale ocean wide regional variations in the composition of ferromanganese oxide concretions are largely due to broad regional changes in the environment of deposition on the sea floor. Seamount areas, for example, have nodules and encrustations distinctively different from those in abyssal regions, more or less irrespective of their geographic location. However, within the abyssal environment, there are more subtle regional variations in the composition of the concretions which form the subject of most of this section. It should be noted that it is only within the abyssal environment that ore grade nodules rich in Ni, Cu and Zn have been found, and thus an understanding of the factors leading to concretion variability within this environment should aid in the location of other ore grade deposits.

5.9.1   The Pacific Ocean

Ocean wide regional variations in the composition of Pacific nodules and encrustations were first described by Mero (1962) and Skornyakova *et al.* (1962). Following H. W. Menard, Mero recognized four types of deposits: iron-rich nodules found in parts of the south and west Pacific and near Central

America; manganese-rich nodules found in parts of the eastern Pacific; copper and nickel-rich nodules found in the central and eastern Pacific and cobalt-rich nodules centred on topographic highs in the central, southern and western Pacific. Cronan (1967) confirmed these findings on the basis of further analyses, and subdivided the Pacific Ocean into broad compositional regions (Table 11). Other workers who have described the regional geo-chemistry of Pacific nodules include Price and Calvert (1970); Goodell *et al.* (1971); Horn *et al.* (1973); Piper and Williamson (1977); Arrhenius *et al.* (1979) and Calvert (1978). Single element plots of the regional compositional variability of Pacific nodules (Cronan, 1967; Arrhenius *et al.*, 1979; Calvert, 1978) and others indicate that manganese generally tends to be high in the eastern Pacific, especially in the continental borderland where diagenetic remobilization of buried manganese and its separation from other elements is important, and decreases in a westerly direction (Fig. 45). The behaviour of iron is largely the reverse of that of manganese, being generally low in eastern Pacific nodules except in those from some near continental areas (Mero, 1965) and increases towards the west and south-west. It is also high on some ridges. The regional variability of minor elements in Pacific nodules

Table 11. Average composition of manganese nodules from different regions of the oceans (in wt. %) (after Cronan and Tooms, 1969; Cronan, 1975b; Moorby, 1978).

	1	2	3	4	5	6	7	8	9
Mn	15·19	16·22	13·54	15·54	9·55	19·75	16·65	19·84	15·26
Fe	23·17	22·41	21·84	20·37	20·27	18·53	22·93	12·95	24·44
Ni	0·270	0·245	0·188	0·225	0·140	0·361	0·249	0·637	0·227
Co	0·287	0·539	0·372	0·439	0·301	0·488	0·438	0·381	0·095
Cu	0·13	0·047	0·048	0·047	0·070	0·126	0·105	0·095	0·200
Pb									
Zn	0·098	0·058	0·056	0·059	0·062	0·071	0·064	0·058	0·065
Ca	2·02	2·66	2·92	3·27	9·41	2·33	1·96	8·39	1·63
Mg	1·79	1·47	2·69	1·42	1·28	1·63	1·32	2·88	2·22
Al									
Na	1·68	1·52	1·38	2·31	1·60	1·57	1·47	1·01	2·06
K	0·48	0·29	0·26	0·31	0·45	0·47	0·37	0·32	0·57
Ba									
Mo									
V									
Cr									
Ti									
Mn/Fe	0·66	0·72	0·62	0·77	0·47	1·06	0·73	1·53	0·62
Depth (m)	4339	1227	2388	2440	2877	3107	3934	838	5115

1 = North-western Atlantic Basin, 21 samples.
2 = Isolated Atlantic seamounts, 7 samples.
3 = Mid-Atlantic Ridge at 45°N, 18 samples.
4 = Central Mid-Atlantic Ridge, 4 samples.
5 = Northern Mid-Atlantic Ridge, 4 samples.

6 = North-eastern Atlantic Basin, 6 samples.
7 = Cape Verde Basin, 3 samples.
8 = Blake Plateau, 7 samples.
9 = South of Blake Plateau, 3 samples.

Table 11—cont.

	10	11	12	13	14	15	16	17	18
Mn	23·67	16·07	12·98	23·45	23·05	17·18	13·96	16·87	15·71
Fe	17·88	19·95	25·85	13·68	18·10	20·26	13·10	13·30	9·06
Ni	0·549	0·266	0·244	0·952	0·482	0·258	0·393	0·564	0·956
Co	0·138	0·327	0·179	0·208	0·676	0·406	1·127	0·395	0·213
Cu	0·182	0·118	0·105	0·500	0·078	0·058	0·061	0·393	0·711
Pb							0·174	0·034	0·049
Zn	0·106	0·109	0·084	0·178	0·116	0·156			
Ca	1·59	2·66	1·92	1·50	2·39	4·78			
Mg	1·41	1·56	1·91	1·99	1·34	1·22			
Al									
Na	2·42	2·72	2·36	2·42	1·46	1·77			
K	0·73	0·91	0·91	0·76	0·37	0·37			
Ba							0·274	0·152	0·155
Mo							0·042	0·037	0·041
V							0·054	0·044	0·036
Cr							0·0011	0·0007	0·0012
Ti							0·773	0·810	0·561
Mn/Fe	1·32	0·80	0·50	1·71	1·27	0·84	1·07	1·27	1·73
Depth (m)	3082	4258	3696	4924	1836	2718	1757	5001	5049

	19	20	21	22	23	24	25	26	27
Mn	15·85	22·33	19·81	16·61	16·5	17·5	1·71	13·4	12·5
Fe	22·22	9·44	10·20	13·92	16·5	14·7	43·9	17·4	19·4
Ni	0·348	1·080	0·961	0·133	0·800	0·285	0·133	0·275	0·119
Co	0·514	0·192	0·164	0·595	0·120	0·264	0·033	0·443	0·205
Cu	0·077	0·627	0·311	0·185	0·204	0·094	0·064	0·065	0·088
Pb	0·085	0·028	0·030	0·073	0·058	0·128	0·016	0·161	0·092
Zn					0·112	0·056	0·048	0·053	0·051
Ca					3·09	2·00	0·64	3·91	2·11
Mg									
Al					1·84	1·73	1·21	1·72	2·54
Na									
K									
Ba	0·306	0·381	0·145	0·230					
Mo	0·040	0·047	0·037	0·035					
V	0·065	0·041	0·031	0·050					
Cr	0·0051	0·0007	0·0005	0·0007					
Ti	0·489	0·425	0·467	1·007					
Mn/Fe	0·71	2·36	1·94	1·19	1·0	1·2	0·04	0·77	0·64
Depth (m)	1146	4537	4324	3539	3120	3180	1720	2240	3920

10 = Argentine Basin, 4 samples.
11 = Brazil Basin, 9 samples.
12 = Drake Passage—Scotia Sea, 36 samples.
13 = Cape Basin, 4 samples.
14 = Walvis Ridge, 3 samples.
15 = South of Africa, 4 samples.
16 = Mid-Pacific Mountains, 5 samples.
17 = West Pacific, 23 samples.
18 = Central Pacific, 9 samples.
19 = Southern Borderland Seamount Province, 5 samples.
20 = North-east Pacific, 10 samples.
21 = South-east Pacific, 8 samples.
22 = South Pacific, 11 samples.
23 = Mozambique Channel, 4 samples.
24 = Southern African Plateaux, 7 samples.
25 = African Continental Borderland, 2 samples.
26 = Indian Ocean Seamounts and aseismic ridges, 19 samples.
27 = Mid-Indian Ocean ridge system, 19 samples.

Table 11—cont.

	28	29	30	31	32	33
Mn	22·1	12·8	12·6	11·6	15·3	15·1
Fe	7·6	15·5	16·1	13·0	12·0	11·4
Ni						
Co	0·113	0·190	0·256	0·150	0·139	0·173
Cu	0·991	0·150	0·115	0·166	0·241	0·355
Pb	0·065	0·097	0·104	0·120	0·071	0·087
Zn	0·119	0·066	0·049	0·048	0·064	0·071
Ca	1·33	1·89	1·59	1·30	1·27	1·35
Mg						
Al	2·75	3·03	3·27	3·07	2·48	3·64
Na						
K						
Ba						
Mo						
V						
Cr	0·0036		0·0028			
Ti	0·324		1·18			
Mn/Fe	2·9	0·83	0·78	0·89	1·3	1·3
Depth (m)	5090	4600	5010	5277	4455	5320

28 = Central Indian Basin, 22 samples.   31 = Mozambique Basin, 4 samples.
29 = Crozet Basin, 8 samples.   32 = Somali Basin, 2 samples.
30 = Madagascar Basin, 15 samples.   33 = Wharton Basin, 5 samples.

is not dependent upon that of the major elements, although within the abyssal environment a co-variance between some major and minor elements is observed (Calvert and Price, 1977a). Nickel, copper, molybdenum and zinc are enriched in eastern Pacific nodules rich in manganese, other than in those from continental borderland areas, and are especially abundant in the pelagic north-eastern equatorial Pacific with Ni also being enriched in parts of the south-eastern Pacific (Fig. 46). They tend to decrease in concentration towards the south and west Pacific, and reach their lowest concentrations on topographic elevations in these areas. Cobalt, lead, tin, titanium and vanadium generally co-vary with iron but also vary independently (Skornyakova and Andrushchenko, 1970), Co and Pb reaching their greatest enrichments on seamounts in the western and southern Pacific (Fig. 47).

A different approach to the representation of the regional geochemistry of Pacific nodules and encrustations has been provided by Howarth *et al.* (1977). These authors applied a computer based non-linear mapping technique to geochemical data on Pacific ferromanganese oxide concretions published by Mero (1965) and Cronan (1967). Two hundred and twelve analyses from these data sets were used and the samples were classified into six groups based on their contents of Mn, Fe, Ni, Co, Cu, Pb and Ti

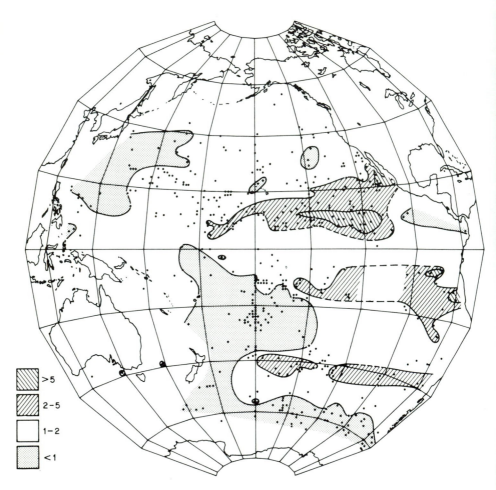

Fig. 45. Distribution of Mn/Fe ratios in ferromanganese nodules from the Pacific (from Calvert, 1978).

(Table 12). Four of the groups (1–4) were found to form parts of a fairly homogeneous population when plotted on a non-linear map (Fig. 48), with groups 5 and 6 reasonably well separated from them. The non-linear mapping reflected considerable compositional variation between the samples, with Mn increasing from groups 1 to 6, the maximum values of Fe, Co, Pb and Ti all occurring in group 2, and Ni and Cu attaining their maximum values in group 5 (Table 12) confirming previous observations on inter-element associations in the deposits (section 5.7.5). When plotted on a map of the

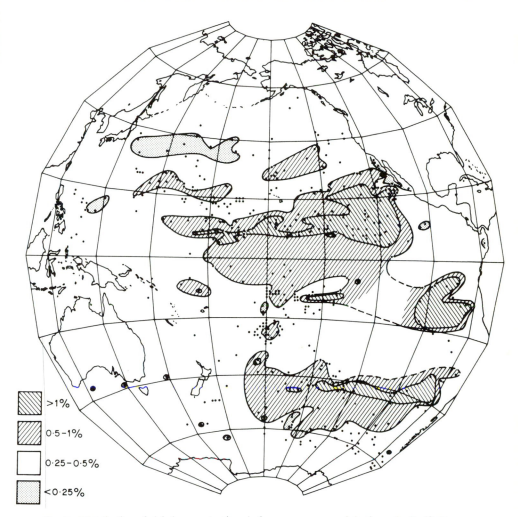

Fig. 46. Distribution of nickel concentrations in ferromanganese nodules from the Pacific Ocean. Copper shows a very similar distribution (from Calvert, 1978).

Pacific (Fig. 49) the regional distribution of the samples assigned to the six groups showed a degree of geographic dependency. Group 6 samples rich in Mn plot off the coasts of the Americas, group 5 samples rich in Mn, Ni and Cu occur in an east–west belt in the eastern Pacific around latitude 10°N, and group 2 samples rich in Fe, Co, Pb and Ti plot in the western Pacific and in parts of the South Pacific. These results confirm the observations of previous workers based on single element plots, and emphasize that the regional geochemistry of Pacific nodules largely reflects a more or less con-

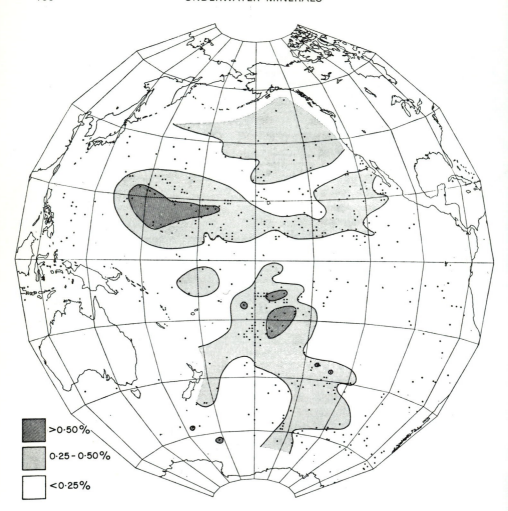

Fig. 47. Distribution of cobalt concentrations in ferromanganese nodules from the Pacific Ocean (from Calvert, 1978).

tinuous spectrum of element variations which nevertheless approximates to the regional element groupings proposed by previous workers. The technique could be used to advantage in other oceans, especially in comparison with the Pacific data, in order to outline other areas containing group five "ore grade" deposits.

Table 12. Group compositions based on non-linear mapping of normalized arithmetic data on Pacific nodules. From Howarth *et al.* (1977).

	Mn (%)	Fe (%)	Ni (p.p.m.)	Co (p.p.m.)	Cu (p.p.m.)	Pb (p.p.m.)	Ti (p.p.m.)
Group 1 (*n* = 30)							
Mean	10·98	11·49	4042	2248	2930	1046	5380
Standard error	0·65	0·71	428	277	409	114	684
Group 2 (*n* = 58)							
Mean	15·58	15·16	3735	6009	1894	1238	10079
Standard error	0·51	0·28	198	416	158	104	478
Group 3 (*n* = 59)							
Mean	17·67	11·86	6997	2996	4479	863	6066
Standard error	0·36	0·28	229	207	205	72	300
Group 4 (*n* = 35)							
Mean	22·07	8·73	11059	2719	8617	796	4315
Standard error	0·46	0·30	252	208	317	71	351
Group 5 (*n* = 14)							
Mean	26·99	5·80	14936	1655	12481	420	2920
Standard error	0·84	0·55	1296	243	1182	73	360
Group 6 (*n* = 8)							
Mean	34·29	4·23	7640	636	2820	256	1564
Standard error	2·87	1·51	2958	241	774	99	371

n = number of samples.

5.9.1.1 *Abyssal nodules*

Regional variations in the composition of abyssal nodules in the Pacific have been described by Price and Calvert (1970). Using the data of Mero (1965), Barnes (1967a) and Cronan (1967), these authors noted regional variations in Mn/Fe, and certain minor element ratios in abyssal manganese nodules throughout the Pacific Ocean. Subsequent work has amplified these trends (Figs 45, 46 and 47). In addition, Calvert and Price (1977a) examined a more limited suite of nodules and associated sediments from the eastern and central Pacific using factor analysis, and found that the deposits could be divided into two groups. Those from the northern tropical region had high factor scores for Mn, Mg, Ba, Cu, Mo, Ni and Zn, while those from the central southern equatorial region had higher than average factor scores for Fe, Ti, P, Ca, As, Co, Pb, Sr, Y and Zr. The Mn-rich nodules had high Mn/Fe ratios and high contents of minor elements associated with the Mn phase which was todorokite. The Mn-poor nodules had Mn/Fe ratios of about 1 and higher than average contents of minor elements associated with the

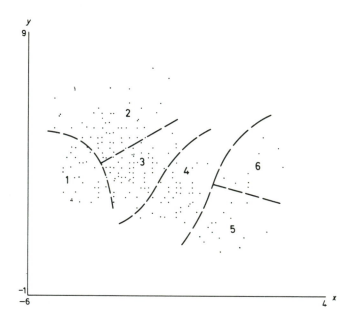

Fig. 48. Non-linear mapping of manganese nodule compositions from the Pacific Ocean on the basis of normalized Mn, Fe, Co, Ni, Cu, Pb and Ti. Numbered areas (1–6) refer to sample groups assigned on basis of mapping from 7 into 2 dimensions (from Howarth *et al.*, 1977).

Fe phase and contained δ MnO$_2$ as their principal manganese mineral. There was every gradation between these two end members.

Similar observations to those of Calvert and Price (1977a) have been made in nodules from small areas in the Pacific (section 5.8.2) and even within single nodules. Raab (1972) noted that discoidal nodules from the Pacific "ore zone" which appear to have remained *in situ* throughout most of their growth history, were enriched in Fe, Co and Pb on their upper sides and in Mn, Ni, Cu, Mo and Zn on their lower sides (see also section 5.3.1). The upper sides contained δ MnO$_2$ and the lower sides contained todorokite. As mentioned, several workers such as Fewkes (1975), Greenslate (1975), and Calvert and Price (1977a) have interpreted these observations in terms of precipitation of metals largely from sea water on the upper surfaces of the nodules, and from interstitial waters as a result of diagenetic remobilization on their lower surfaces.

It is evident from the work summarized in the preceding two paragraphs that a ferromanganese oxide consisting mainly of δ MnO$_2$ precipitated from sea water and, superimposed upon it, one consisting mainly of todorokite possibly formed partly in response to diagenetic processes within the underly-

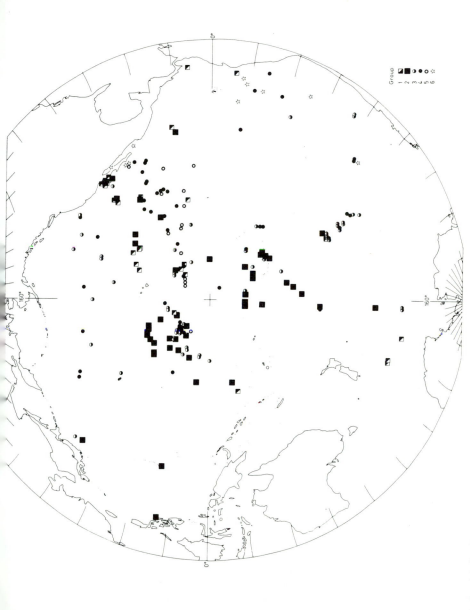

Fig. 49. Spatial distribution of non-linear mapping groups in the Pacific Ocean, on Lambert's equal-area projection (from Howarth *et al.*, 1977).

ing sediments, can be recognized throughout the Pacific basin. The sea water end member with a Mn/Fe ratio near unity is probably best represented by oceanic seamount nodules which grow on rock surfaces largely free of sediment. By contrast the diagenetic end member with a high Mn/Fe ratio is probably best represented by the buried undersides of the Mn, Ni and Cu-rich ore grade nodules in the north-eastern tropical Pacific. Between the two, there is a continuous gradation of deposits which receive their constituents from both sources in varying proportions.

It is likely that the sea water component of Pacific nodules is fairly uniform in composition over the whole ocean basin. This is supported by the relatively small variation in the Mn/Fe ratio of seamount nodules throughout the ocean irrespective of their location (Cronan, 1977a). Variations in the Mn/Fe ratio of bulk nodules from the abyssal Pacific must therefore largely be due to variations in the rate of supply of diagenetically remobilized manganese to the deposits, which in turn influences their minor element content.

The factors affecting the rate of supply of diagenetically remobilized manganese to abyssal nodules have been the subject of much investigation. Rapid rates of sediment accumulation are well known in continental margin areas and, as mentioned, lead to organic matter being preserved within the sediments. Post-depositional oxidation and breakdown of this organic matter leads to the diagenetic reduction and remobilization of manganese which then migrates to the sediment surface to give deposits with high Mn/Fe ratios in the manner described already. Price and Calvert (1970) suggested that rapid sedimentation in abyssal areas also might result in a similar effect. On this basis, abyssal nodules with high Mn/Fe ratios might be expected to occur in areas where sediment accumulation is rapid. However, it was subsequently pointed out that the ratio is also high in areas where sedimentation rates are very low (Cronan, 1972a, 1974; Piper and Williamson, 1977; Calvert et al., 1978). Thus sedimentation rates alone cannot be invoked to account for variations in the Mn/Fe ratio of abyssal nodules throughout the Pacific.

Several workers have discussed variations in the Mn/Fe ratio and minor element content of Pacific nodules in terms of organic productivity in the overlying surface waters (Greenslate et al., 1973; Cronan, 1975a; Piper and Williamson, 1977; Calvert, 1978). The suggestion of Correns (1941), Arrhenius (1963) and Greenslate et al. (1973) that sinking organic remains transport elements to the sediment–water interface provides a mechanism for fluxing them in abundance to forming nodules underlying areas of high organic productivity. Furthermore, the decay of organic material on the sea floor could lower the redox potential of the depositional environment leading to the diagenetic redistribution of Mn and the formation of todorokite as will be described shortly. Regional variations in biological productivity in the surface waters of the Pacific may therefore have a considerable influence on regional variations in the composition of manganese nodules on the underlying sea floor.

5.9.1.2 *Formation of ore grade nodules*

Ore grade manganese nodules which represent the diagenetic end member of the sequence already described were first recognized in the Pacific by Mero (1965). They contain combined Ni, Cu and Co roughly about or in excess of 3%, are rich in manganese, have a high Mn/Fe ratio, and contain todorokite as their principal mineral phase. The extent of these deposits was recognized as large by mining companies and some others, and the compilation of Horn and his co-workers (Horn *et al.*, 1973) showed them to occupy a broad zone of the north-eastern tropical Pacific (Fig. 33). They lie under the northern margin of the equatorial zone of high biological productivity on what is largely a very porous siliceous ooze substrate. Of critical importance in the formation of these deposits is the depth of the sea floor in relation to the calcium carbonate compensation depth. As described, most high grade deposits in the North Pacific, and at least in some parts of the South Pacific also (Pautot and Melguen, 1979), lie at or below the depth at which calcium carbonate dissolves and thus are able to receive metals from the dissolution of sinking biogenic remains. This factor, together with diagenetic redistribution of metals within the sediments, is thought to be largely responsible for the distinctive composition of these deposits (Greenslate *et al.*, 1973; Cronan, 1975a; Calvert and Price, 1977a and others).

A simplified composite model for the formation of ore grade nodules in the Pacific based on the work of Raab (1972), Horn *et al.* (1973), Greenslate *et al.* (1973), Cronan (1975a), Marchig *et al.* (1976), Hartmann and Muller (1976), Calvert and Price (1977a) and Burns and Burns (1978, 1979) is as follows. Organisms containing metals extracted from surface waters in the region of high biological productivity in the Pacific sink to the ocean floor after death. Both their soft and hard parts start to dissolve within the water column, but some fraction of the soft organic material reaches the ocean floor, perhaps protected from extensive decay above the lysocline by the hard parts, to be oxidized and broken down within the uppermost sediments below the lysocline. Additional metals, particularly nickel, copper and zinc, may be picked up from sea water as organically complexed cations as the dead organisms sink. The breakdown of biogenic material on the sea floor and its reaction with phases in the sediment, as well as liberating metals to the interstitial waters for nodule formation, causes a local reduction in the redox potential of the uppermost sediments resulting in diagenetic redistribution of the more mobile metals such as manganese and the formation of todorokite-rich nodules. Other metals such as nickel and copper diffuse through the very topmost sediments to become incorporated in todorokite on and in the buried portions of the manganese nodules. The concentration of such metals continues to increase within the nodules so long as todorokite continues to form in them as a result of post-depositional chemical reactions, and the nodules as a whole remain permeable to the metal-bearing percolating solutions. The tops of the nodules receive their metals from sea water. The high Mn, Ni and Cu content of the deposits would thus be a function first of an enhanced rate of supply of these metals to the sediments via sinking organisms and their post-depositional redistribution, and secondly because of the presence in the deposits of a mineral phase, todorokite, which is able to accommodate the metals.

Evidence to support the model is forthcoming from interstitial water studies. Hartmann and Muller (1976) have found enrichment factors of Mn, Cu, Zn and Ni in the interstitial waters from the Pacific ore zone over their concentrations in sea water of, respectively, 12–19, 5–28, 3–4 and 2–5. All of these metals except zinc tended to have highest concentrations in the interstitial waters of the topmost sediments (0–2 cm), suggesting that diffusion from buried sediments was not the source of the enriched metals. Redox potentials were found to increase slightly with depth, indicating that much of the oxidation of organic matter was complete before appreciable burial. These authors considered that metal release from the sediments is greatest at the surface, perhaps in the first two or three mm, and calculated that the resulting fluxes were more than sufficient to account for Mn, Ni, Cu and Zn in the accompanying nodules. Additional evidence to support the model has been presented by Marchig and Gundlach (1979). These authors found that manganese micronodules were undergoing selective dissolution and liberating Mn, Ni and Cu with increasing burial in the topmost few centimetres of the radiolarian ooze underlying ore grade nodules in the north-eastern equatorial Pacific, probably as a result of reaction with organic material.

The formation of nodules as a result of diffusion of metals within the uppermost oxidized sediments rather than by remobilization of metals from more deeply buried anoxic sediments, as is thought to be the case in diagenetic nodules formed in continental borderlands, might partly account for the compositional differences between the two varieties. In the case of the latter, minor elements such as Ni, Cu etc. could remain behind in organic material preserved within the anoxic sediments. In the case of ore grade nodules in the north-eastern equatorial Pacific the underlying sediments below a few centimetres depth are highly oxidized and contain little or no organic matter in which the minor elements could be fixed. They must therefore either accrete with the nodules or micronodules, or diffuse into the overlying sea water. In regard to the second possibility, Marchig *et al.* (1976) have noted that some nodule forming elements are enriched in the near bottom sea water overlying the ore zone. Thus, metals diagenetically remobilized from sediments into sea water could be contributing to that fraction of the nodules precipitated from sea water as well as that fraction precipitated within the sediment or in nodules at the sediment–water interface.

The possible restriction of the diagenetic redistribution and diffusion of elements to a thin zone in the uppermost sediments of the "ore zone" has important implications in terms of variable growth of nodules. It would account for the seemingly higher growth rates on the equatorial bulges of *in situ* nodules noted previously and would suggest that a uniform distribution of elements over the surface of nodules will only occur if they are buried or rolled about in the sediments in a regular manner. It would also help to explain some of the variable internal structures of nodules as different parts of the deposits could be growing by different mechanisms at different times due to periodic rolling or burial.

5.9.2 Atlantic Ocean

Knowledge of the regional geochemistry of Atlantic Ocean nodules and encrustations is based on many fewer samples than are available from the Pacific Ocean (Smith *et al.*, 1968; Mero, 1965; Cronan, 1975b). Nevertheless it is evident from the data of Cronan (1975b) that the Atlantic Ocean does not exhibit smooth trends in the composition of nodules in quite the same way as is found over much of the Pacific. Its greater topographic complexity leads to an environmental differentiation of the deposits largely based on bathymetry which is independent of their geographic locations. Furthermore, continental and volcanic source influences on the deposits seem to be greater than appears to be the case in the Pacific.

Manganese is highest in Atlantic deposits in deep water areas on either side of the Mid-Atlantic Ridge and in deposits from the Blake Plateau and Walvis Ridge (Fig. 50) in which todorokite appears to be the principal mineral phase. By contrast, iron is highest in samples from the Drake Passage and Scotia Sea area where it sometimes exceeds 40% (Fig. 51) and is generally slightly enriched in δMnO_2 deposits as a whole over its concentration in those rich in todorokite. Nickel is highest in the Cape Basin where it ranges up to 1·5% and is somewhat lower over the remainder of the South Atlantic. It is generally lower still in the North Atlantic, especially on elevated areas such as the Mid-Atlantic Ridge. The distributions of copper and zinc are similar in some respects to that of nickel, these elements being generally highest in basins and low in elevated areas of the ocean. Cobalt varies in more or less an opposite manner to Ni, Cu and Zn, being highest on elevated features such as seamounts and lower in basins, although the latter feature

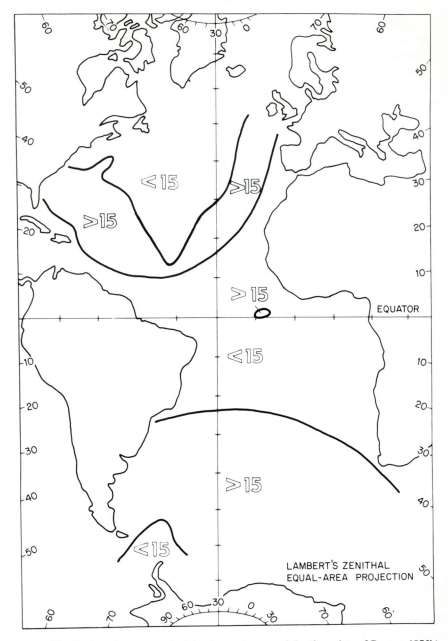

Fig. 50. Distribution of manganese in Atlantic manganese nodules (from data of Cronan, 1975b).

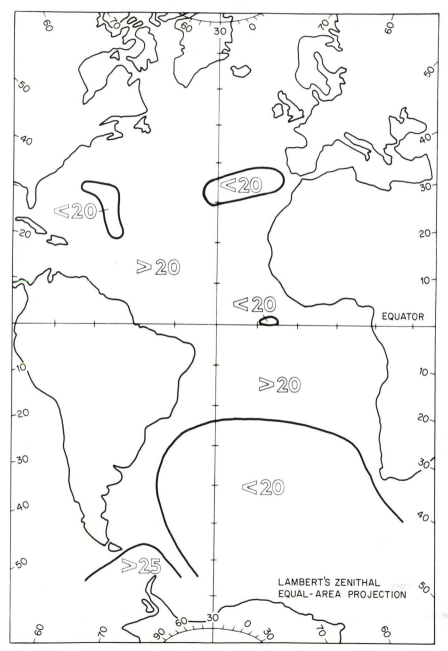

Fig. 51. Distribution of iron in Atlantic manganese nodules (from data of Cronan, 1975b).

is not very distinct. These variations are shown in Table 11. Correlations of Ni, Cu and Zn occur with manganese. None of the minor elements appear to correlate with iron.

Examination of the Mn/Fe ratios of the abyssal Atlantic nodules alone does not reveal the striking variations found in the Pacific. Nevertheless the average Mn/Fe ratios of deposits in the different basin areas listed by Cronan (1975b) do range from 0·65 to 1·72 (Table 11), the lowest being in the northwestern Atlantic and the highest in the Cape Basin where the highest average Ni, Zn and Cu contents occur. Furthermore samples from the equatorial zone tend to be somewhat enriched in Mn and Ni. The significance of these conclusions is tempered by the limited data on which they are based, but if they are valid, suggest that an association of Ni, Cu and Zn with nodules of high Mn/Fe ratio occurs in the Atlantic just as in the Pacific, but rarely except in the Cape Basin do these elements approach ore grade. On the whole, however, the data available on Atlantic nodules and encrustations suggest the diagenetic supply of metals to the deposits is of limited importance, most of the metals probably being precipitated from normal sea water or liberated from terrigenous detritus, with some possible supply of metals from volcanic sources at the Mid-Atlantic Ridge.

5.9.3   The Indian Ocean

The regional geochemistry of Indian Ocean nodules and encrustations appears largely to reflect the physiography of the Ocean. The Indian Ocean can be divided into a series of basins and elevated areas each of which tend to have ferromanganese oxide deposits of fairly well defined composition (Cronan and Tooms, 1969; Bezrukov and Andrushchenko, 1972; Summerhayes and Willis, 1975; Cronan and Moorby, 1976; Frakes and O'Brien, 1980; Cronan and Moorby, in preparation). Average compositions of concretions from different physiographic provinces within the ocean are given in Table 11.

Manganese is highest in nodules from the Central Indian Basin, and somewhat lower in the Wharton Basin and to the south-west of Australia. It is intermediate to low in the basins of the southern and western Indian Ocean, and lowest of all on the mid-ocean ridge system. Just as in the Pacific, concretions from near the continental margins are characterized by very variable manganese contents. As would be expected, iron varies more or less the reverse of manganese. It is lowest in concretions from the Central Indian Basin and reaches its highest concentrations in encrustations from the mid-ocean ridge system, isolated topographic highs, and some continental margin areas. The minor elements in Indian Ocean concretions tend to behave in a similar manner as elsewhere. Nickel, copper and zinc are generally en-

riched in basin nodules where the Mn/Fe ratio is high, particularly in the
Central Indian and Wharton Basins, and are much lower in elevated areas
(Cronan and Moorby, in preparation). Copper is intermediate but Ni and
the Mn/Fe ratio are high in the south-east Indian Ocean basins (Frakes and
O'Brien, 1980). Cobalt by contrast is generally low in samples from basin
areas and highest on seamounts. However, uncharacteristically it is also high
in the Madagascar Basin (see Appendix). These trends are illustrated in
Fig. 52.

The causes of the regional variations in the composition of abyssal Indian
Ocean nodules are likely to be the same as in the Pacific and Atlantic Oceans.
Thus, the high Mn/Fe ratio nodules may receive a substantial diagenetic
component, while those with low Mn/Fe ratios probably receive their constituents largely from sea water. The geographic distribution of Mn/Fe ratios
in the deposits would support this contention. Deposits in the Somali,
Wharton and Central Indian Basins where, in general, the Mn/Fe ratios are
highest, are located in the tropics where biological productivity is likely to
be higher than in mid latitudes. Thus, one could expect a significant flux
of organisms to the sea floor in such areas which could lead to the accumulation of organic material, a depression of the redox potential in the uppermost
few centimetres of the sediments, the diagenetic redistribution of manganese
and other elements in this layer, and the formation of todorokite which in
turn would favour the enrichment of nickel, copper and zinc in the deposits.
Local factors may be of importance in influencing the low Mn/Fe ratios of
Madagascar and Mozambique Basin samples, possibly local sources of iron.
The bottom water flow in the Madagascar Basin is from the direction of
the mid-ocean ridge, and some iron from ridge crest sources may thus be
transported into the basin. In the Mozambique Basin, because of its location
near a major land mass, continental sources of iron may be leading to its
enrichment in ferromanganese oxide concretions, just as has been proposed
in marginal basin concretions in the Atlantic Ocean.

It is in the Central Indian Ocean Basin that the highest grade nodules have
been found to date in the Indian Ocean. These samples approximate to the
diagenetic end members of the series already described in the Pacific and
are similar in composition to Pacific ore grade nodules, being enriched in
Mn, Ni, Cu, Zn and todorokite (Table 11). The distribution of these nodules
is not known in any detail. Those ore grade samples found so far occur
between about 8° and 15° to the south of the equator in an area of siliceous
ooze sedimentation below the calcium carbonate compensation depth.
Knowledge of the productivity of the overlying waters in this part of the
Indian Ocean is scant. However, G. S. Sharma (personal communication)
has suggested that divergence may occur along the boundary of the south
equatorial current and the equatorial counter current which could lead to

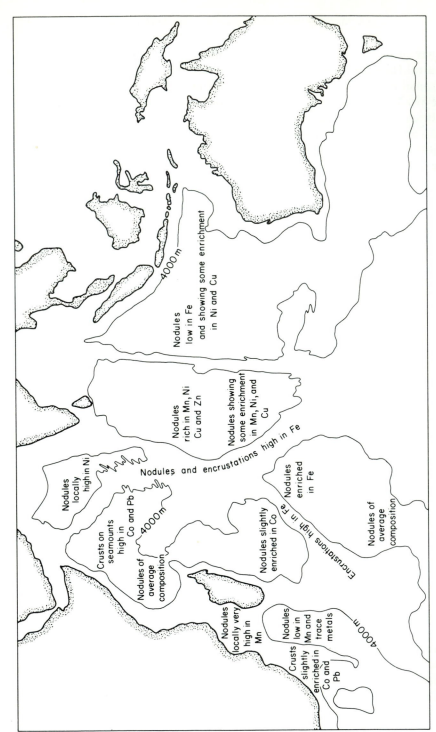

Fig. 52. Regional variability in the composition of Indian Ocean manganese nodules and encrustations (compiled from data in Appendix and the published literature).

upwelling promoting increased productivity. The fact that siliceous ooze is an important substrate in this region points to high productivity and hence the flux of organic remains to the sea floor being higher in the region than further to the south where red clay predominates. It is possible therefore that the manganese nodules in this part of the Central Indian Ocean Basin may be forming in a similar manner to those in the ore zone of the Pacific. More detailed studies in the Central Indian Basin are required to test this hypothesis.

6

Metalliferous Sediments

6.1 Introduction

In this chapter, metalliferous sediments are taken to include all deposits rich in iron, manganese and several other elements found in association with submarine volcanic activity throughout the World Ocean. Evidence to date indicates that the deposits are forming intermittently all along the World Mid-Ocean Ridge system, and also occur in association with submarine volcanism in some island arcs. In addition, deposits of the same type overlie older oceanic crust on the flanks of all the major ocean ridges, and similar possibly genetically related deposits occur within the stratigraphic column on land (Chapter 7). Of the major elements in the deposits, iron appears to be primarily derived from volcanic sources at spreading centres or other areas of submarine volcanic activity. Sources for the remaining elements are less clear. Isotopic evidence has indicated that some of these have at least a partial volcanic origin but that some are also in part derived from sea water.

Mid-ocean ridge metalliferous sediments have been described in detail by Bostrom and Peterson (1966) and subsequently by Bostrom and various co-workers in the late 1960s and early 1970s. Most of the material they studied was taken from the East Pacific Rise and this has remained an area of intensive metalliferous sediment investigations. However, similar deposits have been reported on the Mid-Atlantic Ridge and the Central Indian Ocean Ridge and related deposits in the Red Sea have received a great deal of attention.

Basal metalliferous sediments overlying oceanic crust on the flanks of active ocean ridges were discovered during the Deep Sea Drilling Project and were first described by von der Borch and Rex (1970). These were considered to be analogous to mid-ocean ridge crest metalliferous sediments on the basis of stratigraphic and geochemical evidence (von der Borch and Rex, 1970;

Cronan *et al.*, 1972), and were thought to have moved from the ridge to their present positions as a result of sea floor spreading. Like ridge crest metalliferous sediments, they occur in all the major oceans.

Island arc varieties of metalliferous sediments are of more recent discovery than those on mid-ocean ridges. Marine deposits from adjacent to the volcano of Santorini in the eastern Mediterranean are iron-rich and have been described by Bonatti *et al.* (1972a), Puchelt (1972) and Smith and Cronan (1975); and from the south-western Pacific by Ferguson and Lambert (1972), Bertine (1974) and Cronan and Thompson (1978). These deposits are similar in many respects to those on mid-ocean ridges.

6.2   Constituents of Metalliferous Sediments

Metalliferous sediments, like most marine sediments, are polygenetic in that they can derive their components from more than one source (Chapter 1). Such sources can include material from the continents (terrigenous), organic agencies (biogenic), precipitates from normal sea water (authigenic), the products of submarine weathering and alteration of ocean floor rocks (hal-myrolytic), precipitates from hot aqueous solutions (hydrothermal) and primary volcanic contributions (magmatic). Each of these sources is likely to vary in importance throughout the oceans.

As described in Chapter 1, terrigenous constituents of marine sediments enter the oceans through rivers and coastal erosion and by wind transport. Their average composition is similar to that of the crustal rocks from which they have been derived. Much of this material is precipitated in near-shore areas, particularly the coarser particles, and never reaches the deep sea. Some of the finer particles, however, do reach the deepest parts of the oceans far from land and thus lead to an enrichment in deep-sea sediments of those elements which have affinities for fine-grained minerals. However, few of the metalliferous sediments discussed in this chapter are thought to have derived more than a small portion of their constituents from terrigenous sources, and indeed terrigenous material must often be regarded as a diluent of the metalliferous constituents of such sediments.

Biogenic constituents of marine sediments comprise the skeletons of marine organisms, although the remains of soft parts are also preserved under certain conditions. The role of biological agencies in enriching metals in marine sediments and their potential in contributing to metalliferous sediment formation can be resolved into indirect and direct methods of enrichment.

An example of the indirect method of enrichment is the decay of material of biogenic origin leading to the development of reducing conditions in the sediment which can, in turn, result in the precipitation of certain metals from sea water which would otherwise not precipitate. Turekian and Bertine (1971) consider that molybdenum, uranium and some other elements were enriched in Mid-Atlantic Ridge sediments they examined as a result of deposition from sea water under anaerobic (reducing) conditions. Analogous metal enrichments occur in near-shore anaerobic sediments (Manheim, 1961). High accumulation rates of biogenic constituents over much of the World Mid-Ocean Ridge system, because of its elevation above the calcium carbonate compensation depth, would favour the development of local reducing conditions within the sediment column. However, it should be emphasized that available data indicate that oxidizing conditions prevail at the surface over most of the World Mid-Ocean Ridge System, and under such conditions anaerobic deposition of metals from sea water will not take place.

The direct role of biological agencies in contributing to metalliferous sediments is more straightforward. Planktonic organisms accumulate metals in the surface waters of the oceans by metabolic processes and by adsorption. These elements are released to deep waters after the death of the organisms as a result of the dissolution of their shells on sinking, and also by the oxidation of their soft parts. Carbonate organisms do not dissolve appreciably on settling until they reach the lysocline (Chapter 1) and complete dissolution occurs only at the calcium carbonate compensation depth. Such dissolution liberates metals into the water column or at the sediment surface, if it coincides with the zone of dissolution. These metals are available for incorporation into the sediments by adsorption, complexing, direct precipitation, or other mechanisms. In this way a variety of metals originally concentrated by biological agencies can become progressively enriched in slowly accumulating sediments beneath the calcium carbonate compensation depth due to their continual extraction from the surface waters of the oceans. In general, the greater the surface biological productivity, the greater will be the transfer of metals from surface waters to bottom waters, and the deeper will be the calcium carbonate compensation depth. Regional variations in productivity could therefore cause regional variations in the flux of metals to the sea floor, and thus in the composition of the underlying sediments. Furthermore, marine plankton can vary considerably in composition (Oldnall, 1975) and thus the variable distribution of plankton species in the oceans may also have an important effect on the transport of metals to the sediment–water interface. However, most of the crest of the World Mid-Ocean Ridge System where metalliferous sediments are accumulating is above the calcium carbonate compensation depth and much of it is also above the lysocline. Thus we can expect biological transport of metals from the surface of the oceans to be of·limited importance in enriching metals in metalliferous sediments on the shallowest parts of the mid-ocean ridges, but to assume increasing importance with increasing depth, and be at a maximum in those parts of the mid-ocean ridge below the calcium carbonate compensation depth such as in some of the deeper parts of oceanic fracture zones.

Volcanic contributions to the sediments described in this chapter can be divided into two categories. Hydrothermal leaching of crustal rocks by circulating sea water under elevated temperatures (Corliss, 1971; Spooner and Fyfe, 1973) and from residual primary magmatic solutions (Bostrom, 1973).

Investigations on the role of circulating sea water at the crests of mid-ocean ridges and in other submarine volcanic areas have indicated a possible sea water interaction with crustal rocks to depths of a few kilometres (Lister, 1972; Spooner and Fyfe, 1973; Spooner, 1977). Evidence of chemical reactions between this sea water and the newly formed volcanic rocks has been presented by a number of authors and is supported by leaching experiments (Corliss, 1971; Ellis and Mahon, 1964; Bischoff and Dickson, 1975; Seyfried and Bischoff, 1977 and Seyfried and Mottl, 1977). Corliss (1971) found that the interiors of some Mid-Atlantic Ridge basalt flows were depleted relative to the flow margins in several elements enriched in mid-ocean ridge metalliferous sediments, and concluded that the differences resulted from the removal of these elements from the interiors of the flows by hydrothermal leaching. Bischoff and Dickson (1975) have conducted experiments on the leaching of basalt with sea water at 200°C (although actual sub-sea floor temperatures may be much higher than this) and 500 bars which indicated that sufficient of certain metals could be dissolved from the basalt to account for the metal concentrations found in ridge crest metalliferous sediments, thus supporting the hydrothermal leaching model for the origin of at least a proportion of the constituents in such deposits. Al, Fe, Mn, Zn, Ni, Cu and Pb were determined in solutions extracted from the basalt–sea water reactions during a period of 4752 h. The concentrations of Al, Zn and Pb were so low as to be at or below the experimental limits of the method, while Fe and Mn increased to a maximum of 35 p.p.m. and then decreased to 5 p.p.m., and Ni and Cu reached 0·2 p.p.m. by the end of the experiment. Fe, Mn, Cu and Ni were enriched by two to three orders of magnitude over their concentration in normal sea water, sufficient to be considered as a dilute ore forming solution (Krauskopf, 1967). Additional experiments making sea water react with basalt under hydrothermal conditions by Mottl and Seyfried (1977) have indicated that the ratio of water to rock effective during alteration has a considerable effect on the quantities of metals leached. Two types of sub-sea floor hydrothermal systems can occur: rock dominated and sea water dominated. The distinction between the two is thought to result largely from the role of sea water magnesium in generating and maintaining acidity. According to Mottl and Seyfried, in sea water dominated systems during reaction with basalt, H^+ is produced by the uptake of sea water Mg and

OH^- in the form of a $Mg(OH)_2$ component in smectite or chlorite. So long as high concentrations of magnesium and silica are maintained in solution, the rate of H^+ production exceeds that of H^+ consumption by silicate hydrolysis reactions and the pH stays acid. As a result, high concentrations of heavy metals such as Fe, Mn and Zn can be taken into solution. In rock dominated systems, the chemical reactions produce a neutral to slightly alkaline solution which has a more limited ability to take transition metals into solution. Thus sea water dominated systems are those which can produce acid metal-rich hot springs from which metalliferous sediments could form. By contrast rock dominated systems produce hydrothermal solutions which are rather depleted in metals and from which metalliferous sediments would be unlikely to form in any abundance.

An alternative viewpoint on the source of the metals in submarine metalliferous sediments is that they are derived from deep-seated magmatic sources (Bostrom, 1973). Bostrom considered that carbonate-rich emanations from the mantle enriched in Fe, Mn, P, Ba and U, and depleted in Al, Ti, Si and Th, may play a major role in the concentration of the first group of these elements in mid-ocean ridge sediments.

It is difficult to provide a relative evaluation of the role of sea water–rock interaction as opposed to magmatic activity in forming metalliferous sediments, especially as the latter is less amenable to direct observation than the former. There is little doubt that some of the metals enriched in metalliferous sediments are lost from basalt as a result of hydrothermal leaching. Whether this can provide 100% of each of the enriched metals in metalliferous sediments is not established, and would require detailed balance calculations based on the amount of basalt, sediment and sea water involved. Although the evidence for deep-seated magmatic sources of some metals found in metalliferous sediments is not as conclusive as that for hydrothermal leaching, it would be unreasonable to exclude magmatic contributions to ridge crest sediments entirely. Some of the metals enriched in the sediments are amongst those concentrated in the late stage fluids of magmatic crystallization and, on ascent, the latter might be expected to mix with sea water circulating within the oceanic crust to produce composite solutions of variable composition. On this basis, both hydrothermal leaching of the oceanic crust and late stage magmatic solutions could contribute to the formation of submarine metalliferous sediments, probably in variable proportions as dictated by local circumstances.

The role of submarine weathering of crustal rocks in supplying elements to metalliferous sediments is somewhat contentious. The division between submarine weathering (halmyrolysis) and hydrothermal leaching, must, of necessity, be rather arbitrary, as the former will increase in importance relative to the latter with decreasing temperature. Submarine weathering is probably best defined as the slow alteration of rocks at the temperature of normal oceanic bottom water. That basalt alteration could provide some of the material of normal pelagic sediments has been well known since the work of Murray and Renard (1891). Its possible role in contributing metals to active ridge sediments is more contentious, and has been discussed by Bertine (1974) and Horowitz and Cronan (1976). Where there has been a long gap between lava extrusion and the deposition of the oldest datable sediments, submarine weathering may lead to the enrichment of some metals in the deposits. However, there is no evidence that this process can lead to metal enrichments on the scale necessary to form highly metalliferous sediments, and its role in the formation of such deposits is likely to be rather limited.

Evidence for sea water supplying elements to metalliferous sediments comes from isotope and REE data. Dymond et al. (1973) have shown that the $^{87}Sr/^{86}Sr$ ratios in East Pacific Rise metalliferous sediments are the same as in sea water indicating a sea water source for the strontium in the deposits. Similarly REE distribution patterns in metalliferous sediments are similar to those in sea water (Dymond et al., 1973) indicating a sea water source for the bulk of these elements too. Similar conclusions for a considerable fraction of a variety of elements in East Pacific Rise basal metalliferous sediments were reached by Cronan and Garrett (1973) on the basis of geochemical partition analysis. Most of the Fe, Cu and Zn were thought to have been precipitated from hydrothermal solutions. By contrast much of the Mn, Co, Ni and Pb were thought to have been precipitated from sea water, possibly catalysed by Fe oxides. Further work by Cronan (1976a) on a larger number of samples and elements indicated that a variety of other elements might also be at least partially derived from sea water.

The role of brines in the formation of submarine metalliferous sediments is not entirely clear. The highest grade metalliferous sediments in the Red Sea, those in the Atlantis II Deep, have precipitated from a brine. Furthermore, high temperature experimental leaching of rocks with saline solutions by Ellis and Mahon (1964) has shown that the leaching capacity of the solution increases with increasing salinity. Thus it is likely that a brine will be a more effective leaching agent for metals than normal sea water. However, experimental evidence obtained by Seyfried and Bischoff (1977) indicates that sufficient metal concentrations can be taken into solution to give rise to high grade metalliferous sediments without the necessity of a brine being formed. Furthermore, some metal concentrations in the hydrothermal solutions at Matupi Harbour T.P.N.G. (Ferguson and Lambert, 1972) are similar to those in the Atlantis II Deep (Table 27) but the solutions are much less saline than the latter. It appears therefore that it is not necessary that a brine be generated in order to take sufficient concentrations of metals into solution to form high grade metalliferous sediments. However, the brines do protect the sulphides in the Atlantis II Deep from oxidation and destruction by maintaining a reducing environment, and thus are probably necessary for the long-term preservation of the deposits.

Summarizing available evidence, it is clear that there are several potential sources of the enriched constituents in metalliferous sediments. The most important is likely to be submarine hydrothermal activity, with material precipitated from sea water and derived from submarine weathering of the oceanic crust of lesser importance. Biological supply of metals to the deposits is likely to be of limited importance above the lysocline, but to assume an increasingly important role with increasing depth. Thus, in the case of most metalliferous sediments we are dealing with composite polygenetic deposits whose nature varies depending on the relative importance of the various possible sources of their constituents.

6.3   Red Sea Deposits

Metalliferous sediments in the Red Sea offer the greatest economic potential of any such deposits so far found. They occur in a number of deeps in the Median Valley of the Red Sea and are still in the process of formation. The earliest indications that anomalous deposits were present on the floor of the Red Sea were high temperatures and salinities in the bottom waters, recorded in 1948 during the Swedish Deep Sea Expedition (Bruneau et al., 1953). These indications were confirmed some eighteen years later when further measurements were made and the area was subjected to a detailed survey by the Woods Hole Oceanographic Institution aboard the "Chain" in 1966. Metalliferous sediments and brines were sampled at this time and the results of the work were published in a volume edited by Degens and Ross (1969). Subsequent investigations were carried out by the Applied Geochemistry Research Group at Imperial College aboard the "Towertie" and "Nereus" and by Preussag A. G. aboard the "Valdivia". These investigations resulted in the finding of about a dozen or so brine pools and several areas floored by metalliferous sediments (Fig. 53).

The metalliferous sediments in the Red Sea represent a deposit forming during the early stages of ocean evolution (Chapter 8), at a time when sea floor spreading has restarted after a long period of quiescence (Girdler and Styles, 1974). Most of the mineralization occurs in the northern Red Sea where the Median Valley is well developed. According to Bignell (1975b), the major deeps in this area occur where transform faults intersect the Median Valley, and he has suggested that the discharge of metal enriched brines from which many of the metalliferous sediments are deposited are controlled by

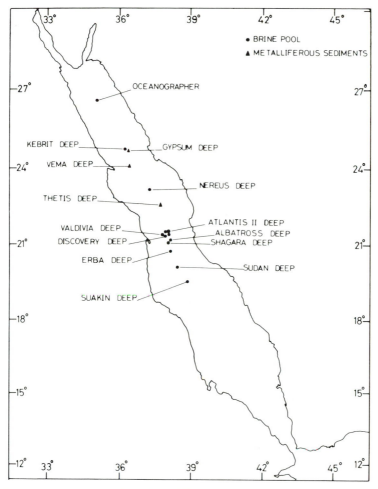

Fig. 53. Location of brine pools and metalliferous sediments in the Red Sea (from Bignell *et al.*, 1976a).

this transform faulting. The mechanism proposed involves changes in iso-static equilibrium during glacial salinity cycles promoted by the ice ages. During the past 100 000 years, there appear to have been several periods of lowered sea level and increased salinity in the Red Sea during which it became an enclosed basin. Evaporation during such periods would have considerably reduced the size of the Red Sea and thus would have disturbed its isostatic equilibrium. At the end of each glacial salinity cycle, return to normal conditions would result in isostatic readjustment, possibly opening fracture zones and allowing brines in transform faults to seep into the Median Valley and there precipitate the metals that they contain.

6.3.1 Sediment facies

One of the characteristic features of Red Sea sediments is the considerable diversity that they often exhibit both vertically and laterally over relatively small distances. This diversity was recognized in the Atlantis II Deep area by Bischoff (1969). Further investigations by Backer and Richter (1973), Hackett and Bischoff (1973), Bignell (1975a) and Bignell *et al.* (1976a) on sediments from the Atlantis II and other deeps resulted in the extension of Bishchoff's (1969) original classification of Red Sea sediments into six major sediment groups and several sub-facies. The major groups are oxides, sulphides, sulphates, carbonates, silicates and normal Red Sea sediments. Of these groups, the sulphides, oxides and silicates are those containing the greatest metal enrichments.

Normal Red Sea sediments form the main sediment type within the Median Valley of the Red Sea, and consist typically of carbonates with various admixtures of terrigenous materials. Foraminifera, pteropods and coccoliths are the principal organisms contributing to the deposits, with quartz, feldspars and clays the main terrigenous constituents. These sediments normally contain a minor ferromanganese oxide component.

The sulphide group of sediments which is the group of principal economic importance can be divided into two sub-facies: (a) mixed sulphides of Fe, Cu and Zn and (b) pyrite.

The mixed sulphides occur as grey, fine-grained massive beds. Sphalerite is the dominant mineral present with pyrite, chalcopyrite and marcasite also occurring in variable concentrations. In the Atlantis II Deep, this facies contains the highest concentrations of zinc, copper and silver thought to occur in the Red Sea (Table 13). These elements co-vary with sulphur (Bischoff, 1969). Bignell (1975a) analysed samples from two sulphide zones in the Atlantis II Deep and obtained concentrations of zinc, copper and iron over 10%, 2% and 15% respectively. However, even higher values of zinc and copper can occur in thin laminations within the deposits (H. Backer, personal communication, 1974).

The origin of the mixed sulphide facies in the Red Sea has been the subject of considerable discussion. According to Bischoff (1969), the main problem concerns the source of the sulphur, which could form from reduction of dissolved sulphate, or leaching of sulphur from magmatic rocks, or both. There is general agreement that the metals have been leached from volcanic rocks and transported by the brine, probably as chloride complexes. It has been speculated that the deposits could form on the mixing of two brines, one

Table 13. Chemical analyses of the sulphide facies of Red Sea sediments (from Bignell, 1975a).

	Ca (%)	Al_2O_3 (%)	Fe (%)	Mn (%)	Zn (%)	Cu (%)	Ni (p.p.m.)	Co (p.p.m.)	Cd (p.p.m.)	Pb (p.p.m.)	Hg (p.p.b.)	Li (p.p.m.)	Sc (p.p.m.)
Mixed sulphide facies													
Atlantis II Deep (SU_2)	3·70	2·81	15·74	1·11	10·93	2·22	130	185	430	1850	3100	11	4
Atlantis II Deep (SU_1)	9·70	1·72	20·31	2·81	5·31	1·34	94	125	200	1090	1140	44	6
Atlantis II Deep (Sulphide/silicate facies)	5·70	1·74	25·71	0·17	11·40	0·83	60	260	320	1430	3140	12	9
Erba Deep	10·64	4·11	16·60	0·61	0·34	0·06	45	40	80	90	N/D		
Pyrite facies													
Erba Deep	12·50	5·20	26·50	0·50	0·05	0·03	60	110	55	120	N/D		
Gypsum Deep	29·10	0·18	29·10	0·09	0·05	0·67	13	45	45	145	155	35	3

	K (%)	Mg (%)	Ag (p.p.m.)	Mo (p.p.m.)	V (p.p.m.)	Ga (p.p.m.)	Sn (p.p.m.)	Ti (p.p.m.)	Sr (p.p.m.)	Ba (p.p.m.)
Mixed sulphide facies										
Atlantis II Deep (SU_2)	0·8	0·6	120	330	140	58	42	460	480	1700
Atlantis II Deep (SU_1)	0·7	0·8	75	85	68	23	22	580	1100	4000
Atlantis II Deep (Sul/Sil)	0·9	0·7	100	130	71	32	6	97	110	380
Pyrite facies										
Gypsum Deep	0·1	0·2	ND	2	32	ND	ND	58	2700	430

ND = not detected.
N/D = not determined.

rich in H_2S and the other in metals (Bischoff, 1969). Such a process has been known to occur in storage tanks in the Cheleken geothermal brines (Lebedev, 1967). Metal-poor brines rich in H_2S occur in the Kebrit and Oceanographer Deeps, and the periodic mixing of such brines with those containing base metals might account for the known occurrences and distribution of the mixed sulphide facies (Bignell, 1975a). However, an alternative mechanism advanced by Bischoff (1969) involves cooling of metal chloride complexes in high temperature equilibrium with sulphides on discharge, and the consequent supersaturation and precipitation of sulphide minerals. Shanks and Bischoff (1977) have suggested that the sulphide in the Atlantis II Deep brine is precipitated in the Deep because of the increased concentration of free metal ions caused by dissociation of chloride complexes. However, precipitation may also occur prior to discharge at temperatures as high as 150°C with the sequence of mineral appearance determined by the temperature at which a given sulphide mineral first becomes supersaturated. They predict, for example, that chalcopyrite is the only sulphide precipitating in the region where the brine temperature is between 150–100°C.

The pyrite facies occurs within the main sulphide zone of the Atlantis II Deep, and in Gypsum Deep where it forms the matrix between large gypsum crystals. It is also found in Suakin, Erba, Kebrit, Nereus and Sudan Deeps. It contains high concentrations of iron and varying concentrations of base metals. In the Atlantis II Deep it exhibits high concentrations of copper but is low in zinc. In general comparison with the mixed sulphide facies, the pyrite facies contains a higher iron content and a lower base metal content (Bignell *et al.*, 1976a).

The silicate group of sediments has been found in the Atlantis II, Thetis and Erba Deeps. The sediments are fine-grained and contain large amounts of intermixed amorphous material. Bignell (1975a) has divided them into the smectite, chamosite and amorphous silicate facies.

The smectite facies is the most widely distributed of the three. In the Atlantis II Deep, it comprises the upper 4–6 m of sediments, and has precipitated recently from the brine. In it, Bischoff (1972) has reported the presence of an iron-rich nontronite, confirmed by Goulart (1976). According to Bischoff (1969), FeO, Fe_2O_3 and SiO_2 are the main chemical constituents of the smectite facies. Metal concentrations are highly variable, but the facies is enriched in Zn, Pb, Hg, Cu and Ag (Table 14). Precipitation of the smectite facies from the brine probably results from the cooling of the latter and its mixing with Red Sea water. Bischoff (1969) has suggested that the high Fe^{2+} of the deposits probably reflects its formation in a zone of limited oxygen availability, probably lower in the brine than the level at which Fe oxide precipitation is taking place.

The chamosite facies occurs within the Thetis Deep, where it is intermixed

Table 14. Chemical analyses of the silicate facies of Red Sea sediments (from Bignell, 1975a).

	Ca (%)	Al$_2$O$_3$ (%)	Fe (%)	Mn (%)	Zn (p.p.m.)	Cu (p.p.m.)	Ni (p.p.m.)	Co (p.p.m.)	Cd (p.p.m.)	Pb (p.p.m.)	Hg (p.p.b.)
Atlantis II Deep											
Ferroan nontronite	2·22	0·37	9·72	0·06	6940	1810	7	20	42	440	1370
Green smectite	5·50	1·20	21·50	0·22	5200	2800	ND	25	60	510	2750
Brown montmorillonite	2·74	0·52	8·90	1·15	2060	1640	7	20	16	300	930
Mixed layer mont/illite	1·79	0·10	3·57	0·04	40	186	ND	ND	ND	70	170
Thetis Deep											
Chamosite	1·40	4·00	39·50	0·72	1440	1120	73	63	ND	72	125

	K (%)	Mg (%)	Ag (p.p.m.)	Mo (p.p.m.)	V (p.p.m.)	Ga (p.p.m.)	Su (p.p.m.)	Ti (p.p.m.)	Sr (p.p.m.)	Ba (p.p.m.)	Li (p.p.m.)	Sc (p.p.m.)
Atlantis II Deep												
Ferroan nontronite	0·5	0·4	68	110	63	20	2	130	200	270	ND	9
Green smectite	3·0	0·5	4	13	61	12	ND	23	130	210	ND	4
Thetis Deep												
Chamosite	0·5	3·0	ND	9	95	ND	16	960	1300	160	28	10

ND = not detected.

with the magnetite facies. It is rich in iron, magnesium and aluminium. It is also enriched to a lesser degree in Zn, Cu, Ni, Ti, Sr and Hg. Mn is low.

A variety of other silicates have been found in the Atlantis II Deep deposits, several of them unidentified. Backer and Richter (1973) reported a brown fibrous silicate in the sulphide zone intermixed with hematite. Rosch and Scheurmann (1974) considered it to be a metastable transitional phase. Backer and Richter (1973) also found a Mg-rich phyllosilicate in the channel through which brine enters the Deep. Hathaway (cited in Bignell, 1975a) reported finding a variety of other silicates in the Atlantis II Deep sediments, including palygorskite, sepiolite and mixed layer clays. Other silicates have been reported by Bignell *et al.* (1976a) and by Goulart (1976) who found in addition to the iron-rich nontronite mentioned above, a montmorillonite–beidellite of continental derivation, and a mixed layer montmorillonite–chlorite formed by the submarine alteration of volcanic glass.

The oxide group of metalliferous sediments comprises iron and manganese oxides and hydroxides in the form of goethite, hematite, magnetite, lepidocrocite and manganite, together with seemingly amorphous manganiferous and ferromanganiferous or limonitic material.

The limonite facies is widespread in Red Sea metalliferous sediments and occurs in Kebrit, Gypsum, Vema, Nereus and Thetis Deeps where beds vary from one to several metres in thickness. Well crystallized goethite is a major component of this facies, and so is "ferrihydrite", an unstable iron oxide which may be a precursor of hematite. The principal chemical components of the limonite facies are iron, oxygen and silica, the iron mainly being present as Fe_2O_3. Zinc is generally enriched in this facies, possibly due to co-precipitation with iron oxides, and copper is enriched in the Thetis and Kebrit Deep occurrences of this facies, with mercury overall also somewhat enhanced (Table 15). The formation of iron hydroxides involves the oxidation of Fe^{2+} to Fe^{3+}, which is occurring extensively within the upper part of the brine in the Atlantis II Deep (Hartmann, 1973). The oxidation probably results from oxygen diffusing into the brine from sea water and reacting according to the equation

$$2Fe^{2+} + \tfrac{1}{2}O_2 + 5H_2O = 2Fe(OH)_3 + 4H^+$$

After deposition the limonite may be altered to goethite by dehydration.

The lepidocrocite facies occurs as well crystallized layers a few centimetres in thickness, and is generally present within the limonitic sequences. Iron concentrations range up to 50–60%, and some layers are also enriched in cobalt, copper, lead and zinc (Table 15).

The hematite facies is common in the Atlantis II and Thetis Deeps where it is often mixed with other oxides. It occurs in a pure form near the incoming hot brine in the Atlantis II Deep (Backer and Richter, 1973) where it may

Table 15a. Chemical analyses of the iron oxide facies of Red Sea sediments (from Bignell, 1975a).

	Ca (%)	Al₂O₃ (%)	Fe (%)	Mn (%)	Zn (p.p.m.)	Cu (p.p.m.)	Ni (p.p.m.)	Co (p.p.m.)	Cd (p.p.m.)	Pb (p.p.m.)	Hg (p.p.b.)
Limonite facies											
Kebrit Deep	14·96	2·76	30·80	0·17	1010	340	30	5	N/D	80	75
Gypsum Deep	1·64	0·84	50·70	0·35	2370	145	9	ND	15	92	88
Vema Deep	2·27	0·53	57·70	0·05	1020	12	10	ND	N/D	23	50
Nereus Deep	0·35	0·92	54·60	0·45	6650	59	ND	8	5	670	123
Thetis Deep	1·29	0·64	64·50	0·98	1980	910	5	40	ND	54	110
Atlantis II Deep	0·30	1·93	63·16	0·26	1456	116	9	ND	ND	35	70
Lepidocrocite facies											
Atlantis II Deep	1·43	0·67	51·43	0·36	790	40	50	ND	ND	20	45
Nereus Deep	10·61	1·20	35·00	2·00	950	850	20	40	ND	40	245
Thetis Deep	1·63	0·37	60·47	1·28	1740	3950	ND	105	ND	76	105
Gypsum Deep	1·22	0·66	54·35	0·19	1780	280	10	ND	18	175	120
Hematite facies											
Atlantis II Deep	5·88	1·03	35·29	0·29	1200	7350	ND	60	ND	280	350
Magnetite facies											
Thetis Deep	1·32	0·91	67·75	0·21	1320	4670	13	120	ND	80	113

ND = not detected.
N/D = not determined.

Table 15b. Chemical analyses of the iron oxide facies of Red Sea sediments (from Bignell, 1975a).

	K (%)	Mg (%)	Ag (p.p.m.)	Mo (p.p.m.)	V (p.p.m.)	Ga (p.p.m.)	Sn (p.p.m.)	Ti (p.p.m.)	Sr (p.p.m.)	Ba (p.p.m.)	Li (p.p.m.)	Sc (p.p.m.)
Limonite facies												
Kebrit Deep	0·8	2·8	ND	17	9	ND	6	900	2600	150	56	11
Gypsum Deep	0·4	1·0	ND	35	45	ND	ND	630	170	130	ND	15
Vema Deep	0·6	1·4	ND	30	11	ND	ND	490	1240	74	10	14
Nereus Deep	0·3	0·3	7	32	32	ND	ND	210	2100	6200	ND	12
Thetis Deep	0·2	0·4	4	42	1200	12	24	290	690	1300	ND	14
Lepidocrocite facies												
Nereus Deep	0·5	1·0	ND	25	180	5	26	930	115	315	ND	10
Magnetite facies												
Thetis Deep	0·3	2·2	ND	28	350	6	15	3000	105	190	ND	18

ND = not detected.

have formed as a result of transformation from goethite as a result of increased temperature (Bischoff, 1969). It is high in Fe_2O_3 and is also enriched in Cu and to a lesser extent Zn, Pb, Co and Hg (Table 15).

The magnetite facies is present both as pure layers of magnetite and inter-mixed with other oxides, and occurs in the Atlantis II and Thetis Deeps. Its major chemical components are FeO, Fe_2O_3 and SiO_2 and in Thetis Deep the facies contains high copper concentrations and is enriched to a lesser extent in Zn, Co, Pb, Hg, Ti, V and Ba (Table 15). Magnetite coexists with hematite in the south-western basin of the Atlantis II Deep, and may result from alteration of the hematite with increased temperature (Hackett and Bischoff, 1973). However, its occurrence in Thetis Deep may result from different factors, as Bignell (1975a) has reported that interbedded layers of limonite are unaltered.

The manganite facies occurs in the Atlantis II, Nereus, Shagara and Thetis Deeps, and in Chain Deep B where it contains 30–35% Mn and may represent an overflow deposit from the Atlantis II Deep. The manganite occurs around the edge of the presently active brine in the Atlantis II Deep, as will be described shortly. Chemically it consists of Mn_3O_4 and Fe_2O_3, with fairly high concentrations of Zn, Cu, Pb and Hg (Table 16). Occasionally Zn concentrations of as much as 1% occur (Bignell, 1975a). Hartmann (1973) considered that manganese hydroxides are forming in the transition zone between brine and sea water in the Atlantis II Deep by the oxidation of Mn^{2+} diffusing from the anoxic brines below. Where this transition zone directly overlies the sea floor, Mn hydroxides are deposited instead of sinking back into the underlying brine and being dissolved again.

Sulphate group minerals occur in the form of gypsum in Kebrit and Gypsum Deeps, and as anhydrite in Atlantis II and Thetis Deeps. In addition, Bischoff (1969) has reported barite as a minor component in the Atlantis II Deep deposits. Both the anhydrite and gypsum contain high concentrations of calcium but only minor concentrations of other elements (Table 17). Indeed, it is possible that even a proportion of the latter may result from minor admixtures of other material in the samples analysed, and, if so, would indicate a high degree of purity of sulphate deposits in the Red Sea.

Carbonate group minerals represented by rhodocrosite, manganosiderite and siderite occur in the Atlantis II and Gypsum Deeps usually in the form of thin layers and laminations. These minerals are generally intimately inter-mixed with representatives of other facies and thus it is difficult to closely characterize their composition. Nevertheless certain elements such as Ca, Mn, Fe, Zn, Cu and Pb are variably enriched in the deposits (Table 18).

Table 16. Chemical analyses of the manganite facies in Red Sea sediments (from Bignell, 1975a).

	Ca (%)	Al$_2$O$_3$ (%)	Fe (%)	Mn (%)	Zn (p.p.m.)	Cu (p.p.m.)	Ni (p.p.m.)	Co (p.p.m.)	Cd (p.p.m.)	Pb (p.p.m.)	Hg (p.p.b.)
Thetis Deep	6·50	1·51	20·50	15·48	7500	860	55	20	5	220	420
Nereus Deep (Core 70–14)	4·25	0·60	29·50	20·20	13500	360	10	15	15	290	720
Nereus Deep (Core 496)	4·00	0·65	32·00	15·50	13000	480	5	ND	ND	250	680
Chain Deep B	3·41	1·07	12·93	35·37	12195	1341	35	60	ND	220	180
Shagara Deep	15·56	2·56	3·89	15·56	2111	122	15	20	N/D	67	N/D

	K (%)	Mg (%)	Ag (p.p.m.)	Mo (p.p.m.)	V (p.p.m.)	Ga (p.p.m.)	Sn (p.p.m.)	Ti (p.p.m.)	Sr (p.p.m.)	Ba (p.p.m.)	Li (p.p.m.)	SC (p.p.m.)
Thetis Deep	0·3	4·6	ND	15	280	8	64	540	980	140	ND	6
Nereus Deep (Core 70–14)	0·3	1·4	ND	11	220	ND	50	140	580	380	ND	ND
Nereus Deep (Core 496)	0·3	1·7	ND	11	53	6	52	110	820	620	ND	ND
Chain Deep B	0·3	3·2	ND	85	108	6	108	190	750	1900	ND	ND

ND = not detected.
N/D = not determined.

Table 17. Chemical analyses of the sulphate facies in Red Sea sediments (from Bignell, 1975a).

	Ca (%)	Al$_2$O$_3$ (%)	Fe (%)	Mn (%)	Zn (p.p.m.)	Cu (p.p.m.)	Ni (p.p.m.)	Co (p.p.m.)	Cd (p.p.m.)	Pb (p.p.m.)	Hg (p.p.b.)
Anhydrite											
Atlantis II Deep	20·99	ND	ND	ND	ND	ND	ND	ND	ND	ND	
Gypsum											
Gypsum Deep	18·50	ND	0·02	ND	30	60	ND	ND	ND	ND	18

ND = not detected.

Table 18. Chemical analyses of the carbonate facies (from Bignell, 1975a).

	Ca (%)	Al$_2$O$_3$ (%)	Fe (%)	Mn (%)	Zn (p.p.m.)	Cu (p.p.m.)	Ni (p.p.m.)	Co (p.p.m.)	Cd (p.p.m.)	Pb (p.p.m.)	Hg (p.p.b.)
Rhodochrosite											
Atlantis II Deep	17·30	2·94	6·49	9·41	2270	227	22	ND	5	32	22
Siderite											
Gypsum Deep	2·35	0·29	55·88	0·04	1770	647	7	7	14	400	190
Gypsum Deep	1·06	0·80	51·25	0·45	1380	72	14	ND	33	105	70

ND = not detected.

6.3.2   Atlantis II Deep

Deposits in most of the metalliferous sediment bearing deeps in the Red Sea
have been described by Backer and Schoell (1972) and Bignell *et al.* (1976a).
Of these, only the Atlantis II Deep deposits are likely to be of immediate
economic importance, and thus they deserve detailed consideration. Furthermore, the Atlantis II Deep is the only deep in which metalliferous sediment
formation is definitely known to be taking place at the present time, and
thus its investigation can provide us with information about the processes
involved in the formation of such deposits.

The Deep is situated in the Median Valley of the Red Sea at about $21 \cdot 5°$N,
$38°$E, in an area of faulted and fractured topography (Backer, 1973). It is
elongated and covers an area of about 60 km^2 (Fig. 54). Chain and Discovery
Deeps are situated to the south of the Atlantis II Deep, and are thought
to be connected to it by both overflow and sub-sea floor channels.

Hydrographic investigations in the Atlantis II Deep have shown the
presence of two brines, a lower one with a salinity of $25 \cdot 7\%$ and a temperature
of $56 \cdot 5°$C in 1966 which had risen to $60°$C in 1972, and an upper one with
a salinity of $13 \cdot 5\%$ and a temperature of $44 \cdot 3°$C in 1966 which had risen to $50°$C
in 1972. These temperature variations indicate that the Atlantis II Deep
contains an active hydrothermal system, and that the ore body it contains
is still in the process of formation. Schoell and Hartmann (1972) have
suggested that the brine enters the deep from beneath the south-west basin,
and spreads out horizontally. Between the brines there is an intermediate
layer about 5 m thick, whereas above the upper brine there is a gradual
transition to overlying $22°$C sea water.

Chemically the Atlantis II brines are enriched in sodium and calcium
relative to sea water, and are considerably depleted in magnesium and SO_4^{2-}
(Table 19). The brines are enriched relative to sea water in the minor elements
Fe, Mn, Zn and Cu (Hartmann, 1973) (Table 19). The $60°$C brine in 1972
was slightly acidic and had a low redox potential. Dissolved oxygen is absent
from the brines within the Deep, but is present in the transition zone above
it. No H_2S has been detected by direct measurements, but its presence has
been inferred from the occurrence of sulphides in the south-west basin of
the Deep.

The origin of the high metal concentrations in the Atlantis II Deep brine
has been the subject of considerable discussion. Craig (1966, 1969) has shown
that the Atlantis II Deep brine is derived from normal Red Sea water. According to Shanks and Bischoff (1977), this water attains high salinity by leaching
Miocene evaporites that are composed mainly of halite and anhydrite. At
the same time the brine is heated along the geothermal gradient and the high
chloride content enables high concentrations of metals to be carried in

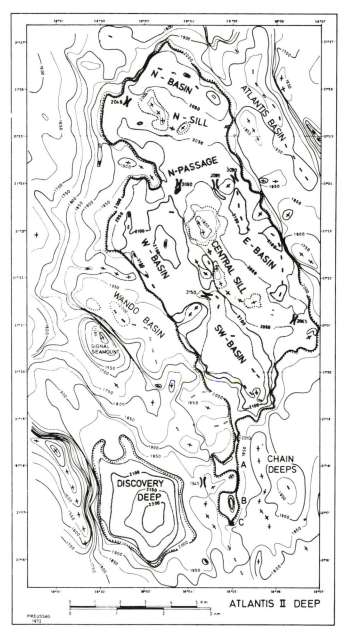

Fig. 54. Bathymetric chart of the Atlantis II Deep area, Red Sea. ELAC narrow beam echo sounder (30 kHz ± 1·4° beam width). Contours in metres, corrected after Matthews. Decca hi-fix navigation. Track space 400 m, within the Atlantis II Deep and Chain Deeps 100 m. Dotted line = uppermost echo reflector on top brine (from Backer and Schoell, 1972).

Table 19. Composition of geothermal brines and sea water of the Red Sea (mg/kg) (from Shanks and Bischoff, 1977).

	Atlantis II Deep, lower brine mass	Atlantis II Deep, upper brine layer	Red Sea deep water
Na	92600	46900	12500
K	1870	1070	450
Mg	764	1190	1490
Ca	5150	2470	470
Cl	156030	80040	22500
SO_4	840	2260	3140
Total CO_2 (as HCO_3^-)	140	150–175	140
Ba	0·9	—	0·020–0·004
Cu	0·26	0·017	0·020–0·001
F	$\leqslant$·02	—	1·5
Fe	81·0	0·2	0·062–0·0001
Li	4·4	—	0·200–0·072
Mn	82·0	82·0	0·009–0·0001
Pb	0·63	0·009	0·00004–0·00002
Si	27·6	—	2·6
Zn	5·4	0·15	0·048–0·001

Data from Brewer *et al.* (1965), Miller *et al.* (1966), and Brewer and Spencer (1969). Trace element data listed under Red Sea deep water are ranges observed in normal oceanic waters (Brewer, 1965).

solution as chloride complexes. As it circulates, the brine comes into contact with intrusive volcanic rocks in the axial rift zone of the Red Sea where it is heated to perhaps 250°C and more, and further altered by chemical reactions with the hot basalts. Anhydrite becomes insoluble at higher temperatures and is precipitated while calcium is leached out of the rocks. Basalt alteration products remove magnesium from the brine and the pH falls to about 5. Dissolved oxygen is depleted. During this process the hot circulating brine leaches considerable amounts of metals from the volcanic rocks through which it passes and it is this process which is thought to be responsible for its high metal concentrations (Shanks and Bischoff, 1977).

Because the Atlantis II Deep is an active geothermal system, it lends itself to the direct study of the ore forming processes that are taking place in it. Iron, copper and zinc start to precipitate from the 60°C brine as sulphides, especially in the south-west basin of the Deep where the brine is entering. According to Shanks and Bischoff (1977) the sequence of precipitation on cooling is chalcopyrite, galena, sphalerite and finally iron monosulphide. According to Bischoff (1969), the formation of the iron silicates most likely takes place after sulphide deposition but prior to the oxidation of Fe^{2+} to

Fe^{3+} and the formation of iron oxides, probably low in the brine column. Iron oxides are precipitated within the transition layer between the two brines and in the $50^\circ C$ brine, due to the oxidation of Fe^{2+} to Fe^{3+}. Where the $50^\circ C$ brine overlies the $60^\circ C$ brine, the oxides and oxyhydroxides sink into the lower brine and dissolve. However, where the $50^\circ C$ brine directly overlies the sea floor around the margins of the deep, iron hydroxides precipitate out. In a similar manner, manganese is oxidized and precipitated at the higher Eh and pH above the $50^\circ C$ brine, its precipitation later than iron probably being a function of both its slower rate of oxidation and the well known separation of these elements in solution with increasing pH (Krauskopf, 1957). Where the upper transition zone overlies the sea floor, manganese oxides settle out leading to a zone of manganese enrichment around the

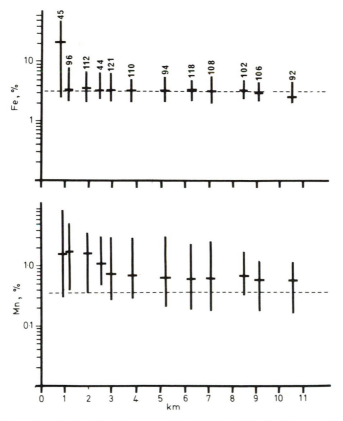

Fig. 55. Range (vertical bars) and average values (horizontal bars) of ore metals in sediment cores from around the Atlantis II Deep with distance from major metalliferous sediments. Broken lines represent background values in sediments from axial valley sides (from Bignell *et al.*, 1976b).

Deep outside that of iron enrichment. Bignell *et al.* (1976b) have shown from the study of sediment cores that manganese enrichment in sediments around the Deep occurs up to 11 km from the Deep, due to the dispersion of Mn most probably in a fine particulate form. The separation of manganese from iron is also clearly shown (Fig. 55). Thus within the Atlantis II Deep, we are able to observe the geochemical fractionation of sulphides, silicates, iron and manganese oxides together with associated minor metals as a result of changing physicochemical conditions as is illustrated in Fig. 56. Deposits in the other Deeps were probably formed in a similar manner and, as will be described later, metalliferous sediments on mid-ocean ridges in the open ocean may be the end members of such a fractionation sequence.

The sediments of the Atlantis II Deep have been described by Bischoff (1969), Backer and Richter (1973), Hackett and Bischoff (1973), Bignell (1975a) and Bignell *et al.* (1976a) among others, and reflect a complex succession of events leading to the deposition of the various sediment facies at different times, or at different places at the same time. Backer and Richter (1973) and Bignell (1975a) have described several major lithostratigraphic units from which the depositional history of the Deep can be established. These are the detrital oxidic pyritic zone, the lower sulphide zone, the central oxidic zone, the upper sulphidic zone, and the amorphous silicate zone.

The detrital oxidic pyritic zone contains the oldest sediments within the Atlantis II Deep, having commenced deposition about 25 000 years ago. It contains a mixture of marl, iron oxides and pyrite. The lower sulphide zone contains the oldest major metalliferous sediments within the Deep, which were deposited about 10 000 years ago. The sediments consist of sulphides, silicates and manganosiderite. The central oxidic zone represents the end of a period of relatively stable conditions, as it contains a very variable sequence of deposits, often mixed. Hematite and magnetite are important minerals while beds of gypsum and anhydrite have a local occurrence. The upper sulphidic zone consists of sulphides, silicates and locally, carbonates. Individual sulphide layers may contain as much as 20% zinc. The amorphous silicate zone is the uppermost zone over much of the Deep and is being formed at the present time. It is dark brown in colour consisting principally of iron silicates, but including sulphides, anhydrite and iron oxides. The source of the modern brine forming these sediments is in the south-west basin, in contrast to the likely sources of some of the brines from which the earlier zones were formed.

Sediments from the south-west basin of the Deep differ from those in the rest of the Deep due to local factors probably related to the influx of brine from below the south-west basin. The uppermost sediment unit in the south-west basin is considerably enriched in sulphides, and contains a massive sulphide layer at its base.

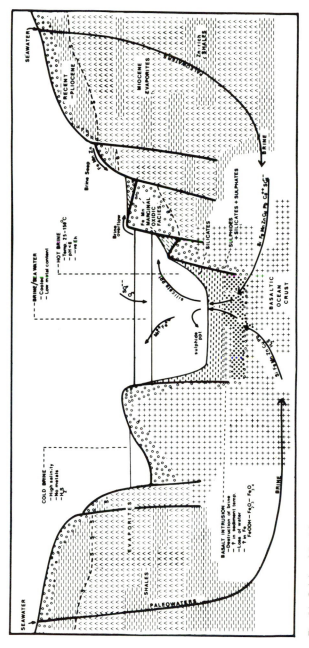

Fig. 56. Origin of Red Sea deposits (after Backer, 1973; from Bignell, 1978, reproduced by permission of Crane Russak, New York).

The processes leading to metalliferous sediment formation in the Atlantis II Deep can briefly be summarized as follows.

(a) Normal Red Sea water percolates through sub-surface evaporites and attains a high salinity.
(b) The brine circulates down under the Red Sea and is heated to 200 C+, or so, in contact with recent volcanic rocks in the axial rift area.
(c) Chemical reactions take place between the brine and the volcanic rocks leading to the enrichment of a number of metals in the brine.
(d) As the brine discharges on the floor of the Red Sea it precipitates its metals in the form first of sulphides, then iron silicates, then iron oxides and finally manganese oxides.

The deposition in the Atlantis II Deep of the different sediment facies described reflects changing depositional conditions, sources of brine and brine composition with time. As mentioned, Bignell (1975b) considered that metalliferous sediment deposition in the Atlantis II Deep was triggered at discrete times in the past by changes in sea level and other factors, and has not been a continuous process. As these factors affected the Red Sea at large, metalliferous sediment deposition in the other less explored Deeps is likely to have been triggered by similar mechanisms and may parallel the sequence of deposits in the Atlantis II Deep.

6.4   Mid-Ocean Ridge Metalliferous Sediments

Mid-ocean ridge metalliferous sediments can be divided into two general varieties. These are "normal" widely dispersed background deposits forming over large areas of the mid-ocean ridges, and "anomalous" deposits super-imposed upon them in certain small areas.

6.4.1   Anomalous metalliferous sediments

Superimposed on more homogeneous normal mid-ocean ridge metalliferous sediments are sometimes found sharp, very localized variations in composition, indicating an extreme fractionation of the metals concerned. However, information accumulated to date indicates that these are rather exceptional deposits of very localized extent. Among such anomalous deposits are iron-rich sediments from Amph. 2D (Bonatti and Joensuu, 1966), basal sediments from DSDP 236 (Cronan et al., 1974), manganese-rich sediments from the crest of the Mid-Atlantic Ridge at 26°N (Scott et al., 1974; Rona, 1976), sharply differentiated iron and manganese deposits from the axial valley of the Gulf of Aden, the FAMOUS area, and the Galapagos area (Cann et al., 1977; Hoffert et al., 1978; Corliss et al., 1978) and sulphide deposits in the

Gulf of California (Lonsdale, 1978) and on the East Pacific Rise (Francheteau
et al., 1979). In some respects, the manganese-rich varieties of these deposits
bear greater similarity to some manganese encrustations than to metalliferous
sediments and are likely to be transitional between the two. The nature of
the transition will be explored more fully in a later chapter, while individual
examples will be considered here.

6.4.1.1 *East Pacific Rise at 8°S*

One of the first anomalous metal-rich deposits to be found on a mid-ocean
ridge was at Station Amph. 2D on a basaltic topographic high at the axis
of the East Pacific Rise (Bonatti and Joensuu, 1966). Exceptionally iron-rich
deposits were found, containing 32·5% Fe, with lesser amounts of Si (8·2%)
lower Al and Mn (0·5% and 1·94% respectively) and very low Ni, Co, Cu,
Zn and Ba. They were considered to be hydrothermal in origin.

6.4.1.2 *DSDP 236 Western Indian Ocean*

Basal sediments from DSDP 236 in the Western Indian Ocean (01°40·62'S,
57°38·85'E) have been found to be enriched in iron, up to 28%, and low in
many other elements (Cronan *et al.*, 1974). These deposits may be analogous
to the iron-rich deposits of hydrothermal origin from Amph. 2D on the East
Pacific Rise, described above.

Table 20. Compositions of layers within the largest fragment of a TAG area
manganese deposit (sample 13–21), in comparison with more normal North Atlantic
ferromanganese oxide encrustations (from Scott *et al.*, 1974).

		Composition				
Sample	Location	Mn (%)	Fe (%)	Co (p.p.m.)	Ni (p.p.m.)	Cu (p.p.m.)
T3–72D 253–13–21	26°08'N, 44°45'W					
Sequence of samples	a top 5 mm	39·2	0·011	18	100	12
through layers of 13–21	b 6 mm	38·5	0·078	25	790	119
	c 6 mm	38·6	0·106	25	660	93
	d 5 mm	39·4	0·070	20	200	23
	e 3 mm	39·2	0·072	18	400	23
	f 8 mm	39·1	0·038	16	270	19
	g 8 mm	39·3	0·036	14	50	11
T3–71D 160–10G	30°08'N, 42°29'W	9·8	18·1	2720	1280	880
T3–71D 148–2B	26°07'N, 25°21'W	14·1	16·1	7200	2200	750
T3–71D 254–15–2	26°33·9'N, 44°30'W	11·2	16·4	9480	900	300
T3–72D 255–19–3	26°16·9'N, 45°6·3'W	11·0	18·6	4950	1110	405

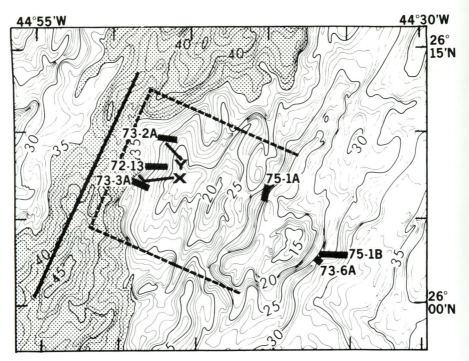

Fig. 57. Bathymetric map (McGregor and Rona, 1975) contoured in hundreds of metres showing axis (solid line) of rift valley (shaded) of the Mid-Atlantic Ridge at latitude 26°N., two profiles (*X, Y*) along which temperature measurements and bottom photographs were made concurrently, and dredge stations at the south-east wall of the rift valley (TAG 1972–13 [*72–13*], TAG 1973–2A [*73–2A*] TAG 1973–3A [*73–3A*]) and along a ridge (unshaded) trending orthogonal to the axis of the rift valley (TO–75AK61–1A [*75–1A*], TO–75AK59–1B [*75–1B*], TAG 1973–6A [*73–6A*]). The approximate known area of the TAG Hydrothermal Field is indicated (dashed line). (From Rona, 1976.)

6.4.1.3   *The TAG area*

The TAG area is at the crest of the Mid-Atlantic Ridge at 26°N (Fig. 57). Hydrothermally deposited manganese oxide crusts have been recovered from several dredge stations in a hydrothermal field on a transverse ridge forming the east wall of the rift valley within the area. The crusts are compositionally extremely pure, containing up to 40% manganese with only trace quantities of other elements (Table 20) and grew at rates of up to 200 mm per million years. They occur on a talus of basalt fragments, as veins in basalt, encrustations, or as a matrix of breccia of altered basaltic fragments. The deposits always occur in association with inferred faults through which the hydrothermal solutions have probably discharged. That the system is still active is evinced by recently measured bottom-water temperature anomalies (Rona, 1978b).

The time period over which the TAG hydrothermal deposits have been forming has been deduced (Rona, 1976) from their rates of accumulation and the local half-rate of sea floor spreading (1·3 cm per year). Assuming a constant accumulation rate, the manganese deposits have been accumulating over a time period of several hundred thousand years. Observations from bottom photographs and recovered rocks suggest that the hydrothermal discharge channels become clogged when hydrothermal minerals seal off a portion of the discharge zone (Rona, 1976). The talus is thought ultimately to develop into the breccia by such a cementation process.

Chemical analyses of the thin sediment cover in the TAG hydrothermal field has revealed an overall enrichment of manganese relative to the Atlantic average (Cronan et al., 1979) and higher than normal manganese accumulation rates (Scott et al., 1978). This would suggest that not all of the hydrothermal manganese is precipitating near the vents, but that some of it is being flushed into the bottom waters to become well mixed and precipitate relatively uniformly over the whole TAG area. Betzer et al. (reported by Rona, 1978a) have found a 20-fold enrichment of manganese in weak acid soluble particulate matter over the TAG area compared with elsewhere. The exploration significance of this in locating hydrothermal mineral deposits on mid-ocean ridges will be discussed in Chapter 9. Certain sediment samples were also found to be enriched in iron and copper. One of these samples was close to a known hydrothermal vent in the area, and the metal enrichments could have been caused by hydrothermal activity.

6.4.1.4 *The Gulf of Aden*

One dredge haul in the Gulf of Aden, Discovery Station 6243, 12°35·0′N, 47°39·9′E (2260 m), brought up thin fragments of ropy basalt lava, together with lumps of brown ferromanganese oxide and very friable lumps of yellow to green crumbly material. The under surfaces of the lavas are coated with spongy Fe-Mn oxides. These are considered by Cann et al. (1977) to be different components of hydrothermal deposits formed on the floor of the Gulf of Aden.

Cann et al. (1977) have divided the Gulf of Aden hydrothermal deposits into four classes: (i) hard ferromanganese oxide; (ii) soft ferromanganese oxide; (iii) yellow to green friable material; and (iv) orange powdery Fe oxides. The composition of the deposits is given in Table 21. The hard and soft ferromanganese oxides exhibited no marked compositional differences from each other. X-ray diffraction showed them to be poorly crystalline and to consist of variable proportions of todorokite and birnessite. The oxides are

Table 21. Chemical analyses of Gulf of Aden hydrothermal deposits (from Cann *et al.*, 1977). (a) Analyses of ferromanganese oxides. (b) Analyses of smectite (d) and of mixtures of smectite, ferromanganese oxide, and iron oxide (e and f).

(a)

	1 2c	2 2c	3 3B	4 3M	5 3T	6 5
Si(%)	4·79	5·38	4·04	2·32	3·38	1·97
Al	1·11	1·11	0·84	0·06	0·69	0·34
Fe	6·39	1·31	1·53	4·52	0·76	1·51
Mn	34·22	34·89	37·33	38·83	39·82	42·45
Mg	1·09	2·21	2·01	1·60	1·50	2·17
Ca	1·41	1·74	1·49	1·50	1·55	1·52
Na	3·53	2·57	2·75	3·04	2·90	3·07
K	1·13	1·54	1·57	1·28	1·21	1·62
H_2O^+	9·16	8·13	9·90	10·97	9·78	10·11
CO_2	1·30	1·74	0·99	0·26	0·52	0·73
S(p.p.m.)	1650	1100	1800	1050	900	1450
Ti	2000	1600	1100	200	700	800
Co	37	75	28	13	2	25
Ni	390	900	670	14	22	375
Cu	77	110	203	9	8	83
Zn	215	445	780	18	22	385
Ga	3	5	4	0	0	2
Ge	2	2	1	2	2	1
Rb	12	19	12	6	11	8
Sr	375	350	325	340	215	335
Y	6	11	11	1	2	7
Zr	47	63	42	15	18	28
Ba	1650	2000	1100	1000	530	660

(b)

	1 10(d)	2 12(d)	3 24(d)	4 31(d)	5 31(e)	6 32(f)
Si(%)	22·12	22·14	21·94	21·76	10·21	14·93
Al	0·33	0·10	0·10	0·10	0·28	0·09
Fe	22·75	19·14	22·89	24·17	23·49	16·16
Mn	<0·1	<0·1	<0·1	<0·1	10·38	10·94
Mg	1·80	1·67	1·94	1·89	1·11	1·75
Ca	0·55	0·46	0·47	0·51	1·82	0·56
Na	1·24	1·02	1·27	1·45	2·37	2·00
K	3·41	3·05	3·57	2·73	1·08	2·39
H_2O^+	8·50	6·54	8·32	7·62	13·86	8·24
CO_2	1·24	0·66	2·65	0·92	2·12	0·44
S(p.p.m.)	400	700	450	700	1550	900
Ti	250	—	200	200	620	—
Co	12	2	1	3	7	—
Ni	6	4	3	1	35	100
Cu	0	0	0	0	2	17
Zn	2	0	2	2	47	96
Ga	0	0	0	0	1	0
Ge	0	0	1	0	1	1
Rb	73	79	80	59	9	41
Sr	47	32	40	55	413	147
Y	2	1	2	2	6	2
Zr	7	2	9	7	27	13
Nb	2	1	1	1	0	0
Ba	120	40	65	70	400	420

much richer in manganese than typical oceanic manganese nodules, and are poor in most minor elements, like those from the TAG hydrothermal field. The yellow to green friable and crumbly material is considered by Cann *et al.* (1977) to be a smectite. Compositionally, the material is an alkaline ferric-iron hydrated silicate. Other components are at low levels, including trace elements (Table 21). The bright orange powdery iron oxides occurred as veins and coatings associated with lumps of smectite and mixed smectite-Mn oxide, and are X-ray amorphous.

6.4.1.5 *The FAMOUS area, Mid-Atlantic Ridge near 37°N*

During submersible dives, two hydrothermal deposits were found at a depth of about 2700 m on the southern wall of a transform fault offsetting the axial valley of the Mid-Atlantic Ridge (Hoffert *et al.*, 1978). Each of the deposits extends over an area of about 600 m² and they are 200 m apart. They consist of asymmetrically elongated ridges 40 m long, 15 m wide and less than 3 m thick, and exhibit east-west fissure like vents (Fig. 58). The deposits are thickest closest to the vents and were probably delivered through them.

According to Hoffert *et al.* (1978), two main types of deposits were found

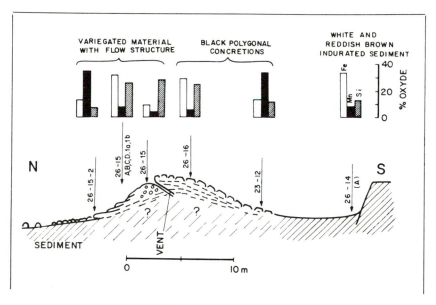

Fig. 58. Schematic cross-section of part of the FAMOUS hydrothermal field (from Hoffert *et al.*, 1978).

Table 22. Chemical analyses of hydrothermal deposits and associated material from Transform fault "A" in the FAMOUS area. (IGN) indicates ignition loss at 1000 C (from Hoffert *et al.*, 1978). (Reproduced by permission of Gauthier-Villars Publishing Co.)

	Fe-Mn-rich concretions				Clay-rich hydrothermal material						Miscellaneous	
	cyp 74-23-12 black	cyp 74-26-15-2 black	cyp 74-26-15-1 a dark green	cyp 74-26-15-1 b dark green	cyp 74-26-15 A yellowish green	cyp 74-26-15 B yellowish green	cyp 74-26-16 yellowish green	cyp 74-26-15 C black	cyp 74-26-15 D white	cyp 74-26-14 A brownish red	cyp 74-26-14 sediment	cyp 74-26-15 basalt
Weight (%)												
SiO_2	16·6	8·7	45·5	36·4	30·2	41·9	44·4	41·0	39·0	24·7	1·7	49·6
Al_2O_3	1·7	0·7	0·2	0·4	0·2	0·2	0·2	3·2	5·9	0·4	0·5	15·7
Fe_2O_3	16·3	13·7	37·9	38·6	32·3	35·1	35·6	29·9	20·8	40·6	1·1	8·8
Mn_3O_4	37·2	40·3	1·07	3·78	6·68	4·69	3·88	4·69	4·01	11·5	0·18	0·18
MgO	3·7	2·68	2·91	2·73	2·77	2·72	2·84	4·39	5·24	2·92	0·68	8·42
CaO	2·3	7·3	0·6	2·9	2·9	1·2	0·8	4·4	9·5	3·0	51·7	10·8
Na_2O	2·47	1·47	1·71	1·70	1·93	1·91	1·84	2·13	1·83	1·75	0·09	2·05
K_2O	0·97	0·28	3·23	2·77	3·00	2·80	3·35	2·28	1·55	1·76	0·05	0·59
TiO_2	0·08	0·04	0·02	0·02	0·02	0·02	0·02	0·20	0·38	0·03	0·05	0·85
IGN	15·93	20·11	6·22	9·53	9·13	7·94	6·95	8·14	9·94	12·89	42·9	0·94
TOTAL	97·25	95·28	99·14	98·81	98·81	98·46	99·66	100·33	98·15	99·55	98·86	97·93
Fe/Mn	0·43	0·33	34·45	9·93	4·70	7·27	8·93	6·19	5·04	3·43	5·92	47·38
Si/Al	6·55	8·35	152·79	61·11	134·93	140·64	149·07	8·60	4·44	41·46	2·29	2·12
Sr (p.p.m.)	353	615	59	300	223	221	149	257	217	383	383	102
Ba	589	703	43	63	73	100	56	101	72	122	6	313
V	321	108	5	270	27	30	48	101	117	472	5	—
Ni	570	172	2	116	20	28	33	66	71	225	2	—
Co	91	73	4	8	9	2	2	10	27	10	2	—
Cr	13	9	—	8	10	11	9	62	84	4	5	—
B	204	170	75	529	532	576	592	461	293	442		
Zn	126	40	6	36	5	6	9	24	79	84	5	8
Ga	5	9	2	5	5	5	5	5	13	5	2	
Cu	275	137	46	88	64	66	49	73	60	135	26	100
Mn	267 877	290 200	7705	27 219	48 096	33 768	27 939	33 768	28 876	82 811	1296	1296

in both hydrothermal fields. The first of these were black Fe-Mn oxide concretions consisting principally of manganese oxides and hydroxides with a small amount of clay. The second was a clay-rich hydrothermal material containing much smectite, hydromica and small amounts of Fe-Mn concretions. In addition rare grains of pyrite have been reported by Hekinian (1979). The composition of the deposits are listed in Table 22. The Fe-Mn concretions are higher in Mn, Ba, V, Ni, Co and Cu and lower in Fe, Si and K than the clay-rich hydrothermal material (Table 22). The deposits exhibit a chemical and mineralogical zonation, with the clay-rich Fe-Si material most abundant near the vents and the Fe-Mn rich concretionary material increasing in abundance away. The Fe-Mn concretionary material itself showed some mineralogical zonation with manganite being present near the vents while rancieite became prominent away. Furthermore, the Fe-Mn concretionary material was chemically distinct from ferromanganese oxide encrustations on basalts in the general vicinity, indicating a different origin for the latter, most probably from normal sea water.

6.4.1.6   *The Galapagos region*

Mounds of hydrothermal sediments are located in a band 20 km south of the Galapagos Rift at about 00°36′N 86°06′W (Corliss *et al.*, 1978). They reach heights of 15–20 m, are up to 50 m in diameter, and occur in linear arrays sub-parallel to the trend of the spreading axis (Londsdale, 1977). Bottom photography of the mounds from a submersible showed massive outcrops of dark coloured material with some bright yellow patches and bands (Corliss *et al.*, 1978). The mounds occur in a high heat flow zone with individual values of greater than 30 heat flow units (von Herzen *et al.*, 1977). The composition of the mound deposits are shown in Table 23 and their mineralogy in Table 24. The deposits can be divided into three types: first, manganese crusts on the tops of the mounds that are mixtures of todorokite and birnessite; secondly, nontronite; and thirdly X-ray amorphous Fe oxide material (Corliss *et al.*, 1978). The manganese crusts range from soft plates to hard veins. Some crusts are more than 6 cm thick. The amorphous iron oxides coat some of the crusts. The nontronite samples occur as yellow-green to dark green crusts or as lumps of semi-lithified mud. The deposits exhibit strong fractionation of iron from manganese in keeping with other hydrothermal deposits described above and are quite different from more normal ferromanganese oxide encrustations on exposed basalt, just like in the FAMOUS area. They are thought to have formed as a result of elements fluxing out of the rocks immediately below the mounds, being derived from alteration of the underlying basalt. The percolation of the hydrothermal fluids through the sediment, a green organic-rich carbonate

Table 23. Composition of dredged samples from the Galapagos Hydrothermal Field (from Corliss *et al.*, 1978).

	TB1	TB2	TB3	TB4	TB5	TB6	TB7	DM1	DM2	A1	A2	N1	N2	N3	N4	N5
Major elements (%)																
Na	2·29	2·1	3·8	2·98	3·46	2·28	4·03	—	1·11	—	—	1·19	1·03	1·21	0·09	0·20
Mg	1·97	1·81	0·85	1·42	0·75	2·07	0·67	—	0·88	—	—	1·44	1·71	1·27	1·01	1·01
Al	0·20	0·27	0·27	0·01	0·28	0·15	0·16	1·33	1·32	0·09	0·55	0·01	0·02	0·26	1·12	0·83
Si	0·65	0·92	1·2	0·11	1·06	0·91	0·70	5·17	17·5	15·1	11·4	22·4	24·8	18·8	20·8	13·4
K	0·55	0·62	0·32	0·92	0·36	1·17	0·27	—	0·46	—	—	1·74	1·86	0·83	0·64	0·50
Ca	1·19	1·34	1·6	1·31	1·69	1·82	1·72	2·46	2·1	1·07	1·7	0·49	0·08	1·02	6·7	17·2
Mn	51·1	50·1	50·2	50·8	50·3	46·7	51·0	22·6	15·1	7·29	8·41	0·20	0·18	0·35	0·34	1·14
Fe	0·31	0·33	0·19	0·03	0·26	0·57	0·14	17·3	10·2	27·3	27·6	25·7	23·2	27·4	11·8	8·33
Minor elements (p.p.m.)																
Sc	0·76	0·97	0·95	0·18	0·86	0·54	0·62	11·5	7·1	0·48	1·8	0·20	0·19	0·84	3·9	2·6
Cr	5·1	5·1	2·8	3·6	3·2	2·6	4·0	40·8	16·3	5·9	10·7	3·4	4·1	6·8	18·9	12·0
Co	8·7	8·1	2·9	1·3	3·5	5·9	2·4	503·0	247·0	1·6	4·8	0·35	0·91	1·6	11·7	7·0
Ni	496·0	850·0	122·0	76·0	158·0	1480·0	103·0	7770·0	4540·0	71·0	54·0	3·0	14·0	27·0	101·0	58·0
Cu	99·0	186·0	48·0	30·0	65·0	264·0	29·0	400·0	380·0	36·0	60·0	2·3	8·0	2·9	152·0	86·0
Zn	301·0	753·0	245·0	38·0	163·0	1070·0	75·0	774·0	524·0	150·0	151·0	28·0	29·0	55·0	375·0	244·0
As	4·3	3·7	27·0	40·0	4·9	18·0	2·5	180·0	120·0	59·0	24·0	5·2	2·9	11·8	2·1	1·0
Sb	32·0	54·0	9·0	21·0	20·0	42·0	5·5	23·0	13·0	8·1	3·9	1·3	0·90	1·9	1·4	3·5
Ba	2490·0	3160·0	1230·0	1231·0	1530·0	1300·0	1000·0	1440·0	760·0	320·0	1090·0	75·0	68·0	600·0	1930·0	2090·0
Hf	—	0·19	0·10	0·06	0·15	—	—	11·0	7·2	0·19	0·55	0·11	—	0·11	0·68	0·29
Th	0·12	0·14	0·14	0·02	0·18	0·09	0·11	13·0	7·7	—	0·03	—	—	0·12	0·58	0·55
Rare earth elements (p.p.m.)																
La	3·2	3·9	2·5	0·8	3·1	3·7	1·8	175·0	92·0	6·8	6·6	2·9	2·2	5·2	5·3	4·6
Ce	3·4	4·4	1·8	1·0	2·5	1·5	1·3	207·0	113·0	—	4·2	2·9	2·3	2·2	4·8	4·2
Nd	0·4	—	—	—	—	—	—	—	73·0	—	—	—	—	—	—	—
Sm	0·39	0·43	0·40	0·07	0·56	0·75	0·26	26·9	15·5	0·61	0·96	0·66	0·49	0·54	1·2	0·89
Eu	0·16	0·14	0·12	0·12	0·10	0·16	0·09	8·8	4·3	0·21	0·32	0·18	0·15	0·16	0·25	0·23
Tb	0·08	0·08	0·07	0·01	0·07	0·09	0·06	5·4	2·7	0·13	0·16	0·04	—	0·05	0·20	0·14
Yb	0·51	0·70	0·56	0·22	0·53	0·66	0·43	27·6	14·0	—	0·99	0·38	0·30	0·83	1·2	1·2
Lu	0·13	0·17	0·10	0·05	0·13	0·17	0·09	4·1	2·4	0·09	0·15	0·03	0·03	0·20	0·22	0·16
Todorokite/ birnessite	20·0	2·0	0·1	0·1	0·1	0·01	<0·01									

Table 24. Mineralogical description of samples from the Galapagos Hydrothermal Field (from Corliss *et al.*, 1978).

Sample	Dredge	T/B[a]	Mineralogy of sample
TB1	5	20	Almost pure todorokite, very well crystallized, with slight amount of birnessite. There is a well defined 1·47 Å peak, not related to known todorokite or birnessite peaks.[b]
TB2	5	2	Well crystallized todorokite with some birnessite. Possible nontronite and barite present. Well defined 1·47 Å peak appears again.
TB3	7	0·1	Well crystallized birnessite with a minor amount of todorokite. 1·47 Å peak is well defined again, and "associated" 1·82 Å and 2·15 Å peaks also are present.
TB4	3	0·1	Well crystallized birnessite with a minor amount of todorokite. A small 1·47 Å peak is present.
TB5	5	0·1	Well crystallized birnessite with a minor amount of todorokite. 1·47 Å, 1·82 Å, 2·15 Å peaks all again present.
TB6	3	0·01	Almost pure birnessite, well crystallized, with very minor todorokite, calcite and quartz.
TB7	7	<0·01	Almost pure birnessite, well crystallized, with only hints of todorokite. 1·47 Å peak has returned in strength, and 1·82 Å, 2·15 Å peaks are again present.
DM1	4	—	Essentially pure δMnO_2, with minor quartz present. Slight hump at $\sim 6 \cdot 9$ Å possible phillipsite or birnessite.
DM2	4	—	δMnO_2 with slight amount of plagioclase.
A1	5	—	Generally X-ray amorphous, with slight amounts of birnessite and nontronite.
A2	7	—	Generally X-ray amorphous, but with slight amount of a plagioclase.
N1	5	—	Nontronite, very well crystallized. A strong 060 peak at 1·518 Å in the random mount shows that it is primarily a dioctahedral clay.
N2	5	—	Well crystallized nontronite, as in N1.
N3	7	—	Almost pure nontronite, not quite so well crystallized as N1. Hint of birnessite.
N4	7	—	A mixture of calcite and fairly well crystallized nontronite.
N5	5	—	A mixture of calcite and fairly well crystallized nontronite.

[a] T/B refers to the peak area ratio of the 9·7 Å todorokite peak to the 7·2 Å birnessite peak.
[b] The 1·47 Å, 1·82 Å and 2·15 Å peaks resemble a synthetic Na-Mn mineral reported by Wadsley (1950).

siliceous ooze, was thought to have resulted in their cooling slowly under reducing conditions leading to the precipitation of the nontronite. Under more oxidizing conditions, near the mound surfaces, the Fe and Mn oxides have precipitated.

Deep-sea drilling in the Galapagos region during Leg 54 of the Deep Sea Drilling Project has confirmed the presence of the mounds, and provided an additional indication of their thickness (Hekinian *et al.*, 1978) (Fig. 59). The uppermost cores from the mounds contain a similar assemblage of materials to that recovered during the submersible operations (Table 25). The Fe-Mn oxides grade down into the green clays, a gradation discernible even though the sections had suffered drilling disturbance. Water temperatures of 8–10 C were recorded inside the mounds, indicating that they are still active.

Table 25. Composition of Galapagos hydrothermal sediment from DSDP sites 424 and 424 A with other sediment types for comparison (from Hekinian *et al.*, 1978). (Reproduced by permission of Gauthier-Villars Publishing Co.)

	1	2	3	4
Fe(%)	21·6	5·06	7·25	11·96
Mn(%)	0·10	0·48	33·0	19·78
Ni(p.p.m.)	16	211	81	6340
Co(p.p.m.)	22	101	16	3350
Pb(p.p.m.)	60	68	48	846
Zn(p.p.m.)	35	165	126	680
Cu(p.p.m.)	14	323	39	3920
Al(%)	0·12	8·4	0·15	3·06
Mg(%)	2·54	2·1	1·65	1·71

1 = Average values in 11 Galapagos green clays from Mounds Area.*
2 = Average of Pacific pelagic clay (Cronan, 1969c; Turekian and Wedepohl, 1961).
3 = Ferromanganese concretions from Mounds Area.*
4 = Average of Pacific manganese nodules (Cronan, 1972a).
* Analyses by Atomic Absorption Spectrophotemetry.

Studies on the composition of hydrothermal fluids discharging from the Galapagos Rift to the north of the mounds, have given an indication of the composition of the solutions forming submarine hydrothermal deposits (Edmonds reported by Corliss, 1979). Five hot springs were located and sampled during a diving programme by the submersible "Alvin". Around the springs there were both abundant living organisms, including giant clams, and the remains of dead organisms. Milky streams of water were observed debouching on the sea floor with temperatures of 10–11°C near the vents, falling off rapidly on mixing with sea water. The solutions were free of dissolved oxygen and all but one contained H_2S indicating their reducing

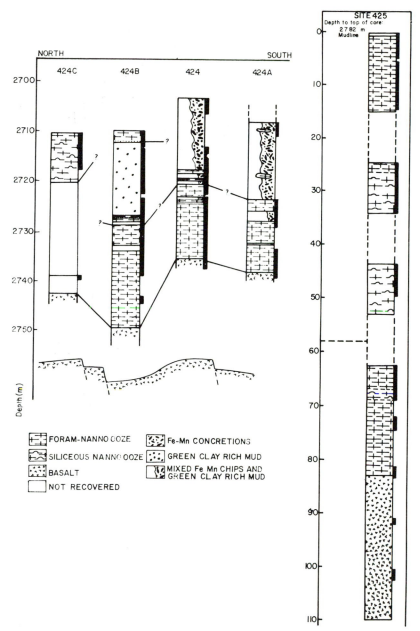

Fig. 59. Lithology columns for the holes drilled in the Galapagos spreading centre area. Holes 424, 424A, 424B and 424C, were drilled approximately 300 m apart from each other at about 22 km south of the spreading axis. Hole 425 was drilled about 65 km north of the spreading axis. Holes 424 and 424A are on or near a topographic high (mound). (From Hekinian *et al.*, 1978.)

nature. Manganese was being flushed into sea water through the vents, while iron was discharged from one vent in abundance, but not from the others. In the latter instances it may have reacted with H_2S and precipitated as a sulphide at depth. There was no Cd, Cu or Ni in the solutions, all these presumably having been precipitated with the H_2S below the sea floor. Evidence for sulphide precipitation on the sea floor was observed in the form of iron sulphide pinnacles seen in one area. In that situation, the hydrothermal solutions must have been escaping at high enough temperatures on to the sea floor so that they precipitated sulphides at the surface. Particulate matter escaping from the vents, as detected on 0·4 μm filters included sulphur particles, iron sulphide crystals, and possibly saponite.

6.4.1.7 *Gulf of California at 27°18′N*

A diving programme in the Gulf of California during 1977 recovered hydro-thermal deposits in the axial rift valley near 27 18′N (Lonsdale, 1978), which were surrounded by dead clam shells just as in the Galapagos area. Most of the material recovered is composed of well crystallized authigenic talc. Included within this material in veins and in scattered crystals is pyrrhotite with subsidiary amounts of copper and zinc sulphides. The pyrrhotite crystals are similar to those reported as having been produced in sea water/basalt interaction experiments (Hajash, 1975). The outer crust of the material collected is a thin layer of ferromanganese oxide and calcium phosphate. The presence of the dead molluscs associated with the deposit indicates that, as in the Galapagos Rift, it was formed fairly recently as a result of the mixing of hydrothermal fluids with cold sea water and the precipitation of the metals contained therein. For sulphides to be precipitated on the sea floor, the temperature of discharge must have been relatively high. Additional sulphide precipitation might be expected below the sea floor in this situation.

6.4.1.8 *East Pacific Rise at 21°N*

Hydrothermal sulphide deposits comprising sphalerite, chalcopyrite, mar-casite and pyrite were found during submersible dives by the French diving saucer "Cyana" in February and March, 1978. They contain up to 29% zinc and up to about 6% Cu in bulk samples. The deposits occurred on the flanks of a 20–30 m deep depression, about 200 m west of an extrusion zone where the youngest lavas in the region occur. They are less than 1 km from the spreading axis.

The deposits occur in the form of mounds about 10 m high and 3–4 m wide aligned parallel to the EPR crest, and have been described by Hekinian (1979) and Francheteau *et al.* (1979). Some of the deposits are porous, their mass being composed of a labyrinth of small channels or tubes separated by thin walls. This framework is composed of white translucent silica as well as the sulphides. The tubes and channels presumably provided paths for the discharge of the hydrothermal solutions.

In addition to the mounds, three other types of deposit were found to occur. Flattish encrustations composed of the same material as the mounds, bright yellow or orange 10–20 cm wide conelets which lie around the mounds and which contain native sulphur, and yellow and red-brown travertine-like flows. In some cases the sulphide is associated with a reddish brown ochre of iron oxides containing up to 80% or 90% Fe_2O_3. This is thought to result from the oxidation of the iron sulphide.

Chemically the deposits are very heterogeneous. Iron, copper, zinc and sulphur are abundant, while cobalt, lead, cadmium and silver are of lesser abundance. Silver reaches concentrations of 1 to 1·5% in some samples. Some small quantity of clay is also present. Manganese appears to be absent from the deposits.

Subsequent to the French discovery, further submersible operations on the East Pacific Rise at 21°N during 1979 have demonstrated that the metalliferous deposits are much more extensive than first found (R. Harmon, personal communication, 1979; H. Holland, personal communication, 1979). They occur intermittently along several kilometres of the ridge crest, and comprise various Fe, Cu and Zn sulphides. Furthermore, active vents through which sulphide-bearing solutions were discharging at temperatures of up to 350°C (with presumably higher temperatures below the sea floor) were also found, the sulphide minerals precipitating in the water column and settling out on the sea floor around the vents. The vents occur in the form of chimneys several metres high out of which five or more metre high plumes of sulphide minerals in suspension are discharged. Within the vents the hydrothermal solutions are clear, indicating that the sulphide minerals precipitate on cooling and mixing with sea water. The force of the plumes detaches pieces of the chimneys which deposit on the sea floor. Eventually, the chimneys must be destroyed by this process. The most abundant minerals found were chalcopyrite in crystals up to 4–5 mm in size, and sphalerite. Some anhydrite was also present.

The discoveries on the East Pacific Rise at 21°N are most important as they demonstrate that sulphide minerals can precipitate in abundance on the sea floor in an elevated situation, and it is likely that more such occurrences will be found both on mid-ocean ridges and in island arcs.

6.4.2 Normal mid-ocean ridge metalliferous sediments

On retrieval, most mid-ocean ridge and basal metalliferous sediments (discussed together here because of their supposed similarity of origin) are characteristically dark brown, fine-grained, seemingly amorphous deposits. They are usually very poorly consolidated, although some of the more deeply buried basal varieties are sometimes partially lithified. The deposits are often mixed or interbedded with varying amounts of biogenic calcium carbonate reflecting their usual formation above the calcium carbonate compensation depth. Such sediments contain anomalous quantities of many base and precious metals such as cobalt, copper, lead, molybdenum, nickel, silver and zinc (Table 26), and according to Field *et al.* (1976) they constitute an important resource for the future.

Table 26. Composition of East Pacific Rise metalliferous sediments.

	1	2	3
Fe(%)	18·00	20·07	5·06
Mn(%)	6·00	6·06	0·48
Ni(p.p.m.)	430	460	211
Cu(p.p.m.)	730	790	323
Pb(p.p.m.)	152	100	68
Zn(p.p.m.)	380	470	160

1 = Ridge crest metalliferous sediments (Bostrom and Peterson, 1969).
2 = Basal ridge flank metalliferous sediments (Cronan, 1976a).
3 = Average Pacific deep-sea clay (Turekian and Wedephol, 1961; Cronan, 1969c).

The constituents of the deposits include grains and globules of iron oxides a few micrometres to a few tens of micrometres in diameter, together with micromanganese nodules, biogenic remains, including fish debris, fragments of submarine volcanic rocks and their alteration products such as palagonite and zeolites, and clay minerals (Dymond *et al.*, 1973; Cronan, 1976a). Normally the content of terrigenous material is low. Ultra-slow scan X-ray diffraction procedures have been used in the identification of some of the seemingly amorphous material in the deposits. Dymond *et al.* (1973) found a variety of mineral phases in basal metalliferous sediments from the flank of the East Pacific Rise, including goethite, psilomelane, barite, phillipsite, montmorillonite and phosphate, in addition to terrigenous, biogenic and volcanic constituents. Those portions of the sample insoluble in hydrochloric acid appeared to have a mineralogical composition similar to that of normal pelagic sediments.

Average metal values on a carbonate free basis of both ridge crest and basal metalliferous sediments are shown in Table 26 together with data on normal pelagic clays for comparison. In general, on a carbonate free basis the deposits are enriched in Fe, Mn, Ni, Cu, Pb and Zn and are depleted in Si, Al and Ti, relative to normal pelagic clays. Other elements that are enriched, at least in Pacific varieties of metalliferous sediments, include Tl, Lu, Tm, Tb, Pr, La, Ag, Yt, Rb, Ge, Ga, B, Be, Li, Cd, V, Hg and U (Bostrom and Peterson, 1969; Cronan, 1974; Cronan 1976a). Data on trace elements in metalliferous sediments from other oceans are not so abundant as in the Pacific, but these too appear to be enriched in many elements.

Work on inter-element relationships in metalliferous sediments has indicated that Fe and Mn are closely correlated, and that many of the minor elements follow both (Cronan, 1976a). Geochemical partition studies (section 6.7.1) have shown, however, that Fe and Mn are largely in separate phases and that the minor elements are variably partitioned between these phases with, for example, the bulk of the Ni and Co associated with the manganese phases, the bulk of the Cu and Zn with the iron phases and Pb more evenly divided (Cronan, 1976a). The correlation between Fe and Mn implies either a common source for these constituents or the precipitation of one catalysing the precipitation of the other.

Although normal mid-ocean ridge metalliferous sediments are relatively homogeneous, detailed studies on small areas of ridge crests have revealed variations in the composition of the sediments over small distances. For example, sediments from within the median valley of the Mid-Atlantic Ridge near 45°N show considerable variations in their content of Hg, As, Mn and Fe over distances of a few tens of kilometres, and the differences are even greater if sediments from immediately adjacent to the valley are included (Cronan, 1972b). Iron was found to be highest near what was thought to be a submarine volcano (F. Aumento, personal communication, 1971) possibly the source of the metal. Manganese, by contrast, was quite low in the iron-rich sediment but increased away from the area of iron enrichment. Cronan (1972b) considered this to reflect the separation of these metals with changes in pH and Eh away from a volcanic source, possibly akin to the processes operating around the Atlantis II Deep in the Red Sea. These variations indicate that the processes that lead to the formation of even widely dispersed ridge crest metalliferous sediments can be non-uniform in nature and are likely to depend on both the sources of the metals and the nature of the depositional environment.

6.5 Bauer Deep Deposits

Metalliferous sediments from the Bauer Deep on the Nazca Plate between the East Pacific Rise and the Galapagos Rise in the south-eastern Pacific deserve special mention as they comprise an extensive deposit of metalliferous sediments whose metals may be present in sufficient abundance to be of economic value in the future (Heath et al., 1973). Sayles and Bischoff (1973) consider that metalliferous sediments may occupy the whole basin below the calcium carbonate compensation depth, from 5° to 22°S. Because they occur below the calcium carbonate compensation depth, absolute metal concentrations in Bauer Deep sediments are higher than in East Pacific Rise crest sediments which are variably diluted by calcium carbonate. For this reason, comparisons of them with East Pacific Rise crest sediments are usually made on a carbonate-free basis.

Near-surface Bauer Deep metalliferous sediments resemble the non-carbonate fraction of basal and ridge crest metalliferous sediments from the East Pacific Rise, but differ from them in several important mineralogical and chemical respects. Mineralogically, they are predominantly composed of an iron-rich smectite, and also contain significant amounts of ferro-manganese oxide compounds, low concentrations of biogenic silica, calcium carbonate, phosphorite, volcanic glass and terrigenous materials (Sayles and Bischoff, 1973; Dymond et al., 1973). The iron smectite has also been identified in basal and ridge crest metalliferous sediments from the East Pacific Rise but is present in lower concentrations than in the Bauer Deep. According to Eklund (1974), at least four mineral phases were identified in one Bauer Deep core that he analysed. These were Fe smectite (SiO_2 52·3%; Fe_2O_3 29·7%; MgO 6·1%; Al_2O_3 2·4%; K_2O 2·0%), todorokite (MnO_2 74·9%; MgO 3·1%; Fe_2O_3 1·6%), ferromanganese hydroxyoxide, in part goethite (MnO_2 36·2%; Fe_2O_3 25·4%; SiO_2 15·1%; MgO 3·3%; CaO 2·1%; Al_2O_3 1·7%) and phosphatic fish debris (CaO 45·2%; P_2O_5 34·4%). Various minor and trace metals were found to be preferentially concentrated in the iron, manganese and phosphatic mineral phases. These were nickel, zinc, copper and cobalt in the first, copper and nickel in the second, and lanthanum in the third (Field et al., 1976).

Chemical differences between Bauer Deep and East Pacific Rise metalliferous sediments are possibly in part dependent upon their mineralogical differences. Sayles and Bischoff (1973) reported that the geochemistry of the Bauer Deep sediments that they studied was similar to that of the non-carbonate fraction of sediments from the East Pacific Rise described by Bostrom and Peterson (1969), but that silicon was considerably higher, probably due to the presence of the smectite. Fe, Mn, Al and Ti were intermediate between Bostrom and Peterson's sediments from the crest and flanks of the East Pacific Rise. Dymond et al. (1973) found Mn and Fe to be lower and Ni and Si to be higher in Bauer Deep sediments than in East Pacific Rise crest and basal metalliferous sediments. Indeed, Ni is anomalously high in Bauer Deep sediments relative to most others from the Nazca Plate (Field et al., 1976), a fact that would contribute to their possible future economic value. In addition, slightly higher Mn and similar Fe values on a carbonate free basis to those encountered by Sayles and Bischoff (1973) were reported by McMurtry (1975) in an additional core from the Bauer Deep. Heath and Dymond (1977) have further analysed a number of surface sediments from the Deep and find them to be enriched in Al, Si, Co, Ni, Ba and REE.

The origin of the Bauer Deep metalliferous sediments has been the subject of considerable controversy, which can be reduced to two main schools of thought. Data of Anderson and Halunen (1974) and McMurtry and Burnett (1975) appearing to show high heat flow values and high metal accumulation rates within the Bauer Deep were interpreted as indicating local hydrothermal activity and metal supply within the Deep itself. However, Lyle and Dymond (1976) have questioned the validity of the accumulation rate data on the basis of possible errors in the assumed values for bulk density of the sediments. Andersen and Halunen considered that a jump in spreading from the fossil Galapagos Rise spreading centre to the present East Pacific Rise spreading centre about 6 million years ago may have resulted in the reinitiation of hydrothermal circulation beneath the Bauer Deep, resulting in the formation of metalliferous sediments. If this hypothesis is correct, it has important implications in exploration for metalliferous sediments in other areas, as it implies that metalliferous sediment formation is not necessarily restricted to spreading centres, but may also result from intra-plate vulcanism.

An alternative view on the origin of the Bauer Deep metalliferous sediments proposed by Dymond *et al.* (1973) is that they precipitate from solutions at the East Pacific Rise crest, and are transported as fine particulates down the flank of the Rise to deposit beneath the calcium carbonate compensation depth in the Bauer Deep. Heath and Dymond (1977) consider the increased smectite in Bauer Deep sediments to be due to diagenetic reactions between iron oxides and biogenic silica during such transport processes. This alternative hypothesis might explain some of the compositional differences between Bauer Deep and East Pacific Rise metalliferous sediments, as the latter could scavenge material from sea water during their transport to the Bauer Deep. In this regard, the relative enrichment of nickel in Bauer Deep sediments is of significance, as Cronan and Garrett (1973) have shown that this element is largely associated with the ferromanganese oxide component of Pacific metalliferous sediments which could scavenge it from normal sea water.

As the Bauer Deep has a depth only slightly greater than that of the local calcium carbonate compensation depth, a possible additional supply of metals to the sediments can be expected from the surface waters as a result of the dissolution of sinking organic remains. Oldnall (1975) has calculated that significant amounts of Ba, Zn, Pb and Sr may have been contributed to the sediments in this manner, and biogenic supply of other metals is possible

(Dymond *et al.*, 1977). Furthermore, dissolution of siliceous organisms will also be taking place and this could release silica to promote smectite formation.

The stratigraphic record within the Bauer Deep is of importance in any discussions on an East Pacific Rise as opposed to a local Bauer Deep source for Bauer Deep metalliferous sediments. Site 319 of the Deep Sea Drilling Project was drilled in the Bauer Deep (Yeats and Hart, 1976) and encountered a complete sequence of chemically anomalous sediments. The sediments could be divided into three major groups (Dymond *et al.*, 1977): first, surface sediments recovered between 0 and 8 m below sea floor which have relatively high concentrations of Al, Si, Co, Ni, Ba and REE; secondly, intermediate sediments recovered between 8 and 25 m depth which also have high concentrations of Si but lower Al, Co, Ni, Ba and REE contents than surface sediments; thirdly, basal sediments recovered between 25 and 107 m depth which are rich in Fe, Mn, Cu and Zn. Dymond *et al.* (1977) noted an increase in nickel and cobalt in the near-surface sediments relative to those from greater depths and large variations in the manganese, iron, copper and zinc contents of the basal sediments. They were able to confirm that Bauer Deep surface sediments are richer in Al and Ni than surface sediments from the East Pacific Rise, as was noted previously by Dymond *et al.* (1973); that sediments from site 319 are higher in Fe and Mn and lower in Al than normal pelagic sediments; and that basal and intermediate sediments from site 319 are similar to East Pacific Rise surface sediments. Accumulation rates of Mn, Fe, Cu and Zn had been highest in the basal sediments, implying a hydrothermal source for a considerable portion of these elements. The depositional site would have been near the crest of the spreading Galapagos Rise at the time these sediments were deposited, and thus the sediments are presumably analogous to other basal metalliferous sediments in the southeast Pacific. If so, the chemical differences between these and the recent surface sediments in the Bauer Deep would imply that the latter were not the result of local hydrothermal activity and the volcanic influence on them was less than on rise crest sediments. The lower manganese accumulation rate in the upper sediments would not be at variance with these conclusions.

Summarizing available evidence, the Bauer Deep sediments would appear to be polygenetic. It is difficult to make a strong case for local hydrothermal activity within the Deep, but it cannot be ruled out altogether. Some supply of material from the East Pacific Rise is probable, but is difficult to quantify accurately. There can be little doubt that the dissolution of organisms is supplying metals to the sediments. Furthermore, the protected situation of the Bauer Deep between two rises and on the seaward side of a major oceanic trench system would limit terrigenous sedimentation in it. Under these circumstances, the precipitation of authigenic minerals such as ferromanganese oxides and the concomitant scavenging from sea water of additional metals that would take place, must be admitted as a probable major influence on the composition of Bauer Deep sediments.

6.6   Off Mid-Ocean Ridge Metalliferous Sediments

Several occurrences of submarine metalliferous sediments have been reported from areas other than on mid-ocean ridges, usually from island arcs or related environments. On the whole, however, sediments from such environments have attracted less attention than the mid-ocean ridge varieties.

One of the earliest reports of off-ridge hydrothermal sediment formation was that of Zelenov (1964), on the submarine Banu Wuhu Volcano, In-

Table 27. Compositions of representative samples of the four groups of thermal waters from the Matupi area, and the composition of the fumarole condensate from Tavurvur Gulley. Average sea water composition (from Krauskopf, 1967) is given for comparison. All elements in p.p.m.; ND = not detected (from Ferguson and Lambert, 1972). (Reproduced with permission of the Director, B. M. R., Australia.)

	Tavurvur Gully		Tavurvur Shore	Rabal–Ankaia Shore	Fumarole Condensate, Tavurvur	Average ocean
	Upper	Lower				
Fe	108	18	97	3·5	ND	0·01
Mn	20	15	111	2·7	ND	0·002
Zn	1·35	0·58	2·53	0·03	ND	<0·01
Cu	0·06	0·05	0·05	0·05	ND	0·003
Pb	0·05	0·05	0·09	0·07	ND	0·00003
As	—	0·01	0·02	0·01	ND	0·003
Ca	475	440	395	1030	ND	400
Mg	700	885	1340	1370	ND	1350
Na	1930	2380	13 600	8600	4·3	10 600
K	130	180	756	525	0·3	380
Li	—	0·13	0·42	0·40	—	0·17
B	—	1·0	9·8	5·4	ND	4·6
Cl	1760	2250	22 500	18 000	4	19 000
Br	—	6	76	60	ND	65
I	—	ND (<1)	ND	ND	ND	0·6
SO$_4$	5820	6560	5420	2230	trace	2649
Total diss. solids	11 800	14 000	46 000	34 200	12	34 700
Temp. °C	44	34	65	85	102	
pH (20°C)	3·4	4·8	3·7	6·1	3·5	8·3
Eh	+514	+534	+444	+224	+124	

Table 28. Compositions of the iron-rich precipitates from the Matupi thermal springs. Analyses with lower iron values are diluted by detrital silicate material. To enable direct comparison of minor metal abundances in the precipitates, all the analyses have been normalized to 44% iron (values in parenthesis). Zn, Cu, Pb expressed as p.p.m., other elements as % (from Ferguson and Lambert, 1972). (Reproduced with permission of the Director, B. M. R., Australia.)

Location		Tavurvur Gully		Tavurvur Shore	Rabalankaia Shore
Remarks	Deposit at orifice of low discharge spring	Deposit at bottom of pool beneath orifice	Deposit at bottom of pool about 15 m from spring orifice	Deposit near orifice of high discharge spring just below low tide level	Deposit near orifice of medium discharge spring, between low and high tide marks
	pH = 3·4	pH = 3·6	pH = 4·8		
Fe(%)	44·0	24·3	12·7	25·6	17·6
		(44·0)	(44·0)	(44·0)	(44·0)
Mn(%)	0·034	0·024	0·11	1·03	0·068
		(0·043)	(0·38)	(1·7)	(0·17)
Zn	52	24	187	1150	34
		(43)	(650)	(1980)	(85)
Cu	47	34	20	26	18
		(61)	(70)	(45)	(45)
Pb	<100	<100	<100	<100	<100
Total S(%)	2·43	—	—	1·13	—
Acid Soluble S = %	0·10	—	—	0·12	—
S⁻(%)	0·17	—	—	0·23	—

donesia. Hot jets of iron and manganese-rich solutions were discharging on to the sea floor. Iron and manganese were seen to precipitate as hydroxides about 1 m above the hydrothermal vent, and the surrounding rocks were heavily coated with iron and manganese precipitates. A cloudy suspension, thought to be silica, was observed drifting away from the hydrothermal vent.

One of the best described occurrences of off-ridge metalliferous sediment formation is at Matupi Harbour, New Britain (Ferguson and Lambert, 1972). Not only were sediments precipitating from hydrothermal solutions examined, but the hydrothermal solutions themselves were also analysed. Volcanic thermal waters were reported as being mildly to strongly acid, containing up to 100 p.p.m. Fe, 100 p.p.m. Mn, 2·5 p.p.m. Zn and slightly less than 0·1 p.p.m. Cu and Pb. The Fe, Mn and Zn contents were similar to those occurring in the Atlantis II Deep brines in the Red Sea, but the Cu and Pb were lower. Significantly however, the total dissolved salts and chloride contents of the Matupi thermal springs are much lower than in the Red Sea brines and in some instances are less than in normal sea water. Their composition is shown in Table 27. The compositions of the precipitates from the thermal springs are shown in Table 28. The deposits are enriched in iron oxides with generally variable but low manganese and zinc contents, much lower, in fact than are often found in precipitates from Red Sea brines. Total sulphur in the deposits ranged from 0·5 to 2·5%, largely present in sulphate minerals and detrital pyrite. At two localities where the thermal waters discharge into sea water, metals were rapidly precipitated as a result of sharp changes of acidity and redox potential on mixing. By contrast, where the hydrothermal solutions discharge subaerially the initial precipitate was relatively pure iron oxide. Only when the pH and Eh of the solutions increased away from the discharge point did Mn and Zn precipitate.

Metalliferous sediments from the Cyclades Volcanic Arc in the eastern Mediterranean (Fig. 60) have been described by a number of workers (Butuzova, 1968; Bonatti et al., 1972a; Puchelt, 1972; Smith and Cronan, 1975). The best known examples occur in the caldera of Santorini, and are found within small embayments situated off the channel between two islands, Nea Kameni and Palaea Kameni (Fig. 60). Gases and metal-rich solutions are actively discharging into the sea. The bathymetry of the caldera of Santorini and the surrounding region has been divided into five zones by Smith and Cronan (1975), each of which contains a distinctive sediment type (Fig. 60). These zones are the inner exhalative zone, the outer exhalative zone, the channel zone, the caldera zone and the shelf zone immediately outside the caldera of Santorini.

Within the embayments off the islands in the caldera of Santorini can be observed a fractional precipitation of metals, similar to that occurring in and around the Atlantis II Deep. Iron is highest in solution close to the

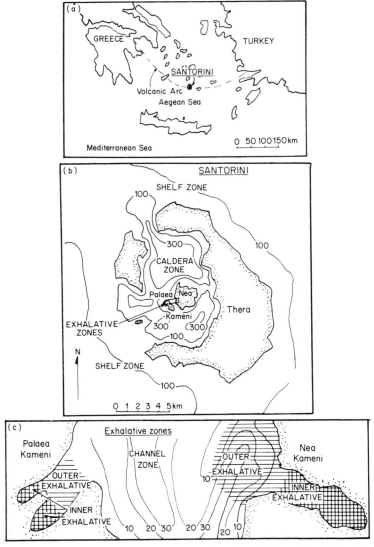

Fig. 60. Metalliferous sediments at Santorini: (a) location of Santorini; (b) location of the deposits and outer zones; (c) exhalative zones (from Smith and Cronan, 1975).

hydrothermal outlets and decreases down the embayments. Iron values of 40% occur in the surface sediments in the inner exhalative zone, decreasing to 7% in the outer exhalative zone. By contrast, aluminium increases with distance from the hydrothermal outlets and is highest in the deep water sediments of the caldera zone suggesting that hydrothermal contributions of this element are negligible in the Santorini caldera. Manganese is relatively low in the iron-rich sediments of the inner exhalative zone, but is considerably enriched in the sediments of the outer exhalative zone, less than 200 p.p.m. and as much as 5500 p.p.m. respectively. This again illustrates the differing behaviour of these metals on mixing of acid hydrothermal solutions with sea water. Zinc is highest in the outer exhalative zone, up to 140 p.p.m., and generally covaries with manganese which may be scavenging it out of solution. Copper values are rather similar throughout the five zones defined by Smith and Cronan (1975) averaging about 25 p.p.m. overall. However, the inner exhalative zone exhibits the highest average copper contents in surface sediments, 34 p.p.m., suggesting a hydrothermal source for this element, and possibly higher concentrations at depth.

Beneath the surface sediments in the Palaea Kameni deposit, there is about half a metre of ferrous carbonate rich sediment, and below this ferrous silicates or sulphates may occur (Puchelt, 1972). In the Nea Kameni deposit a similar sequence of sediments has been reported by Butuzova (1966), who has also reported the formation of iron sulphide. Hydrogen sulphide gas is present in the Nea Kameni embayment, but seemingly not in the Palaea Kameni embayment.

Metalliferous sediments from the Aeolian Island Arc in the western Mediterranean have been described by Honnorez (1969), Honnorez et al. (1973a, b), Honnorez (1979a) and Wauschkuhn and Gropper (1975). The island arc comprises seven islands, and two active volcanoes, Stromboli and Vulcano. In Bahia de Levante off Vulcano Island there is an underwater fumarole field on a fracture which is subject to earthquake activity. Fumaroles on the adjacent land exhibit temperatures in the region of 250°C and are associated with deposits of sulphur and ammonium chloride. However, in 1924–1925 the fumarole temperatures on land went up to over 600°C and sulphide minerals were deposited.

The underwater fumarole field exhibits water discolouration due to colloidal sulphur in suspension. Gases comprising CO_2, H_2S, SO_2 and steam are discharging from the fumaroles. The pH is as low as 2·53 in the fumaroles, but is normal just a few metres away. Iron concentrations of 1 mg/litre are found in the waters directly overlying the fumaroles. The sediment in the fumarole field is a grey tuff containing up to about 40% sulphides including marcasite, pyrite and small amounts of chalcopyrite and arsenopyrite. In some instances pyrite and marcasite can be found replacing titanomagnetite

Table 29. Elemental composition of sediments from the Lau Basin (from Bertine, 1974).

Sample	Location	Water depth (m)	Maximum sediment depth (m)	Heat flow (μcal/cm^2/s)	Depth (cm)	CaCO$_3$ (%)	Al (%)	Si (%)	Ca (%)
7 Tow 123–72G	20 24'S 176 46'W	2730	200	1·04	0–3	42·0	6·4	25·0	5·2
					4–6	45·4			
					8–10	34·6			
					12–14	33·9			
					20–22	30·1			
					30–32	35·7			
					50–52	39·3	4·6	23·3	3·0
					75–77	45·5			
					100–102	37·6			
					140–142	42·3	4·7	19·6	7·6
							5·2	22·6	5·3
7 Tow 123–84G	17 36'S 177 45'W	2406	100	0·76	0–2	67·8	7·8	22·8	2·0
7 Tow 123–88G	16 47·5'S 176 39·5'W	2698	100	4·22	2–5	49·3	5·9	20·3	5·1
7 Tow 123–94G	16 29'S 177 33'W	2328	100	2·29	0–3	65·9	6·7	18·2	10·6
					10–12	80·1			
					20–22	69·0			
					30–32	69·2			
					40–42	72·7	5·5	19·0	15·0
					50–52	69·8			
					60–62	67·7			
							6·1	18·6	12·8
7 Tow 123–105G	15 15·5'S 176 49·4'W	2163	100	6·75	0–3	45·1			
					3–5	36·2			
					5–7	38·4	5·0	21·2	5·7
					9–11	42·0			
					14–16	48·6			
					19–21	64·6			
					30–32	68·8			
					50–52	69·1	2·9	16·1	14·8
							4·0	18·6	10·2
					Average of 5 cores		5·8	18·8[a]	7·1

[a]Corrected for opal content.

Mg (%)	CaCO₃-free Na (%)	K (%)	Ti (%)	Fe (%)	Mn (%)	Cu (p.p.m.)	Zn (p.p.m.)	Cr (p.p.m.)	Ni (p.p.m.)	Co (p.p.m.)	Pb (p.p.m.)	Opal (%)
3·9	5·2	1·0	0·33	11·4	1·4	245	185	55	85	60	27	
				11·7	1·6	225	130	130	75			
				10·6	1·1	230	160	45	75	75		
				11·5	1·2	235	160	80	75			9
				10·3	0·9	165	130	70	45	55		
				10·1	1·0	225	130	40	45			
1·9	5·0	0·8	0·31	11·2	1·2	235	130	35	75	80	33	
				11·5	1·4	220	140	60	75	90		5
				11·0	1·2	210	125	35	50			
1·5	4·1	0·7	0·24	10·7	1·8	315	155	45	85	70		
2·4	4·8	0·8	0·29	11·0	1·3	230	145	60	69	72	30	
2·8	6·3	1·1	0·28	14·2	1·8	330	380	60	215	125	109	
2·0	6·8	0·9	0·34	11·0	1·4	240	150	40	90			
1·9	5·5	0·9	0·26	12·8	0·7	395	210	60	90		76	
				9·2	1·1	375	280	105	225	275		<1
				8·5	0·8	255	215	60	145			
				11·0	1·3	340	200	75	145	180		
2·2	5·9	0·9	0·26	10·5	1·4	350	225	80	165			
				11·4	1·5	380	200	65	150	180		<2
				10·6	1·2	340	190	95	140		77	
2·0	5·7	0·9	0·26	10·6	1·1	348	217	77	151	212	76	
				12·4	2·0	320	195	60	190	165	46	
				12·0	1·5	265	170	140	205			
3·3	4·8	0·5	0·76	13·3	1·5	280	215	120	290	145		
				12·2	1·7	275	185	110	145			6
				10·6	1·9	380	190	145	225	80	49	
				12·4	2·8	355	230	115	200			
				11·6	2·9	390	205	125	160	130		
2·0	7·1	1·1	0·23	10·3	3·0	345	200	95	160			0
2·7	6·0	0·8	0·50	11·9	2·2	327	199	115	196	130	47	
2·4	5·9	0·9	0·33	11·7	1·6	295	178	70	144	135	66	

in the country rock. Chemically, the sediments are low in SiO_2 and rich in Fe and Hg. Towards the fumaroles Cr, Fe, Co, Ni and B and V increase, while Al, Ba, Mn, Si, P, Ca and Mg decrease. Base metals are low in the deposits in comparison with sulphide deposits in the Atlantis II Deep in the Red Sea, but massive sulphide deposits may occur below the fumarole field.

The importance of the sediments off Santorini and Vulcano lies in the information they provide on submarine metallogenesis in a readily accessible part of an island arc system. As mentioned, the sequence of sediments away from the submarine hydrothermal outlets off Santorini with the differential precipitation of iron and manganese, and the possible pre-segregation of sulphides, is analogous in many respects to the situation observed in and around the Atlantis II Deep and elsewhere in much deeper water mid-ocean ridge hydrothermal centres. In these two situations we may be observing directly parts of a general process accompanying a certain type of submarine metallogenesis.

The south-western Pacific Ocean is an example of an island arc/marginal basin complex in which several occurrences of submarine volcanogenic sediments have been recorded (Taylor 1976; Carney, 1975). This area contains both numerous submarine volcanoes, often in quite shallow water, and active spreading centres in the basins behind the island arc. The latter appear to be analogous in many respects to mid-ocean ridge spreading centres and thus can be expected to be overlain by similar metalliferous sediments. Indeed, ferruginous sediments very similar to mid-ocean ridge types have been described from the spreading centre in the Lau Basin by Griffin *et al.* (1972) and Bertine (1974), and hydrothermal barite has been described from a fracture zone offsetting the spreading centre by Bertine and Keen (1975).

The non-biogenic fraction of Lau Basin Rise sediments analysed by Bertine (1974) consists largely of volcanic debris, with abundant montmorillonite and small amounts of partially ordered chlorite in the clay fraction (Griffin *et al.*, 1972). Chemically they are rich in iron and relatively rich in manganese and copper (Table 29). In comparison with mid-ocean ridge sediments, they contain lower iron, manganese, copper, zinc and nickel concentrations than on the East Pacific Rise, being more similar to Mid-Atlantic Ridge deposits. Bertine (1974) concluded that these sediments were formed by the weathering of volcanics with the addition of certain elements from sea water co-precipitated with ferromanganese oxides. However, Bertine also noted that the accumulation rates of Mn, Fe, Cu and Zn, four of the more important elements in submarine hydrothermal systems, were much higher than in most ridge crest sediments. This suggests that a local hydrothermal source of iron and possibly some associated elements may be important on the Lau Basin Rise and thus, by analogy, on other back arc basin spreading centres.

More recently, a regional geochemical reconnaissance survey to seek occurrences of metalliferous sediments in the island arc system of the south-western Pacific has been described by Cronan and Thompson (1978). This work showed several areas of metal enrichment including parts of the Lau Basin, the South Fiji Basin, north-west of Fiji, and near to the New Hebrides and Solomon Islands. Comparison of the element distribution patterns obtained with known patterns associated with submarine volcanism suggested that the New Hebrides region and the Lau Basin might be prime areas to seek high grade metalliferous sediments.

6.7   Geochemical Interrelationships and Origin of Metalliferous Sediments

It is evident from the examples presented in the preceding sections, that submarine metalliferous sediments exhibit a wide range of compositions. Examples include the copper and zinc-rich sulphides of the Red Sea, the iron-rich, minor element poor, sediments from Amph 2D and the basal sediments of DSDP 236, the Mn-rich deposits on the Mid-Atlantic Ridge at 26° N, and all intermediate varieties. Are these unrelated deposits formed under differing conditions, or are they different varieties of the same genetic class of deposit? Although the bulk composition of metalliferous sediments may vary considerably, the composition of their individual constituents is less variable. We are able to determine this by selective partition analysis using chemical leaching procedures.

6.7.1   Partition of elements between constituent phases of metalliferous sediments

Selective partition analysis is a valuable technique in elucidating geochemical interrelationships between different metalliferous sediments because more useful information can be gained from examination of discrete fractions of such polycomponent deposits than can be derived from their bulk analysis. A variety of techniques have been proposed to remove selectively different fractions of marine deposits by chemical leaching. For example, Arrhenius (1963) proposed the use of hydroxylamine hydrochloride to remove the manganese oxide fraction of manganese nodules, and Dymond *et al* (1973) used oxalic acid to dissolve the reducible fraction of East Pacific Rise metalliferous sediments. Possibly the most widely used selective leach technique is either the one developed by Chester and Hughes (1967), or some modification of it.

A modified version of the Chester and Hughes (1967) technique has been applied to a variety of metalliferous sediments by Cronan and Garrett (1973), Cronan (1976a) and Horowitz and Cronan (1976). This method has been described in detail by Cronan (1976a) and involves the use of acetic acid, hydroxylamine hydrochloride, HCl, and HF coupled with $HClO_4$. Samples are leached first with the acetic acid to remove carbonates and loosely sorbed ions, secondly with hydroxylamine hydrochloride to remove the reducible fraction which is largely manganese oxides, thirdly with HCl to dissolve iron oxide and last with HF, $HClO_4$ to dissolve that which is not attacked by the HCl. Although this procedure is not effective in completely removing any particular phase while not attacking the others (no selective leach procedure is), it does result in a reasonable chemical separation of the sediments into their main constituents, which are usually carbonates, manganese and iron oxides and silicate material.

Examination of the partition of elements between the different chemical fractions of a wide variety of metalliferous sediments (Cronan, 1976a; Horder, 1979; Varnavas, 1979; Cronan, unpublished data) illustrates certain regularities in the elements' behaviour. Much of the Mn, Ni, Co and to a lesser extent Pb occur in the reducible ferromanganese oxide fraction, much of the Cu, Zn and Fe and some Si, Al and Mg occur in the HCl soluble Fe oxide and silicate fraction, and much of the Al, Si, Mg and K occur in the detrital silicate fraction. These results indicate that the seemingly different metalliferous sediments of widely varying bulk composition may be different varieties of the same sediment types, in that they contain the same constituents but in differing proportions. For example, the manganese-rich deposits from the Mid-Atlantic Ridge at 26°N consist mostly of manganese oxide and little iron oxide, the iron-rich deposits from DSDP 236 and Amph 2D contain mostly iron oxide and little manganese oxide, while other anomalous mid-ocean ridge sediments contain variable concentrations of both phases and silicates, well exemplified by the Gulf of Aden, FAMOUS and Galapagos deposits as well as by many normal more widely dispersed metalliferous sediments on mid-ocean ridge crests. However, in each of these cases the different end member constituents, iron oxides, manganese oxides, and iron silicates are similar in composition. It is the proportions in the mix that vary.

6.7.2   Fractional precipitation

A model to account for the compositional differences between the different varieties of metalliferous sediments described can be based on the observed sequence of deposits in and around the Atlantis II Deep. This is because the sequence of precipitates in and around the Atlantis II Deep include most of the varieties of metalliferous sediments found elsewhere in submarine volcanic areas. Such metalliferous sediments can be viewed as different products of one general ore forming process. The sulphides on the East Pacific Rise at 21 N may be regarded as the analogues of the sulphides forming near to the discharge point of the hydrothermal fluids in the south-west basin of the Atlantis II Deep. The iron silicates and associated iron oxides in the FAMOUS and Galapagos areas, and in the Gulf of Aden, may be regarded as the analogues of the iron silicates and oxides which occur over much of the floor of the Atlantis II Deep. The manganese oxides in the TAG area, although compositionally very pure, may be the equivalent of the manganese oxides near the margin of the Atlantis II Deep. Finally, the widely dispersed mixed Fe and Mn oxides occurring over mid-ocean ridges at large may be the equivalents of the widely dispersed oxides found in the dispersion halo around the Atlantis II Deep (Cronan, 1976b). It is evident therefore that in and around the Atlantis II Deep we may be observing a general process of submarine metalliferous sediment formation in microcosm. The sulphides on the East Pacific Rise at 21 N would represent early formed precipitates from hydrothermal solutions, the iron-rich silicate and oxide deposits from the various localities mentioned would represent intermediate formed precipitates, and the manganese oxide deposits in the TAG area would represent last formed precipitates. The widely dispersed iron and manganese-rich sediments most probably represent precipitates from iron and manganese-bearing solutions which discharged from the hydrothermal vents into the overlying sea water, together with particulate oxides flushed out from the vents, to be dispersed over a wide area. Because of the nature of their precipitation process, these deposits have been able to scavenge additional metals from sea water (Cronan, 1976a).

The spatial relationships on the sea floor between the different varieties of the deposits described above will depend largely on the physicochemical conditions at the point of hydrothermal discharge. Discharge of hydrothermal solutions into a highly oxidizing environment such as unrestricted normal sea water is likely to lead to the rapid oxidation of iron and to sharp variations in the Fe/Mn ratio of the precipitates over short distances, such as in the FAMOUS and Gulf of Aden deposits. Where the hydrothermal solutions discharge into less oxidizing or reducing conditions, separation of the metals will take place over greater distances as the physicochemical properties of the environment, particularly its pH and Eh, change more gradually. The Atlantis II Deep provides the best example of this. A similar effect may be taking place in the Galapagos region where high biological productivity and concomitant high organic sedimentation rates are giving rise to a low Eh in the sediments resulting in the precipitation of hydrothermal iron silicates such as nontronite prior to deposition of Fe/Mn oxides. The deposits from Santorini and like instances where the separation of the metals is taking place over tens to hundreds of metres, are intermediate between the rapidly oxidized Gulf of Aden and FAMOUS type deposits on the one hand, and the slowly oxidized Atlantis II Deep type deposits on the other, probably because the solutions debouch into channels which are partially restricted rather than into the open sea.

Some confirmation of metal fractionation processes on the sea floor is forthcoming from experimental work. Seyfried and Bischoff (1977) have reacted the solutions obtained from hydrothermal leaching of basalts with sea water at various dilutions. They observed a rapid and quantitative removal of iron, presumably as hydrated ferric oxide, at all dilutions. By contrast, independent of the dilution factor, manganese remained in solution and demonstrated no tendency to precipitate as a discrete phase nor to co-precipitate with iron. This behaviour may possibly be attributed to the somewhat slow oxidation of Mn^{2+} at a pH of < 9 (Stumm and Morgan, 1970). The behaviour of SiO_2 varied with the dilution factor. At a 1 : 1 dilution SiO_2 decreased in solution from 617 to 130 p.p.m., a level thought to have been maintained by the solubility of amorphous SiO_2. A slight removal of Mg from solution was also apparent at this dilution. The precipitate from this reaction was dominated by amorphous SiO_2 and was thought to be reflected in the natural state by the barite/opal deposits of the Lau Basin described by Bertine and Keen (1975) (section 6.6). Diluting the altered sea water after reaction with basalt with three parts normal sea water resulted in a significant removal of Mg, partial removal of SiO_2, and increase in pH. This was thought to be due to the formation of a hydrated Mg silicate. Diluting the altered sea water with normal sea water in the ratio 1 : 39, resulted in the hydrothermally derived SiO_2 remaining in solution and the bulk precipitate being relatively pure amorphous Fe oxide. This was thought to be analogous to the Fe-rich metalliferous sediments found on the crest of the East Pacific Rise. Thus the results of these mixing experiments indicate that the mixing ratio of hydrothermal solution with sea water as well as the physicochemical nature of the solutions themselves is of great importance in determining the composition of the precipitates formed. Iron is precipitated under most conditions. SiO_2 forms the major part of the precipitate at low dilutions, Mg silicate forms at intermediate dilutions, but neither SiO_2 nor Mg precipitate significantly at high dilutions, resulting in an iron-rich precipitate. Hydrothermal precipitates can thus range from almost pure SiO_2 to pure ferric oxide depending upon the mixing conditions, a range that is observed on the sea floor.

So far the problem of metal fractionation associated with hydrothermal circulation and discharge has been discussed in only two dimensions. Again, analogy with the Atlantis II Deep can help to develop the model in three dimensions (Cronan, 1976b). The sulphides precipitating within the Atlantis II Deep are doing so under elevated temperatures and reducing conditions.

These conditions are likely to be very rare at the surface of mid-ocean ridges in the open ocean. However, where high temperatures and reducing conditions are maintained up to the point of hydrothermal discharge, base metal sulphides will precipitate on the sea floor as on the East Pacific Rise at 21°N, and the remaining metals will escape into sea water to precipitate elsewhere. Where downward flowing sea water mixes with and cools the ascending hydrothermal solutions, subsurface precipitation of sulphides is likely to take place and lower temperature hydrothermal precipitates, first silicates and then oxides are likely to occur on the sea floor, or just below, as in the FAMOUS and Galapagos areas and in the Gulf of Aden, their vertical distribution depending, among other factors, on the Eh, pH and temperature gradient in the ascending fluids. In such circumstances, manganese is likely to precipitate either above or adjacent to the iron deposits, as occurs in the Galapagos area and in the Gulf of Aden. Finally, where extensive cooling and mixing of the hydrothermal solutions takes place below the sea floor, most of the hydrothermal minerals will precipitate subsurface and the final precipitates, manganese oxides, will precipitate on or near the sea floor as in the TAG area. Thus a three-dimensional model for metalliferous sediment formation on mid-ocean ridges would include precipitation of metals from the same hydrothermal solution both within the crust and at the surface, but any or all of the precipitates could form on the sea floor given the maintenance of high temperatures and reducing conditions until hydrothermal discharge. The model is illustrated in Fig. 61.

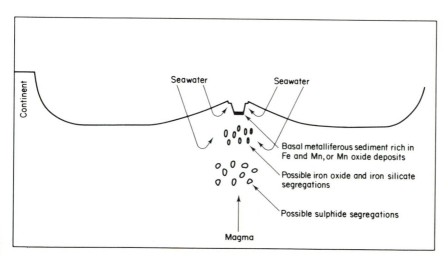

Fig. 61. Idealized hypothetical section of mid-ocean ridge showing possible sequence of mineral deposition (not to scale).

The three-dimensional model receives support from at least two sources. First, dredged rocks from parts of the mid-ocean ridges have been found to contain disseminated sulphides within them (Bonatti *et al.*, 1976a; Chapter 7), although no massive sulphide deposits have yet been encountered. Secondly, the geological sections and sequences of metals precipitated in the massive sulphide-bearing ophiolite sequences in the Troodos Massif and elsewhere which are thought to have been formed under oceanic conditions, are similar to those described here for modern mid-ocean ridges. These occurrences will be discussed more fully in Chapter 7.

In spite of the probability described above that most hydrothermal sulphides will precipitate below the sea floor in open ocean submarine volcanic areas subject to unrestricted circulation of oxidizing bottom waters, conditions for base metal sulphide formation can occur locally on the sea floor in such regions. Examples from the East Pacific Rise at 21°N and the Gulf of California have been mentioned. Cann (1979) has suggested that the temperatures required to form base metal sulphides on the ocean floor in the open ocean are only likely to be found in the axial zone of mid-ocean ridges, and has calculated that there may be only one base metal sulphide deposit exposed per 100 km or so of ridge crest at any one time. Francheteau *et al.* (1979) have suggested that hydrothermal base metal sulphides may be more prevalent on fast spreading ridges than on slow spreading ones, based on the lack of such deposits found to date on open ocean mid-ocean ridges other than on the East Pacific Rise (see also Chapter 8). However, because of their proximity to the ridge axis such deposits are likely to be covered over by lavas soon after formation, which, coupled with their likely oxidation under the oxidizing conditions prevailing on open ocean mid-ocean ridges, means that few if any will be preserved indefinitely. Under these circumstances, in order to find sulphides of any size and value preserved in the open ocean, it would be necessary to seek a volcanically active area sufficiently removed from the ridge axis to render unlikely the deposits being covered over by lavas, and which exhibits a restricted environment where reducing conditions independent of those produced by the volcanism could prevail. Island arcs and mid-ocean ridge fracture zones may contain such areas (Cronan, 1976b).

As described, metalliferous sediments of the oxide variety have been reported on the sea floor in association with submarine volcanism in island arcs (Ferguson and Lambert, 1972; Bertine, 1974; Smith and Cronan, 1975). In these situations, sulphide minerals may be precipitating below the sea floor. However, that sulphide minerals can precipitate on the sea floor in an island arc setting is evinced by the occurrence of sedimentary sulphide deposits of geologically recent age on land in the Solomon Islands (Taylor, 1974). The conditions under which sulphides could precipitate and be preserved on the sea floor in an island arc would include a restricted circulation of sea water leading to reducing conditions, structural depressions in which the deposits could be ponded, and, naturally, the occurrence of submarine volcanic activity. All these conditions could be met in some of the deep basins in island arcs.

The probability of sedimentary base metal sulphides occurring in oceanic fracture zones is high. These features are volcanically active, exhibit high heat flow thought to result from hydrothermal circulation, expose great thicknesses of the oceanic crust to circulating hydrothermal fluids which could leach metals from it, are sufficiently deep to have restricted circulation in places leading to reducing conditions, and contain basins which could pond hydrothermal precipitates. Bonatti *et al.* (1976b) and Honnorez (1979b) have reported a minor occurrence of hydrothermal pyrite of recent origin in the Romanche Fracture Zone in the Atlantic and Honnorez (1979b) also reported the finding of iron sulphide enriched in As, Hg, Tl and other metals in a fracture zone off Baja California. Cronan (1977b) has suggested that a combination of high biological activity in the surface waters coupled with a restricted circulation at depth, such as might occur in fracture zones underlying equatorial areas of high biological productivity, might lead to stagnation and reducing conditions in the bottom waters because of organic decay, which would be suitable for sulphide deposition. Such situations might be the most favourable for base metal sulphide deposition *and preservation* on the deep ocean floor. The recent reports of sulphides in the Gulf of California (Lonsdale, 1978) and in the Galapagos region (Corliss *et al.*, 1978), both areas of high biological productivity, would lend support to this conclusion.

7

Sub-surface Deposits

Sub-sea floor mineral deposits have been mined intermittently on continental shelves for many years, mostly from shafts sunk on the adjacent land areas. As the continental shelf is a natural extension of the land, mineral deposits occurring near coastal areas can, in some instances, be expected to extend offshore. Mining these deposits from land presents no great difficulties so long as the deposits do not occur too far offshore or too near the sea floor. Problems of mine ventilation and transport become severe if the lateral shafts are too long, and flooding of the workings becomes a problem if they are not buried sufficiently. By contrast, sub-surface mineral deposits have never been mined in the deep sea. Indeed, their occurrence under the deep-sea floor has yet to be proved, although analogies with certain rock sequences on land suggest that sulphide minerals probably do occur there.

7.1 Continental Shelves and Lakes

7.1.1 Coal

The most important and longest mined offshore bedded deposit is coal, first recovered more than 350 years ago off Scotland where a shaft was sunk from an artificial island (Austin, 1967). Many areas where coal is mined on land contain coal seams offshore. In Japan, for example, by 1972 undersea coal production had accounted for 38% of the total coal production, and the world's total sub-sea floor coal production at that time was about 30 million tonnes.

Offshore coal mining in Japan dates back to 1860 when mining offshore was extended off the coast of western Kyushu. Since then, many more undersea coal seams have been found off eastern Hokkaido and western Kyushu, with over 300 million tonnes of proven coal reserves recoverable (Wang and McKelvey, 1976). Workings extend to more than 5 km offshore.

Coal mining from seams under the UK continental shelf commenced during the last century, and some of the mines have reached 6·4 km out to sea (Dunham and Sheppard, 1969). Offshore drilling carried out in the 1960s indicated reserves in the order of 550 million tonnes off the coasts of Durham and Northumberland alone.

Undersea coal deposits are known from many other continental shelf areas. In the future, an increasing proportion of the world's coal supply may come from offshore areas. *In situ* gasification and other methods of extraction without transporting the coal may be used in the future to utilize coal deposits presently beyond the limits of sub-sea underground mining (Wang and McKelvey, 1976).

7.1.2   Metallic minerals

Many metallic minerals are known to occur in rocks underlying the continental shelf areas of various countries. These are mostly extensions offshore of mineral deposits which have been exploited on land.

The tin ores off Cornwall in the United Kingdom are one of the best known examples of offshore mineralization. According to Dunham and Sheppard (1969), many of the lodes were found because they outcropped in cliff faces, and some of the mines started as open cuts or by driving adits into the cliffs. Some of these lodes were followed out to sea, as, for example, in the Botallack and Levant mines in the St Just-Lands End district (Fig. 62). Many other lodes in the region may also extend offshore. Favourable areas include the St Agnes-Perranporth district, and south of the Godolphin Granite in the Marazion-Porthleven area. According to Dunham (1969), there is good evidence that the belt of granite plutons with which the tin lodes are associated extends westwards past the Scilly Isles to perhaps 160 km out to sea. Thus, there is no reason why the mineral belt should not continue for this distance too, although this would be difficult to prove as it would pass beneath Cretaceous sediments.

Iron is another metal which has been recovered offshore. The Jussaro Island Mine off Finland and mines off the island of Elba, and off Cockatoo Island in Australia, are examples. Sub-sea iron deposits also occur off Bell Island, Newfoundland (Wang and McKelvey, 1976). The ore in the Jussaro Mine, which is magnetite, was discovered by magnetic methods, and was subsequently developed from shafts both on the mainland and from an island (Dunham, 1969). Hematite occurs in the south Cumberland-Furness iron ore field in the UK, and the last operating mine, at Hodbarrow, extracted ore beneath the estuary of the River Duddon (Dunham and

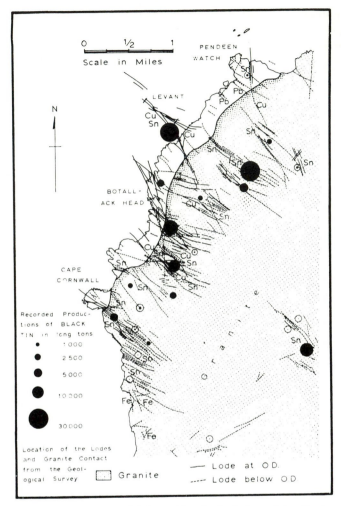

Fig. 62. Positions of past and potential tin workings in the St Just mining district of Cornwall (from Dunham and Sheppard, 1969; after Garnett).

Sheppard, 1969) where it was necessary to build a sea wall to protect the workings. Additional deposits may occur offshore.

7.1.3 Evaporites

Evaporites occur under a number of continental shelf areas. Under the North Sea for example, Upper Permian Zechstein salt deposits occur, in places thickened to thousands of metres in salt pillows and domes (Kent 1966, reported in Dunham, 1969). Dunham (1969) believed that potash seams might also be present. However, the deposits are unlikely to be of any great economic interest in view of the large land based reserves of evaporites.

7.1.4 Sulphur

Sulphur deposits are associated with salt domes in the Gulf of Mexico. One such deposit occurs under about 620 m of sediments 11·2 km seawards of Grand Isle, Louisiana. It covers an area of more than 1 km², and varies from 67–129 m in thickness (Mero, 1965). The deposit has been mined using a modification of the Frasch process, which involves pumping heated sea water down into the deposit to melt the sulphur. The latter is then forced up a pipe to the surface. Sulphur probably occurs associated with other salt domes in the offshore area, as about 10% of those drilled on land have been found to have associated sulphur deposits (Mero, 1965).

7.1.5 Sub-lacustrine minerals

Extensively mineralized areas on land which are covered by large numbers of lakes, such as the Canadian Shield and the Baltic Shield, almost certainly contain mineral deposits in the rocks underlying the lakes. One such example has been outlined in the Great Lakes. There is evidence that copper deposits occurring on the Keweenaw Peninsula, Lake Superior, may extend in bedrock offshore. Geophysical and sampling work carried out by the University of Wisconsin has indicated some specific target areas where prospects for bedrock mineralization appear to be quite good (Nebrija et al., 1976).

7.2 The Deep Sea Floor

The prevalent view on the origin of mid-ocean ridge basalts, which comprise most of the deep ocean floor underlying sediments, is that they are formed by partial melting of mantle material between 30 and 100 km depth below the sea floor, and at temperatures of 1250–1300°C (Sleep, 1975). Ringwood (1966) has estimated that when 20 to 40% melting of the mantle has occurred, liquids will separate from it, but this may be a slight over-estimation (J. R. Cann, personal communication, 1979). Czamanske and Moore (1977) consider that this early formed melt contains virtually all of the sulphur in that part of the mantle being melted, and conclude that as increasing amounts of silicate melt are formed, sulphide melt will be continually dissolving into it. On this basis, and assuming 0.03% as the concentration of S in the mantle (Ringwood, 1966), and 0.08% as the juvenile sulphur content of basalt (Moore and Fabbi, 1971), Czamanske and Moore (1977) consider that the basalt liquid melted from the mantle may contain a sulphide melt phase until 37.5% of the mantle source region has been melted. On the basis of paragenetic relationships in DSDP Leg 34 basalts, Mathez and Yeats (1976) believe that a sulphide liquid phase existed in the basaltic magma prior to eruption. Similar conclusions have been reached by Czamanske and Moore (1977) who considered that this is the usual situation associated with the eruption of submarine basalt. They believe that the bulk of this sulphur is in solid solution in basaltic glass, but that up to 1.5% of the sulphur is contained in immiscible sulphide globules.

7.2.1 Magmatic sulphide globules

Sulphide globules in ocean floor basalts, which range in diameter from 5 to 500 μm, have been investigated by several workers (e.g. Moore and Calk, 1971; Mathez, 1976). They contain considerable amounts of Ni and Cu as monosulphide solid solution and intermediate solid solution, together with some pentlandite (Czamanske and Moore, 1977). These authors consider that the globules may have persisted in the basaltic melt since partial melting of mantle material, or may have exsolved as the melt became sulphur saturated in a high-level magma chamber. About one-third of the Cu and commensurate amounts of S, Ni, and Fe from the magma are thought to have been involved in globule formation in the samples studied by Czamanske and Moore (1977). However, only one globule, ranging between 30 and 270 μm was found per 6.1 cm^2 in these samples, the globules averaging only 0.0036% of the material analysed.

A detailed study of sulphide globules has been made in DSDP Leg 37 drill cores from the Mid-Atlantic Ridge by MacLean (1977). Globules composed of pyrrhotite, chalcopyrite and pentlandite were found in basalt glass, fine-grained basalt, gabbro and peridotite. The globules in the basalt glass were all less than 8 μm in diameter, but those in the gabbro and peridotite were larger, up to 150 μm in diameter, and in them the sulphide minerals were frequently cleanly separated from each other. The Ni and Cu contents of the sulphides in these cores are similar to those found in sulphide globules in basalt by other workers, and their grade and Ni/Cu ratios are also similar to magmatic sulphide ores from Sudbury, Canada and Noril'sk, USSR, found in association with gabbroic and noritic rocks. The sulphides in the DSDP Leg 37 cores would not, of course, in themselves, constitute an ore deposit as they are not nearly abundant enough. However, their

composition does indicate the presence of Ni and Cu in the right proportions to form ore bodies should a mechanism be available for concentrating
and segregating the sulphide minerals.

7.2.2 Disseminated and vein sulphides

In addition to sulphide globules, the DSDP Leg 37 basalts described above,
and many other samples of deep sea basalts contain disseminated and/or
vein sulphide, mostly pyrite. In the Leg 37 samples, pyrite represents about
99% of the sulphide minerals present, and occurs as vesicle fillings, fracture
linings and as mineral coatings comprising about 0·49% of the basalt samples
analysed. It has a close spatial distribution with smectite, calcite and other
alteration minerals, and represents a post magmatic mineral formed during
hydrothermal alteration of the basalt (MacLean, 1977).

Sulphide mineralization has been reported in other rocks from mid-ocean
ridges. Dmitriev et al. (1970) have reported sulphide occurrences in rocks
from the Carlsberg Ridge. Bonatti et al. (1976a) have described Fe-Cu sulphide mineralization in metabasalts from the equatorial Mid-Atlantic Ridge
which offers direct evidence of redistribution of metals within the oceanic
crust. The mineralization occurred in metabasalts from 0°56·6′S, 24°30·8′W
close to the intersection of the Romanche Offset Zone with the western
axial segment of the Mid-Atlantic Ridge, and in metabasalts from 10°51′N,
41°48′W on the northern wall of the Vema Fracture Zone. The Romanche
Offset Zone samples contain sulphide mineralization in veins generally less
than 1 mm thick and as isolated aggregates disseminated within the rock.
The mineral assemblage consists of pyrrhotite and pyrite scattered in the
microcrystalline basaltic matrix, and chalcopyrite in veins. The main sulphide phase in the Vema Fracture Zone samples is chalcopyrite, commonly
rimmed by a thin alteration zone of Fe hydroxide. According to Bonatti
et al. (1976a), these two examples of Fe-Cu mineralization resemble the
"stockwork" and "disseminated" mineralization found in sulphide ore
bodies on land and probably precipitated from hydrothermal solutions
which circulated through fractures in the oceanic crust, leaching out sulphur
and metals on passage and deriving additional sulphur from the reduction
of sea water sulphate.

7.2.3 Massive sulphide deposits: the example of Cyprus

To date massive sulphide deposits have not been found on the ocean floor
but as discussed in Chapter 6 there are several indications that they are
present. Some of the most powerful evidence for this comes from the study

of sulphide deposits associated with ophiolite sequences on land, one of the best described of which is probably that in Cyprus.

Ophiolite sequences are vertical successions of basic and ultrabasic rocks overlain by marine sediments and are generally considered to represent fragments of ancient ocean floor, now emplaced on land. However, whether or not they are truly representative of modern ocean floor has not been established. They have been found in many parts of the world including Italy, Newfoundland, and Cyprus. Bonatti *et al.* (1976c), for example, have described ophiolites in the northern Appenines of Italy in which metalliferous sediments occur in chert formations directly overlying basalts in a manner analogous to that of metalliferous sediments on modern spreading centres. Iron and copper ore deposits occur within the basalts, pyrite and chalcopyrite being the main minerals present.

As mentioned, probably one of the most intensively studied ophiolites and associated mineralization is in Cyprus, in the Troodos Massif (Constantinou and Govett, 1972; Elderfield *et. al.*, 1972; Robertson and Hudson, 1973; Robertson, 1975; Spooner, 1977). Metalliferous sediments consisting of Fe-rich, Mn-poor "ochres" are intimately associated with sulphide ores within a basaltic lava sequence, and Mn-rich "umbers" overlie the lavas. The similarity of these deposits to modern mid-ocean ridge metalliferous sediments is one reason why massive sulphide deposits similar to those in Cyprus are thought to form underneath metalliferous sediments within the modern ocean crust.

The upper Cretaceous ophiolitic sequence of the Troodos Massif in Cyprus actually contains, not just one, but approximately 20 cupriferous pyrite hydrothermal ore bodies. The deposits consist, in general, of lens shaped bodies of massive sulphide ore (pyrite and chalcopyrite with showings of sphalerite, marcasite and galena) semi-conformably intercalated within pillow lavas, and underlain by a stockwork which extends down into a sheeted dyke complex, itself indicative of formation at a spreading ridge (Spooner, 1977; Parmentier and Spooner, 1978). Fluid inclusion, stable isotope and other geochemical studies suggest that the deposits formed within the discharge zones of hydrothermal circulation systems in which sea water was the convecting fluid (Fig. 63), deriving its metals from alteration of the rocks through which it passed and its sulphur from the same source and sulphate reduction (Spooner, 1977; Spooner and Bray, 1977; Heaton and Sheppard, 1977; Parmentier and Spooner, 1978). These studies lend further support to the belief that the Cyprus deposits are the ancient analogues of deposits which may be forming under modern spreading centres.

If we accept that the Cyprus ore deposits described above are the analogues of the assumed modern massive sulphide deposits within the oceanic crust,

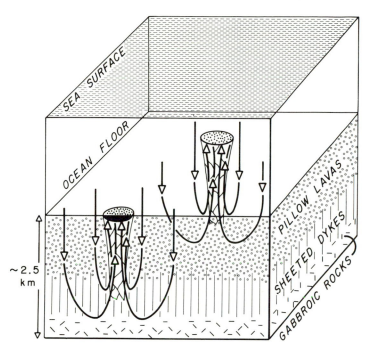

Fig. 63. Schematic three-dimensional diagram of the geologically inferred mode of hydrothermal convection, metamorphism and mineralization within the upper Cretaceous ophiolitic sequence of the Troodos Massif, Cyprus. General metamorphism is thought to have occurred in the zones of recharge flow, whereas the cupriferous pyrite ore deposits are thought to have formed at the positions of discharge of approximately axially symmetric plumes of rising hot fluid of sea water origin. (From Spooner, 1980.)

certain features of the former can tell us about the likely nature and occurrence of the latter. According to Parmentier and Spooner (1978), and Spooner (1978) the following features are of relevance:

(a) The stockworks beneath the massive ore are approximately elliptical or sub-circular in cross-section, suggesting that the geometry of discharge consisted of axially symmetical jets of hot fluid.

(b) The upper part of the rock sequence, including the pillow lavas and the sheeted dykes, shows evidence of alteration to a depth of 2–3 km, a value consistent with the supposed depth of sea water circulation under modern mid-ocean ridge spreading centres, and not inconsistent with sea water being the hydrothermal fluid from which the deposits were formed.

(c) The sulphide ore bodies are distributed fairly regularly along the northern pillow lava outcrop of the Troodos Massif at an approximate spacing of $2 \cdot 6 \pm 1 \cdot 4$ km, suggesting that the hydrothermal plumes were separated by a distance similar to the thickness of the permeable layer. This would be consistent with a convective model for their origin.

(d) The radii of mineralized stockworks is about one-tenth of the mean half spacing between ore deposits, and their depth is about 200 m. The tonnages of the different ore bodies are generally comparable, about 3·5–4 million tonnes each, suggesting that a similar quantity of fluid flowed upward at each discharge centre.

(e) Homogenization temperatures of fluid inclusions in three of the Cyprus mineralized stockworks suggest that the temperature of the rising hydrothermal plumes was 300–350°C. This is in good agreement with a value of about 300°C estimated for the temperature of the Galapagos Ridge axis hydrothermal fluid prior to discharge (Edmond, 1978) and is consistent with the more than 300°C maximum measured in hydrothermal plumes discharging on the East Pacific Rise at 21°N (section 6.4.1.8).

Cann (1979) has reviewed the likely availability of sulphide ores in the oceanic crust, both on the basis of the Troodos Massif examples and the sequence of rock types found on modern mid-ocean ridges. He pointed out that, at or near the sea floor, sulphide deposit formation would only be likely to take place within the axial region of a mid-ocean ridge because it is only in such a situation that temperatures would be high enough. However, sulphides precipitated on the sea floor at a spreading axis would soon be covered by later lava flows. Cann estimated that perhaps one deposit in every 100 km of ridge axis, or some 500 deposits along the whole of the World Mid-Ocean Ridge System, might be exposed on the sea floor at any one time. The remainder would be buried to increasing depths by successive lava flows as they moved away from the spreading axis under the influence of sea floor spreading.

On the basis of observations and concepts such as those reviewed in the previous paragraphs, and most importantly, assuming comparability of ophiolite associated massive sulphides with those thought to be forming at modern spreading centres, we might expect to find sulphide deposits every few kilometres along the axis of the World Mid-Ocean Ridge system, but perhaps only one every 100 km or so exposed at the surface.

8

Interrelation between Sub-sea Mineral Deposits and their Relationship to Ocean Evolution

So far in this book, different types of underwater mineral deposits have been considered as separate entities. In this chapter I propose to explore some of the interrelationships between the deposits to determine to what extent they have features in common. In any such discussion, an understanding of the relationship of the deposits to various stages of ocean evolution is necessary, as well as being of considerable importance in its own right, and therefore this topic will be discussed first.

8.1 Ocean Evolution

Ocean evolution was introduced briefly in Chapter 1, but now requires fuller treatment. Blissenbach and Fellerer (1973) have described five stages of ocean evolution of relevance to mineral forming processes on the sea floor. These are the early and advanced graben stages prior to continental break-up, and the early, advanced and late continental drift stages.

The development of a new ocean basin commences with the early graben stage (Fig. 64a) characterized by tensional faulting. Possible modern examples of this include the East African Rift and the Basin and Range Province of the United States. The central blocks of the graben subside while the margins rise to give a long valley bounded by steep walls. The deposits accumulating within the graben depend upon the climate and relief, and are predominantly clastic. In arid regions, coarse-grained alluvial fans occur at the foot of the flanking uplands, whereas in more humid climates the graben is often the site of major river and lake systems. Volcanic activity

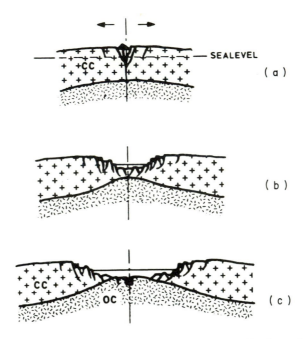

Fig. 64. Early stages of ocean evolution: (a) early graben stage; (b) advanced graben stage; (c) early drift stage. cc = continental crust, oc = oceanic crust (from Blissenbach and Fellerer, 1973).

is widespread in grabens, giving rise to the large thicknesses of volcanic rock sometimes interbedded with sediment.

According to Blissenbach and Fellerer (1973) the advanced graben stage is reached when sea water enters the rift and floods it (Fig. 64b). This gives rise to narrow elongated seas flanked by elevated areas. Evaporite deposition is common during the advanced graben stage of ocean evolution, especially in low latitudes, as is demonstrated by the large thicknesses of Miocene evaporites flanking the Red Sea. The margins of the North Atlantic are also thought to contain evaporite deposits considered to have been formed when the Atlantic was at an early stage of rifting (Pautot et al., 1970). Other characteristic sediments of the advanced graben stage include coarse clastics derived from the adjacent land area, organic-rich reducing sediments where basin topography or other factors lead to stagnation, and the products of volcanic activity.

Blissenbach and Fellerer (1973) define the early drift stage of ocean evolution as beginning when the continental crust is torn apart and sea floor spreading begins (Fig. 64c). The basin is then divided into a marginal area underlain by continental crust and a central rift underlain by oceanic crust.

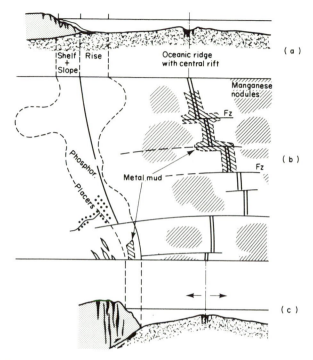

Fig. 65. Middle and late stages of ocean evolution: (a) advanced drift stage; (b) distribution of mineral deposits in an ocean basin at the advanced drift stage; (c) late drift stage (modified from Blissenbach and Fellerer, 1973).

The modern Red Sea is a good example of an ocean basin in its early drift stage, in which new sea floor is being created by the extrusion of fresh basalts in the central rift zone.

The early drift stage grades into the advanced drift stage by continued continental separation. The central rift of the early drift stage gradually changes to a mid-ocean ridge as the older sea floor away from the spreading centre cools and subsides (Fig. 65a). The modern Atlantic Ocean can be taken as an example of the advanced drift stage of ocean evolution. Normal pelagic sedimentation processes prevail, with terrigenous deposits abundant near the continents and a volcanic input of material near the mid-ocean ridge.

The late drift stage occurs when crustal plates generated at different spreading centres collide and subduction occurs (Fig. 65c). A good example of subduction resulting from the collision of oceanic and continental crust is to be found along the western margin of South America, whereas subduction associated with the collision of two oceanic plates is thought to occur in the south western Pacific.

8.2   Mineral Deposits Associated with Various Stages of Ocean Evolution

Of the various mineral deposits found on the sea floor, the occurrence of some can be related to specific stages of ocean evolution. By contrast others appear to bear no relationship to ocean evolution at all. Amongst the latter can be included aggregates and placers and some minor authigenic minerals. These minerals can occur in lakes, rivers and in near-shore areas during both early and advanced stages of ocean evolution. They will not therefore be considered further in the present context. Of the remaining minerals, metalliferous sediments can form during all stages of ocean evolution but the varieties change as ocean evolution proceeds, while manganese nodules and phosphorites only form in abundance during one stage of ocean evolution.

8.2.1   The early stage of ocean evolution

During the Early and Late Graben stages of ocean evolution, volcanic activity can be expected to give rise to both epigenetic and syngenetic ore deposits. Epigenetic deposits would be formed in veins in both the walls and floor of a volcanically active graben structure, and stratiform deposits may form in lakes on the graben floor on precipitation from hydrothermal fluids.

Examples of the latter are rare, possibly because few lakes in active grabens are known, and those studied such as the ones in East Africa are rather remote and inaccessible. Nevertheless, Degens *et al.* (1972) have reported the formation of sphalerite globules within the waters of Lake Kivu in East Africa, which, coupled with locally high heat flow values, was thought to indicate a hydrothermal souce for the zinc. Mineral rich solutions and high heat flow also occur in the Salton Sea, California, a large lake sitting above the supposed extension of the East Pacific Rise under the head of the Gulf of California (Elders *et al.*, 1972).

Undoubtedly the best known examples of mineral deposits associated with the early drift stage of ocean evolution are those in the Red Sea, already described in Chapter 6. There, a combination of volcanic activity, hydrothermal leaching of basalts and possibly other rocks such as black shale, and the discharge of the resulting solutions into restricted basins with fractional precipitation of their metals, results in a complex sequence of deposits. Faulting associated with the rifting of the basin may be largely responsible for the siting of the brine and metalliferous sediment-filled deeps at their present locations (Bignell, 1975b).

The occurrence of hydrothermal mineral deposits in the Red Sea associated with the early drift stage of ocean evolution implies that other similar deposits should occur along the margins of older ocean basins, but are either deeply buried by more recent sediments or thrust up on to the continents if continental collision has taken place. To date, no such deposits have been found around the margins of modern oceans, which are Mesozoic to Tertiary in age. However, some Palaeozoic deposits thought to be of this type have been found on land, possibly as a result of thrusting associated with continental collision (Sillitoe, 1978). The possibility of finding Red Sea type deposits underlying rifted continental margins surrounding modern oceans is quite likely, if deep drilling is employed. Characteristically, very great thicknesses of sediment occur at such margins, which have not yet been penetrated to basement.

According to Blissenbach and Fellerer (1973) the early North Atlantic probably exhibited conditions suitable for the generation of metalliferous muds of the Red Sea type. These conditions would have included concentrated hydrothermal activity in a narrow central rift zone within a trough closed at both ends, and deeps resulting from tectonic activity. The most likely areas for the occurrence of such metalliferous sediments were thought to be those closest to the continental margins, especially those adjacent to areas of evaporite formation.

That the formation of Red Sea type deposits has occurred in the Atlantic is indicated at DSDP 105 in the western North Atlantic. At this site there is about 50 m of multi-coloured sediments of probable Mesozoic age containing abundant Mn and Fe oxides together with sphalerite and pyrite. These deposits resemble the metalliferous sediments of the Red Sea both in appearance and composition, although they are of lower grade, but are not directly comparable to them stratigraphically for they occur overlying 350 m of Mesozoic sediments. Nevertheless their formation during an early stage of the evolution of the Atlantic Ocean does suggest that a more detailed search for such deposits around the margins of this ocean and in other rifted continental margin areas, might find additional examples.

8.2.2 Mature stage of ocean evolution

The mature stage of ocean evolution is characterized by a wide ocean with a well developed mid-ocean ridge flanked by broad areas of pelagic sedimentation (Fig. 65). All three major oceans fulfil these criteria. Excluding placers, three types of mineral deposit are associated with mature ocean basins, a continuation of metalliferous sediment formation carried over from the early stage of ocean evolution, phosphorite formation, and manganese nodule formation (Fig. 65b).

8.2.2.1 *Metalliferous sediments*

The bulk of metalliferous sediments found to date on mature mid-ocean ridges differ from those in the Red Sea in several respects, particularly in their normal lack of sulphides. Their hydrothermal constituents probably largely represent material flushed out of hydrothermal vents as fine-grained particulates, although some precipitation of residual species in solution such as manganese is also likely. Transport and mixing of such constituents by bottom currents prior to their precipitation can probably account for their relative homogeneity over large areas of mid-ocean ridges. However, as discussed in section 6.7.2, given suitable depositional conditions, there is no reason why high grade metalliferous sediments containing sulphides should not occur on the sea floor in areas such as fracture zones or in locally restricted areas.

Notwithstanding their relative homogeneity compared with Red Sea sediments and the anomalous mid-ocean ridge sediments described in Chapter 6, the composition of the bulk of mid-ocean metalliferous sediments is not entirely uniform.

Comparison of the average concentrations of certain elements in modern ridge crest metalliferous sediments from different oceans (Cronan, 1974) demonstrates that there are inter-ocean compositional differences between the deposits. Those from the East Pacific Rise are the most metalliferous and those from the Mid-Atlantic Ridge the least so. In addition comparison of the composition of basal metalliferous sediments of different ages demonstrates large compositional differences and differences in metal accumulation rates (Cronan, 1976a; Leinen and Stakes, 1979). Both the inter-ocean and intra-ocean comparisons demonstrate a correlation between the iron content of the sediments and the spreading rate of the sea floor at the time that they were formed (Bostrom, 1973; Cronan, 1974, 1976a), with the most iron-rich sediments being formed on the fastest spreading ridges. This correlation may be due to the composition of volcanic solutions being related to the rate of spreading of the ridge. Fast spreading ridges such as the East Pacific Rise are more active than slow spreading ridges such as the Mid-Atlantic Ridge in terms of the generation of new oceanic crust, and the rate at which ocean crust is generated could influence the composition of the metalliferous sediments, as described below. However, variations in the input of terrigenous materials which varies from ocean to ocean, and which has probably varied in the past, can also affect the bulk composition of mid-ocean ridge metalliferous sediments by their dilutive effect.

Scott (1978) has suggested a structural control on differences in the composition of sediments from fast and slow spreading ridges. According to Scott (1978), fast spreading ridges are characterized by fewer and more widely spaced fractures than the slow spreading ridges, which means that the surface area of rock exposed to circulating sea water is lower on fast than on slow spreading ridges. It follows from this that the water/rock ratio will be lower on slow spreading ridges than on fast spreading ridges, which in turn will influence the chemistry of the solutions formed by rock/water interaction (section 6.2). Where there are low water/rock ratios, i.e. in rock dominated systems on slow spreading ridges, the chemical reactions that take place result in smaller amounts of metals being taken into solution than in water dominated systems on fast spreading ridges, and thus smaller amounts of metals are available for precipitation on discharge of the solutions on the sea floor. Furthermore, those metals taken into solution on slow spreading ridges during early stages of circulation when a water dominated system, might, for a period, prevail, will probably be precipitated before discharge on to the sea floor due to the increasing pH as the water/rock ratio changes towards that of a rock dominated system. Thus not only might variations in the water/rock ratio be one explanation for average differences in the bulk composition of metalliferous sediments between the fast spreading East Pacific Rise, the intermediately spreading Central Indian Ocean Ridge and the slow spreading Mid-Atlantic Ridge, but they might also help to determine possible variations in the nature of sub-sea floor precipitates from hydrothermal solutions under different ridges, and thus the relative as well as the absolute amounts of metals available for discharge into sea water.

8.2.2.2 Phosphorites

Although they are continental margin deposits, phosphorites occur principally at the margins of mature ocean basins (Chapter 4) and are thought to be formed largely as a result of upwelling associated with a well developed current system. Immature ocean basins at an early stage of drifting do not have such well developed current systems as mature ocean basins and thus would be unlikely to exhibit upwelling on the scale required for phosphorite formation. On this basis, therefore, phosphorites can be considered to be a product of a mature stage of ocean evolution, rather than just happening to occur around the margins of mature ocean basins.

There are only two areas of the world where phosphorite is known to be forming at present, off Peru and Chile and off south-west Africa. Both of these areas exhibit strong upwelling associated with a predominantly northward moving current system. Other phosphorite deposits along the western margins of the continents were formed in the past, possibly under current systems more intense than those presently found in these areas. Changes in the nature of currents could result from plate movements leading to the changing configuration of mature ocean basins with time, which in turn would influence the locations of phosphorite formation. In the Atlantic Ocean, for example, the extensive bedded phosphorites found off north-west Africa commenced deposition in the Cretaceous and finished forming in the Tertiary (Summerhayes, 1970; McArthur, 1974). The configuration of the Atlantic and perhaps other factors must have been conducive to intense upwelling leading to the phosphorite formation in that area at that time, and have since changed. Detailed reconstruction of the palaeo-oceanography of past phosphorite forming areas would be a way of testing such a hypothesis.

8.2.2.3   *Manganese nodules*

Manganese nodules are the characteristic and by far the most abundant mineral deposit on the floors of mature ocean basins. They occur in greatest quantities on the broad undulating areas between mid-ocean ridge systems and the abyssal plains which border the continental margins in areas without a marginal trench system.

Certain of the prerequisites for extensive ferromanganese oxide deposition reviewed in Chapter 5 are common only in mature ocean basins. For example, they require highly oxidizing conditions in which to grow; this necessitates free bottom-water circulation which is characteristic of large deep ocean basins. In small ocean basins like the Black Sea or the Red Sea which are enclosed or restricted, ferromanganese oxide deposits either do not form at all or only form around the oxidizing margins of the basin. As the deposits precipitate from sea water, they also require low rates of deposition of associated sediments to enable them to accumulate to any great extent. Apart from some rare areas near desert coastlines or on marginal topographic elevations, such conditions are only met in the deep ocean basins far from land. Furthermore, most deep ocean nodules probably accumulate slowly and thus would have required long periods of stable conditions to reach their present abundance in areas such as the north-east equatorial Pacific. Such conditions would be unlikely to prevail during the early drift stage of ocean evolution.

In general, the volume of ferromanganese oxides deposited within an ocean basin is time-dependent, and thus will increase as the ocean matures. For example, Cronan (1967) observed thin manganese encrustations on rocks from the crest of the Carlsberg Ridge, but thicker encrustations on rocks on its older flanks. Similarly Aumento *et al.* (1968) found manganese encrustations to thicken away from the axis of the Mid-Atlantic Ridge in a regular manner as the sea floor aged, implying time-dependent growth at a rather constant rate by precipitation from sea water. Although nodules and encrustations have been reported on the East Pacific Rise, they are quantitatively much less abundant than in the older basins to the west, again implying time-dependent deposition. Nevertheless, it should not be thought that the nodules we find in abyssal regions far from the mid-ocean ridges commenced their growth at the ridge and thus are of the same age as the basement underlying the sediments on which they rest. Nodules probably only grow to a finite size dependent on their bottom environment, before they are buried or break up (Chapter 5; Bender *et al.*, 1966; Heye, 1975), and thus most nodules are probably very much younger than the underlying basement.

8.2.3   Late stages of ocean evolution

The late stage of ocean evolution is characterized by the consumption of plate margins by subduction. The fate of sea floor mineral deposits actually on sub- duction will be the subject of the next section. Here, deposits formed on the sea floor during the late drift stage of ocean evolution will be considered.

Mineral formation on the sea floor during the late drift stage of ocean evolution can be associated with the collision of two plate margins com- posed of oceanic crust. Under these conditions, a volcanically active island arc can form (Fig. 66) in which some of the volcanic activity will be on the

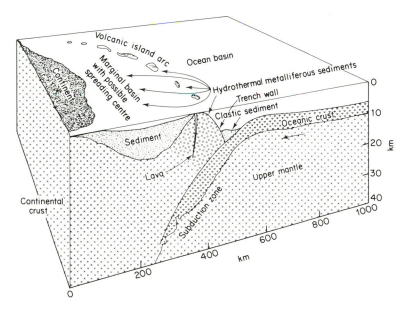

Fig. 66. Island arc and trench with possible locations of metalliferous sediments.

sea floor in the arc and some associated with back arc basin spreading centres. This can give rise to submarine metalliferous sediments in the same way as during the early and mature drift stages of ocean evolution (Fig. 66). Examples of such deposits have been described from the Banu Wuhu Volcano, Indonesia, the Lau Basin and Matupi Harbour, at the Indian–Pacific Plate Boundary (Chapter 6), and from Santorini and Vulcano in the Mediterranean (Smith and Cronan, 1975; Honnorez, 1969). The conditions required for the formation of such deposits are similar to those during the early and mature stages of ocean evolution (Chapter 6).

8.2.4   Fate of sea floor mineral deposits on subduction

Of the various types of mineral deposit found on or under the sea floor, only those on sediments associated with oceanic crust, or within the crust itself, namely metalliferous sediments, manganese nodules, some minor authigenics, and sub-deep sea floor deposits, are liable to subduction. Placers, aggregates and phosphorites occurring on continental shelves and margins should not become involved in the subduction process.

Sub-sea floor mineral deposits such as sulphides together with metalliferous sediments formed at mid-ocean ridges and directly overlying basement are most susceptible to subduction in trench zones. Sillitoe (1972) has suggested that porphyry copper ores in orogenic belts bordering subductive plate boundaries, such as in the Andes, may result from partial melting of subducted ocean crust and the metalliferous sediments on it. However, some of the latter may be scraped off on to the overriding plate or take part in diagenetic reactions prior to the subduction leading to the return of some of their metals to the sea floor and thus to the ocean system. On this basis, sub-sea floor mineral deposits would be permanently lost to the ocean system on subduction, to be compensated for by new deposits forming under mid-ocean ridges. By contrast sea floor metalliferous sediments may be only partially lost with some components of them, particularly their manganese oxides (see below) and associated metals, being returned to the sea floor.

The fate of at least some metals in manganese nodules in and near trench zones will be quite different from that of mineral deposits contained within the oceanic crust. Ferromanganese oxide minerals are diagenetically unstable on burial under anything but the most highly oxidizing conditions, and thus buried examples of them have only been commonly found in oxidized slowly accumulating pelagic sediment sequences on the deep ocean floor. On translation towards active continental margins as a result of sea floor spreading, off South America for example, nodules will become buried by increasing amounts of detrital sediments from the continent and organic sediments possibly formed by continental margin upwelling. Reducing conditions will be encountered at shallow depth within the sediments and will lead to the eventual dissolution of the nodules. The manganese will return to the sediment surface to precipitate as manganese-rich diagenetic nodules commonly found seawards of the trench system in the eastern Pacific (Mero, 1965; Appendix, this volume). However, once the trench system itself is reached, the Eh at the sediment surface will probably be too low to permit even the formation of diagenetic manganese-rich continental margin nodules and the manganese together with some associated metals should be returned to sea water. By contrast, where manganese nodules approach a trench system at the margin of two oceanic plates, as in the south-western Pacific for example, burial of nodules is less likely. Nodules found seawards of the Tonga-Kermadec Trench, for example, do not exhibit the diagenetic features of their south-east Pacific counterparts. Nevertheless, once they enter the trench system, if they survive that long, rapid sedimentation should soon bury the nodules and lead to their dissolution. On dissolution, some of the metals in the nodules such as Fe, Si, Al, and perhaps some minor metals too, could remain fixed in the buried sediments as sulphides or other minerals, eventually to be subducted, but most of the manganese should always eventually return to the sea floor. On this basis therefore, sedimentary manganese would appear not to be a subductable element in the oceans and must have been continually accumulating in the ocean basins throughout geological time. This may well account for the observed higher concentration of manganese in oceanic sediments than in most other units of the earth's crust, which has intrigued geochemists since first noted over one hundred years ago.

Because the deep sea floor is normally subducted, examples of it are only rarely preserved on the continents and thus deep sea mineral deposits are hardly ever found in the stratigraphic record. Metalliferous sediments associated with ophiolites are an exception to this general rule, but these are rare and some may not be true deep ocean floor deposits but have originated in ancient continental margin areas now incorporated into continental land masses. True deep sea manganese nodules are very rare in ancient sediments. Both the subduction of the sea floor on which they rest and their diagenetic instability would mitigate against their preservation. For the latter reason, even continental margin and lacustrine nodules rarely survive deep burial to be entombed in ancient sediments. The survival of the known examples required exceptional conditions which have been well documented by Jenkyns (1977).

8.3   Deposit Interrelationships

The existence of the main mineral deposits, aggregates, placers, phosphorites, metalliferous sediments and manganese nodules, for the most part separated in space on the ocean floor, implies a general lack of relationship between them. This, however, is not necessarily so in all cases. Detrital deposits such as placers and aggregates appear to have little in common with the other deposits, and probably exhibit no relationship to them, at least no chemical relationship. They are therefore again excluded from the ensuing discussion. However, certain relationships can be drawn between manganese nodules, metalliferous sediments and phosphorites which have a bearing on the genesis of these deposits and this will form the subject of the remainder of this chapter.

8.3.1   Phosphorite-ferromanganese oxide interrelationships

A physical interrelationship between phosphorite and manganese nodules has been observed on the Campbell Pleatear (Summerhayes, 1967a) and on the Blake Plateau (Pratt and McFarlin, 1966; Manheim, 1972), amongst other places. The phosphorite sometimes acts as a nucleus for ferromanganese oxide deposition, and in some instances the two phases are inter-layered and intergrown.

Chemical interrelationships between phosphorus and ferromanganese oxide compounds have been noted by Winterhalter (1966), Winterhalter and Siivola (1967) and Glasby (1970). Nodules from near-shore environments are richer in phosphorus than are their deep water counterparts, and, in general, the phosphorus is concentrated in the iron-rich phases. The possibility exists that a ferric phosphate phase may form but Winterhalter and Siivola (1967) noted that there was more iron in the concretions that they examined than could be accommodated in ferric phosphate. They suggested that phosphorus in these concretions was more likely to occur as a result of the scavenging by ferric hydroxide of the PO_4^{3-} anion than due to its precipitation as ferric phosphate.

The occurrence of phosphorus in mid-ocean ridge metalliferous sediments has been reviewed by Calvert (1978). Berner (1973) found it to be enriched in East Pacific Rise sediments and to be accumulating rapidly, but concluded that it was of sea water rather than hydrothermal origin. Froelich et al. (1977) more or less confirmed these observations. Its enrichment may be due to the scavenging effect of the freshly precipitated iron and manganese oxides in ridge crest sediments, and in this regard it may be acting in a similar way to some of the minor metals enriched in these sediments (Chapter 6).

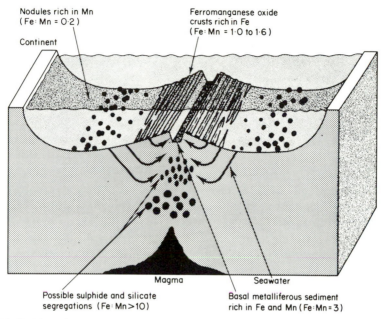

Fig. 67. Fe/Mn ratios in the ferromanganese continuum and associated deposits.

8.3.2 Manganese nodule-metalliferous sediment interrelationships

As will be evident from Chapters 5 and 6, manganese nodules, encrustations and metalliferous sediments have a considerable number of differences. However, they do exhibit a more or less continuous range of compositions. If the deposits are considered solely in terms of their Fe/Mn ratio (Fig. 67) it is evident that, in general, the ratio is highest in early formed metalliferous sediments such as in the sulphide, silicate and oxide deposits in the Atlantis II Deep of the Red Sea (sections 6.3.2 and 6.7.2) and thus by implication within the oceanic crust underlying spreading centres. It is lower in the more widely dispersed later products of metalliferous sediment formation such as East Pacific Rise crest and basal ferromanganese oxide-rich metalliferous sediments, lower still in ferromanganese oxide encrustations on the flanks of mid-ocean ridges, even lower in manganese nodules from abyssal regions, and lowest of all in diagenetically formed continental margin nodules. It is possible to explain this variation in terms of a predominantly hydrothermal source of the iron and manganese at mid-ocean ridges, with a decreasing hydrothermal influence away from mid-ocean ridges and an increasing contribution of elements from normal sea water, directly precipitated in the case of encrustations and some nodules but diagenetically recycled through the interstitial waters of the sediments in the case of nodules with highest Mn/Fe ratios. Of course, there are exceptions to this general rule. Manganese-rich hydrothermal deposits can form at active spreading centres such as in the TAG area, etc. (Chapter 6), but these are of small volume relative to the bulk of oceanic ferromanganese oxide deposits and represent an extreme fractionation of metals under somewhat exceptional conditions. Likewise, Fe-rich crusts occur in continental margin areas where the depositional conditions are unsuitable for manganese precipitation. These too are quantitatively unimportant. Iron-rich crusts also occur on seamounts or other rock outcrops in predominantly sediment covered areas in ocean basins well away from mid-ocean ridges, probably because they are unable to receive manganese via the diagenetic process, and may receive iron and some other elements from the alteration of their volcanic substrate. In spite of these exceptions, ferromanganese deposits on the ocean floor can be regarded as representing a continuum ranging from Fe-rich deposits near the primary volcanic source of the metals to manganese-rich deposits far from such sources.

On this basis, therefore, manganese nodules and metalliferous sediments can be regarded not as different deposits, but different varieties of the same genetic class of deposits.

9

Exploration Methods

The history of marine mineral exploration is, among other things, a history of accidental discoveries. Until relatively recently, few attempts had been made to explore for undersea minerals in anything like a systematic way. The chance nature of the discoveries made is well illustrated by the finding of the metal-rich brines and sediments in the Red Sea (page 176). As mentioned, standard oceanographic measurements during the Swedish Deep Sea Expedition in the late 1940s provided the first indication of an anomalous situation in the Red Sea (Bruneau *et al.*, 1953). Elevated water temperatures and salinities were recorded at a depth of 1937 m near 21°10′N, 38°09′E, in what is now known to be the Atlantis II Deep region. It was not until 1959, however, that elevated salinities were found in the vicinity of the Atlantis Terrace (Neumann and McGill, 1962), and the presence of metalliferous sediments within the Atlantis II Deep was not confirmed until the mid 1960s. If we take into account the fact that the Atlantis II Deep is more or less directly under the main shipping lane through the Red Sea, and that numerous oceanographic vessels had passed over it conducting scientific observations, it is evident that the likelihood of finding such deposits by chance is rather small. How many other metal-rich deposits might occur on other parts of the World Mid-Ocean Ridge System which have rarely, if ever, been passed over by oceanographic vessels? The history of our discovery of the Atlantis II Deep deposits illustrates the need for a systematic approach to marine mineral exploration.

A necessary prerequisite for any undersea mineral exploration is a suitable vessel, the nature of which will depend on the type and location of the deposits being sought. Shallow water inshore deposits such as placers, for example, can be surveyed using quite small vessels of limited endurance. By contrast, exploration for deep water deposits far from land, such as manganese nodules, requires a much larger and more sophisticated vessel. The nature of the sampling operations to be used will also affect the choice of ship. Bottom sampling using free fall corers or grabs (section 9.1.2) can be conducted from a much smaller vessel than those able to support a winch suitable for wire lowered samplers (section 9.1.2). Other constraints on the choice of ship for survey operations are the number of berths required for survey personnel, the type of sea conditions likely to be encountered and the amount of equipment to be carried. Ideally, each operation should be evaluated individually and an appropriate vessel selected.

In this chapter the principal methods employed in marine mineral exploration will be discussed and their application to different types of undersea minerals described. For convenience they have been divided into direct and indirect methods, the first group relying mainly on visual and sampling techniques and the second on geophysical and geochemical methods.

9.1 Direct Methods of Undersea Mineral Exploration

9.1.1 Visual

Undoubtedly the most direct approach to exploration for sea floor mineral deposits is to attempt to observe their whereabouts on the sea floor. In shallow water this approach relies heavily on divers, and in deeper water on manned submersibles.

Divers have been employed occasionally in exploration for sand and gravel deposits and placers, and have also been involved in providing basic geological information on the shallower portions of continental shelves. As mentioned in Chapter 7, on land geological features do not stop at the sea shore but continue under water, often for considerable distances. Sometimes the only way in which these features can be properly mapped is by using geologically trained divers (Eden *et al.*, 1969; Eden and Binns, 1973; Garnett, 1962).

In deeper water, visual observations can only be made from manned submersibles. Such vehicles have been little used to date in undersea mineral exploration, but the Franco-American submersible operations in the FAMOUS area on the Mid-Atlantic Ridge, where some metalliferous sediments have been found, point the way to how such devices might be used. The discovery of base metal sulphides on the East Pacific Rise at 21°N was made from a manned submersible (Francheteau *et al.*, 1979).

A more common approach to visual exploration of the sea floor is the use of cameras and underwater television. Underwater photography has been a well established tool in marine geological investigations for many years (Hersey, 1967) and has found a widespread application in the search for marine mineral deposits. Cameras have been designed which can take a sequence of photographs of the sea floor simply by being towed just above the bottom and triggered periodically (Laughton, 1967). Free fall cameras have also been designed, similar in the principle of their retrieval to free fall grabs (section 9.1.2). However, a limitation of underwater photography is that the camera has to come to the surface and the photographs be developed before any information on the bottom deposits can be obtained. This means there can be a considerable delay between obtaining data and their evaluation and thus exploration cannot be directed continuously. A solution to this problem is in the use of underwater television, in which there have been considerable advances in the past few years. Using underwater television, the sea floor can be monitored continuously and a videotape recording made for permanent reference. In this way, the sea floor can be examined in detail, and the positions of mineral deposits, boulders and rock outcrops noted. Underwater TV cameras can remain submerged for long periods of time, giving them an additional advantage over deep sea cameras. Kaufman and Siapno (1972a) have reported continuous underwater TV operations for up to five days in water depths of 4000 to 5000 m. However, underwater television does have its limitations. Normally, because of the lack of light in the deep sea and the limits of the resolution of the camera systems, only relatively small areas of the sea floor can be brought into view at any one time, not always enough to give an image of medium to large-scale features. Another limitation is the slow speed at which the cameras have to be towed, and thus the amount of ship time consumed in underwater TV operations is relatively large. Deep tow devices (section 9.3) can help to overcome some of these difficulties, and in spite of its limitations underwater TV can give the equivalent of thousands of still photographs in any given time period, and has the advantage of continuity.

Unmanned submersibles are being used increasingly as vehicles for underwater camera and TV operations, as well as for sampling. They have a particularly important application in exploration for manganese nodules on the deep sea floor. Lenoble (1980) has described three submersibles designed for this purpose. The first is a light towed vehicle named RAIE which determines its depth by means of a pressure gauge, its distance above the sea floor with a precision depth recorder (PDR), and its velocity by means of doppler sonar. RAIE carries cameras to photograph nodules, and "flies" at a distance of about 10 m above the sea floor. It also has a capacity to carry TV. The second is a heavy towed vehicle named PARC-ERIC which has the capacity to carry a large TV system and handle sampling tools by a mechanical arm under direction from the surface (Charles, 1974). The third is a free submersible named EPAULARD controlled by an acoustic system and able to take pictures of the sea floor and measure other parameters. RAIE is designed mainly for general sea floor survey work in order to delineate areas favourable for nodule exploration. PARC-ERIC and EPAULARD incorporate acoustic positioning and are designed to undertake more detailed surveys of the sea floor.

9.1.2 Sampling

Probably the simplest sea floor sampling devices are the dredge and the corer. The former is used to sample surface deposits on the sea floor like nodules or placers, or to break off samples of outcropping rocks, and the latter to obtain a section of sea floor sediments.

Dredging involves pulling a wide mouthed rigid frame attached to a net or basket (Fig. 68) along the sea floor behind a slow moving ship. While

Fig. 68. Deep-sea dredge.

this usually obtains some material, the representativeness of the samples is questionable. What is almost certain is that in most cases the dredge does not give a truly representative composite sample of the whole length of the sea floor that it has traversed. It probably comes into contact with the bottom only occasionally, particularly in rugged terrain, and "flies" above the bottom for the remainder of the traverse. The sample obtained may thus only represent the place where the dredge first came into contact with the sea floor and filled. Alternatively, material collected in the dredge may be partially or wholly discharged on subsequent contacts with the sea floor, and new material picked up. It is evident therefore that dredging can only

Fig. 69. Shipek grab.

be expected to obtain samples of sea floor materials, not necessarily in proportion to their relative abundance.

Partially to overcome some of the problems caused by dredging, various types of sea floor grab have been designed (Fig. 69). The advantage that they have over dredges is that they only sample the sea floor at one point, and thus the sample can be more precisely located than those obtained from dredging. Furthermore, the area of the sea floor sample is known, which is very useful for statistical purposes when computing mineral abundances. However, grabs do have their disadvantages, not least of which is a tendency to underrepresent the area of sea floor sampled. They also sometimes fall on their sides and close without obtaining any material at all, or samples get jammed in the jaws thus allowing finer material to fall out of the grab on retrieval. Failure to obtain a mineral sample with a grab does not mean therefore that nothing was present on the sea floor which could be sampled, nor if the jaws of the grab are jammed partially open are the contents of the grab, if any, likely to be representative of the material originally sampled.

As mentioned, dredges and grabs only sample the topmost deposits on the sea floor. If penetration beneath the sediment surface is required, one of several types of corer has to be used. The simplest and most commonly employed is a gravity corer, but various other corers of differing sophistication are also frequently used.

The gravity corer is a simple steel pipe, usually lined with a detachable plastic tube called a core liner, which is driven into the sea floor by a heavy weight (Fig. 70). Sometimes, especially in shallow water, it is operated by disengaging the ship's winch and allowing the corer to fall to the sea floor under its own weight. More normally, however, the corer is lowered to the sea floor at a much slower speed, which considerably reduces its depth of penetration into the sediments. A common solution to the latter problem is to use a device which releases the corer some 15 to 20 m above the sea floor on a slack wire of this length allowing it to fall to the bottom unimpeded. Gravity corers give a reasonably representative sample of the uppermost sediments on the sea floor but rarely is penetration greater than 3 m and the section is often compressed and somewhat disturbed.

A more advanced coring device is the piston corer (Fig. 71), which was designed to avoid the problem of sediment compression and to obtain longer cores than those normally obtainable by gravity coring. It contains a piston at the base of the corer which is released when the corer penetrates the sediments. The corer then moves into the sediment while the piston remains at the sediment surface thus creating a suction effect within the corer which has the effect of increasing penetration. However, if the corer does not fill, the sediments obtained can be disturbed by excessive suction as the corer is

Fig. 70. Gravity corer.

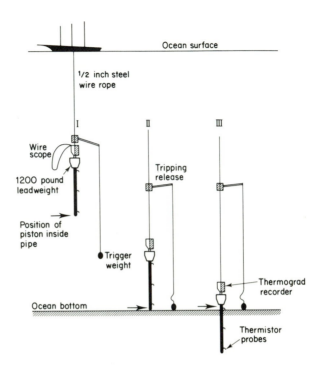

Fig. 71. Piston corer and attached heat flow apparatus (from Rona, 1972 after Talwani, 1964).

pulled out of the sediment. The use of a piston that splits on core retrieval can partially overcome this problem.

In order to obtain undisturbed samples of the uppermost metre or so of marine sediments, various box corers have been designed. They work on the principle of a wide box being pushed gently into the sediments on the sea floor under a heavy weight, in contrast to a narrow tube being plunged into the sea floor at high speed, as is the case with gravity and piston coring. A commonly used box corer is the Reineck Corer (Fig. 72) which has a maximum penetration of about half a metre. After penetration, the box is closed underneath by a swinging spade.

Coring in shallow water sediments of variable lithology poses consider-able problems as the corer is often stopped at the first change in lithology, especially if it encounters a coarse sediment layer. Partly to overcome this difficulty, but mainly to obtain long cores in continental shelf areas, various types of vibrocorer (Fig. 73) have been developed. The mechanics of their operation differ, but all work on the principle of the corer entering the sediments with a vibratory motion rather than just on impact under gravity.

Fig. 72. Reineck Corer.

Vibrocorers are widely used in the search for placer deposits, for example in locating cassiterite off Cornwall (Beckmann, 1975), and in proving the vertical extent of offshore sand and gravel deposits. Their depth of penetration is almost always much greater than that of conventional coring devices, but the representativeness of the samples that they take is questionable in some circumstances. Where, for example, the sediments consist of sands with a finer-grained heavy mineral assemblage, the vibratory action of the corer could lead to a partial separation of the two, and thus to the retrieval of an unrepresentative sample.

Fig. 73. Vibrocorer.

Fig. 74. Rock drill.

Another piece of sea floor sampling equipment is the rock drill (Fig. 74). This is simply a rotating drill which operates within a frame on the sea floor, driven from a power source aboard ship. It has received relatively widespread use in continental shelf areas, and a version has also been developed for deep sea use (Brook and Gilbert, 1968).

When sampling in areas of metalliferous sediments, especially if volcanically active, it is often useful to take bottom-water samples as well as sediment cores. The usual way of taking sea water samples is to lower a series of water bottles on a wire and trigger their closure from the surface using a messenger. However, this method is not altogether suitable if samples are required from very close to the bottom, especially in areas of rugged topography, as it is difficult to position the bottles accurately above the sea floor without them hitting it. One method that has been devised to overcome this problem is to rig a water bottle for "bottom tripping" (Fig. 75). In other words, rather than triggering the bottle closure using a messenger from the surface, it is closed by contact with the bottom. Of course, the bottle itself should not hit the sea floor because the sediment stirred up on impact would make the water sample useless for chemical analysis. In practice, the trigger mechanism can be a heavy grab slung under the bottle, its weight keeping the bottle open. As the grab hits the sea floor the weight comes off the bottle which closes immediately taking a sample of bottom water as far above the sea floor as the wire length between the bottle and the grab. In this way, a bottom-water sample uncontaminated by disturbed sediment can be taken and a bottom-sediment sample obtained at the same time. A free fall version of this sort of water sampler has also been developed.

One of the most significant advances in sea floor sampling techniques is the development of the free fall sampler. The samplers themselves are, of course, similar to wire-lowered devices, being either grabs (Fig. 76) or corers (Fig. 77) of one type or another. The collective difference between them and the wire-lowered sampling equipment lies in their being allowed to fall to the sea floor unattached to any wire, and to return to the surface under their own buoyancy. Different free fall samplers differ in the detail of their operation, but all function on the basis of a weight being discharged on the sea floor, the loss of which enables the sampler to be pulled back to the surface by floats. In the case of most grabs, a weight is discharged when the grab hits the sea floor and closes. In the case of free fall corers, the core barrel and weights remain on the sea floor while the core liner attached to buoyant spheres returns to the surface. The use of free fall sampling equipment greatly increases the amount of material that can be obtained in a given time, thus considerably reducing ship time costs. In addition, it allows samples to be fairly precisely located relative to each

Fig. 75. Water bottle rigged for bottom tripping with a Shipek grab.

Fig. 76. Free fall grab.

Fig. 77. Free fall corer.

other, as a whole line of free fall instruments can be dropped to a pre-determined set pattern. However, free fall corers have the limitation that they can only penetrate up to about 2 m into the sediments.

Of increasing importance in undersea mineral exploration are integrated systems for both surveying and sampling. Kaufman and Siapno (1972a) have reported a dredge used in conjunction with an underwater TV system, the dredge being suspended from the TV housing. The principle of opera-tion is that when the TV frame sets down, the dredge scrapes across the sea floor. In this way samples can be obtained during a TV survey, thus eliminating the need for separate dredge lowerings and ensuring that the area sampled is the area being observed.

In spite of the relatively high level of sophistication of some of the more advanced sampling devices, improvements are still both desirable and possible. One field where further equipment development would be most useful is that of serial sampling by remote control. Ideally, serial sampling equipment should be able to take samples from predetermined positions, precisely located one to another, and to take further samples on command. Some form of visual monitoring of the operation, such as TV, would also be desirable. Different types of equipment would be required for different sampling operations, nodules or sediments for example, and thus the avail-

ability of various types of sampling equipment in a modular form would
be of value. The development of a system for *in situ* analysis of deposits
(section 9.2.2.2) to complement the serial sampling would be a logical im-
provement on the latter.

9.2   Indirect Techniques of Undersea Mineral Exploration

9.2.1   Geophysical exploration

The use of geophysical methods in undersea mineral exploration is well
established. Precision depth recording, for example, is a prerequisite for any
undersea sampling operation, seismic exploration techniques are achieving
an increasing use, and electrical and magnetic methods are of potential value
under some circumstances.

9.2.1.1   *Precision depth recording*

A knowledge of the topography of the ocean floor is of paramount importance in exploration for undersea mineral deposits. Such knowledge is
obtained by use of an echo sounder or precision depth recorder (PDR).

The basic components of a PDR system include an acoustic transducer,
a sonar transceiver, and a recorder. The acoustic transducer acts as a sound
source and a hydrophone to receive the echoes of sound waves transmitted
to the sea floor.

In addition to providing an image of the sea floor, precision depth recording can be used to determine the presence of mid-water reflectors. This
application has proved particularly useful in exploration for brine filled
basins in the Red Sea, as the density interface between the brine and sea
water is sometimes observable at depth (Swallow, 1969; Pugh, 1969) (Fig.
78). However, this approach does not have a uniform applicability in exploration for metal-rich deposits, as experience in the Red Sea has shown
that not all metalliferous sediments are associated with brines, and indeed
that not all brines are metalliferous (Backer and Schoell, 1972). Nevertheless,
the presence of mid-water reflectors on PDR records would certainly provide
targets for subsequent sampling operations to determine whether a metalliferous deposit is present. The application of 3·5 kHz PDR profiling in manganese nodule exploration has been presented in section 5.4.1.

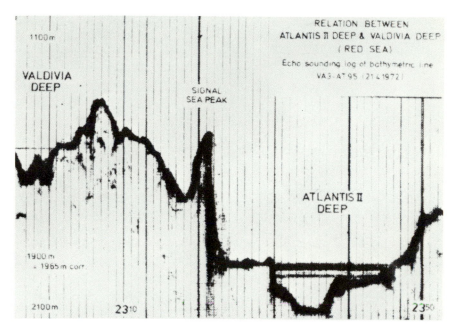

Fig. 78. Original echo sounding log of a profile in the Red Sea rift valley from Valdivia Deep (23.00: 21°20·3′N: 37°56·9′E.) to Atlantis II Deep (23.50: 21°21·2′N; 38°08·0′E). ELAC narrow beam echo sounder 30 kc ± 1·4° beam width. Direction of the section 86°. The horizontal echoes correspond to the surface of brine layers (from Backer and Schoell, 1972).

9.2.1.2 *Side scan sonar*

Side scan sonar systems are mounted in such a way that an acoustic beam is projected sideways to the sea floor at an angle, rather than vertically down under the ship as with a PDR. Furthermore, whereas PDR beams are fan shaped, side scan sonar beams are cone shaped. They give an oblique picture of the sea floor to the side of the ship, as shown in Fig. 79. The resolution of the systems depends on a variety of factors, including the distance above the sea floor at which they are towed. Side scan sonar has achieved only limited application in undersea mineral exploration to date. However, as described in Chapter 2, sand waves and ribbons can show up very clearly on the sea floor using such a system. Side scan sonar has a considerable potential in manganese nodule exploration. As mentioned in Chapter 5, manganese nodules vary considerably in abundance on the sea floor, and tend to be concentrated on hill slopes and in gently rugged areas, rather than on smooth plains. A deep-sea side scan sonar such as GLORIA (Rusby and Somers, 1977) could therefore be towed over a nodule bearing

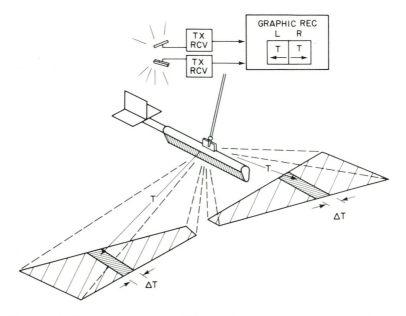

Fig. 79. A side-looking sonar system in which sound sources are mounted to project sound laterally from a vehicle towed by a ship to obtain a sonar display of the ocean bottom analogous to an oblique aerial photograph (from Rona, 1972; after Clay *et al.*, 1964).

area to delineate different topographic settings in sweeps several tens of kilometres wide. Samples of nodules from each of the settings could then be retrieved to determine the most favourable bathymetric situation for both high grade and abundance, and the side scan sonar then used to find other examples of such a setting in the nodule bearing region at large. In addition, high resolution side scan sonar towed near the sea floor as part of a "deep tow" package may have an application in outlining manganese nodule fields by the roughness of the sea floor.

9.2.1.3 *Seismic methods*

Seismic exploration methods can be divided into two varieties, seismic reflection and seismic refraction. The latter is of use in delineating the deep structure of the oceanic crust and thus has little or no application in exploration for undersea mineral deposits. Seismic reflection, on the other hand, does have some applications in this regard. The method utilizes the differing velocity of sound waves in different materials. When the reflections of sound pulses transmitted to the sea floor are expressed graphically, discontinuities are recorded as a result of differences in the density of the materials through which the sound waves pass. Rona (1972) has described the application of various seismic methods in exploration on continental shelves. Sub-sea floor penetration by different systems is determined by their frequency band and by the energy level of the sound source. High resolution shallow penetration systems are of greater use than others in undersea mineral exploration, because most deposits of any economic interest are either on the sea floor or buried under only a shallow overburden. Some sparker and boomer systems tend to give relatively deep penetration (Rona, 1972) of use in delineating sub-surface structures in bedrock under the sea floor, for example in oil exploration. Other systems, including air guns which eject a bubble of air into the sea, can be varied in capacity to

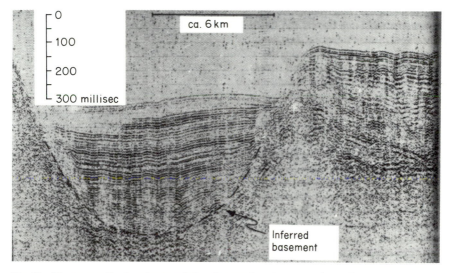

Fig. 80. Air gun profile showing ponded sediments in a basement depression.

give either shallow or deep penetration, and are of great use in determining the thickness of unconsolidated sediment over bedrock (Fig. 80). It is this last application which is of most use in undersea mineral exploration. Placer deposits, for example, may occur just above bedrock in ancient sediment filled river channels on continental shelves, now submerged due to the post glacial rise in sea level (Chapter 2). Because they often lack topographic expression on the sea floor, the best way of locating these channels is by using a shallow penetrating seismic device. Similarly, in areas of metalliferous sediment occurrence, shallow penetrating seismic devices can allow an estimate of the total thickness of the sediment column to be made. Seismic methods also have an application in exploration for manganese nodules. They are of use in delineating sediment covered areas on which nodules occur, and in picking out obstacles on and just below the sea floor which could hamper nodule mining.

9.2.1.4   *Electrical methods*

The application of electrical methods to geophysical exploration on continental shelves has been reviewed by Rona (1972) and Francis (1977). There are two groups of methods. One utilizes natural electric currents flowing through the sea floor to locate small-scale features such as electrically conductive ore bodies. The other utilizes the application by man of electric fields to the sea floor. Voltages are measured between electrodes inserted into the ocean bottom, differences in electrical response between pairs of electrodes reflecting differences in the resistivity of the intervening rocks.

Francis (1977) has provided an assessment of the relative usefulness of three electrical exploration methods in the marine environment. These are the earth resistivity, self potential and induced polarization methods. All three are purely electrical and none of them have an application in exploration for anything other than buried ore bodies. Francis considered the usefulness at sea of the self potential method to be limited relative to its usefulness on land, because self potential anomalies at sea are likely to be too small in relation to other sources of potential gradient to be easily measurable. He also considered the induced polarization method to be of little use in undersea exploration, leaving only the earth resistivity method as having a potential application. The success at sea of the earth resistivity method, which measures differences in the electrical resistance of the rocks through which a current is passed, depends on whether or not a significant fraction of the total current passed between electrodes in the sea can be made to penetrate the sea bed. An appreciable current fraction can be made to do this only if the spacing of the towed electrodes is significantly greater than the water depth. If this condition is fulfilled, towed electrode arrays can detect variations in the resistivity of the sea bed, and thus lead to the delineation of areas of potential bedrock mineralization. This was evinced by the finding of sulphide mineralization on the UK continental shelf using the method. However, the need to space the electrodes at distances much greater than the water depth makes it unlikely that the earth resistivity method will ever have an application anywhere at sea other than on continental shelves.

9.2.1.5 *Magnetic methods*

Magnetic methods of sea floor exploration depend on measuring anomalies in the local geomagnetic field produced by variations in the intensity of the magnetization of sea floor rocks and sediments. The magnetic susceptibility of the sea floor depends largely on its content of magnetic minerals. Rocks and sediments containing highly magnetic minerals exhibit a stronger magnetic signature than others which contain fewer magnetic minerals.

Magnetic measurements are made at sea using a ship or airborne towed magnetometer. The study of magnetic anomalies on the ocean floor has been of great importance in contributing to our understanding of the origin of the oceans and the development of the theory of plate tectonics (Vine and Matthews, 1963; Vine, 1966; Le Pichon, 1968) but has not yet found much application in sea floor mineral exploration. This is largely because three of the four main groups of sea floor mineral deposits, manganese nodules, phosphorites and metalliferous sediments, exhibit no magnetic properties which could be used to pinpoint their location. Even when sea floor minerals are magnetic, for example some placer sands, being only a surface or near surface phenomenon they contribute little to the total intensity of the magnetic field on the sea floor. Magnetite-bearing deposits would lend themselves to detection by magnetic methods, especially with deep tow instrumentation, as might some other iron and titanium-rich minerals, but probably few other undersea mineral deposits could be located in this way.

Magnetic survey methods do, however, have an indirect application in the search for metalliferous sediments associated with active spreading ridges. The oceanic crust on either side of spreading ridges exhibits parallel zones of normal and reversely magnetized rocks, the direction of magnetization being aligned with that of the earth's magnetic field at the time of the rocks' formation. Subsequent alteration of these rocks by hydrothermal activity can lead to a disturbance of their magnetic signature and in some cases a reduction in the intensity of the remanent magnetization (Ade-Hall *et al.*, 1971). Severe disturbance of the magnetic signature of mid-ocean ridge crest basalts has been observed in the TAG area at the crest of the Mid-Atlantic Ridge at 26°N resulting in a low in residual magnetic intensity (McGregor and Rona, 1975; Rona *et al.*, 1976; Rona, 1978a) thought to be the result of alteration of the sea floor rocks by hydrothermal solutions associated with the TAG hydrothermal field. Such magnetic lows have been observed in other areas of submarine hydrothermal activity, for example in the Atlantis II Deep in the Red Sea (Rona, 1978a), and, if such disturbances of normal mid-ocean ridge magnetic patterns are a common feature associated with submarine hydrothermal activity, exploration for magnetically disturbed areas on mid-ocean ridge crests could provide useful targets for subsequent bottom sampling in attempts to find hydrothermal ore bodies.

9.2.1.6 *Gravity*

The measurement of gravity at sea can tell us about the density of the sea floor. Local fluctuations in gravity can be caused by both variations in rock type, and structural variations below the sea floor (Rona, 1972). However, as stressed when discussing other geophysical exploration methods, the fact that undersea minerals are essentially a surface phenomenon and thus will not contribute significantly to the local gravity field, severely limits the use of gravity techniques in locating them. Even sub-sea floor mineral deposits would be unlikely to affect significantly the gravity patterns as recorded from a ship.

9.2.1.7 *Heat flow*

Heat is continuously being lost from the sea floor, largely as a result of the decay of radioactive elements within the oceanic crust. However, superimposed on this background heat flow are local increases caused by submarine volcanic activity. Heat flow is generally much higher over active mid-ocean ridges than in the basins on either side, but measured values are rather variable due to convective circulation of sea water. There are also localized areas of high heat flow in some island arc environments and intra-plate volcanic provinces (Sclater and Menard, 1967). Definition of such areas presents targets for exploration for submarine hydrothermal sediments.

In addition to high heat flow in submarine volcanic areas, water temperature anomalies are sometimes observed in the bottom waters. The best examples of these are in the Red Sea where the brines of the Atlantis II Deep range in temperature up to $60°C$ (Chapter 6). However, smaller temperature anomalies have been reported in other submarine volcanic areas, such as over the TAG hydrothermal field for example (Rona *et al.*, 1975; Rona, 1978b) and in the Galapagos region (Weiss *et al.*, 1977). The presence of water temperature anomalies in submarine volcanic areas is a good indication of the occurrence of hydrothermal activity, but searching for such anomalies is not the best way of locating hydrothermal deposits. Heat is dispersed from the hydrothermal source very rapidly through sea water, and the temperature anomalies may thus occur only in the immediate vicinity of the hydrothermal vent and only when the hydrothermal system is active, hence limiting its chance of detection. Sediment studies are more valuable in locating hydrothermal deposits (section 9.2.2.1) because they can contain a permanent record of the hydrothermal activity.

9.2.2   Geochemical exploration

Geochemistry can be applied to undersea mineral exploration in two ways: analytical investigations on recovered material, and *in situ* measurements on the sea floor. It is a valuable supplement to direct and geophysical exploration methods in that it can be used to pinpoint target areas and high grade deposits in a way that the other methods cannot (Cronan, 1978a).

9.2.2.1   *Analysis of recovered material*

Chemical analysis of sea-bottom samples can aid in exploration for all four main types of undersea mineral deposits. The methods rely on the recovery and analysis of sediments associated with the deposits and the interpretation of analytical data obtained on them to pinpoint the deposit site.

The concept of dispersion is important in submarine geochemical exploration. It is based on the observation that elements are dispersed away from many undersea mineral deposits in a way that can be used to aid in the location of the deposits. Such dispersion can occur either by lateral movement of elements away from the deposits in detrital phases like heavy minerals and other particulates, or by the migration of elements through the water column in solution or in fine-grained particulate phases. Each will be considered separately using examples from different types of deposits.

(a) *Placers and lodes*

The general philosophy behind geochemical exploration for submarine placer deposits and outcrops of metal bearing lodes on the sea floor is that metals in the sediments in a particulate form, usually as heavy minerals, should decrease in concentration away from the deposit, and that by measuring this decrease it ought to be possible to project the concentration gradients back to the metal source. Naturally, in an environment as complex as the littoral and near-shore zone it would be naïve to expect simple linear dispersion gradients of metals away from their source, and much of the work that has been done on developing geochemical exploration methods for placers has been aimed at elucidating the mechanism of dispersal of the metals in relation to such complex factors as sea floor topography, wave action, and current patterns.

One of the earliest attempts to apply geochemical exploration methods in the search for placer mineral deposits was in Mounts Bay, Cornwall (Tooms *et al.*, 1965). The mineral in question was cassiterite, either eroded from the abundant tin lodes and old mine workings near the Cornish coast, or from outcrops of submarine lodes. Tooms *et al.* (1965) found the amount of tin decreased in the fine fraction of the sediments with increase in depth and distance from the shore, highest tin concentrations being found in small bays. This would suggest that the principal source of the tin in Mounts Bay sediments is from streams draining the hinterland, and not from the outcrop of submarine lodes. However, further work by Tooms (1969) was aimed at refining this conclusion. A good fit was found between the decrease in tin in the surface sediments with increase in distance

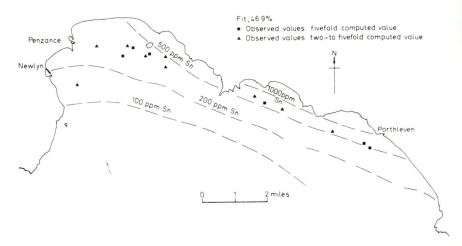

Fig. 81. Computed cubic trend surface of -80 mesh tin in marine sediments, Mount's Bay, Cornwall. After Hazelhoff Roelfzema (from Tooms, 1969).

offshore, and a cubic trend surface (Fig. 81), which is the pattern which would be expected if the dominant source of the tin was from the land. However, a number of samples were also found which had tin concentrations greatly in excess of the computed values, which might have reflected local sources of the tin. Several traverses were made across projected extensions of lodes offshore and of known bedrock mineralization. The results from the latter over the Wherry Mine, which had been worked from an offshore shaft, indicated an increase of tin in certain size fractions of the sediments which could be related to bedrock mineralization. However, the pattern was not clear enough to be certain about this.

Yim (1978) has described exploration for tin off North Cornwall. Surface

sediments from the region between St Agnes Head and Portreath are enriched in tin, thought to have been derived from the dispersion of tin from
land through the discharge of mine tailings offshore by streams. Some slight
tin enrichment was found in the basal sediments near the supposed offshore
extension of the Towanwrath tin lode probably related to bedrock mineralization.

Moore and Welkie (1976) and Moore (1979) have described a method for
placer exploration developed in the search for noble metal placers off Alaska
(Chapter 2). The method relies on certain element and textural associations
being found in areas of placer mineral occurrence. In sediments associated
with marine platinum placers, positive correlations were found between V,
Ni, Cu, Zn and Mn, and in sediments associated with gold placers between
V, Fe, Co, Ni, Cu and Zn. Correlations with textural parameters were also
apparent.

On the basis of the information summarized above, it is evident that
geochemical exploration for placers and lodes on continental shelves has
considerable potential. Nevertheless, the dispersion of minerals as particulate phases away from a mineral deposit is likely to be rather limited. Such minerals could become trapped in depressions as they move
across the sea floor. In addition, energy from waves and tides would be
likely to distort any symmetrical dispersion of minerals round a deposit,
and would also lead to their mixing with other phases such as sand and
shell. Geochemical exploration for anomalies associated with placer and
lode minerals should thus be conducted by taking close spaced samples in
the supposed vicinity of a deposit, with the sampling being concentrated,
for lodes, in sediments immediately overlying bedrock. Care should be
exercised to avoid false geochemical anomalies such as those associated
with metal scavenging from sea water by highly adsorptive phases such as
iron and manganese oxides, and due to contamination from land mining
operations such as occurs off Cornwall.

(b) *Phosphorites*

As described in Chapter 4, phosphorites can occur in continental margin
areas either in the form of unconsolidated deposits, or as bedrock outcrops.
The use of instrumental methods in their location on the sea floor is reviewed in section 9.2.2.2 and the use of direct sampling techniques in this
regard is briefly discussed here.

Studies on the continental shelf off north-west Africa have shown that
bedded phosphorites of Cretaceous and Tertiary age outcrop at various
places on the sea floor (Tooms and Summerhayes, 1968; Summerhayes
et al., 1972). Sampling of sediments on this shelf and their subsequent

analysis has indicated considerable variations in the phosphorus content of the sediments which can be related to phosphorite outcrops (Fig. 18). A narrow belt of phosphate-rich sediment surrounded by sediments of lower P content has been found at or near the shelf break in various places, and in at least one instance extends down to a depth of about 1200 m. Summerhayes et al. (1972) consider the main source of the phosphorus in the sediments to be from the erosion of phosphorite rock outcrops during Pleistocene lowerings of sea level. This phosphorus, largely in the form of detrital sand-sized grains of phosphorite, was redistributed by currents along the Pleistocene shoreline and tended to be concentrated either among or immediately seawards of the present rock outcrops. Such a distribution is evident from comparison of the P_2O_5 distribution in Fig. 18 with the locations of the phosphorite rock outcrops marked.

The erosion of phosphorite rock at outcrop and the dispersion of detrital phosphorite away from it has an obvious potential in exploration for bedded phosphorites on the continental shelf. However, as is evident from Fig. 18, one cannot simply measure phosphorus concentration gradients in sediments and project back to the source assuming a homogeneous distribution of P around the source rock. The dispersion of detrital phosphorites on the sea floor, like that of other detrital particles, will depend on wave and current patterns, and on the redistribution of material during past regressions and transgressions of the sea over continental shelf areas during glacial periods. Nevertheless, if these complicating factors are appreciated, and assuming a knowledge of the recent geological history of the shelf area in question, the distribution of phosphorus in the sediments could be used to delineate areas of likely outcrops of phosphorite rock.

(c) *Metalliferous sediments*

The development of geochemical exploration techniques for locating submarine metalliferous sediments of hydrothermal origin has utilized the distribution of elements both within sea water and within the sediment surrounding ore bodies. Detection of geochemical anomalies in sea water relies essentially on the ore forming process being in operation at the time that the survey is done. By contrast, geochemical exploration based on analysis of bottom sediments can be used to find mineral deposits that were formed in the past but which are still present near the sediment–water interface.

(i) *Element dispersion in sea water*. An investigation into metal dispersion in sea water as an aid to submarine mineral exploration has been reported by Holmes and Tooms (1972). These workers obtained water samples over and around the metal-rich Atlantis II and Nereus Deeps in the Red Sea, which they analysed for both dissolved and particulate metals. The effect

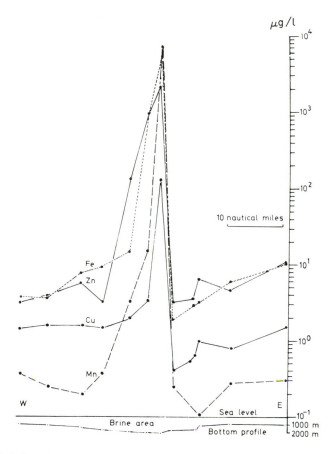

Fig. 82. Variation of dissolved metal species in near bottom water, west-east across Atlantis II Deep (no samples from brine) (from Holmes and Tooms, 1972).

of the Atlantis II brines on the levels of dissolved Fe, Mn, Cu and Zn in the near bottom waters was very marked (Fig. 82). Maxima of these elements occurred immediately over the brine and anomalies extended laterally several kilometres to the west. There was, however, no reflection of this enrichment in the surface waters overlying the Deep. Data on dissolved species in the near bottom water over and around the Nereus Deep revealed less marked lateral variations, but the near bottom particulates did disclose an anomaly. Strong Fe, Mn and Zn maxima occurred over the brine area, and to the east the metal content of the particulates remained elevated over a distance of about 1·6 km. Along the median valley of the Red Sea to the south of the Nereus Deep, dissolved Fe and Zn exhibited

an anomaly over a distance of at least 24 km. These data indicate that care-
ful close spaced bottom-water sampling in areas of submarine hydrothermal
activity can help to delineate areas of high metal values. However, the
probable rapid mixing of the metal-rich waters with the overlying sea water
limits the vertical extent of the anomaly and thus the likelihood of detecting it at the sea surface.

More recently, another approach of relevance to geochemical exploration
for submarine hydrothermal ore bodies has been described by Lupton *et al.*
(1977), based on helium isotope studies in the Red Sea. These authors found
an approximate 3000-fold enrichment of ^{3}He in the Red Sea brines of
hydrothermal origin relative to its content in sea water, indicating helium
to be a sensitive indicator of hydrothermal emanations from ocean floor
basalts. On this basis, helium isotope measurements made on deep sea
water samples collected from other submarine volcanic areas may be of use
in locating hydrothermal activity.

(ii) *Element dispersion in sediments.* The selective dispersion of metals
through sea water from a submarine hydrothermal orebody can leave a
permanent chemical imprint on the surrounding sediments which may be
of great value in geochemical exploration for the deposit. Large-scale examples of such cases have been well documented in the sediments surrounding the Atlantis II and Nereus Deeps in the Red Sea (Bignell *et al.*, 1976b).

As described in Chapter 6, various metalliferous sediments are being
precipitated in the Atlantis II Deep as a result of the mixing of hot metal-
rich brines with sea water. In addition, some phases escape from the Deep
altogether and precipitate in the surrounding sediments. The latter process
can be illustrated by a comparison of the distribution of Fe and Mn in
sediment cores from around the Deep (Fig. 55). Iron is enriched in the
sediments both within and immediately adjacent to the Deep, but drops
off to background levels only a kilometre or so away. By contrast,
manganese remains elevated in the sediments for at least 10 km from the
Deep and may be high even beyond that. The reasons for this selective
dispersion have already been explained (section 6.7). Both metals are
oxidized and precipitated in the waters overlying the Deep, but the later
oxidation of Mn than of Fe is probably responsible for its more widespread dispersion around the Deep.

The selective dispersion of Mn from Fe around the Atlantis II Deep
gives rise to dispersion haloes for these metals as illustrated in Fig. 83.
The presence of dispersion haloes such as these are of great potential value
in locating base metal sulphide deposits of hydrothermal origin on the sea
floor. The sulphide deposits themselves may be only of limited areal extent
and thus if one were to attempt to locate them by sampling on a grid

basis, the sampling points would have to be very close together. When, however, the sulphides are surrounded by a dispersion halo of manganese in the sediments many times the size of the deposit itself, a much wider grid could be employed just to locate the dispersion halo, after which the manganese values in the samples can be contoured and the concentration gradients extrapolated to give the most likely location of the sulphide deposit. More detailed sampling could then be employed in this area. This approach would be time saving relative to small-scale grid sampling over the whole of an area of interest for hydrothermal sulphides.

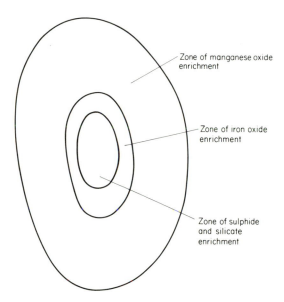

Zone of manganese oxide enrichment

Zone of iron oxide enrichment

Zone of sulphide and silicate enrichment

Fig. 83. Schematic distribution of Fe and Mn around a hydrothermal ore body, based on studies around the Atlantis II Deep in the Red Sea.

Partly in order to test the general validity of the dispersion halo concept developed from studies around the Atlantis II Deep, the dispersion of metals away from submarine hydrothermal vents off Santorini, in the eastern Mediterranean, was investigated by Smith and Cronan (1975). It was found that Mn was selectively fractionated from Fe over a distance of a few tens of metres away from the hydrothermal source (Fig. 84) just as occurs on a larger scale around the Atlantis II Deep. Iron was being contributed to the waters immediately adjacent to the hydrothermal vents in high concentrations but was being rapidly oxidized and precipitated. By contrast, manganese was quite low in the sediments immediately adjacent

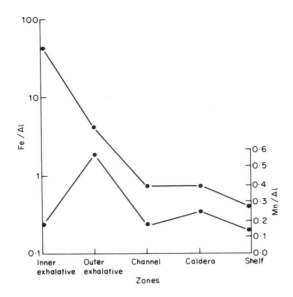

Fig. 84. Selective fractionation of Mn from Fe in sediments off Santorini (modified from Smith and Cronan, 1975).

to the vents, remaining in solution, but increased with distance away reaching a maximum outside the zone of maximum Fe concentration.

As described in section 6.4.1.3 recent studies on sediments around the TAG hydrothermal field on the Mid-Atlantic Ridge near 26°N (Cronan *et al.*, 1979) have indicated that in an elevated area of the mid-ocean ridge system subjected to unrestricted circulation of bottom waters, simple dispersion gradients of metals away from hydrothermal vents such as are found in and around the Atlantis II Deep do not appear to occur. In the TAG area, most of the hydrothermal manganese is precipitated immediately adjacent to the vents, but some manganese is probably being flushed out of the vents in a particulate form to become well mixed in the bottom waters. It is probably the precipitation of this manganese that is leading to the fairly uniform enrichment of manganese relative to the Atlantic average in sediments throughout the TAG area (Cronan *et al.*, 1979). Thus a general enrichment in manganese may be more typical in sediments surrounding an open ocean hydrothermal centre, than a dispersion halo containing a well marked gradient of increasing manganese values towards the hydrothermal source, such as is found in the more restricted Atlantis II Deep.

So far, discussion of element dispersion patterns in sediments as an aid to geochemical exploration has centred on the behaviour of metals in bulk sediment samples. This approach is most useful when there are only minor contributions to the sediments from non-hydrothermal sources, as in the exhalative zones off Santorini, or when the hydrothermal dispersion is major as in the Red Sea. In many submarine volcanic areas neither of these situations are found. Along most of the World Mid-Ocean Ridge System, the possible sub-sea floor selective fractionation of metals described previously (section 6.7.2) would result in only the late stage precipitates from the fractionation process being discharged on the sea floor, and their abundance is likely therefore to be limited. Furthermore, the crest of the World Mid-Ocean Ridge System is almost uniformly above the calcium carbonate compensation depth, resulting in the accumulation of large amounts of carbonate sediment which will dilute any hydrothermal precipitates that may have been formed. Input of detrital sediments can also be locally high on some portions of mid-ocean ridges. In such situations, the combination of limited supply of hydrothermal precipitates coupled with their dilution by carbonate and/or detrital phases, could make the identification of dispersion patterns using only bulk sample analyses very difficult. Under these circumstances, it is more logical to examine the geochemistry of the phases containing the hydrothermally supplied elements rather than the bulk sediments as a whole. This can be done by using a selective chemical leach procedure to remove diluent phases and concentrate only the phases of interest. Obvious examples of this approach are to use dilute acetic acid to remove the carbonate fraction in order that any variation in the manganese–iron ratio in the remaining fraction can be examined in detail, or to extract the authigenic fraction from the diluent fractions and examine it separately (Cronan, 1978a).

One problem that may be encountered in attempting to delineate dispersion haloes of hydrothermal Mn from either analysis of bulk samples or leached residues is that manganese of diagenetic origin may also contribute to the total manganese content of the sediments. A good example of this is to be found in the caldera of Santorini. Some manganese of hydrothermal origin is bypassing the exhalative zones adjacent to the hydrothermal vents (section 6.6) and is being dispersed, probably as particulate MnO_2, into the caldera (Smith and Cronan, 1978). This results in somewhat elevated Mn values in the caldera sediments relative to those on the open shelf surrounding Santorini. However, superimposed on this hydrothermal manganese is an additional supply of manganese from within the sediments as a result of the diagenetic remobilization of buried MnO_2 and its reprecipitation at the surface in the manner described previously. Simple chemical analysis will not enable a distinction between these two sources of manganese to be made. However, a possible solution to this problem is to examine the composition of the manganese oxide fraction itself by use of the hydroxylamine hydrochloride leach procedure (section 6.7.1). Hydro-thermally dispersed manganese dioxide will probably have scavenged some minor elements from sea water, particularly Zn (Bignell *et al.*, 1976b) which should be reflected in the minor element content of the hydroxylamine hydrochloride soluble fraction of the sediments. By contrast, manganese dioxide of diagenetic origin is known to be very poor in trace metals (Lynn and Bonatti, 1965; Price, 1967, and others) because many of the normally associated metals are left behind in the sediments, possibly as sulphides or organic complexes (Price and Calvert, 1970). Thus by analysis of the hydroxylamine hydrochloride soluble fraction of surface sediments for minor elements it may be possible to determine the source of the MnO_2. How-ever, if it is being contributed from two or more sources, this approach will probably not work and recourse will have to be made to sedi-ment coring rather than surface sampling in order that buried sediments can be examined for direct evidence of Mn reduction and remobiliza-tion.

Elements other than iron and manganese are also of potential value in geochemical exploration for submarine hydrothermal ore bodies. Mercury is an element of considerable use in land based geochemical exploration, and does have a widespread dispersion around the Atlantis II Deep (Bignell *et al.*, 1976b). Arsenic is another element of potential value in this re-gard (Cronan, 1972b). However, the distribution of these, and other elements, around submarine hydrothermal deposits may be complicated by their being scavenged from sea water by iron oxide and manganese dioxide and this possibility would have to be taken into account in assessing their use in geochemical exploration.

The great advantage of sediment analysis over other methods in the search for submarine hydrothermal ore bodies is that it can help to find the highest grade deposits in a way that other methods cannot (Cronan, 1978a), and using shipboard analysis results can be obtained as the survey proceeds. Furthermore the use of the method is not restricted only to the location of deposits forming at the present time but is equally applicable to the probably much more numerous deposits formed in the recent past and still exposed on the sea floor. Perhaps the best example of the latter application is in the Red Sea where some of the highest metal concentra-tions in the sediments are not associated with either brines or current vol-canic activity. It is only by the analysis of bottom sediments that such deposits can be detected.

(d) *Manganese nodules*

Geochemical exploration for manganese nodules on the sea floor cannot be approached in the same way as for other sub-sea mineral deposits

(Cronan, 1979), as nothing is dispersed from the nodules which can be used in their detection. Unlike placers and phosphorites, they are not subjected to mechanical redistribution processes which fractionate their constituents and disperse them around the deposit. Similarly, although they can receive contributions from hydrothermal solutions, they are not analogous to Red Sea type deposits with their associated dispersion haloes. Indeed, as mentioned previously, any hydrothermal contributions to them are likely to be from the residual solutions of a submarine hydrothermal system. Geochemical exploration for ore grade manganese nodules must therefore rely either on a routine grid sampling and analysis programme in nodule bearing areas, which has been the most common method used to date, or on a predictive approach based on a thorough understanding of the factors leading to valuable metal enrichment in the deposits.

Grid sampling methods have been used with a considerable degree of success in outlining potential manganese nodule mine sites on the sea floor. One problem, however, has been to determine the most effective grid interval to be used. Lenoble (1976) has described a statistical approach to this problem, concluding that a sample spacing of about 2 km is necessary to characterize fully a nodule bearing area. Fellerer (1975) has described a multi-phase approach to nodule exploration, using the north-east equatorial Pacific as a model area. Based on sampling and other operations, some 10% of this area was selected for detailed exploration and about 2·5% for intense surveys. In the latter area, a three phase approach to exploration was used. Phase 1 was a bathymetric and seismic survey, using a bathymetric grid of 5·6 × 14·8 km and a somewhat larger grid for seismic lines. After mapping, about 50% of the area was adjudged suitable for sampling which involved taking several samples at each survey point on about a 5·6 km grid. Finally, in phase 3, about 25% of the phase 1 area was selected for underwater TV survey.

The predictive approach to nodule exploration relies on being able to define the factors, particularly the depositional conditions, which lead to metal enrichment in ore grade nodules, and, by considering where and to what degree these factors might prevail in the oceans at large, attempting to predict the likely occurrence of ore grade deposits. Factors leading to metal enrichment to ore grade in north-east equatorial Pacific nodules have been discussed (section 5.9.1.2). They are thought to form as a result of the fluxing of metals from surface waters by sinking organic remains and their diagenetic uptake by nodules after liberation on organic decay. What is important in the present context is that with knowledge of how these ore grade nodules form, and consideration of where else the same processes could occur, other areas may be delineated as having a potential for high grade nodule formation. A good example of this application is the delineation of the central Indian Ocean as a potential area of high grade nodules on the basis of its comparability with the north-eastern equatorial Pacific (Cronan and Moorby, 1976; Cronan, 1978b).

One very important geochemical exploration tool in determining the depositional environment most conducive to high grade manganese nodule formation, is a knowledge of the depth over which calcium carbonate is dissolving. As described in Chapter 5, in some areas nodules are both most abundant and of highest grade in a narrow depth interval which coincides with the lysocline, where maximum organic dissolution and uptake of metals by forming nodules is taking place. The position of the lysocline is known to within a few hundred metres over most of the oceans, but can vary within this range dependent on local conditions. In order to fix its position precisely, it is necessary to take sediment samples for $CaCO_3$ analysis at close intervals over the probable depth range of the lysocline. The $CaCO_3$ content of the sediments will decrease with depth, and by plotting one against the other, the depth range of maximum dissolution can be established and nodule exploration concentrated there.

In spite of the lack of any dispersion from nodules of an exploration significance, there is at least one way in which studies of sediments associated with nodules may help to give a clue to nodule composition. That is by examining the composition of their micronodule fraction. Micronodules separated from sediments associated with ore grade nodules in the north-eastern equatorial Pacific have been examined by Friedrich (1976) who found Ni and Cu enrichment in the nodules to be reflected by Ni and Cu enrichment in the micronodule fraction of the sediments. However, the time consuming nature of the sample preparation procedure precludes the use of this approach as an exploration tool.

A different approach to the problem of determining the composition of the micronodule fraction of sediments associated with nodules has been attempted by Cronan and Moorby (unpublished). This was to use the hydroxylamine hydrochloride leach technique, described previously, on sediments associated with nodules, and to compare the composition of the reducible manganese dioxide fraction with that of both whole nodules and that of their reducible fraction. This approach was adopted because the valuable metals Ni and Cu are concentrated in the reducible manganese dioxide fraction of nodules (Cronan, 1977b). The philosophy behind this work was that the manganese oxide phases of both nodules and associated sediments might be similar in composition if formed by similar processes, and therefore selective analysis of the sediments might give an indication of the composition of the associated nodules. The study indicated that interrelationships do occur between some individual elements determined in the same fractions of both nodules and sediments. However, there were really too few samples of nodules *and* associated sediments analysed from the same stations to draw any firm conclusions on the value of this approach as an exploration tool, and more work is required to evaluate its use in this regard. An important problem in trying to use nodule–sediment inter-relationships for exploration, or for any other purpose, is, as mentioned in section 5.4.2, the fact that the nodules and associated sediments are often likely not to be contemporaneous. This may account for the lack of success of most workers in this endeavour.

Even if feasible, an exploration method for nodules based on analysis of their associated sediments would not, of course, be used if it were possible to mount a sampling programme at sea to collect the nodules themselves for analysis. Its use would be in enabling areas worthy of exploration for nodules to be delineated on the basis of existing sediment collections.

9.2.2.2   In situ *analysis*

In order to avoid having to retrieve large numbers of samples from the sea bed for analysis in submarine geochemical exploration, *in situ* analysis of the sea floor using nuclear techniques has been proposed by several workers. The advantages of such an approach are obvious. If it were possible to receive a continuous record of the composition of the sea floor from a sea bed analyser, geochemical maps could be constructed during the course of a marine survey with a considerable saving in time over con-ventional techniques of sampling, analysis and data reduction. Nevertheless some bottom sampling would always be required as a control on the in-strumental results. Two approaches to *in situ* analysis proposed utilize the measurement of natural radioactivity, and induced radioactivity using a Californium 252 source.

(a)   *Natural radioactivity*

Certain minerals in marine sediments are sufficiently radioactive for this property to be used in their detection. Uranium, thorium and their decay products occur in certain heavy minerals and in phosphorites (Summerhayes *et al.*, 1970; Noakes *et al.*, 1974). For example, heavy mineral assemblages which contain monazite, epidote, sphene and zircon often contain significant amounts of thorium and its daughter products, whereas as described pre-viously phosphorite deposits can be high in uranium and its daughter pro-ducts.

The first application of *in situ* measurements of natural radioactivity in phosphorite exploration has been described by Summerhayes *et al.* (1970). These workers developed a submersible scintillation counter which measured total sea floor radioactivity, the detector being a sodium iodide crystal housed in a sea bed container (Fig. 85). Gamma spectrum analysis of deposits from the phosphorite-rich area off north-west Africa showed that elevated levels of radioactivity were due to uranium and its decay products present in the phosphorites. A reconnaissance survey using the instrument demonstrated its usefulness in detecting variations in the radioactivity of the sea floor which could be related to the occurrence of phosphorite rock outcrops and phosphoritic sediments.

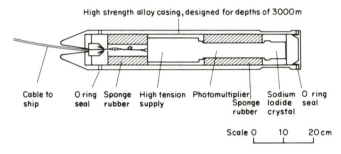

Fig. 85. Submersible scintillation counter: schematic section (from Summerhayes *et al.*, 1970).

Noakes *et al.* (1974) have described research into techniques which could measure and differentiate between natural radioactivity from uranium associated with phosphorite deposits and from thorium associated with heavy minerals. One system, mounted in a towed sled, contained four gamma-ray detectors consisting of thallium activated sodium iodide crystals, and was used to determine the total natural radioactivity of areas of the sea floor. The signals from the detectors after being summed and amplified were fed into a two-channel strip chart recorder set to discriminate between different energy levels of radiation. An additional static system utilizing a lithium drifted germanium detector was used for the identification of specific isotopes in order to differentiate between thorium and uranium decay products. Tests of the towed gamma-ray detectors showed that gamma-ray emitting materials could be detected on the sea floor, which were subsequently identified as heavy mineral bearing sands and silts. Tests using the static Ge (Li) detector system enabled gamma-ray spectra from heavy minerals and phosphorites to be differentiated.

Probably the most highly developed towed gamma spectrometer for measuring natural radioactivity on the sea floor has been described by Miller and Symons (1973) and Miller *et al.* (1977). The gamma-ray detecting probe, containing a NaI (Tl) crystal, is enclosed in a long flexible tube, or

Fig. 86. Towed sea bed gamma spectrometer developed by AERE Harwell and I.G.S. (UK) (after Bowie and Clayton, 1972 and Miller *et al.*, 1977).

"eel" (Fig. 86) which minimizes snagging and the loss of the equipment on the sea floor. The system continuously monitors the total radioactivity and gamma energy bands characteristic of potassium, uranium and thorium, at speeds of up to 7 knots. Satisfactory operation of the spectrometer obviously depends on the rear half of the "eel" which contains the detector remaining in contact with the sea bed. In order to achieve this, the length of the cable attaching the "eel" to the ship is adjusted to compensate for changes in water depth and ship speed. The "eel" can be towed for up to 24 hours, after which it is retrieved for inspection to determine any wear. Between traverses, the "eel" is towed a few metres above the sea floor which enables a measurement of "background" gamma radiation from sea water to be monitored. Not only is the system capable of detecting radioactive element bearing minerals on the sea floor, but it also has considerable application in sea bed geological mapping. Different rock and sediment types on the sea floor tend to have characteristic levels of radioactivity and radioelement ratios which can be continuously monitored and contoured. The ensuing maps reflect the geology of the sea floor and can provide a basis for the critical location of bottom sampling sites, thereby ensuring maximum representivity of the samples and minimizing the total number of bottom samples required to characterize any area of sea floor.

(b) *Californium 252*

One of the earliest methods proposed for *in situ* sea floor analysis was to irradiate the sea floor using the man-made isotope Californium 252. Senftle *et al.* (1969) conducted experiments to show the feasibility of using *in situ* neutron activation from a ^{252}Cf source on the sea floor, followed by detection of neutron capture gamma radiation using a germanium (lithium) drifted crystal. Californium 252 undergoes spontaneous fission (2·6 year half life) and can provide a sustained neutron yield.

The development of an *in situ* neutron activation system on this principle specifically for manganese nodule exploration has been described by Lange and Biemann (1975). It was designed to utilize neutron induced prompt gamma radiation from a ^{252}Cf source which is recorded by a Ge (Li) detector as described above. A spectrum is generated from which the height of the characteristic lines of each element are measured and the element concentrations determined. The system was constructed to be mounted on a sled which is lowered to the sea floor. A suction nozzle picks up the nodules which are transported through a pipe into a separator where they are washed free of clay and other adhering foreign materials. After cleaning, the nodules fall into an analysis chamber where they are analysed and the data transmitted to the ship.

9.3 Summary: Integration of Marine Mineral Exploration Systems

In this chapter various methods of undersea mineral exploration, both tried and innovative, have been discussed. A prerequisite for any undersea exploration is a suitable vessel in which exploration equipment can be housed. Standard geophysical techniques such as precision depth recording and seismic profiling are common to most undersea mineral exploration surveys. Various sampling methods are also normally used. In more sophisticated surveys, refined geophysical techniques such as magnetics and side scan sonar may be used, as may detailed sampling for geochemical exploration purposes. Underwater TV is a component of advanced phases of exploration, and *in situ* analysis of the sea floor may become an increasingly important activity in the future.

There has been a tendency in recent years to move towards the construction of all-purpose integrated mineral exploration vessels. These have the advantage that many different sorts of operations can be conducted from the one vessel, thus obviating the need to move equipment and personnel from ship to ship. Multi-purpose mineral exploration vessels must be capable of working in the most difficult environments in deep water far from land, and be able to stay at sea for at least 3–4 weeks at a time. Precise navigation systems are therefore an important component of such vessels. All purpose mineral exploration vessels must also be able to deploy a range of geophysical and sampling devices, sometimes simultaneously. An adequate winch system is therefore a necessity, coupled with a launch for the retrieval of free fall samplers whilst the main vessel is engaged in geophysical or wire-lowered operations. Such vessels have been developed in several countries, and one is illustrated schematically in Fig. 87.

An important development in sea floor exploration in recent years which has considerable potential in the search for undersea minerals is the "Deep Tow". This enables an integrated package of geophysical instruments to be towed near the sea floor rather than at the sea surface, thus considerably increasing the resolution obtained (Spiess and Mudie, 1970; Spiess *et al.*, 1976). The system includes a narrow beam precision depth recorder, a side scan sonar, a 3·5 kHz echo sounder to delineate details of shallow structure, stereo photography and a proton magnetometer. Water sampling equipment can also be attached. Coupled with a TV system such a package could be a powerful tool in deep sea mineral exploration.

Obviously, the ultimate aim of any marine mineral exploration programme is to determine the composition of materials on the sea floor. As mentioned, there have been some attempts to integrate the taking of samples

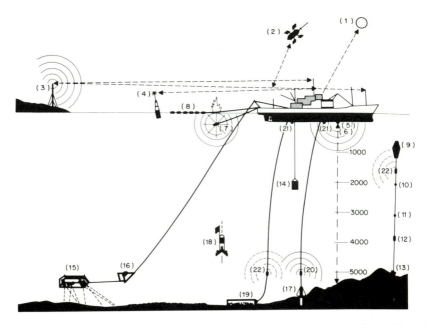

Fig. 87. All purpose mineral exploration vessel. *Navigation:* (1) stars; (2) satellites; (3) radio navigation; (4) navigation buoy (transponder/radar). *Bathymetry:* (5) narrow beam sounder and sediment echograph; (6) various depth recorders. *Reflection seismic:* (7) airgun; (8) streamer with hydrophones, analogue and digital registration. *Oceanographic survey:* (9) underwater measuring chain with localizable buoy; (10) current meter; (11) thermometer; (12) water pressure gauge; (13) cut-off anchor; (14) bathysonde (continuous measurement of temperature, salinity, sound velocity, pressure). *Survey of ore deposits:* (15) deep diving probe with TV camera, still camera and lights; (16) depressor platform; (17) corer for sampling sediment with nodules; (18) free fall sampler; (19) bulk sampling of nodules for metallurgical tests. *Location of launched survey gauges:* (20) pinger; (21) hydrophone; (22) transponder (from Mining Engineering, April, 1975).

for analysis with underwater TV operations, so that a picture of the material on the sea floor can be obtained prior to its being sampled (Kaufman and Siapno, 1972b). However, in general, few attempts have been made to develop integrated sampling and observational tools, and there is a great need for new developments in this field. For example, the coupling of a TV system with an underwater *in situ* analytical device would be a great advance over present techniques. Similarly, the integration of serial sampling devices with underwater TV would be most useful. Ultimately, the most desirable undersea mineral exploration package would be one which enables all the parameters required to evaluate a deposit to be continuously monitored at the same time. This aim is certainly not beyond the scope of present day technology.

10

Exploitation

The exploitability of underwater mineral deposits depends on a variety of factors. Among these can be included their nature, their ease of extraction, their distance from processing plants or markets, their processability if significantly different from that of similar land based deposits, the likely effect on the environment of their extraction and the cost of preventing or repairing environmental damage, and their ownership. The economic feasibility of exploiting each deposit must therefore be based, in part, on the individual characteristics of that deposit. This is particularly so in the case of near-shore minerals such as placers and aggregates which are of limited areal extent, bulky in nature, and which vary greatly in grade and abundance from one locality to another. Detailed consideration of the relationship between the various factors affecting the exploitability of underwater mineral deposits is beyond the scope of this book, but certain of them will be reviewed in general terms.

10.1   Resource potential

Much has been written about the resource potential of undersea mineral deposits. Mero (1965) reviewed in a generally optimistic manner the value of a wide range of deposits from manganese nodules to deep sea clays and ooze. Many subsequent evaluations have been rather more circumscribed in their approach, whilst nevertheless admitting that some deposits do have a considerable potential value.

In discussing the economic value of underwater mineral deposits, it is important to distinguish between resources and reserves. The recoverable metals in underwater mineral deposits that are economically workable in the current locally prevailing economic circumstances, are reserves (see for example Archer, 1976). By contrast, those metals in deposits with a lower grade or abundance that may be workable at some time in the future, coupled with the reserves, constitute resources. Thus resources may become reserves with changing economic and technological circumstances. It is evident that data on average grade of underwater mineral deposits through-out the oceans are no more meaningful in an economic sense than average crustal abundances of elements on land, and such data can only be used in resource estimates with extreme caution. Pasho and McIntosh (1976) have shown how data of this sort can become confused with reserves and re-sources. Quoting the famous and well intentioned speech by Ambassador Pardo (Malta) at the United Nations, concerning the amounts of metals in manganese nodules based on the data of Mero (1965), Pasho and McIntosh pointed out that such numbers are misleading and incorrect in that they imply that the metals concerned are economically recoverable in the quanti-ties mentioned. In this chapter, the terms reserves and resources will be used in the sense defined by Archer (1976).

10.1.1   Aggregates

Marine aggregates consisting principally of sand and gravel are, in terms of value, the most important underwater mineral deposit being mined at the present time, other than oil. For example, about 13% of all UK gravel production and 19% of Japan's sand and gravel production came from off-shore areas prior to 1976 (Cottell, 1978; NOAA, 1976). Amounts of sand and gravel actually mined included about 20 million tonnes a year by the UK, and 10 million tonnes a year by Holland (NOAA, 1976). As can be seen from Table 30, the total amount of sand and gravel recovered from the UK offshore area has increased steadily over the past two decades.

Several factors are of importance in determining the resource potential of offshore aggregates. Naturally, the grade and quality of the deposit are of prime importance in this regard, but so is its distance from potential markets. Because aggregates are a bulky commodity of relatively low value per tonne, transportation costs are very important in assessing their value, and they must serve local markets to be utilizable. Much of the sand and gravel dredged in the British sector of the North Sea, for example, is used in the Thames Valley and in the Low Countries, and that off north-east England is used between Humberside and Newcastle (Archer 1973b). Some is also exported to Germany (Cottell, 1978). Thus, it is only possible to estimate the resource potential of aggregates in terms of local markets and prices.

As can be seen from Table 30, until about 1963 offshore production of sand and gravel by the UK was increasing at about 3% a year. From 1963 to 1971 the rate increased by about 15% a year. This increase was due to

Table 30. Production of sand and gravel in Great Britain (from Archer, 1973b).

Year	Total Million tonnes	Marine dredged Million tonnes	Percentage
1959	68·4	3·9	5·7
1960	76·0	4·2	5·5
1961	85·1	4·3	5·1
1962	85·3	4·1	4·8
1963	88·7	4·4	5·0
1964	106·3	5·8	5·5
1965	102·4	7·2	7·0
1966	106·1	7·5	7·1
1967	112·2	8·7	7·8
1968	114·5	12·0	10·5
1969	112·6	13·5	12·0
1970	113·3	13·6	12·0
1971	114·5	13·5	11·8

Marine dredged figures: Crown Estates Commissioners and Department of the Environment.

a number of factors, not least among them being the growing need for sand and gravel for construction purposes in the UK and neighbouring countries, and the increasing restrictions being placed on extraction of the commodity from sources on land. Increases in land values related to building and agricultural purposes, coupled with the environmental disturbance associated with open pit mining, have conspired to make aggregate mining on land more costly and difficult, and sometimes prohibited it altogether. If one adds to these factors the depletion of land resources of the deposits, it is evident why the marine aggregate industry has increased so much in importance and will probably continue to do so in the future.

The development of the offshore sand and gravel industry in the United States has been much slower than in Western Europe. There are a number of reasons for this, but it is mainly because the land reserves are so large that sand and gravel requirements have not had to be met from offshore sources. However, this situation is changing as a result of increased urbanization, resource depletion on land, the increasing amenity value of recreational land in the vicinity of urban centres where sand and gravel is most needed, and the heavy road and rail costs in moving sand and gravel. (It has been estimated that the cost of aggregates on land doubles with transport 16 km from the source.) The resources of sand and gravel off the United States have been estimated by Cruickshank and Hess (1975) to be as much as 1400 billion tonnes. Deposits are scattered over much of the United States continental shelf in quantities from an estimated mere 5 million tonnes

Table 31. Resources of sand and gravel in selected areas of the US Continental Terrace as estimated by various workers (from N.O.A.A., 1976).

Location	Quantity estimated[a]
Maine	94 million m³
Massachusetts Bay	44 million m³
Rhode Island	108 million m³
Long Island Sound	100 million m³
Long Island South Shore	5254 million m³
New Jersey	2730 million m³
Delaware–Maryland	168 million m³
Virginia	15 million m³
North Carolina	172 million m³
Florida East Coast	2271 million m³
Southern California	458 million m³
Eastern Lake Michigan	"large quantities"
New Jersey (gravel)	7·6–23 billion m³
New England (sand)	450 billion tonnes
New England (gravel)	31 billion tonnes
California, Russian River	100 million tonnes
California, Redondo Beach	5 million tonnes
California, total	"considerably less than Atlantic"
Alaska, southeast	"large quantities"
Hawaii, Oahu	370 million tonnes

[a] Some of the estimates are in nature of reserves; some are in nature of resources.

at Redondo Beach, California, to as much as 450 billion tonnes off New England in general (Table 31).

Calcareous shell is locally important for use in the manufacture of cement, and for other construction purposes. The distribution of high grade shell is very patchy on the sea floor, and the deposits sometimes exist in the form of shell banks. Such deposits have been found in the north-eastern Irish Sea, off the Isle of Man, for example (Cronan, 1969b), and sand waves consisting of shell sand have been found in the Moray Firth off Scotland (Archer, 1973b). Shell sand has been extracted off Iceland for the cement industry for some time (Chapter 2) and off the United States for use as aggregate.

10.1.2 Placers

Placer mining is most developed off south-east Asia where cassiterite is being recovered in a number of areas. The exploration and development of the shallow coastal cassiterite deposit at Takuapa, West Thailand, can be used as an example of how placer resource evaluation is carried out and some of the problems that can arise (McDonald and Tong, 1978). This deposit was prospected in the late 1950s and 1960s using banka drilling equipment. The method of evaluation was the same as that used in the evaluation of alluvial tin deposits on land. The result of the initial prospecting indicated a rich tin deposit of about 81 km² in extent, but generally of thicknesses limited to an average of 1–1·2 m, with less than 0·3 m in places. However, a low mining efficiency obtained in early mining operations prompted a revaluation of the original reserve estimates. This investigation revealed that there had been a considerable over-evaluation of the thin alluvium deposits, and a re-evaluation of the deposit took place. This work showed that the standard method for evaluation of alluvial deposits is liable to result in over-estimation in those with a thickness of less than about 1 m, due mainly to the small volume of sample that can be obtained from the bore with standard equipment. Evaluation of such deposits using other methods would therefore be prudent (McDonald and Tong, 1978).

There are extensive deposits of placer minerals in areas other than southeast Asia (Chapter 2) but they have not been exploited to such a great extent. Many of the deposits are only marginally economic to work. For example, mining of offshore tin took place in St Ives Bay, Cornwall, in the mid 1960s for a short period, but was soon discontinued because of bad weather, harbour difficulties, and poor recovery (Penhale and Hollick, 1968). Wilcox et al. (1972) have made a preliminary estimate of the economic potential of marine placer mining off the USA, and concluded that even in the case of the highest grade placer minerals, mining the deposits was not economically justified. Metal prices have increased considerably since that estimate was made, but so have costs, and it may still not be profitable to mine most US offshore placer minerals.

It is evident from the above that placer mineral mining may only be economically viable for certain periods and in certain situations, and except for a few deposits, the returns are likely to be rather small. Local circumstances or changes in the metal markets could, however, substantially alter this picture for better or worse.

10.1.3 Phosphorite

The worldwide distribution of phosphorite deposits has been reviewed in Chapter 4, but insufficient information is available on grade and abundance within areas of phosphorite occurrence to enable their resource potential to be determined.

An important factor inhibiting serious consideration of the resource potential of marine phosphorites is the abundance of extensive deposits on land. The United States, a major user of phosphates for agricultural purposes is, because of its large land phosphorite resources, an exporter of phosphate rock. Large terrestrial phosphorite deposits also occur in Africa, Australia and Asia. However, as in the case of sand and gravel extraction on land, advanced countries are re-evaluating their land use priorities to the extent that environmental, amenity and recreational considerations are becoming more important than resource considerations. Thus, although the US, for example, may have large land reserves of phosphorite, use of the land for other purposes may inhibit their development thus increasing the US dependence on other sources. Under these circumstances, marine phosphorite mining might become worthwhile in the future.

10.1.4   Metalliferous sediments

Estimates of the resource potential of metalliferous sediments have only been made in the Red Sea, where mining feasibility studies have been carried out. Elsewhere on mid-ocean ridges, the deposits found to date are too low grade to be considered as a resource. However, this does not mean that as yet undiscovered high grade metalliferous sediments do not occur in submarine volcanic areas other than the Red Sea (Chapter 6), for exploration has not been directed towards finding them.

An estimate of the economic worth of the Atlantis II Deep deposits in the Red Sea has been provided by Hackett and Bischoff (1973) on the basis of coring within the Deep in 1969. Correcting for the salt content of the cores, zinc and copper were expressed on both a dry salt free basis and a wet *in situ* basis. Volume estimates of the deposits were made based on an isopach map of the Deep obtained through the coring, the Deep being divided into three areas representing partially separate basins. Grades and volumes of the deposits calculated are given in Table 32. From these, the value of the deposits was estimated as $2·33 billion at 1972 prices.

A more detailed exploration survey of Atlantis II Deep and other deeps in the Red Sea was commenced in 1971/72 by a German group of companies including Preussag AG. A mining feasibility study was commenced by the same group for the Red Sea Commission in 1976/77. Backer (1979) has estimated that about 2·5 million tonnes available reserves of Zn occur in Atlantis II Deep sediments, with 0·6 tonnes of Cu and 0·009 tonnes of Ag.

10.1.5   Sub-sea floor deposits

The resource potential of sub-sea floor mineral deposits varies depending upon the deposit type and its location. According to Wang and McKelvy

Table 32. Volumes and grades for Atlantis II Deep (from Hackett and Bischoff, 1973).

	Area I
Volume	$36 \cdot 39 \times 10^7$ m³
Specific gravity	$1 \cdot 56$
Zn	$4 \cdot 99 \times 10^3$ g/m³ Zn (total) $20 \cdot 2 \times 10^5$ tonnes
Cu	$0 \cdot 936 \times 10^3$ g/m³ Cu (total) $3 \cdot 8 \times 10^5$ tonnes
	Area II
Volume	$18 \cdot 95 \times 10^7$ m³
Specific gravity	$1 \cdot 58$
Zn	$2 \cdot 05 \times 10^3$ g/m³ Zn (total) $4 \cdot 34 \times 10^5$ tonnes
Cu	$0 \cdot 79 \times 10^3$ g/m³ Cu (total) $1 \cdot 56 \times 10^5$ tonnes
	Area III
Volume	$28 \cdot 67 \times 10^7$ m³
Specific gravity	$1 \cdot 67$
Zn	$2 \cdot 51 \times 10^3$ g/m³ Zn (total) $8 \cdot 06 \times 10^5$ tonnes
Cu	$0 \cdot 835 \times 10^3$ g/m³ Cu (total) $2 \cdot 67 \times 10^5$ tonnes
	Total for Atlantis II Deep
Volume	$84 \cdot 01 \times 10^7$ m³
Specific gravity	$1 \cdot 60$
Zn	$3 \cdot 48 \times 10^3$ g/m³ Zn (total) $32 \cdot 7 \times 10^5$ tonnes
Cu	$0 \cdot 869 \times 10^3$ g/m³ Cu (total) $8 \cdot 2 \times 10^5$ tonnes

(1976), any mineral that was worth more than \$15–20 a tonne at 1976 prices and extends offshore from the coast as a large thick deposit beneath impervious rock may be economically recoverable. The value of coal seams extending out under the sea from coal fields on land can be proved at least as far from the coast as the limit from which the coal can be extracted with current technology, as has been done by the National Coal Board off north-east England (Dunham and Sheppard, 1969). Proving metallic mineral lodes under the sea floor is more difficult because of their greater complexity, but has been done off Cornwall.

The economic potential of massive sulphide deposits presumed to be present within the oceanic crust has been considered by Spooner and Bray (1977), assuming their comparability with the ore deposits of the Troodos Massif in Cyprus (Chapter 7). They are one or two orders of magnitude smaller, 0·5 to 15 million tonnes with up to 4% Cu, than porphyry copper deposits, the main source of the world's copper. Thus, Cyprus type deposits are not of great relative value even when occurring on land. Taking into account the technological difficulties of exploration and mining, their economic importance under the sea is likely to be negligible for the foreseeable future.

10.1.6 Manganese nodules

More controversy has surrounded the resource potential of manganese nodules than any other underwater mineral deposits.

Their possible value as a mineral resource was apparently recognized during the "Challenger" Expedition by J. Y. Buchanan, the expedition chemist, who commented to this effect in a letter to his father (Glasby, 1977a). However, it was not until the work of Mero (1959, 1965) that serious consideration was given to the mining of manganese nodules. They are now thought of primarily as a source of nickel and to a lesser extent of copper, cobalt and manganese with perhaps molybdenum, vanadium, zinc and other metals as by-products. It has also been reported (NOAA, 1976) that nodules can adsorb up to 200% of their weight of SO_2, and thus they may find applications as exhaust gas scrubbers in industrial power plants and in controlling automobile emissions.

Mero first considered that the elements Mn, Ni, Cu and Co would be the prime ore metals in manganese nodules, with Mo, Pb, Zn, Zr, some rare earths and possibly Fe, Al, Ti, Mg and V being of lesser value. Mero considered that even if only 10% of the nodule deposits on the ocean floor proved economic to mine, there would be sufficient supplies of many metals to last for thousands of years at present rates of their consumption by mankind. He also outlined some of the indirect advantages of manganese nodule mining. For example, he pointed out that the exploitation of manganese nodules could provide raw materials for expanding populations thus eliminating one of the causes of war between nations in historical times. He also suggested that the mining of manganese nodules could enable some land mines of the metals concerned to be closed down, thus reducing the effects of environmental pollution from land mining operations. Another point he made which has often been quoted is that, ocean wide, manganese nodules are forming at a rate faster than many of the metals they contain are being consumed, and thus the world could be faced with a situation of working deposits which are growing faster than they could be mined.

Mero's beliefs regarding the resource potential and mining of manganese nodules fall at one end of a spectrum of opinion on this matter which ranges from very optimistic to highly pessimistic. Opinion is still divided as to the true resource value of manganese nodules in terms of simple mineral economics, let alone the other possible advantages of mining them. Nevertheless, Mero's work has served to focus attention on the possibility of deep sea mining, and has lead directly to much of the subsequent work in the field.

Mining company interest in mining manganese nodules commenced around the mid 1960s and has generally been increasing ever since. Concurrent with this interest came more conservative estimates than those of Mero on the resource potential of manganese nodules. Many of the data collected by the mining companies, mostly in the north-eastern Pacific equatorial zone, have never been released publicly and thus it is not possible to evaluate some statements by industry regarding the potential worth of manganese nodule deposits. However, since the mid 1960s increasing amounts of analytical data on manganese nodules have come into the public domain, primarily as a result of scientific work in universities (Menard *et al.*, 1964; Mero, 1965; Barnes, 1967a; Cronan, 1967; Glasby, 1970; Skornyakova and Andrushchenko, 1970; Goodell *et al.*, 1971; Bezrukov and Andrushchenko, 1972; Horn *et al.*, 1973; Greenslate, 1975; Cronan, 1975b; Meylan and Goodell, 1976; Calvert and Price, 1977a, Calvert *et al.*, 1978; Appendix, this volume; and many others) and these have formed the basis of most, if not all of the published manganese nodule resource evaluations that have been made.

Following the work of Mero (1965), several attempts were made to refine our knowledge of the distribution of high grade nodules (Cronan, 1967; Price and Calvert, 1970; Horn *et al.*, 1973; and others). Using published data, Horn and co-workers catalogued the distribution and composition of nodules throughout the World Ocean and showed that the area of highest grade nodules was an east–west zone in the north-eastern equatorial Pacific (Chapter 5).

Since the work of Horn and co-workers in outlining the regional variability of nodules, most subsequent work in this field has been aimed at calculations of reserves, resources and mine site identifications. There are several problems which have to be taken into account in this sort of endeavour. First, few of the chemical data used were collected for resource evaluation purposes and certain assumptions have to be made before they can be employed, principally that an analysis of a nodule from a single site is representative of other nodules at that site. This assumption is often unfounded as sometimes parts of nodules rather than whole nodules have been analysed (Horn *et al.*, 1973) and different morphological populations of nodules at individual sites can exhibit considerable compositional differences (Cronan and Tooms, 1967b). In order to overcome such problems it has generally been assumed in resource calculations that variations in the chemical representivity of analytical data on nodules are random and in a large enough sample population will tend to cancel each other out (Archer, 1976, 1979; Fraser, 1979). Secondly, the abundance data used in resource calculations are not always reliable. Most abundance estimates are based on nodules observed in sea-bottom photographs, but these can only be accurately expressed in terms of true abundance if the sizes of the nodules are known. This is a difficult parameter to gauge unless the deposits are sampled, because nodules are often markedly non-uniform in morphology (Chapter 5) and buried portions commonly differ in shape from exposed portions (Raab and Meylan, 1977). In the absence of measurements, nodule sizes have to be assumed. Furthermore, nodules are sometimes buried in the upper few centimetres of sediments (Sorem *et al.*, 1978) and thus cannot be taken into account in abundance calculations. Abundance estimates have also been made on the basis of recovery in free-fall grab samplers. However, these may also not be very reliable as they tend to underestimate the amount of nodules present. Another problem in resource estimation relates to the fact that data on grade and abundance are often obtained on different deposits, individual samples in the case of the chemical data and bottom photographs in the case of the abundance data.

An important factor in the estimation of manganese nodule reserves is the relationship between nodule grade and abundance. In making such estimations, most workers have assumed that the two vary independently. However, this concept has been challenged by Menard and Frazer (1978) who conclude that the two variables are inversely correlated. However, the data on which this conclusion is based may not be sufficient to sustain it. First, estimations of grade and abundance were sometimes made on samples from adjacent areas, rather than on the same samples. In view of the local variability in nodule grade and abundance reviewed in Chapter 5, this approach is questionable. Secondly, at many of the sites the nodules were collected with grab samplers, which, as mentioned, tend to underrepresent nodule abundance. Two small areas where a negative correlation between grade and abundance was found had only between 10 and 20 sample sites each, possibly too small a number to be representative. Even where larger populations were used, the scatter of points was considerable, indicating much local variability in the relationship between grade and abundance. Menard and Frazer admit that not all sample populations chosen show a negative correlation between grade and abundance, and some have been reported as showing a positive correlation between these two variables (Pautot and Melguen, 1979). Conceptually, a negative correlation between grade and abundance implies a finite amount of metals to be incorporated in nodules, all of which is utilized. There is no evidence for this. Further, a logical extension of the suggestion that nodules form in abundance within the lysocline as a result of carbonate dissolution (section 5.4.2) would be that grade and abundance should be positively correlated, as a reduced sedimentation rate would favour increased nodule abundance and an increased metal supply as a result of the dissolution would favour increased nodule grade. Indeed, as mentioned, such has been found in some areas of the South Pacific (Pautot and Melguen, 1979) and has also been noted in the North Atlantic by Addy, (1978). Thus, it is clear that both positive and negative correlations occur between nodule grade and abundance in different areas, as well as their often being no correlation at all between them.

In spite of the problems involved in manganese nodule reserve calculations, it is possible to arrive at some generalized order of magnitude estimates of the reserves of metals available in manganese nodules on the ocean floor, the longer-term resource potential of the deposits, and the number of first generation mine sites. In order to do this, certain cut-off grades and abundances have to be assumed. Many workers have concluded that the average abundance of nodules required for a first generation mine is 10 kg/m^2 or more (Fig. 88) with a minimum of 5 kg/m^2 (Archer, 1979; Bastien-Thiery *et al.*, 1977). According to Kildow *et al.* (1976), average and cut-off contents of 2·27% and 1·18% combined Ni and Cu, the two elements of greatest economic importance in the nodules, are likely to be necessary to support a first generation mining operation. Furthermore, in addition to using parameters such as nodule grade and abundance in estimating reserves of manganese nodules on the ocean floor, other factors of considerable importance in an underwater mining operation such as bottom topography and sea state have also to be taken into account. For example, one of the companies involved in the development of nodule mining has estimated that in order to support a viable mining operation, more than 50% of the mine site must be minable and that climatic and hydrographic conditions should be such that mining could take place on average for 300 days per year. Another factor of importance is the bearing strength of the sediments in that this influences the nature of the nodule collecting device that can be used. There are still many imponderables in assessing the potential of the sea floor for nodule mining, and these may not be fully resolved until nodule mining actually starts.

On the basis of grade and abundance values similar to those outlined in the previous paragraph, namely average Ni + Cu of about 2·2% and a nodule abundance of approximately 10 kg/m^2, Frazer (1977) has estimated that there are between 14 and 56 first-generation mine sites currently identifiable. Archer (1976) has estimated between 44 and 166, Holzer (1976) has estimated between 80 and 185 and Archer (1979) has estimated between 60 and 95. The methods used to obtain these values are given by the respective authors, as are the mine site criteria on which they are based. Using both available data and personal assessments, Pasho and McIntosh (1976) have estimated that there is a 50% chance of there being more than 30 mine sites in the north-eastern equatorial Pacific alone, a 95% chance of there being more than five mine sites and only a 5% chance that there are more than 140 mine sites that will be commercially exploitable before the year 2000.

The concept of prime areas has been used as an additional method in

Fig. 88. Abundant cricket ball sized nodules on the sea floor of the Indian Ocean.

the assessment of nodule reserves. Prime areas have been defined by Archer as areas in at least part of which there are deposits of relatively abundant nodules with significantly higher grades than elsewhere. Available data indicate that the largest such area occurs in the north-eastern equatorial Pacific between the Clarion and Clipperton fracture zones, about 3·4 million km² between 7°N–15°N and 120°W–155°W, Archer (1979). A second area of about 0·8 million km² lies to the south-west of Hawaii. Outside the North Pacific, estimates of prime areas are less reliable. Archer considers that there may be about 1 million km² of prime area in the South Pacific with relatively small amounts in the Atlantic and Indian oceans, giving a total of approximately 6·5 million km² or less than 2% of the sea floor

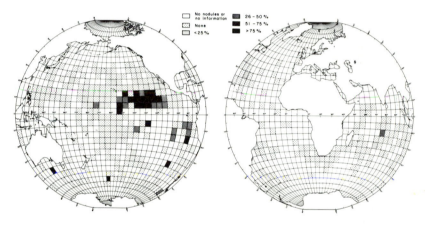

Fig. 89. Percentage of manganese nodule analyses above the required average mine grade (Cu + 2·2 Ni ⩾ 3·76%) (from Frazer, 1977, reproduced by permission of Crane Russak, New York).

for the total prime area. However, only part of this area will meet the specifications for first-generation mine sites, Archer estimates this to be only 2·2 million km². Maps of prime areas (Fig. 89) have been produced by Frazer (1977) and potential reserves of nodules are given in Table 33.

Estimation of manganese nodule resources poses greater problems than the estimation of reserves, because in doing so one has to attempt to predict the grade and abundance that will be workable far ahead in time. Archer has assumed that the eventual lower limits of nodule grade and abundance necessary to support a mine will be about 0·88% combined Ni + Cu and an abundance of 2·5 kg/m,², i.e. about half the cut-offs assumed for potential reserves, and concludes that about 17·5 million km² of the sea floor may contain about 165 000 million tonnes of nodules with grades and abundance

Table 33. Potential reserves and resources in nodules (from Archer, 1979).

	Potential reserves	Resources
Assumed minimum grade (% Ni + Cu)	1·76%	0·88%
Average grade (% Ni + Cu)	2·29%	1·57%
Assumed minimum abundance (wet kg/m²)	5	2·5
Assumed average nodule diameter (cm)	3·68	3·68
Average abundance (wet kg/m²)	15	13·5
Estimated area with this grade and abundance (million km²)	2·2	18·5
Total nodules (wet million tonnes)	33 000	250 000
Total nodules (dry million tonnes)	23 000	175 000
Assumed average Ni grade	1·26%	0·86%
Ni content (million tonnes)	290	1500
Assumed average Cu grade	1·03%	0·71%
Cu content (million tonnes)	240	1240
Assumed average Co grade	0·25%	?
Co content (million tonnes)	60	?
Assumed average Mn grade	27·5%	?
Mn content (million tonnes)	6000	?

greater than these values. However, many of these nodules would be un-workable for a variety of reasons, and thus the 165 000 million tonnes should be regarded as the approximate maximum value for total nodule resources that can be derived from currently available data.

It cannot be emphasized too strongly that reserve and resource estimations of manganese nodules are fraught with uncertainty. They are founded on a limited data base and involve several assumptions that have not as yet been fully tested. As more data become available, they are likely to be revised considerably. For example, an upward revision of only 2% in the proportion of nodules with grade suitable for first-generation mining and revision of minimum abundance requirements from 10 kg/m² to 5 kg/m², lead to an upward revision of the number of first-generation mine sites by as much as 38% (Archer, 1979). Large areas of the oceans have been poorly explored for nodules and some, such as the Central Indian Ocean (Cronan and Moorby, 1976), may contain substantially more ore grade nodules than has hitherto been thought. Nevertheless, according to Archer, present data suggest that first-generation mine sites are likely to total nearer to 100 than 10 or 1000 and that the quantities of Mn, Ni and Cu that would become available as a result of manganese nodule mining are likely to be neither enormously less nor enormously greater than the amounts of these metals that remain to be mined on land. The admitted uncertainty of such estimates, although carefully worked out on the basis of the best available data, constitute a most eloquent plea for further exploration and evaluation of manganese nodules by public institutions, so that before the deposits do start to be mined the true nature and value of the resource can be gauged with accuracy.

10.2   Mining methods

Both existing and proposed methods for mining underwater mineral deposits vary considerably in complexity. Least sophisticated are the simple dredgers used in the extraction of sand and gravel in shallow waters, and most sophisticated are the proposed manganese nodule mining systems. It is not possible to generalize about underwater mining systems because they vary according to the nature and depth of the minerals being mined. Systems for each environment of underwater mineral deposition will therefore be considered separately.

10.2.1   Shallow water deposits

10.2.1.1   *Aggregates*

The principal method of recovering sand and gravel at sea is by use of a suction dredger. Most of the dredgers in use off the United Kingdom have a capacity of about 2000 tonnes, although some large vessels are also used (Archer, 1973b). Both forward and trailing suction pipes are employed, the trailing pipes being used to facilitate the coverage of a wide area where the deposits are thin.

10.2.1.2   *Placers*

Placer deposits are mineable using a variety of techniques. Among these can be included bucket dredging, suction dredging, grab dredging and the use of a mobile dredging platform.

(a) *Bucket dredging*

Tin dredging off Thailand has been carried out using bucket dredging since the early years of this century. The first dredge was powered by steam, had a ladder 24 m long that supported a band of 38 buckets of capacity 0·204 m³ each, and was capable of dredging to 12 m below the water line (Hewett, 1978). Since that time more refined bucket dredgers have been employed. Two such dredgers built for work in Indonesian waters incorporate several of the latest features in bucket dredgers. One of them is equipped with 0.84 m³ buckets for dredging up to 46 m below the water line, and hydraulic buffer mechanisms are being employed to counteract the effect of sea swell which causes the digging point to move in relation to the sea bed. The other has 0·623 m³ buckets and is also able to dredge up to 46 m below the water line.

All bucket dredgers work on the principle of a continuous dragline dredge (Fig. 90) with buckets scooping up the bottom deposits and transporting them up a ladder to the ship. Such dredgers have generally been limited to shallow sheltered waters because of their constuction, but recently

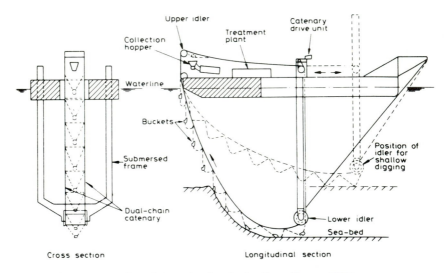

Fig. 90. Arrangement of continuous dragline dredge (from Hewett, 1978).

attempts have been made to adapt them for deeper water work. Two methods have been investigated. First, to mount the buckets and ladder on a semi-submersible pontoon, and secondly, to mount them on a standard type pontoon fitted with vertically adjustable dampening plates at the corners. Features important in bucket dredgers designed to operate in exposed waters include designing a pontoon and superstructure that will withstand gale force winds, greater freeboard than that of dredgers working in sheltered areas, articulation at the ends of the ladder to ensure bottom contact as the dredger pitches and heaves and to dampen down shock as the buckets come into contact with the sea bed, and finally a sophisticated dredge mooring system (Hewett, 1978).

(b) *Suction dredging*

Suction dredging has been used extensively in tin mining operations, as in the recovery of sand and gravel. Two types employed are the suction cutter and the trailing suction dredge. The suction cutter dredge comprises a movable suction pipe with a cutter head mounted on its lower end to break up the deposits and direct them into the suction pipe. By contrast the trailing suction dredge operates by the suction pipe trailing behind the dredger and is of greater use in sweeping up thin deposits of unconsolidated sediments. A version of the latter was constructed to mine the Takuapa offshore tin deposit in Thailand (McDonald and Tong, 1978). As mentioned in section 10.1.2, this deposit has a very limited thickness and is thus not suitable for bucket dredging. A wide area has to be dredged per unit time in order to get a reasonable return. This in turn necessitates high mobility of the dredge which, coupled with the other considerations, led to the construction of a side trailing suction dredge to mine the deposits. The side trailing assembly consists of two pipes of 40·6 cm diameter, coupled together in lengths of 6·09 m and normally operates at an angle of approximately 40–45°. The trailing pipes are joined to fixed pipes at the hull of the dredger by means of flexible reinforced rubber hoses. The extremities of the suction pipes are joined to twin dragheads which comprise two shoes with four apertures each. High pressure water jets discharged from a device attached to the leading edge of the drag head help break up material prior to suction into the pipe and up to the dredger (McDonald and Tong, 1978).

(c) *Grab dredging*

Grab dredgers use large clam shell grabs lowered to the sea floor on flexible steel cables. For example, a converted freighter equipped with twin grabs was used to mine placer tin in the Phukett Island area, Thailand, between 1957 and 1967. More recently Hewett (1978) has proposed a multi-grab dredge which would be suitable for dredging deeper than is possible with bucket dredgers. Grabs to retrieve the bottom deposits would be positioned on both the port and starboard sides of the dredger, and their operation staggered in such a way as to ensure a constant dredged input (Fig. 91).

(d) *Mobile platform*

Beckmann (1975) has described the use of a walking platform to mine placer minerals in very shallow water where they are often concentrated. If successful, this would overcome the problem of grounding that would confront a normal suction dredger working immediately seawards of the surf zone. The platforms could move by alternately sliding one frame on a

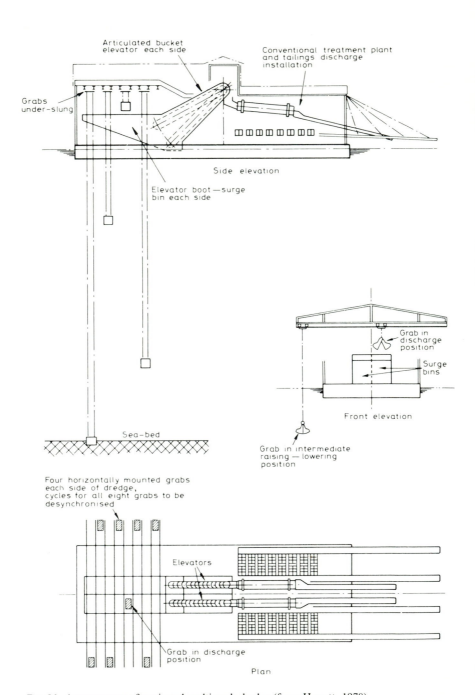

Articulated bucket
elevator each side

Conventional treatment plant
and tailings discharge
installation

Grabs
under-slung

Side elevation

Elevator boot—surge
bin each side

Grab in
discharge
position

Surge
bins

Front elevation

Sea-bed

Grab in intermediate
raising — lowering
position

Four horizontally mounted grabs
each side of dredge,
cycles for all eight grabs to be
desynchronised

Elevators

Grab in discharge
position

Plan

Fig. 91. Arrangement of projected multi-grab dredge (from Hewett, 1978).

second and could attain a speed of about 0·8 km per hour. Such platforms have been built for offshore construction purposes in the United States. Operationally, they can walk from the shore, across a beach, through the surf zone and into shallow water offshore. They are able to equalize their load in such a way that they can traverse rocky areas and irregularites.

10.2.2   Deep-sea deposits

The proposed collection of deep-sea deposits such as manganese nodules and Red Sea metalliferous sediments in commercial quantities has resulted in the development of completely novel mining technologies. This has been

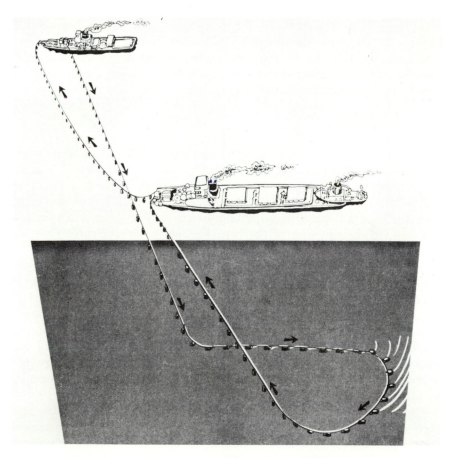

Fig. 92. Two-ship continuous-line bucket system for nodule mining (from *Mining Engineering,* April, 1975).

conditioned by the two main features that have to be taken into account in deep-sea mining, the great depth of the deposits concerned and their occurrence, in the case of the nodules (from the commercial point of view although not in fact), essentially as a single layer at the sediment surface. The great depth of the deposits poses problems concerning the system used for raising them, such as weight, response to surface support movements, water resistance and manoeuvrability, etc. The mining system must cover a wide area in order to achieve an economic production, about 10 000–15 000 tonnes a day, while the dredge head must only penetrate a few centimetres into the sediments in order to avoid collecting disproportionate amounts of unwanted sediment.

Two mining systems are being developed for the recovery of manganese nodules, a mechanical system called the CLB system and a hydraulic system. The CLB system consists of a continuous loop to which collecting buckets are attached (Fig. 92) and which travel to and from the sea floor in a conveyor belt like manner. Hydraulic systems are based on a pipe lowered from the mining ship to the sea floor at the bottom of which is attached a nodule collecting device (Fig. 93).

10.2.2.1 *The CLB System*

The CLB system involves dredging using dredge buckets spaced at intervals along a cable loop, the cable rotating continuously from a surface vessel or vessels to the sea floor. This system carries out both a collecting and a raising function. As originally conceived, the CLB system was to be operated from a single ship, however problems with this approach including possible entanglement of the two sides of the dredge cable have resulted in the development of a two ship system.

In order to raise an economically viable amount of nodules from the ocean floor, i.e. to maintain a predetermined daily output, the various operational parameters in the CLB system have to be carefully chosen. Important factors are the capacity of the dredge buckets and hence the amount of nodules that they can recover, the transit speed of the buckets over the sea floor and hence the rotation speed of the cable, the weight of the buckets and hence the thickness and strength of the cable, and the spacing of the buckets along the line. These factors have been treated numerically by Gauthier and Marvaldi (1975).

The recovery efficiency of the dredge buckets in terms of nodules, and their ability to exclude sediments associated with the nodules are critical factors in the CLB system. As a bucket traverses the sea floor, it collects only a certain proportion of the nodules present. Thus bucket design has to be such that collection of nodules is maximized while collection of associ-

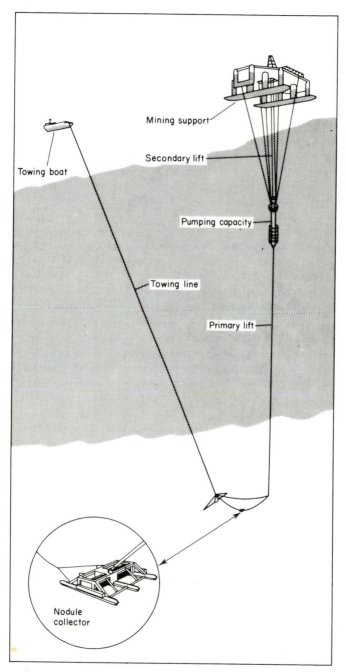

Fig. 93. CORANO hydraulic lift concept for nodule mining (from AFERNOD publicity literature, reproduced by permission).

ated sediments is minimized. The strength of the cable is another important factor in the design of the CLB system. The large capacity mining systems envisaged, which may average as much as 10 000–15 000 tonnes of nodules a day, would require cables with breaking strength in the order of more than 1000 tonnes. The pulley capacity on the surface vessel is also of critical importance in determining the weight of nodules that can be lifted on the cable and hence the spacing of the buckets. Various parameters of the CLB system as envisaged by Gauthier and Marvaldi (1975) for a production rate of 5000 tonnes of nodules per day are given in Table 34.

Table 34. Comparison of certain parameters in the CLB and hydraulic system of manganese nodule mining (from Gauthier and Marvaldi, 1975).

Daily production	t/day		5000
Concentration of nodules	kg/m²	10	5
Hydraulic system (travelling speed: 0·5 m/s)			
Collecting width	m	12	24
CLB system (Cable speed: 1 m/s)			
Loading of buckets with nodules	t/m³	0·7	0·5
Bucket volume	m³	3	3
Spacing of buckets	m	36	25
Length of run required for loading	m	170	230
Minimum number of dredging buckets		5	9

10.2.2.2 *Hydraulic systems*

The essential components of hydraulic systems of nodule mining are firstly a nodule collecting device and secondly a lift system to raise the nodules to the ship.

Several collecting devices have been patented, and their design has been based on a number of criteria which they have to fulfil. Perhaps most important of these is their ability to collect sufficient tonnages of nodules to maintain a high daily production rate. This means that the collecting device should be wide enough, about 10–15 m, to take in sufficient nodules, but not so large that it loses contact with the sea floor as a result of undulation in the latter. It must be able to move easily over the ocean floor without sinking into the sediment, and be able to scrape off the surface layer of nodules while discarding as much as possible of the associated clay before the nodules are lifted to the surface. Naturally, the collecting device must be sufficiently rugged to withstand impact with rocks and the effects of the enormous pressure on the deep ocean floor, and sufficiently manoeuvrable that major obstacles can be avoided and the sea floor traversed in a manner most consistent with maximum nodule recovery.

Smale-Adams and Jackson (1978) have described one version of a manganese nodule collector. The nodules are collected by hydraulic suction possibly with the aid of nodule dislodging devices such as water jets or tines. The amount of nodules obtained by such a collector is a function of the average nodule abundance, the speed of the collector over the sea floor, its width, and the efficiency with which it works. Smale-Adams and Jackson point out that it may be necessary to provide some method for concentrating nodules from the sediment–water mixture perhaps by taking advantage of differences in settling velocity between the nodules and the other materials collected. It would also be useful to remove heavier solids such as basalt fragments etc., at an early stage of the dredging operation. Smale-Adams and Jackson described a successful test of a hydraulic suction collecting device held in 1975.

Once the nodules have been collected they have to be lifted to the surface. Two methods of doing this have been proposed: by hydraulic pumping with pumps and by air lift. Both methods utilize large diameter pipes up which nodules are swept by fluids.

According to Smale-Adams and Jackson (1978), all the hydraulic lift methods comprise two components, a pipe section and a pump section. The air lift system consists of a large pipe extending from the mining vessel down to the nodule collecting device. A thinner pipe runs part way down the main pipe and discharges high pressure air into it. The air rises through the water in the large pipe and forms a fluid column with a lower density than that of ocean water. This density contrast produces a force which results in an upward flow of fluid in the main pipe and which can flush nodules up the pipe to the surface. An alternative method of lifting nodules to the surface is by the use of hydrocarbons instead of air to reduce the density of the fluid in the upper part of the pipe. Both methods have the advantage that no moving parts below the water line are required, but the hydrocarbon lift method could raise objections on environmental grounds (Smale-Adams and Jackson, 1978).

The centrifugal pump system for mining nodules operates on the principle of immersed centrifugal pumps placed at regular intervals underwater down the dredge pipe. One such system has been described by Mero (1965). The pumps provide the lift required to move the fluid plus nodules up the pipe to the surface. This system may have some advantages over the air lift system in that it would require less energy to lift a given weight of nodules (Tinsley, 1976) and would have a slower upward flow thus reducing abrasion of the dredge pipe, but may have some disadvantages in that there are more moving parts.

10.2.2.3 *Comparison of CLB and hydraulic systems*

A comparative evaluation of the CLB and hydraulic lift system in nodule mining has been attempted by Gauthier and Marvaldi (1975). From Table 34 it can be seen that the width of the collecting device in the hydraulic system has to double in order to obtain a daily production of about 5000 tonnes of nodules when their concentration on the sea floor drops from 10 kg/m² to 5 kg/m². By contrast, the size and spacing of the buckets in the CLB system would have to vary less with a change in nodule concentration. Thus, according to Gauthier and Marvaldi, the CLB system would allow the exploitation of nodules which could not be recovered by the hydraulic system without considerably enlarging the width of the collecting device beyond the 10–15 m or so generally considered feasible. An additional point in favour of the CLB system is that should some of the buckets become clogged with sediments, it would not affect the collecting ability of the remainder of the buckets. By contrast, if a nodule collector comprising part of a hydraulic system became clogged, it might have to be raised to the surface to be cleared, thereby resulting in a considerable loss of production. However, Gauthier and Marvaldi admit that the design of a dredger such as would be employed in the CLB system poses greater problems than the design of a suitable collecting device for a hydraulic nodule mining system, and imply that constructing suitable cables for lifting the buckets might also pose considerable problems. Factors such as these may eventually result in the abandonment of development of the CLB system in favour of a hydraulic lift system for nodule mining.

10.2.2.4 *Mining ship*

In any discussion of manganese nodule mining systems, consideration of the nature and functions of the mining ship is of importance. In order to meet the production requirements of manganese nodules outlined previously, i.e. 5000–15000 tonnes per day, the mining ship should be around 50000 tonnes, and be able to stay at sea for considerable periods. According to Smale-Adams and Jackson (1978), four years would be a reasonable period for the vessel to remain at sea before returning to shore facilities. All food, fuel, stores, repair parts and personnel would be transported to the mining ship by supply vessels. The size of the crew would be around 100–120 persons, with crew changes expected to occur every 30 days or so.

In the case of mining using a hydraulic system, the ship would need to have a derrick to handle the mining equipment, which would be lowered through a moon pool in the ship's hull. Some mechanism would be required to limit movement of the pipe. Other important requirements that would have to be met include adequate pipe stowage, a deployment system for the nodule collecting device, air compression for the air lift system, if used, and a sophisticated navigation and positioning system. Detailed specifications would depend upon the individual requirements of users. According to Smale-Adams and Jackson (1978), the pipe handling system dynamic analyses which have been performed indicate that it is feasible to deploy and recover the pipe string with the collector attached in a sea state of 4 at a maximum speed of 7 m/min and to tow the pipe string and collector at speeds between 1·5 and 2 m/s. The pipe string should be isolated from the ship's angular roll and pitch motions in excess of 1° at all times during deployment. They consider the maximum pipe string drag angle which would occur during mining operations is likely to be less than 25°.

In the case of mining using the two ship CLB system, rather different equipment would be used than in a hydraulic lift system. Cable take-up pulleys, bucket guide ramps, bucket emptying equipment and winches would all be necessary, together with sufficient storage space for the buckets and cables.

10.2.2.5 *Mining of metalliferous muds in the Red Sea*

According to Mustaffa and Amann (1978), mining of the Red Sea metalliferous muds will be done by suction, using a vibration/cutting head with sea water jetting and dilution as an aid to mobilize the mud. The muds will be pumped to the surface in a diluted state through a steel pipe.

10.3   Environmental Considerations

There are many considerations to be taken into account in assessing the possible influence on the marine environment of underwater mining. For example, will there be any permanent change to the environment? Will the affects of the mining be harmful to marine life? Can any disturbance be put right after the mining operation has ceased? These and many other environmental questions are the subject of intensive research at the present time.

Near-shore mining has potentially more likelihood of causing observable environmental damage than in the deep ocean. The mining of sand, gravel and placers in the immediate offshore area or on beaches, could lead to a disturbance in the near-shore equilibrium and the erosion of adjacent coastal areas to redress the balance. Alternatively, offshore sediment transport could be enhanced, possibly necessitating bathymetric charts to be resurveyed in order to maintain safe navigation. Disturbance of fish breeding grounds is another possible effect of shallow water offshore mining.

Other effects of such mining could include the disturbance of underwater cables and petroleum pipelines, and the destruction of trawling grounds by leaving holes or boulders which would make trawling impracticable (Archer, 1973b). The possible effect of near-shore mining on the recreational use of beaches must also be considered. Accelerated beach erosion to replace sand and gravel extracted offshore or the shoreward transport of tailings and spoils from placer mining could be particularly serious in areas of tourist importance. In the United Kingdom, factors such as these are evaluated before the Crown Estates Commissioners grant licences for offshore mining, and similar practices prevail in other countries.

Processing of recovered Red Sea metalliferous muds is likely to involve shipboard flotation, and the discharge of tailings back into the sea at a depth in excess of 400 m. During tests, the tailings plume was monitored to depths in excess of 1000 m, and became more diffuse with time. At the time of writing, intensive studies are underway into the possible environmental effects of such a mechanism of tailings disposal (A. Mill, personal communication).

Much consideration has been given to the possible environmental effect of manganese nodule mining (Amos et al., 1972, 1973, 1977; Dubbs, 1978). In any mining system there will be some disturbance of the bottom environment leading to the re-suspension of sediments. For example, estimates based on the use of the CLB mining system (Amos et al., 1977) indicate that as much as 5×10^4 m^3 of sediment could be disturbed per day. It is obvious that mining companies would want to separate the nodules from their associated sediments as much as possible before lifting them to the surface. Nevertheless this will not be 100% effective. Based on Stokes' Law, fine particles lifted with nodules could take several hundred days to settle again on the ocean floor, and they may be kept in suspension even longer and transported considerable distances by bottom currents. However, evidence to date indicates that disturbed sediment may not settle particle by particle as implied above but flocculate in some manner thus speeding up settling (Amos et al., 1977).

Little is known about the effect of deep ocean mining on bottom dwelling organisms. Turbidity may have a deleterious effect on some species. While 100% coverage of the sea floor is unlikely in any mining operation, those organisms which cannot escape the oncoming dredge will be at best severely disturbed and at worst destroyed. However, repopulation of the mined out area from adjacent untouched areas will occur.

During transport of nodules to the mining ship, some entrained sediment and bottom water could be discharged either at the surface or within the water column. The CLB system may introduce sediment anywhere into the water column, whereas suction type mining systems will discharge bottom water and sediment mainly near the sea surface (Amos *et al.*, 1977). Little is known about the possible fate of such effluent. Ultimately it will probably sink back to the ocean floor, but may become spread over a wide area in the process. However, bearing in mind the relative uniformity of deep sea sediments, this should not cause a great problem.

Even though the concentrations of mining effluents will be very low in the surface waters over a manganese nodule mine site, some effect on surface organisms may be discernible. For example, it is possible that the increase in nutrient concentration due to bringing up nutrient-rich bottom waters could enhance phytoplankton growth in the surface waters (Amos *et al.*, 1973). Conversely, increased turbidity in the surface waters will lower the penetration of sunlight and may decrease primary productivity (Amos *et al.*, 1977). Furthermore, oxidizable organic material settling through the water column may deplete oxygen from the waters through which the particles settle, but probably by an insignificant amount. Some dissolution of raised sediments may occur as they sink but again this will probably be small. Manganese nodules are in equilibrium with sea water and thus dissolution of raised nodule fragments should be minimal.

Although environmental studies associated with proposed nodule mining will continue for some time, the overall results of the work done to date indicate that the disturbances caused by the mining will be very small in comparison with natural processes, and will be unlikely to cause an environmental hazard.

10.4   Legal Considerations

In any underwater mining operation, some sort of title to the deposits has to be secured in order to guarantee the investment capital required to initiate the operation and maintain it during its early stages. This is not a problem in the case of near-shore mineral deposits where the coastal state exercises legal rights, but is in the deep sea.

Coastal states exert or seek to exert jurisdiction over underwater mineral deposits up to at least 12 miles from their coast, and in an increasing number of cases, up to 200 miles. This effectively includes all placers and aggregates which are currently exploitable, or are likely to be exploitable within the foreseeable future, and most if not all phosphorites. Some countries divide seas between them on the basis of a median line. National legislation regarding the exploitation of offshore mineral deposits is very varied in its nature. In the United Kingdom, the Crown Agents have responsibility for licensing mining operations in the whole of the offshore area. By contrast those countries which consist of an aggregate of states or provinces such as Australia, the United States and Canada, have both central government and local legislation regarding offshore mineral exploitation, and in some cases which level of government actually has jurisdiction over the deposits is in dispute. The reader is referred to individual national legislation to learn of the laws prevailing in this regard in different countries.

Mineral deposits lying outside of areas of national jurisdiction include most deep-sea manganese nodules (some fall within 200 miles of land areas) and metalliferous sediments, and it is the manganese nodules which have provoked most legal discussions regarding deep ocean mining beyond the limits of national jurisdiction. The 1958 Geneva Convention confirmed a coastal state's right to exploit minerals adjacent to its shores to a depth of 200 m, or beyond should exploitation be possible. This effectively placed no constraints on a country exploiting the deep-sea bed adjacent to its coast, provided it had the technology to do so. In 1967, the Maltese Ambassador to the UN addressed the matter of the deep-sea bed and urged that it should be reserved for peaceful purposes. An international agency to control its exploitation was proposed. A sea bed committee was established by the UN to study the whole problem of the legal status of the deep-sea floor, and concluded that these questions were related to many other law of the sea questions which should all be considered together.

It is unlikely that deep-sea mining can develop in an orderly fashion without some sort of international agreement. Thus we are unlikely to see the full mineral potential of the deep-sea bed realized until this is accomplished.

References

Addy, S. K. (1978). Prog. Abstr. Fifth Symposium of the International Association for the Genesis of Ore Deposits. Snowbird, Utah, August, 1978, p. 35.

Ade-Hall, J. M., Palmer, H. C. and Hubbard, T. P. (1971). *Roy. Astron. Soc. Geophys. J.* **24**, 137–174.

Aleva, G. J. J. (1973). *Geol. en Mijnb.* **52**, 79–91.

Altschuler, Z. S., Clarke, R. S. and Young, E. J. (1958). *U.S. Geol. Surv. Prof. paper* 314–D, 45.

Altschuler, Z. S., Berman, S. and Cuttitta, F. (1967). *U.S. Geol. Surv. Prof. paper* 575-B, 1–9.

Ames, L. L. (1959). *Econ. Geol.* **54**, 829.

Amos, A. F., Garside, C. Haines, K. C. and Roels, O. A. (1972). *J. Mar. Technol. Soc.* **6** 40–45.

Amos, A. F. Garside, C., Gerard, R. D., Levitus, S. Malone, T. C., Paul, A. Z. and Roels, O. A. (1973). *In* "Inter-University Programme of Research on Ferro-manganese Deposits on the Ocean Floor," Phase 1, Rept, NSF/IODE, Washington, pp. 221–264.

Amos, A. F., Roels, O. A. Garside, C., Malone, T. C. and Paul A. Z. (1977). *In* "Marine Manganese Deposits" (G. P. Glasby, Ed.), pp. 391–437. Elsevier, Amsterdam.

Anderson, R. N. and Halunen, A. J. (1974). *Nature* **251**, 473–475.

Andrews, J. E. (1976). *In* "Marine Geological Investigations in the Southwest Pacific and Adjacent Areas" (G. P. Glasby and H. R. Katz, Eds). UNESCAP Tech. Bull. N. 2, pp. 1–13.

Andrews, J. E. and Friedrich, G. (1980). *In* "International Monograph on the Geology and Geochemistry of Manganese" (I. Varentsov, Ed.). Publishing House of Hungarian Academy of Sciences (in press).

Andrews, J. E. and Meylan, M. A. (1972). *Hawaii Inst. Geophys. Rept.* No. 72–23, 83–111.

Andrushchenko, P. F. and Skornyakova N. S. (1969). *Oceanology* **9**, 229–242.

Archer, A. A. (1973a). *Ocean Management* **1**, 5–40.

Archer, A. A. (1973b). *In* "North Sea Science" (E. D. Goldberg, Ed.) pp. 437–449. M.I.T. Press, Mass.

Archer, A. A. (1976). *In* "Marine Geological Investigations in the Southwest Pacific and Adjacent Areas" (G. P. Glasby and H. R. Katz, Eds). UNESCAP Tech. Bull. No. 2, pp. 21–38.

Archer, A. A. (1979). *In* "Manganese Nodules: Dimensions and Perspectives", pp. 71–81. D. Redel Co. Dordrecht, Netherlands.

Arrhenius G. (1963). *In* "The Sea" (M. N. Hill, Ed.), Vol. 3, pp. 665–727. Interscience, New York.

Arrhenius, G. (1967). *Trans. Am. Geophys. Union* **48**, 604–631.

Arrhenius, G. and Bonatti, E. (1965) *In* "Progress in Oceanography" (M. Sears, Ed.), Vol 3, pp. 7–22. Pergamon, Oxford.

Arrhenius, G., Mero, J. and Korkisch, J. (1964). *Science* **144**, 170–173.

Arrhenius, G., Cheung, K., Crane, S., Fisk, M., Frazer, J., Korkisch, J., Mellin, T., Nakao, S., Tsai, A. and Wolf, G. (1979). *In* "Sur La Genèse des Nodules de Manganese" (C. Lalou, Ed.). Proc. Colloque Internat. du CNRS, 289.

Aumento, F., Lawrence, D. E. and Plant, A. G. (1968). *Can. Geol. Surv. paper* 68-32, pp. 1–30.

Austin, C. F. (1967). *Eng. Min. J.* **168**, 82–88.

Baak, J. A. (1936). "Regional Petrology of the Southern North Sea". Wageningen.

Bachra, B. N., Travtz. O. R. and Simon, S. L. (1965). *Arch. Oral. Biol.* **10**, 731.

Backer, H. (1973). *Erzmetall.* **26**, 544–555.

Backer, H. (1979). *In* "Offshore Mineral Resources", pp. 319–338. Documents B.R.G.M. No. 7—1979, Orleans, France.

Backer, H. and Richter, H. (1973). *Geol. Rundschau* **62**, 3.

Backer, H. and Schoell, M. (1972). *Nature* (*Phys. Sci.*) **240**, 153–158.

Barnes, S. S. (1967a). The formation of oceanic ferromanganese nodules. Unpublished Ph.D. thesis, University of California, San Diego.

Barnes, S. S. (1967b). *Science* **157**, 63–66.

Barnes, S. S. and Dymond, J. (1967). *Nature* **213**, 1218–1219.

Bass, M. N., Moberly, R., Rhodes, J. M., Shih chu-yu and Church, S. E. (1973). Initial Reports of the Deep Sea Drilling Project, 17, pp. 429–503. U.S. Govt Printing Office, Washington, D.C.

Bastien-Thiery, H., Lenoble, J. P. and Rogel, P. (1977). *Eng. Min. J.* **178**, 86–87.

Baturin, G. N. (1969). *Dokl. Acad. Sci. U.S.S.R.*, *Earth Sci. Sect.* **189**, 227–230.

Baturin, G. N. (1971). *Nature* (*Phys. Sci.*) **232**, 61.

Baturin, G. N. and Bezrukov, P. L. (1979). *Marine Geology* **31**, 317–332.

Baturin, G. N., Kochenov, A. V. and Peterlin, V. P. (1970). *Lithol. Miner. Resour.* (*U.S.S.R.*) **3**, 15–26.

Beckmann, W. C. (1975). "Oceanology International 1975", pp. 342–345. BPS Exhibitions Ltd, London.

Bee, A. (1974). The marine geochemistry and geology of the Atlantic continental shelf of Morocco. Unpublished Ph.D. thesis, University of London.

Bell, D. M. (1977). *Chemistry and Industry* 14 July, 1977.

Bender, M. L. (1971). *J. Geophys. Res.* **76**, 4212–4215.

Bender. M. L., Ku, T. L. and Broecker, W. S. (1966). *Science* **151**, 325–328.

Berger, W. (1976). *In* "Chemical Oceanography" (J. P. Riley and R. Chester, Eds), Vol 5, pp. 265–388. Academic Press, London and New York.

Berger, W. H. and von Rad, U. (1972). Initial Reports of the Deep Sea Drilling Project, 14, pp. 787–954. U.S. Govt Printing Office, Washington, D.C.

Bernat, M. and Church, T. M. (1978). *In* "Natural Zeolites, Occurrence, Properties Use" (L. B. Sand and F. A. Mumpton, Eds), pp. 259–267. Pergamon, Oxford.

Bernat, M. and Goldberg, E. D. (1969). *Earth. Planet. Sci. Letts* **5**, 308–312.

Bernat, M., Bieri, R. H., Koide, M, Griffin J. J. and Goldberg, E. D. (1970). *Geochim. Cosmochim. Acta* **34**, 1053–1071.

Berner, R. A. (1969). *Marine Geology* **71**, 253.

Berner, R. A. (1973). *Earth Planet. Sci. Letts* **18**, 77–86.

Bertine, K. K. (1974). *Geochim. Cosmochim. Acta* **38**, 629–640.

Bertine, K. K. and Keen, J. B. (1975). *Science* **188**, 150–152.

Betzer, P. R., Bolger, G. W., McGregor, B. *et al.* (1974). *E.O.S., Trans. Am. Geophys. Union* **55**, 293.

Bezrukov, P. L. and Andrushchenko, P. F. (1972) *Izv. Acad. Nauk. U.S.S.R., Ser. Geol.* **9**, 18–37.

Bezrukov, P. L. and Baturin, G. N. (1976). *In* "Lithology of Phosphorite Bearing Deposits" pp. 20–28. Nauka, Moscow.

Bezrukov, P.L. and Baturin, G. N. (1979). *Marine Geology* **31**, 317–332.

Bezrukov, P. L. and Skornyakova, N. S. (1976). *Am. Assoc. Petrol. Geol. Memoir* (M. T. Halbouty, J. C. Maher and H. M. Lian, Eds), **25**, 376–381.

Bignell, R. D. (1975a). The geochemistry of metalliferous brine precipitates and other sediments from the Red Sea. Unpublished Ph.D. thesis, University of London.

Bignell, R. D. (1975b). *Trans. Instn Min. Metall.* **B 84**, 1–6.

Bignell, R. D. (1978). *Marine Mining* **1**, 209–236.

Bignell, R. D., Cronan, D. S. and Tooms, J. S. (1976a). *In* "Metallogeny and Plate Tectonics" (D. Strong, Ed.). Geol. Assoc. Canada, Spec. Paper, 14, pp. 147–184.

Bignell, R. D., Cronan, D. S. and Tooms, J. S. (1976b). *Trans. Instn Min. Metall.* **B 85**, 273–278.

Biscaye, P. E. (1965). *Geol. Soc. Am. Bull.* **76**, 803–832.

Bischoff, J. L. (1969). *In* "Hot Brines and Recent Heavy Metal Deposits in the Red Sea" (E. T. Degens and D. A. Ross, Eds), pp. 368–401. Springer-Verlag, New York.

Bischoff, J. L. (1972). *Clays and Clay Minerals* **20**, 217–223.

Bischoff, J. L and Dickson, F. (1975). *Earth Planet. Sci. Letts* **25**, 385–397.

Blissenbach, E. and Fellerer, R. (1973) *Geol. Rundschau* **62**, 812–840.

Boles, J. R. and Wise, W. S. (1978). *In* "Natural Zeolites, Occurrence, Properties, Use" (L. B. Sand and F. A. Mumpton, Eds), pp. 235–244. Pergamon, Oxford.

Bonatti, E. (1963). *Trans. N.Y. Acad. Sci.* **25**, 938–948.

Bonatti, E. and Joensuu, O. (1966). *Science* **157**, 643–645.

Bonatti, E., Honnorez, J., Joensuu, O., and Rydell, H. S. (1972a). *In* "The Mediterranean Sea" (D. J. Stanley, ed.), pp. 701–710. Dowden, Hutchinson and Ross, New York.

Bonatti, E., Kramer, T. and Rydell, H. (1972b). *In* "Ferromanganese Deposits on the Ocean Floor" (D. R. Horn, Ed.), pp. 149–165. National Science Foundation, Washington D. C.

Bonatti, E., Guerstein-Honnorez, B. M. and Honnorez, J. (1976a). *Econ. Geol.* **71**, 1515–1525.

Bonatti, E., Guerstein-Honnorez, B. M., Honnorez, J. and Stern, C. (1976b). *Earth Planet. Sci. Letts* **32**, 1–10.

Bonatti, E., Zerbi, M., Kay, R. and Rydell, H. (1976c). *Geol. Soc. Am. Bull.* **87**, 83–94.

Bostrom, K. (1973). *Stockholm Contr. in Geology* **27**, 149–243 (Acta Universitatis Stockholmiensis).

Bostrom, K. and Fisher, D. E. (1969). *Geochim. Cosmochim. Acta* **33**, 743–745.

Bostrom, K. and Peterson, M. N. A. (1966). *Econ. Geol.* **61**, 1258–1265.

Bostrom, K. and Peterson, M. N. A. (1969). *Marine Geology* **7**, 427–447.

Bostrom, K. Peterson, M. N. A., Joensuu, O. and Fisher, D. E. (1969). *J. Geophys. Res.* **74**, 3261–3270.

Bowen, H. J. M. (1956). *J. Mar. Biol. Ass. U.K.* **35**, 451–460.

Bowie, S. H. U. and Clayton, C. G. (1972). *Trans. Instn Min. Metall.* **B. 87**, 215.

Brewer, P. G. (1965). *In* "Chemical Oceanography" (J. P. Riley and G. Skirrow, Eds). Academic Press, London and New York.

Brewer, P. G. and Spencer. D. W. (1969). *In* "Hot Brines and Recent Heavy Metal Deposits in the Red Sea" (E. T. Degens and D. A. Ross, Eds), pp. 174–179. Springer-Verlag, New York.

Brewer, P. G., Riley, J. P. and Culkin, F. (1965). *Deep Sea Res.* **12**, 497–503.

Bricker, O. P. (1965). *American Mineralogist* **50**, 1296–1354.

Brook, J. and Gilbert, R. L. G. (1968). *Deep Sea Res.* **15**, 483–490.

Bruneau, L., Jerlov, N. G. and Koczy, F. (1953). *In* "Reports of the Swedish Deep Sea Expedition" Physics and Chemistry. 3.

Buckland, W. (1829). *Geol. Soc. Lond., Trans. 2nd Ser.* **3**, 223.

Burnett, W. C. (1974). *Hawaii Inst. Geophys. Rept*, No. 74–3.

Burnett, W. C. (1977). *Geol. Soc. Am. Bull.* **88**, 813–823.

Burnett, W. C., and Piper, D. Z. (1977). *Nature* **265**, 596–600.

Burnett, W. C. and Veeh, H. H. (1977). *Geochim. Cosmochim Acta* **41**, 755–764.

Burns, R. G. (1965). *Nature* **205**, 999.

Burns, R. G. and Brown, B. A. (1972). *In* "Ferromanganese Deposits on the Ocean Floor" (D. R. Horn, Ed.) pp. 51–62. National Science Foundation, Washington D.C.

Burns, R. G. and Burns V. M. (1977). *In* "Marine Manganese Deposits" (G. P. Glasby, Ed.), pp. 185–248. Elsevier, Amsterdam.

Burns V. M. and Burns R. G. (1978). *Earth Planet. Sci. Letts* **39**, 341–348.

Burns, V. M. and Burns R. G. (1979). *In* "Sur la Genèse des Nodules de Manganese" (C. Lalou, Ed.). Proc. Colloque International du CNRS No. 289.

Burns, R. G. and Fuerstenau, D. W. (1966). *American Mineralogist* **51**, 895–902.

Burns R. G., Burns, V. M. and Sung. W. (1974). *Geol. Soc. Am. Abs. Progs.* **6** (7) 1029–1031.

Buser, W. (1959). *Int. Oceanogr. Congr. Preprints* **1**, 962–963.

Buser, W. and Grütter, A. (1956). *Schweiz. Mineral. Petrogr. Mitt.* **36**, 49–62.

Butuzova, G. V. (1966). *Proc. Acad. Sci. U.S.S.R., Earth Sci. Sect.* **168**, 215–217.

Butuzova, G. V. (1968). *In* "Geochemistry of Sedimentary Rocks and Ores" (N. M. Strakhov, Ed.), pp. 183–222. Nauka, Moscow.

Callender, E. (1973). *In* "Inter-University Programme of Research on Ferromanganese Deposits of the Ocean Floor", Phase 1, Rept. 105–120. National Science Foundation, Washington D.C.

Calvert, S. E. (1978). *In* "Sea Floor Development: Moving into Deeper Water", pp. 43–73. The Royal Society, London.

Calvert, S. E. and Price, N. B. (1970). *Contrib. Mineral. Petrol.* **29**, 215–233.

Calvert S. E. and Price N. B. (1977a). *Marine Chemistry* **5**, 43–74.

Calvert S. E. and Price N. B. (1977b). *In* "Marine Manganese Deposits" (G. P. Glasby, Ed.), pp. 45–86. Elsevier, Amsterdam.

Calvert, S. E., Price, N. B., Heath, G. R. and Moore, T. C. Jr. (1978). *J. Marine Res.* **36**, 161–183.

Cann, J. R. (1979). *In* Metallogenesis at Oceanic Spreading Centres (Meeting report). *J. Geol. Soc. Lond.* **136**, 621–626.

Cann, J. R., Winter, C. K. and Pritchard, R. G. (1977). *Mineral. Mag.* **41**, 193–199.
Carney, J. N. (1975). Occ. Publ. 7/75 New Hebrides Condominium Geological Survey, Port Vila.
Charles, J. (1974). *In* "Deuxieme Colloque International sur l'Exploitation des Oceans", 6, 209 Bordeaux, France.
Chave, K. E. and Mackenzie, F. T. (1961) *J. Geol.* **69**, 572–582.
Cheney, E. S. and Vredenburgh, L. D. (1968). *J. Sediment. Petrol.* **38**, 1363–1365.
Cherdyntsev, V. V., Kadryov, N. B. and Novichova, H. V. (1971). *Geochemistry International* **8** (2), 211–225.
Chesselet, R. (1975). *Thalassia Jugoslavicci* **11**, 135–138.
Chesselet, R., Jedwab, J., Darcourt, C. and Dehairs, F. (1976). *Trans. Am. Geophys. Union.* **57**, 225.
Chester, R. and Hughes, M. J. (1967). *Chemical Geology* **2**, 249–262.
Church, T. M. (1970). Marine barite. Unpublished Ph.D. thesis, University of California, San Diego.
Church T. M. and Bernat, M. (1972). *Earth Planet. Sci. Letts* **14**, 139–144.
Church, T. M. and Wolgemuth, K. (1972). *Earth Planet. Sci. Letts* **15**, 35–44.
Clay, C. S., Ess. J. and Weisman, I. (1964). *J. Geophys. Res.* **69**, 3823–3825.
Colley, N. M., Cronan, D. S. and Moorby, S. A. (1979). *In* "Sur La Genèse de Nodules de Manganese" (C. Lalou, Ed.). Proc. Colloque International du CNRS No. 289.
Collins, J. F. and Buol, S. W. (1970). *Soil Science* **110**, 111–118.
Constantinou, G. and Govett, J. S. (1972). *Trans. Instn Min. Metall.* **B 81**, 34–46.
Cook, H. E., Zemmels I., and Matti, J. G. (1974). Initial Reports of the Deep Sea Drilling Project, 26, pp. 573–592. U.S. Govt Printing Office, Washington D.C.
Cook, P. J. (1977). *In* "Handbook of Stratabound and Stratiform Ore Deposits", 7 (K. H. Wolf, Ed.) pp. 505–535. Elsevier, New York.
Corliss, J. B. (1971). *J. Geophys. Res.* **76**, 8128–8138.
Corliss, J. B. (1979). *In* "Metallogenesis at Oceanic Spreading Centres". *J. Geol. Soc. Lond.* **136**, 621–626.
Corliss J. B., Lyle, M. Dymond, J. and Crane, K. (1978). *Earth Planet. Sci. Letts* **40**, 12–24.
Correns, C. W. (1941). *Nachr. Acad. Wiss Goettingen, Math. Physik Klasse* **5**, 219–230.
Cottell, D. S. (1978). *Trans. Instn Min Metall.* **A 87**, 84–88.
Craig, H. (1966). *Science* **154**, 1544–1548.
Craig, H. (1969). *In* "Hot Brines and Recent Heavy Metal Deposits in the Red Sea" (E. T. Degens and D. A. Ross, Eds), pp. 208–242. Springer-Verlag, New York.
Craig, J. D. (1975). The distribution of ferromanganese nodule deposits in the north equatorial Pacific. Unpublished M.Sc. thesis, University of Hawaii, 104 pp.
Craig, J. D (1979). *Marine Geology* **29**, 165–186.
Crane, K. and Normark, W. R. (1977). *J. Geophys. Res.* **82**, 5336–5348.
Crerar, D. A. and Barnes, H. L. (1974). *Geochim. Cosmochim. Acta* **38**, 279–300.
Cressman, E. R., and Swanson, R. W. (1964). *U.S. Geol. Surv. Prof. paper*, 313-C, 275.
Cronan, D. S. (1967). The geochemistry of some manganese nodules and associated pelagic deposits. Unpublished Ph.D. thesis, University of London.
Cronan, D. S. (1969a). *Chemical Geology* **5**, 99–106.

Cronan, D. S. (1969b). Institute of Geological Sciences Report 69/8. H.M.S.O., London.

Cronan, D.S. (1969c). *Geochim. Cosmochim. Acta* **33**, 1562–1565.

Cronan, D. S. (1970). Institute of Geological Sciences Report 70/17. H.M.S.O., London.

Cronan, D. S. (1972a). *In* "Ferromanganese Deposits on the Ocean Floor" (D. R. Horn, Ed.), pp. 19–30. National Science Foundation, Washington D.C.

Cronan, D. S. (1972b). *Can. J. Earth Sci.* **9**, 319–323.

Cronan, D. S. (1972c). *Nature* (*Phys. Sci*) **235**, 171–172.

Cronan, D. S. (1973). Initial Reports of the Deep Sea Drilling Project, 16, pp. 605–608. U.S. Govt Printing Office, Washington, D.C.

Cronan, D. S. (1974). *In* "The Sea" (E. D. Goldberg, Ed.), Vol. 5, pp. 491–525. Wiley Interscience, New York.

Cronan, D. S. (1975a). *In* "Oceanology International 1975", pp. 118–120. BPS Exhibitions Ltd, London.

Cronan, D. S. (1975b). *J. Geophys. Res.* **80**, 3831–3840.

Cronan, D. S. (1975c). *Trans, Instn Min. Metall.* **B 84**, 30–32.

Cronan, D. S. (1976a). *Geol. Soc. Am. Bull.* **87**, 928–934.

Cronan, D. S. (1976b). *Nature* **262**, 567–569.

Cronan, D. S. (1976c). *In* "Chemical Oceanography", (J. P. Riley and R. Chester, Eds), Vol. 5, pp. 217–263. Academic Press, London and New York.

Cronan, D. S. (1977a). *In* "Marine Manganese Deposits" (G. P. Glasby, Ed.), pp. 11–44. Elsevier, Amsterdam.

Cronan, D. S. (1977b). *Chemistry and Industry* **14**, 576–578.

Cronan, D. S. (1978a) *Trans. Instn Min. Metall.* **A 87**, 143–146.

Cronan, D. S. (1978b). *Endeavour* (New Series) **2**, 80–84.

Cronan, D. S. (1979). *In* "Offshore Mineral Resources" Documents BRGM 7-1979, Orleans.

Cronan, D. S. and Garrett, D. E. (1973). *Nature* (*Phys. Sci.*) **242**, 88–89.

Cronan, D. S. and Moorby, S. A. (1976). *In* "Marine Geological Investigations in the Southwest Pacific and Adjacent Areas" (G. P. Gasby and H. Katz, Eds), pp. 118–123. UNESCAP Tech. Bull. 2.

Cronan, D. S. and Moorby, S. A. (1980). Geochemistry of manganese nodules from the Indian Ocean (in preparation).

Cronan, D. S. and Thomas, R. L. (1970). *Can. J. Earth Sci.* **7**, 1346–1349.

Cronan, D. S. and Thomas, R. L. (1972). *Geol. Soc. Am. Bull.* **83**, 1493–1502.

Cronan, D. S. and Thompson, B. (1978). *Trans. Instn Min. Metall.* **B 87**, 87–90.

Cronan, D. S. and Tooms, J. S. (1967a). *Deep Sea Res.* **14**, 117–119.

Cronan, D. S. and Tooms, J. S., (1967b.) *Deep Sea Res.* **14**, 239–249.

Cronan, D. S. and Tooms. J. S. (1968). *Deep Sea Res.* **15**, 215–223.

Cronan, D. S. and Tooms, J. S. (1969). *Deep Sea Res.* **16**, 335–359.

Cronan, D. S. *et al.* (1972). *Science* **175**, 61–63.

Cronan, D. S., Damiani, V. V. Kinsman, D. J. J. and Thiede, J. (1974). Initial Reports of the Deep-Sea Drilling Project, 24, pp. 1047–1110. U.S. Govt Printing Office, Washington, D.C.

Cronan, D. S. Rona, P. A. and Shearme, S. (1979). *Marine Mining* **2**, 79–89.

Cruickshank, M. J. (1974). *In* "The Geology of Continental Margins" (C. A. Burk and C. L. Drake, Eds), pp. 965–1000. Springer-Verlag, New York.

Cruickshank, M. J. and Hess, H. D. (1975). *Oceanus* **19**, 32–44.

Cruft, E. F. (1966). *Geochim. Cosmochim Acta* **30**, 375–398.

Czamanske, G. K. and Moore, J. G. (1977). *Geol. Soc. Am. Bull.* **88**, 587–599.
Czyscinski, K., (1973). *Deep Sea Res.* **20**, 555–559.
D'Anglejan, B. F. (1967). *Mar. Geol.* **5**, 15.
Davies, T. A. and Gorsline, D. S. (1976). *In* "Chemical Oceanography" (J. P. Riley and R. Chester, Eds), Vol. 5, pp. 1–69. Academic Press, London and New York.
Dean, W. E. and Ghosh, S. K. (1980). *In* "International Monograph on the Geology and Geochemistry of Manganese" (I. M. Varentsov, Ed.). Publishing House of Hungarian Acad. Sci. (in press).
Dean, W. E. and Schreiber, B. C. (1977). Initial Reports of the Deep Sea Drilling Project, 41, pp. 915–931, U.S. Govt Printing Office, Washington, D.C.
Deer, W. A., Howie, R. A. and Zussman, J. (1963). "Rock Forming Minerals", Vol. IV, "Framework Silicates" Longmans, Green and Co, London.
Degens, E. T. and Ross, D. A. (1969). "Hot Brines and Recent Heavy Metal Deposits in the Red Sea". Springer-Verlag, New York, 600pp.
Degens, E. T., Okada, H., Honjo, S. and Hathaway, J. C. (1972). *Mineral Deposita* **7**, 1–12.
Dingle, R. H. (1975). *Trans. Geol. Soc. S. Afr.* **77**, 261.
Dmitriev, L. V., Barsukov, V. L. and Udintsev, G. B. (1970). *Geokhimiya* **4**, 937.
Dreever, J. I. (1971). *Science* **172**, 1334.
Dubbs, M. (1978). *In* "Oceanology International 1978", Tech. Session C. pp. 43–49. BPS Exhibitions Ltd, London.
Dudley, W. C. (1979). *In* "Sur La Genèse des Nodules de Manganese" (C. Lalou, Ed.) Colloque Internat. du CNRS No. 289.
Dugolinsky, B. (1976a). Chemistry and morphology of deep sea manganese nodules and the significance of associated encrusting protozoans on nodule growth. Unpublished Ph.D. thesis, University of Hawaii.
Dugolinsky, B. K. (1976b). *Ocean Industry* **11**, 88–90.
Dunham, A. C. and Glasby, G. P. (1974). *N. Z. J. Geol. Geophys.* **17**, 929–953.
Dunham, K. C., (1969). *Q.J. Geol. Soc. Lond.* **124**, 101–129.
Dunham, K. C. and Sheppard, J. S. (1969). *Proc. Ninth Commonwealth Min. Metall. Congr.* **2**, 3–25. Institution of Mining and Metallurgy, London.
Dymond, J. R. (1966). *Science* **152**, 1239–1241.
Dymond, J. R., Corliss, J. B., Heath, G. R., Field, C. W., Dasch, E. J. and Veeh, H. H. (1973). *Geol. Soc. Am. Bull.* **84**, 3355–3372.
Dymond, J., Corliss, J. B. and Heath, G. R. (1977). *Geochim. Cosmochim. Acta* **41**, 741–753.
Easton, A. J., Hamilton, D., Kempe, D. R. C. and Sheppard, S. M. F. (1977). *Phil. Trans. Roy. Soc. Lond. A* **286**, 253–271.
Eden, R. A. and Binns, P. E. (1973). *Proc. Third Sci. Symp. of CMAS* (N. C. Flemming, Ed.), pp. 210–214. BSAC Publication.
Eden, R. A., Small, Anne V. F. and McKeown, M. C. (1969). *Marine Geology* **7**, 235–251.
Edmond, J. M. (1978). Chemistry of the hot springs on the Galapagos ridge axis. Second Maurice Ewing Memorial Symposium, abstracts, p. 13. American Geophysical Union, Washington, D.C.
Ehrlich, A. M. (1968). Rare earth abundances in manganese nodules. Unpublished Ph.D. thesis, M.I.T.
Ehrlich, H. L. (1963). *Appl. Microbiol.* **11**, 15–19.
Ehrlich, H. L. (1968). *Appl. Microbiol.* **16**, 197–202.

Ehrlich, H. L. (1972). *In* "Ferromanganese Deposits on the Ocean Floor" (D. R. Horn, Ed.), pp. 63–70. National Science Foundation, Washington, D.C.

Eklund, W. A. (1974). A microprobe study of metalliferous sediment components. Unpublished M.Sc. thesis, Oregon State University, 77 pp.

Elderfield, H. E. (1976a). *In* "Chemical Oceanography" (J. P. Riley and R. Chester, Eds), Vol 5, pp. 137–215. Academic Press, London and New York.

Elderfield, H. E. (1976b). *Marine Chemistry* **4**, 103–132.

Elderfield, H., Gass, I. G., Hammond, A. and Bear, L. M. (1972). *Sedimentology* **19**, 1–19.

Elders, W. A., Rex, R. W., Meidav, T., Robinson, P. T. and Biehler, S. (1972). *Science* **178**, 15–24.

Ellis, A. J. and Mahon, W. A. J. (1964). *Geochim. Cosmochim. Acta* **28**, 1323–1357.

Emery, K. O. (1960). "Geology of the Sea Floor off California". Wiley, New York.

Emery, K.O. and Noakes, L. C. (1968). *Tech. Bull ECAFE* **1**, 95–111.

Ewing. M., Horn, D., Sullivan, L., Aitken, T. and Thorndike, E. (1971). *Oceanol. Int.* **6**, 26–27, 30–32.

Fellerer, R. (1975). *In* "Oceanology International 1975", pp. 121–127. BPS Exhibitions Ltd, London.

Ferguson, J. and Lambert, I. B. (1972). *Econ. Geol.* **67**, 25–37.

Fewkes, R. H. (1975). *E.O.S. Trans. Am. Geophys. Union* **56**, 1000 (Abs).

Field, C. W., Dymond, J., Corliss, J. B. *et al.* (1976). *Am. Assoc. Pet. Geol. Mem.* No. 25, 539–550.

Fisher, R. L., Bunce, E. T. *et al.* (1974). Initial Reports of the Deep Sea Drilling Project, 24. U.S. Govt Printing Office, Washington, D.C.

Foster, A. R. (1970). Marine manganese nodules: nature and origin of internal features. Unpublished M.Sc. thesis, Washington State University, 131pp.

Frakes, L. A. and O'Brien, G. (1980). *In* "International Monograph on the Geology and Geochemistry of Manganese" (I. Varentsov, Ed.). Publishing House of the Hungarian Acad. Sci. (in press).

Francheteau, J., Needham, H. D., Choukroune, P., Juteau, T., Seguret, M., Ballard, R. D., Fox, P. J., Normark, W., Carranza, A., Cordoba, D., Guerrero, J., Rangin, C., Bougault, H., Cambon, O. and Hekinian, R. (1979). *Nature* **227**, 523–528.

Francis, T. J. G. (1977). Institute of Geological Sciences Rept. No. 77/4. H.M.S.O., London.

Frazer, J. (1977). *Marine Mining* **1**, 103–124.

Frazer, J. (1979) *In* "Manganese Nodules. Dimensions and Perspectives", pp. 21–36. D. Redel, Dordrecht, Netherlands.

Friedrich, G. H. (1976). *In* "Marine Geological Investigations in the Southwest Pacific and Adjacent Areas" (G. P. Glasby and H. R. Katz, Eds), pp. 39–53. UNESCAP Tech. Bull. 2.

Friedrich, G. and Pluger, W. (1974). *Meerestechnik* **5**, 203–206.

Friedrich, G. and Roonwal G. S. (1975). *In* "Geowissenschaftilche Untersuchungen auf dem Gebiet der Manganknollen-forshung" (G. Friedrich, Ed.). Bundesministrium fur Forshung und Technologie, Bonn. Res. Rept M 75–02 pp. 151–170.

Friedrich, G., Rosner, B. and Demirsog. S. (1969). *Mineralium Deposita* **4**, 298–307.

Froelich, P. N., Bender, M. L. and Heath, G. R. (1977). *Earth Planet. Sci. Letts* **34**, 351–359.

Frondel, C., Marvin, J. B. and Ito, J. (1960). *American Mineralogist* **45**, 1167–1173.
Fuerstenau, D. W. and Han, K. N. (1977). *In* "Marine Manganese Deposits" (G. P. Glasby, Ed.), pp. 357–390. Elsevier, Amsterdam.
Fuerstenau, D. W., Herring, A. P. and Hoover, M. (1973). *Trans. Soc. Min. Eng. A.I.M.E.* **254**, 205–211.
Gardner, D. E. (1955). *Aus. Bur. Min. Res. Geol. Geophysics. Bull.* **28**.
Garnett, R. H. T. (1962). *Proc. Geol. Assoc.* **73**, 65–81.
Gauthier, M. and Marvaldi, J. (1975). *In* "Oceanology International 1975", pp. 346–349. BPS Exhibitions, London.
Gerard, R., Lanseth, M. and Ewing, M. (1962). *J. Geophys. Res.* **67**, 785–803.
Gillette, N. J. (1961). *N.Y. State Conserv.* **18**, 41.
Giovanoli, R., Stahli, E. and Feitknecht, W. (1970). *Helv. Chim. Acta* **53**, 209–220, 453–464.
Girdler, R. W. and Styles, P. (1974). *Nature* **247**, 7–11.
Glaccum, R. and Bostrom, K. (1976). *Marine Geology* **21**, 47–58.
Glasby, G. P. (1970). The geochemistry of manganese nodules and associated pelagic sediments from the Indian Ocean. Unpublished Ph.D. thesis, University of London.
Glasby, G. P. (1972). *Marine Geology* **13**, 57–72.
Glasby, G. P. (1974). *In* "Annual Reviews in Oceanography and Marine Biology" (H. Barnes, Ed.), Vol. 12, pp. 11–40. Allen and Unwin, London.
Glasby, G. P. (1976). *N.Z. J. Geol. Geophys.* **19**, 707–736.
Glasby, G. P. (1977a). *In* "Marine Manganese Deposits" (G. P. Glasby, Ed.), pp. 1–10. Elsevier, Amsterdam.
Glasby, G. P. (1977b). *N.Z. J. Sci.* **20**, 187–190.
Glasby, G. P. (1978). *Marine Geology* **28**, 51–64.
Glasby, G. P. and Lawrence, P. (1974). *N. Z. Oceanogr. Inst. Charts. Misc. Series* 33–39.
Glasby, G. P. and Read, A. J. (1976). *In* "Handbook of Strata-Bound Straiform Ore Deposits" (K. H. Wolf, Ed.), pp. 295–340. Elsevier, Amsterdam.
Glasby, G. P. and Andrews, J. E. (1977). *Pacific Science* **31**, 363–379.
Glasby, G. P., Tooms, J. S. and Cann, J. R. (1971). *Deep Sea Res.* **18**, 1179–1187.
Glasby, G. P., Tooms, J. S. and Howarth, R. J. (1974). *N.Z. J. Sci.* **17**, 387–407.
Glasby, G. P., Meylan, M. A., Margolis, S. V. and Backer, H. (1980). *In* "International Monograph on the Geology and Geochemistry of Manganese" (I. Varentsov, Ed.). Publishing House of the Hungarian Acad. Sci. (in press).
Glover, E. D. (1977). *American Mineralogist* **62**, 278–285.
Goldberg, E. D. (1954). *J. Geol.* **62**, 249–265.
Goldberg, E. D. (1961a). *Phys. Chem. Earth* **4**, 281–305.
Goldberg, E. D. (1961b). *In* "Oceanography" (M. Sears, Ed.), pp. 583–597. Am. Assoc. Adv. Sci., Washington, D.C.
Goldberg, E. D. (1965). *In* "Chemical Oceanography" (J. P. Riley and G. Skirrow, Eds), pp. 163–196. Academic Press, London and New York.
Goldberg, E. D. and Arrhenius, G. O. S. (1958). *Geochim. Cosmochim. Acta.* **13**, 153–212.
Goldberg, E. D., Koide, M., Schmitt, R. A. and Smith, R. H. (1963). *J. Geophys. Res.* **68**, 4209–4217.
Goldberg, E. D., Somayajulu, B. L. K. and Galloway, J. (1969). *Geochim. Cosmochim. Acta.* **33**, 287–289.
Goodell, H. G. (1965) *Contr. Sediment. Res. Lab. Fla. St Univ.* **11**, 196 pp.

Goodell, H. G., Meylan, M. A. and Grant, B. (1971). *In* "Antarctic Oceanology" (J. L. Reid, Ed), Vol. 1, pp. 27–92. Am. Geophys. Union, Baltimore.
Gorham, E. and Swaine, D. J. (1965). *Limnology and Oceanography*, **10**, 268–279.
Goulart, E. P. (1976). *Geol. Jb*, **D 17**, 135–149.
Graham, J. W. and Cooper, S. C. (1959). *Nature* **183**, 1050–1051.
Grant, J. B. (1967). *Contr. Sediment. Res. Lab. Fla. St. Univ.* **19**, 99 pp.
Greenslate, J. (1974). *Science* **186**, 529–531.
Greenslate, J. (1975). Manganese-biota associations in north-eastern Equatorial Pacific sediments. Unpublished Ph.D. thesis, University of California, San Diego.
Greenslate, J., Frazer, J. and Arrhenius, G. (1973). *In* "Progress on the Origin and Distribution of Manganese Nodules in the Pacific and Prospects for Exploitation" (M. Morgenstein, Ed.), pp. 45–69. University of Hawaii.
Griffin, J. J., Koide, M., Hohndorf, A., Hawkins, J. A. and Goldberg, E. D. (1972). *Deep Sea Res.* **19**, 139–148.
Grill, E. V., Murray, J. W. and MacDonald, R. D. (1968). *Nature* **219**, 358–359.
Guichard, F., Reyss, J. L. and Yokoyama, Y. (1978). *Nature* **272**, 155–156.
Gulbrandsen, R. A. (1966). *Geochim. Cosmochim. Acta* **30**, 769.
Gulbrandsen R. A. (1969). *Econ. Geol.* **64**, 365.
Gulbrandsen, R. A., Kramer, J. R., Beatty, L. B. and Mayer, R. E. (1966). *American Mineralogist* **51**, 819.
Gumbel, W. (1878). *Sitzungsber, Bayer, Akad. Wiss, Math-Phys. K.* **8**, 189–209.
Hackett, J. P. and Bischoff, J. L. (1973). *Econ. Geol.* **68**, 244–256.
Halbach, P. and Ozkara, M. (1979). *In* "Sur La Genèse des Nodules de Manganese" (C. Lalou, Ed.). Colloque International du CNRS No. 289.
Hajash, A. (1975). *Contrib. Mineralogy Petrology* **53**, 205–226.
Harada, K. (1978). *Mem. Fac. Sci. Kyoto Univ.*, Ser. Geol. Min., Vol. XLV, No. 1, 111–132.
Harada, K. and Nishida, S. (1976). *Nature* **260**, 770–771.
Harriss, R. C. (1968). *Nature* **219**, 54–55.
Harriss, R. C., Crockett, J. H. and Stainton, M. (1968). *Geochim. Cosmochim. Acta* **32**, 1049–1056.
Hartmann, M. (1973). *Geol. Rundschau* **62**, 742–754.
Hartmann, M. and Muller, P. (1976). *Proc. Internat. Oceanographic Assembly*, Edinburgh, 1976 (preprints).
Hathaway, J. C. and Sachs, P. L. (1965). *American Mineralogist* **50**, 852–867.
Hawkins, D. B. and Roy, R. (1963). *Geochim. Cosmochim. Acta* **27**, 1047–1054.
Hay, R. L. (1966). *Geol. Soc. Am. Special Paper*, 85.
Hay, R. L. (1978). *In* "Natural Zeolites, Occurrence, Properties, Use" (L. B. Sand and F. A. Mumpton Eds), pp. 135–144. Pergamon, Oxford.
Hays, J. D., Saito, T., Opdyke, N. D. and Burckle, L. R. (1969). *Bull. Geol. Soc. Am.* **80**, 1481–1514.
Heath, G. R. and Dymond, J. (1977). *Geol. Soc. Am. Bull.* **88**, 723–733.
Heath, G. R., Dymond, J. and Veeh, H. H. (1973). Metalliferous Sediments from the Southeast Pacific: the IDOE Nazca Plate Project (unpublished report).
Heaton, T. H. E. and Sheppard, S. M. F. (1977). *Geol. Soc. Lond. Spec. Publ.* **7**, 42–57.
Heezen, D. C. and Hollister, C. (1971). "The Face of the Deep." Oxford University Press, New York.
Hekinian, R. (1979). *In* "Metallogenesis at Oceanic Spreading Centres". *J. Geol. Soc. Lond.* **136**, 621–626.
Hekinian, R., Rosendahl, B. R., Cronan, D. S., Dmitriev, Y., Fodor, R. V.,

Goll, R. M., Hoffert, M., Humphris, S. E., Mattey, D. P., Natland, J., Petersen, N., Roggenthen, W., Schrader, E. L., Srivastava, R. K. and Warren, N. (1978). *Oceanologica Acta* **1**, 473–482.

Hersey, J. B. (Ed.) (1967). "Deep Sea Photography". The John Hopkins Oceanographic Studies 3, Baltimore.

Hewitt, J. A. (1978). *Trans. Instn Min. Metall.* **A 87**, 89–95.

Heye, D. (1975). *Geol. Jb.* **E 5**, 3–122.

Heye, D. (1978). *Marine Geology* **26**, M59–M66.

Heye, D. and Marchig, V. (1977). *Marine Geology* **23**, M19–25.

Hoffert, M., Karpoff, A. M. and Schaaf, A. (1979). *In* "Sur la Genèse des Nodules de Manganese" (C. Lalou, Ed.). Proc. Colloque International du CNRS No. 289.

Hoffert, M., Perseil, A., Hekinian, R. Choukroune, P., Needham, H. D., Francheteau, J. and Le Pichon, X. (1978). *Oceanologica Acta* **1**, 73–86.

Holmes, R. and Tooms, J. S. (1972). *Proc. Fourth Int. Geochem, Explor. Symp.* Inst. Min. Metall. London, 193–201.

Holser, A. F. (1976). Manganese nodule resources and mine site availability. Professional Staff study, U.S. Ocean Mining Admin. August, 1976.

Honnorez, J. (1969). *Mineralium Deposita* **4**, 114–131.

Honnorez, J. (1978). *In* "Natural Zeolites, Occurrence, Properties, Use" (L. B. Sand and F. A. Mumpton, Eds), pp. 245–258. Pergamon, Oxford.

Honnorez, J. (1979a). *In* Metallogenesis at Oceanic Spreading Centres (meeting report). *J. Geol. Soc. Lond.,* **136**, 621–626.

Honnorez, J. (1979b). *In* Metallogenesis at Oceanic Spreading Centres (meeting report). *J. Geol. Soc. Lond.* **136**, 621–626.

Honnorez, J., Honnorez-Guerstein, M., Valette, J. and Wauschkuhn, A. (1973a). *In* "Ores in Sediments" (G. C. Amstutz and A. J. Bernard, Eds). I.U.G.S. ser. A. pp. 139–166. Springer-Verlag, Berlin.

Honnorez, J., Honnorez-Guerstein, M., Tonani, F. and Wauschkuhn, A. (1973b). Present day formation of an exhalative sulphide deposit at Vulcano. Vort. Vulk. Tagung in Bukarest.

Horder, M. F. (1979). Geochemical investigations on deep sea sediments from the Indian Ocean. Unpublished Ph.D. thesis, University of London.

Horn, D. R., Ewing, M., Horn, B. M. and Delach, M. N. (1972). *Ocean Industry* **7**, 26–29.

Horn, D. R., Delach, M. N. and Horn, B. M. (1973). Metal content of ferromanganese deposits of the Ocean. Tech. Rept No. 3 (N.S.F. GX-33616) IODE, NSF Washington, D.C.

Horowitz, A. and Cronan, D. S. (1976). *Marine Geology* **20**, 205–228.

Howarth, R. J., Cronan, D. S. and Glasby, G. P. (1977). *Trans. Instn Min. Metall.* **B 86**, 4–8.

Hubred, G. L. (1970). *Hawaii Inst. Geophys. Rept* 70–18.

Iijima, A. (1971). *Advances in Chemistry*, No. 101, pp. 334–341.

Iijima, A. (1978). *In* "Natural Zeolites, Occurrence, Properties, Use" (L. B. Sand and F. A. Mumpton, Eds), pp. 175–198. Pergamon, Oxford.

Jenkyns, H. C. (1977). *In* "Marine Manganese Deposits" (G. P. Glasby, Ed.), pp. 87–108. Elsevier, Amsterdam.

Johnson, C. E. and Glasby, G. P. (1969). *Nature* **222**, 376–377.

Jones, E. J. (1887). *J. Asiatic Soc. Bengal* **56**, 209–212.

Jones, H. A. and Davies, P. J. (1979). *Marine Geology* **30**, 243–268.

Jones, L. H. P. and Milne, A. A. (1956). *Mineral. Mag.* **31**, 283–288.

Kastner, M. (1976). Initial Reports of the Deep Sea Drilling Project, 35. U.S. Govt Printing Office, Washington, D. C.

Kastner, M. and Siever, R. (1972). Initial Reports of the Deep Sea Drilling Project, 13. U.S. Govt Printing Office, Washington, D.C.

Kastner, M. and Stonecipher, M. (1978). *In* "Natural Zeolites, Occurrence, Properties and Use" (L. B. Sand and F. A. Mumpton, Eds), pp. 199–220. Pergamon, Oxford.

Kaufman, R. and Siapno, W. D. (1972a). Future needs of deep ocean mineral exploration and surveying. Offshore Technology Conference Preprints No. OTC 1514, Dallas, Texas.

Kaufman, R. and Siapno, W. D. (1972b). *In* "Ferromanganese Deposits on the Ocean Floor" (D. R. Horn, Ed.), pp. 263–270. National Science Foundation, Washington, D.C.

Kazakov, A. V. (1937). *Trans. U.S.S.R. Sci. Inst. Fertilisers and Insect Fungicides* **142**, 95.

Kelts, K. and McKenzie, G. (1976). Initial Reports of the Deep Sea Drilling Project, 33, pp. 789–803. U.S. Govt Printing Office, Washington, D.C.

Kempe, D. R. C. and Easton, A. J. (1974). Initial Reports of the Deep Sea Drilling Project, 26, pp. 593–601. U.S. Govt Printing Office, Washington, D.C.

Kildow, J. T., Bever, M. B., Dar, V. K. and Capstaff, A. E. (1976). Assessment of economic and regulatory conditions affecting ocean minerals resource development, prepared by M.I.T. for U.S. Dept. Interior, Ocean Mining Admin., 1146 pp. (unpublished).

Kolla, V. and Biscaye, P. E. (1973). *Marine Geology* **15**, 11–17.

Krauskopf, K. B. (1956). *Geochim. Cosmochim Acta* **9**, 1–32.

Krauskopf, K. B. (1957). *Geochim. Cosmochim. Acta* **12**, 61–84.

Krauskopf, K. B. (1967). "Introduction to Geochemistry". McGraw Hill, New York.

Krishnaswami, S. and Lal, D. (1972). *In* "The Changing Chemistry of the Oceans" (D. Dyrssen and D. Jagner, Eds). Almqvist and Wiksell, Stockholm.

Krishnaswami, S., Somayajulu, B. L. K. and Moore, W. S. (1972). *In* "Ferromanganese Deposits on the Ocean Floor" (D. R. Horn, Ed.). National Science Foundation, Washington, D.C.

Krumbein, W. C. and Garrels, R. M. (1952). *J. Geol.* **60**, 1–33.

Ku, T. L. (1977). *In* "Marine Manganese Deposits" (G. P. Glasby, Ed.), pp. 249–268. Elsevier, Amsterdam.

Ku, T. L. and Glasby, G. P. (1972). *Geochim. Cosmochim. Acta* **36**, 699–703.

Ku, T. L., Knauss, K. G. and Lin, M. C. (1975). *E.O.S. Trans. Am. Geophys. Union* **56**(12) 999 (abs).

Lakin, H. W., Thompson, C. E. and Davidson, D. F. (1963). *Science* **142**, 1568–1569.

Lalou, C. (1980). *In* "International Monograph on the Geology and Geochemistry of Manganese" (I. M. Varentsov, Ed.). Publishing House of the Hungarian Acad. Sci. (in press).

Lalou, C. and Brichet, E. (1972). *C. R. Acad. Sci. Paris. V.* **275**, Sèrie. D., 815–818.

Lalou, C. and Brichet, E. (1976). *Mineralium Deposita* **11**, 267–277.

Lalou, C., Brichet, E. and Ranque, D. (1973). *C. R. Acad. Sci. Paris* **276** D, 1661–1664.

Lancelot, Y., Hathaway, J. C. and Hollister, C. D. (1972). Initial Reports of the Deep Sea Drilling Project **11**, 901–973. U.S. Govt Printing Office, Washington, D.C.

Lange, J. P. and Biemann, W. G. (1975). *Seventh Ann. Offshore, Technol. Conf. Preprints* **2**, 585–592.

Laughton, A. S. (1967). *In* "Deep Sea Photography" (J. B. Hersey, Ed.) pp. 191–206. Johns Hopkins University.

Lebedev, L. M. (1967). *Dokl. Acad. Sci.* **174**, 173–176.

Le Geros, R. Z. (1965). *Nature* **206**, 1003.

Leinen, M. and Stakes, D. (1979). *Bull. Geol. Soc. Am.* **90**, 357–375.

Lenoble, J. P. (1976). "Problems in Ocean Mining Evaluation". Symposium 108, 25th Int. Geol. Cong. Sydney (abs).

Lenoble, J. P. (1980). Technical problems in ocean mining evaluation. *In* "International Monograph on the Geology and Geochemistry of Manganese" (I. Varentsov, Ed.). Publishing House of the Hungarian Acad. Sci. (in press).

Le Pichon, X. (1968). *J. Geophys. Res.* **73**, 3661–3697.

Levinson, A. A. (1960). *American Mineralogist* **45**, 802–807.

Li, Y. H., Bischoff, J. L. and Mathieu, G. (1969) *Earth Planet. Sci. Letts* **7**, 265–270.

Lister, C. R. B. (1972). *Geophys. J. Roy. Astronom. Soc.* **26**, 515–535.

Lonsdale, P. (1977). *Earth Planet. Sci. Letts* **36**, 92–110.

Lonsdale, P. (1978). Submersible Exploration of Guaymas Basin: S.I.O. Report 78-1 Scripps Instn. of Oceanography, University of California.

Lupton, J. E., Weiss, R. F. and Craig, H. (1977). *Nature* **266**, 244–246.

Lyle, M. (1976). *Geology* **4**, 733–736.

Lyle, M. and Dymond, J. (1976). *Earth Planet. Sci. Letts* **30**, 164–168.

Lyle, M., Dymond, J. and Heath, G. R. (1977). *Earth Planet. Sci. Letts* **35**, 55–64.

Lynn, D. C. and Bonatti, E. (1965). *Marine Geology* **3**, 457–474.

MacLean, W. H. (1977). *Can. J. Earth. Sci.* **14**, 674–683.

Manheim, F. T. (1961). *Geochim. Cosmochim. Acta* **25**, 52–70.

Manheim, F. T. (1965). *In* "Symposium on Marine Geochemistry" (D. T. Schink and J. T. Corliss, Eds), Occasional Publication No. 3, pp. 217–276. University of Rhode Island.

Manheim, F. T. (1972). *In* "Ferromanganese Deposits on the Ocean Floor" (D. R. Horn, Ed.), p. 105. National Science Foundation, Washington, D.C.

Manheim, F. T. (1978). *Geochim. Cosmochim. Acta* **42**, 541–542.

Manheim, F. T., Rowe, G. T. and Jipa, D. (1975). *J. Sediment. Petrol.* **45**, 243.

Manheim, F. T., Pratt, R. M. and McFarlin, P. F. (1978). Composition and origin of phosphorites from the Blake Plateau (unpublished).

Marchig, V. and Gundlach, H. (1979). *In* "Sur La Genèse des Nodules de Manganese" (C. Lalou, Ed.). Proc. Colloque International du CNRS No. 289.

Marchig, V. *et al.* (1976). Preprints, Joint Oceanographic Assembly, Edinburgh, 1976.

Margolis, S. V. and Glasby, G. P. (1973). *Geol. Soc. Am, Bull.* **84**, 3601–3610.

Margolis, S. V., Dugolinsky, B. K. and Dudley, W. C. (1979). *In* "Sur La Genèse des Nodules de Manganese" (C. Lalou, Ed.). Proc. Colloque International du CNRS.

Mariner, R. H. and Surdam, R. C. (1970). *Science* **170**, 977–980.

Martens, C. S. and Harriss, R. C. (1970). *Geochim. Cosmochim. Acta* **34**, 621.

Mathez, E. A. (1976). *J. Geophys. Res.* **81**, 4269–4275.

Mathez, E. A. and Yeats, R. S. (1976). Initial Reports of the Deep Sea Drilling Project, **34**, pp. 363–373. U.S. Govt Printing Office. Washington, D.C.

Matthews, D. H. (1962). *Nature* **194**, 368–369.

Matthews, D. H. (1971). *Phil. Trans. Roy. Soc. London* **268**, 551–571.

McArthur, J. M. (1974). The geochemistry of phosphorite concretions from the continental shelf off Morocco. Unpublished Ph.D. thesis, University of London.

McArthur, J. M. (1978). *Mineral. Mag.* **42**, 221–228.

McConnell, D. (1952). *Bull. Soc. fr. Miner. Cristallogr.* **75**, 428.

McConnell, D. (1973). "Apatite". Springer-Verlag, New York.

McDonald, G. C. R. and Tong, W. K. (1978). *In* "Offshore Mineral Exploration", 7–15, Tech. Session C, Oceanology International 1978, Brighton. BPS Exhibitions Ltd, London.

McGregor, B. A. and Rona, P. A. (1975). *J. Geophys. Res.* **80**, 3307–3314.

McKenzie, R. M. (1971). *Mineral. Mag.* **38**, 493–502.

McManus, D. A. *et al.* (1970). Initial Reports of the Deep Sea Drilling Project, 5. U.S. Govt Printing Office, Washington, D.C.

McMurtry, G. M. (1975). Geochemical investigations of sediments across the Nazca Plate at 12°S. Unpublished M.Sc. thesis, University of Hawaii.

McMurtry, G. M. and Burnett, W. C. (1975). *Nature (Phys. Sci.)* **254**, 42–44.

Mellis, O. (1952). *Nature* **169**, 624.

Menard, H. W. (1964). "The Marine Geology of the Pacific". McGraw Hill, New York.

Menard, H. W. (1976). *American Scientist* **64**, 519–529.

Menard, H. W. and Frazer, J. Z. (1978). *Science* **199**, 969–971.

Menard, H. W., Goldberg, E. D. and Hawkes, H. E. (1964). Composition of Pacific Sea-Floor Manganese Nodules. Unpublished Report Scripps Institution of Oceanography.

Mero, J. L. (1959). The mining and processing of deep sea manganese nodules. Unpublished Ph.D. thesis, University of California.

Mero, J. L. (1962). *Econ. Geol.* **57**, 747–767.

Mero, J. L. (1965). "The Mineral Resources of the Sea". Elsevier, Amsterdam.

Meyer, K. (1973). *In* "Papers on the Origin and Distribution of Manganese Nodules in the Pacific and Prospects for Exploration" (M. Morgenstein, Ed.). Hawaii Inst. of Geophysics, Honolulu.

Meylan, M. A. (1974). *Hawaii Inst. Geophys. Rept* H.I.G.-74–9, 158–168.

Meylan, M. A. (1976). *In* "Marine Geological Investigations in the Southwest Pacific and Adjacent Areas" (G. P. Glasby and H. R. Katz, Eds), pp. 92–98. UNESCAP Tech. Bull. 2.

Meylan, M. A. and Goodell, H. G. (1976). *In* "Marine Geological Investigations in the Southwest Pacific and Adjacent Areas" (G. P. Glasby and H. R. Katz, Eds), pp. 99–117. UNESCAP Tech. Bull 2.

Miller, A. R., Densmore, C. D., Degens, E. T., Hathaway, J. C., Manheim, F. T., McFarlin, P. F., Pocklington, H. and Jokela, A. (1966). *Geochim. Cosmochim. Acta* **30**, 341–359.

Miller, J. M. and Symons, G. D. (1973). *Nature* **242**, 184–186.

Miller, J. M., Roberts, P. D., Symons, G. D., Merrill, N. H. and Wormald, M. R. (1977). A towed sea bed gamma ray spectrometer for continental shelf surveys. *In* Internat. Symp. on Nuclear Techniques in Exploration, Extraction and Processing of Mineral Resources, I.A.E.A. Vienna, March, 1977.

Mizuno, A. and Moritani, T. (1976). *In* "Marine Geological Investigations in the Southwest Pacific and Adjacent Areas" (G. P. Glasby and H. R. Katz, Eds), pp. 62–79. UNESCAP Tech. Bull. 2.

Moorby, S. A. (1978). The geochemistry and mineralogy of some ferromanganese oxides and associated deposits from the Indian and Atlantic Oceans. Unpublished Ph.D. thesis, University of London.

Moore, J. G. and Calk, L. (1971). *American Mineralogist* **56**, 476–488.

Moore, J. G. and Fabbi, B. P. (1971). *Contr. Mineralogy Petrology* **33**, 118–127.

Moore, J. R. (1976). Origin and exploration of marine placers. Symposium 108, 1 25th Internat. Geol. Cong. Sydney (abs).

Moore, J. R. (1979). *In* "Offshore Mineral Resources", 131–161, Documents BRGM, 7–1979, Orleans, France.

Moore, J. R. and Welkie, C. J. (1976). Metal bearing sediments of economic interest, coastal Baring Sea. Proc. Symposium on Sedimentation, Alaska Geol. Soc. Anchorage.

Moore, W. S. and Vogt, P. G. (1976). *Earth Planet. Sci. Letts* **29**, 349–356.

Morgenstein, M. (1967). *Sedimentology* **9**, 105–118.

Morgenstein, M. and Felsher, M. (1971). *Pacific Sci.* **25**, 301–307.

Mortimer, C. H. (1971). *Limnology and Oceanography* **16**, 387–404.

Mottl, M. J. and Seyfried, W. E. (1977). *Geol. Soc. Am. Abstr. Prog.* **9**, 1104–1105.

Mumpton, F. A. (1960). *American Mineralogist* **45**, 351–369.

Murray, J. W. and Brewer, P. G. (1977). *In* "Marine Manganese Deposits" (G. P. Glasby, Ed.), pp. 291–326. Elsevier, Amsterdam.

Murray, J. and Irvine, R. (1894). *Trans. Roy. Soc. Edin.* **37**, 721–742.

Murray, J. and Renard, A. F. (1891). Deep Sea Deposits, Rept Sci. Results of Voyage of H.M.S. Challenger (C. W. Thompson, Ed.), H.M.S.O., London.

Murray, L. G. (1969). Proc. Ninth Commonwealth Mining and Metallurgical Congress, Paper 14. Institution of Mining and Metallurgy, London.

Mustaffa, Z. and Amann, H. (1978). Proc. Tenth O.T.C. Houston, Texas (O.T.C. 3188), pp. 1199–1206.

Nebrija, E. L., Young, C. T., Meyer, R. T. and Moore, J. R. (1976). Electrical prospecting for copper veins in shallow water. Offshore Technology Conference preprints O.T.C. 2454, Dallas, Texas.

Nelson, C. H. and Hopkins, D. M. (1972). *U.S. Geol. Survey, Prof. Paper* **689**, 27 pp.

Neumann, A. C. and McGill, D. A. (1962). *Deep Sea Res.* **8**, 223.

Nicholls, G. D., Curl, H. and Bowen, V. T. (1959). *Limnology and Oceanography* **4**, 472–478.

NOAA (1976). Marine Minerals Workshop, U.S. Dept. of Commerce, Washington, D.C. (unpublished report).

Noakes, J. E., Harding, J. L. and Spaulding, J. D. (1974). *J. Marine Tech. Soc.* **8**, 36–39.

Oldnall, R. J. (1975). Possible sources of metals in pelagic sediments with special reference to the Bauer Basin. Unpublished M.Sc. thesis, University of Hawaii.

Opdyke, N. D. and Foster, J. H. (1970). *Mem. Geol. Soc. Am.* **126**, 83–119.

Overeem, A. J. A. van (1960). *Geol. en Mijnb* **39**, 444–457.

Parker, R. J. (1971). SANCOR Mar. Geol. Prog. Bull. No. 2. Dept. of Geol., Univ. Cape Town, 93 pp.

Parker, R. J. and Seisser, W. G. (1972). *J. Sed. Petrol.* **42**, 434–440.

Parmentier, E. M. and Spooner, E. T. C. (1978). *Earth Planet, Sci. Letts* **40**, 33–44.

Pasho, D. W. (1976). *N.Z. Oceanographic Inst. Memoir* **77**, 28 pp.

Pasho, D. W. and McIntosh, J. A. (1976). C.I.M. Bulletin, September, 1976.

Pautot, G. and Melguen, M. (1976). *In* "Marine Geological Investigations in the Southwest Pacific and Adjacent Areas" (G. P. Glasby and H. R. Katz, Eds), pp. 54–61. UNESCAP Tech. Bull. 2.

Pautot, G. and Melguen, M. (1979). *In* "Marine Geology and Oceanography of the Pacific Manganese Nodule Province" (J. R. Bischoff and D. Z. Piper, Eds). Plenum, New York.

Pautot, G., Auzende, J. M. and Le Pichon, X. (1970). *Nature* **227**, 351–354.

Payne, R. R. and Conolly, J. R. (1972). *In* "Ferromanganese Deposits on the Ocean Floor" (D. R. Horn, Ed.), 81–92. National Science Foundation, Washington, D.C.

Penhale, J. and Hollick, C. T. (1968). *Trans. Instn Mining Metall.* **A 77**, 65–73.

Pettersson, H. (1959). *Geochim. Cosmochim. Acta* **17**, 209–213.

Pettijohn, F. J. (1957). "Sedimentary Rocks". Harper and Row, New York.

Petzing, J. and Chester, R. (1979). *Marine Geology* **29**, 253–272.

Piper, D. Z. (1972). *In* "Ferromanganese Deposits on the Ocean Floor" (D. R. Horn, Ed.), pp. 123–130. National Science Foundation, Washington, D.C.

Piper, D. Z. and Williamson, M. E. (1977). *Marine Geology* **23**, 285–304.

Pratt, R. M. and McFarlin, P. F. (1966). *Science* **151**, 1080–1082.

Price, N. B. (1967). *Marine Geology* **5**, 511–538.

Price, N. B. and Calvert, S. E. (1970). *Marine Geology* **9**, 145–171.

Price, N. B. and Calvert, S. E. (1978). *Chem. Geol.* **23**, 151–170.

Puchelt, H. (1972). *In* "Ores in Sediments" (G. Amstutz, Ed.) pp. 227–245. Springer-Verlag, Berlin.

Pugh, D. T. (1969). *In* "Hot Brines and Recent Heavy Metal Deposits in the Red Sea" (E. T. Degens and D. A. Ross, Eds), pp. 158–163. Springer-Verlag, New York.

Pytowicz, R. M. and Kester, D. R. (1967). *Limnology and Oceanography.* **12**, 714.

Raab, W. (1972). *In* "Ferromanganese Deposits on the Ocean Floor" (D. R. Horn, Ed.), pp. 31–50. National Science Foundation, Washington, D.C.

Raab, W. J. and Meylan, M. A. (1977). *In* "Marine Manganese Deposits" (G. P. Glasby, Ed.), pp. 109–146. Elsevier, Amsterdam.

Rawson, M. D. and Ryan, W. B. F. (1978). Ocean Floor Sediment and Polymetallic Nodules, Sheet 1, U.S. Dept of State, Office of the Geographer.

Revelle, R. and Emery, K. O. (1951). *Geol. Soc. Am. Bull.* **62**, 707–724.

Revelle, R., Bramlette, M., Arrhenius, G. and Goldberg, E. D. (1955). *Geol. Soc. Am. Spec. Paper* **62**, 221–235.

Rex, R. W. (1967). *In* "Clays and Clay Minerals" (S. W. Bailey, Ed.), pp. 195–203. Pergamon Press, Oxford.

Riley, J. P. and Sinhaseni, P. (1958). *J. Marine Res.* **17**, 466–482.

Rinaldi, R., Plutz, J. J. and Smith, J. V. (1974). *Acta. Cryst.* **B30**, 2426–2433.

Ringwood, A. E. (1966). *In* "Advances in Earth Science" (P. M. Hurley, Ed.). M.I.T. Press, Cambridge, Mass.

Robertson, A. F. H. (1975). *J. Geol. Soc. Lond.* **131**, 511–531.

Robertson, A. F. H. and Hudson, J. D. (1973). *Earth Planet. Sci. Letts* **18**, 93–101.

Robertson, C. E. (1966). U.S. Geol. Surv. Prof. Paper, 550-D, 178.

Rona, P. A. (1972). NOAA Tech. Rept ERL 238-AOML 8 U.S. Dept of Commerce, 47 pp.

Rona, P. A. (1976). *Marine Geology* **21**, 59–66.

Rona, P. A. (1978a). *Econ. Geol.* **73**, 135–170.

Rona, P. A. (1978b). *Geophys. Res. Letts* **5**, 993–996.

Rona, P. A. (1979). *In* "Metallogenesis at Oceanic Spreading Centres", *J. Geol. Soc. Lond.* **131**, 621–626.

Rona, P. A. (1980). *In* "International Monograph on the Geology and Geochemistry of Manganese" (I. Varentsov, Ed.). Publishing House of the Hungarian Acad. Sci. (in press).

Rona, P. A., McGregor, B. A., Betzer, P. R., Bolger, G. W. and Krause, D. C. (1975). *Deep Sea Res.* **22**, 611–618.

Rona, P. A., Harbison, R. N., Bassinger, B. G., Scott, R. B. and Nalwalk, A. J. (1976). *Geol. Soc. Am. Bull.* **87**, 661–674.

Rosch, H. and Scheurmann, L. (1974). In "Valdivia Wissenchaft Liche Ergebrissel", pp. 54–81. B.F.B., Hannover.

Rossmann, R. (1973). Lake Michigan ferromanganese nodules, Unpublished Ph.D. thesis, University of Michigan.

Rossmann, R. and Callender, E. (1968). Science 162, 1123–1124.

Rusby, J. S. M. and Somers, M. L. (1977). In "A Voyage of Discovery" (M. V. Angel, Ed.), pp. 611–625. Pergamon, Oxford.

Sands, C. D. and Drever, J. I. (1978). In "Natural Zeolites, Occurrence, Properties, Use" (L. B. Sand and F. A. Mumpton, Eds), pp. 269–275. Pergamon, Oxford.

Sano, M. and Matsubara, H. (1970). Suiyokwai—Shi 17, 111–114.

Sayles, F. L. and Bischoff, J. L. (1973). Earth Planet. Sci. Letts 19, 330–336.

Schlee, J. (1964). Pit and Quarry December, 1964.

Schoell, M. and Hartmann, M. (1973). Marine Geology 14, 1–14.

Schoettle, M. and Friedman, G. M. (1971). Geol. Soc. Am. Bull. 82, 101–110.

Schvoerer, M., Dautani, A. and Bechtel, F. (1980). In "Sur La Genèse des Nodules de Manganese" (C. Lalou, Ed.). Proc. Colloque International du CNRS No. 289 (in press).

Sclater, J. G. and Menard, H. W. (1967). Nature 216, 991–993.

Scott, M. R., Scott, R. B., Rona, P. A., Butler, L. W. and Nalwalk, A. J. (1974). Geophys. Res. Letts 1, 355–358.

Scott, M. R., Scott, R. B., Morse, J. W., Betzer, P. R., Butler, L. W. and Rona, P. A. (1978). Nature 276, 811–813.

Scott, R. B. (1978). E.O.S. Trans. Am. Geophys. Union 59, pp. 389 (abs).

Scott, R. B., Rona, P. A., Butler, L. W., Nalwalk, A. J. and Scott, M. R. (1972). Nature (Phys. Sci.) 239, 77–79.

Senftle, F., Duffey, D. and Wiggins, P. F. (1969). Marine Technol. Soc. J. 3, 9–16.

Sevast'yanov, V. F. and Volkov, I. I. (1967). Trudy Inst. Okeanolog. 83, 137–152.

Seyfried, W. E. and Bischoff, J. L. (1977). Earth Planet. Sci. Letts 34, 67–71.

Seyfried, W. E. and Mottl, M. J. (1977). Proc. 2nd Internat. Symp. Rock Water Interaction, I.A.G.C. Strasbourg, IV, pp. 173–180.

Shanks, W. C. and Bischoff, J. L. (1977). Geochim. Cosmochim. Acta 41, 1507–1521.

Sheppard, R. A. and Gude, A. J., III (1968). U.S. Geol. Survey, Prof. paper 597.

Sheppard, R. A. and Gude, A. J., III (1969). U.S. Geol. Survey, Prof. paper 634.

Sheppard, R. A., Gude, A. J., III and Griffin, J. J. (1970). American Mineralogist 55, 1053–2062.

Shima, M. and Okada, A. (1968). J. Japan Assoc. Mineral-Petrol. Econ. Geol. 60, 47–56.

Siddique, H. N. and Rajamanickam, G. V. (1979). In "Offshore Mineral Resources", pp. 233–255. Documents BRGM No. 7-1979, Orleans, France.

Sillen, L. G. (1961). In "Oceanography" (M. Sears, Ed.), pp. 549–581. Amer. Assoc. Adv. Sci. Washington, D.C.

Sillitoe, R. H. (1972). Trans. Instn Min. Metall. B81, 141–148.

Sillitoe, R. H. (1978). Prog. Abstr., Fifth Symposium of the International Association for the Genesis of Ore Deposits. Snowbird, Alta, Utah, August, 1978, p. 175.

Silverman, S. R., Fuyat, R. K. and Weiser, J. D. (1952). American Mineralogist 37, 211.

Simpson, D. R. (1964). American Mineralogist 49, 363.

Skornyakova, N. S. and Andrushchenko, P. F. (1970). In "Sedimentation in the Pacific Ocean" (P. L. Bezrukov, Ed.), part 2, pp. 203–268. Nauka, Moscow.

Skornyakova, N. S., Andrushchenko, P. F. and Fomina, L. S. (1962). Okeanologiya 2, 264–277.

Sleep, N. H. (1975). *J. Geophys. Res.* **80**, 4037–4042.

Smale-Adams, K. B. and Jackson, G. O. (1978). *In* Sea Floor Development: Moving into Deeper Water. *Phil. Trans. Roy. Soc. A* **290**, 125–132.

Smales, A. A. and Wiseman, J. D. H. (1955). *Nature* **175**, 464–465.

Smith, J. D. and Burton, J. D. (1972). *Geochim. Cosmochim. Acta* **36**, 621–629.

Smith, P. A. and Cronan, D. S. (1975). "Oceanology International 1975," pp. 111–114. BPS Exhibitions Ltd, London.

Smith, P. A. and Cronan, D. S. (1978). *In* "Thera and the Aegean World", Proc. 2nd Internat. Scientific. Cong., Santorini, Greece, August, 1978. Nomikos, Bishopsgate, London.

Smith, R. E., Gassaway, J. D. and Niles, H. N. (1968). *Science* **161**, 780–781.

Sneed, E. D. and Folk, R. L. (1958). *J. Geol.* **66**, 114–150.

Sorem, R. K. (1967). *Econ. Geol.* **62**, 141–147.

Sorem, R. K. and Banning, D. L. (1976). *In* "Geology and Geochemistry of site C. Deep Ocean Environmental Study, N.E. Pacific Nodule Province" (J. Bischoff, Ed.). U.S. Geol. Survey. Open File Report, 76–548, 167–216.

Sorem, R. K. and Fewkes, R. H. (1977). *In* "Marine Manganese Deposits" (G. P. Glasby, Ed.), pp. 147–184. Elsevier, Amsterdam.

Sorem, R. K. and Foster, A. R. (1972a). *In* "Ferromanganese Deposits on the Ocean Floor" (D. R. Horn, Ed.), pp. 167–182. National Science Foundation, Washington, D.C.

Sorem, R. K. and Foster, A. R. (1972b). Twenty-fourth Int. Geol. Cong. Montreal, Sect. 8, pp. 192–200.

Sorem, R. K., McFarland, W. A. and Fewkes, R. H. (1978). Prog. Abstr., Fifth Symposium of the International Association for the Genesis of Ore Deposits. Snowbird, Alta, Utah, August, 1978, p. 178.

Sorem, R. K., Fewkes, R. H., McFarland, W. A. and Reinhart, N. R. (1979). *In* "Sur La Genèse des Nodules de Manganese" (C. Lalou, Ed.). Proc. Colloque International du CNRS, No. 289.

Sozanski, A. G. (1974). Geochemistry of ferromanganese oxide concretions and associated sediments and bottom waters from Shebandowan Lakes, Ontario, Unpublished M.Sc. thesis, University of Ottawa.

Sozanski, A. G. and Cronan, D. S. (1976). *Limnology and Oceanography* **21**, 894–898.

Sozanski, A. G. and Cronan, D. S. (1979). *Can. J. Earth Sci.* **16**, 126–140.

Spiess, F. N. and Mudie, J. D. (1970). *In* "The Sea" (A. E. Maxwell, Ed.), Vol. 4, pp. 205–250. Wiley Interscience, New York.

Spiess, F. N., Lowenstein, C. D., Boegeman, D. E. and Mudie, J. D. (1976). Fine scale mapping near the deep sea floor. *In* "Oceans '76". Marine Technology Society, Washington, D.C.

Spooner, E. T. C. (1977). *Geol. Soc. Lond. Spec. Publ.* **7**, 58–71.

Spooner, E. T. C. (1978). Ophiolitic rocks and evidence for hydrothermal convection of sea water within oceanic crust (abs). The Second Maurice Ewing memorial Symposium, abstracts, American Geophys. Union.

Spooner, E. T. C. (1980). *Geol. Assoc. Canada, Spec. paper* **21**, (in press).

Spooner, E. T. C. and Fyfe, W. S. (1973). *Contr. Mineral. Petrol.* **42**, 287–304.

Spooner, E. T. C. and Bray, C. J. (1977). *Nature* **266**, 808–812.

Steinfink, H. (1962). *Acta Crystallographica* **15**, 644–651.

Stonecipher, S. A. (1976). *Chemical Geology* **17**, 307–318.

Stonecipher, S. A. (1978). *In* "Natural Zeolites: Occurrence, Properties and Use" (L. B. Sand and F. A. Mumpton, Eds), pp. 221–234. Pergamon, Oxford.

Straczek, J. A., Horen, A., Ross, M., and Warshaw, C. M. (1960). *American Mineralogist* **45**, 1174–1184.

Stride, A. H. (1963). *J. Geol. Soc. Lond.* **119**, 175–199.

Strunz, H. (1970). "Mineralogische Tabellen." Akademische Verlag-gesellschaft, Leipzig.

Stumm, W. and Leckie, J. O. (1970). "Advances in Water Pollution Research", Vol. 2. Pergamon, New York.

Stumm, W. and Morgan, J. J. (1970). "Aquatic Chemistry". Wiley Interscience, New York.

Suess, E. and Djafari, D. (1977). *Earth Planet. Sci. Letts* **35**, 49–54.

Summerhayes, C. P. (1967a). *N.Z. J. Geol. Geophys.* **10**, 1372–1381.

Summerhayes, C. P. (1967b). *N.Z. J. Mar. Freshwater Res.* **1**, 267–282.

Summerhayes, C. P. (1969). *Bull. N.Z. Dept Scient. Ind. Res.*, No. 190, 92 pp.

Summerhayes, C. P. (1970). Phosphate deposits of the northwest African continental shelf and slope. Unpublished Ph.D. thesis, University of London.

Summerhayes, C. P. and Willis, J. P. (1975). *Marine Geology* **18**, 159–173.

Summerhayes, C. P., Hazelhoff Roelfzema, B. H., Tooms, J. S. and Smith, D. B. (1970). *Econ. Geol.* **65**, 718–723.

Summerhayes, C. P., Nutter, A. H. and Tooms, J. S. (1972). *Sediment. Geol.* **8**, 3–28.

Surdam, R. C. and Sheppard, R. A. (1978). *In* "Natural Zeolites, Occurrence, Properties and Use" (L. B. Sand and F. A. Mumpton, Eds), pp. 145–174. Pergamon, Oxford.

Sverdrup, H. U., Johnson, M. W. and Fleming, R. H. (1942). "The Oceans". Prentice Hall, Englewood Cliffs, New Jersey.

Swaine, D. J. (1962). Tech. Comm. No. 52, Commonwealth Agr. Bureau, Farnham Royal, England, 306 pp.

Swallow, J. C. (1969). *In* "Hot Brines and Recent Heavy Metal Deposits in the Red Sea" (E. T. Degens and D. A. Ross, Eds), pp. 3–9. Springer-Verlag, New York.

Talwani, M. (1964). *Marine Geology* **2**, 29–80.

Taylor, G. R. (1974). *Trans. Instn Min. Metall.* **B83**, 120–130.

Taylor, G. R. (1976). *In* "Marine Geological Investigations in the Southwest Pacific and Adjacent Areas" (G. P. Glasby and H. R. Katz, Eds), pp. 83–91. UNESCAP, Tech. Bull No. 2.

Taylor, S. R. (1964). *Geochim. Cosmochim. Acta* **28**, 1273.

Thompson, G. and Bowen, V. T. (1969). *J. Mar. Res.* **27**, 32–38.

Tinsley, R. C. (1976). *Min. Engng* **28**, 34–37.

Tooms, J. S. (1969). *In* Ninth Commonwealth Mining and Metallurgical Congress, Mining and Petroleum Geology Sect, Paper 3. Institution of Mining and Metallurgy, London.

Tooms, J. S. and Summerhayes, C. P. (1968). *Nature* **218**, 1241–1242.

Tooms, J. S., Taylor-Smith, D., Nichol, I., Ong, P. and Wheildon, J. (1965). *Colston Papers* **17**, 363–391. Butterworths, London.

Tooms, J. S., Summerhayes, C. P. and Cronan, D. S. (1969). *Oceanogr. Mar. Biol. Ann. Rev.* **7**, 49.

Turekian, K. K. (1965). *In* "Chemical Oceanography" (J. P. Riley and G. Skirrow, Eds), Vol. 2. Academic Press, London and New York.

Turekian, K. K. (1977). *Geochim. Cosmochim. Acta* **41**, 1139–1144.

Turekian, K. K. and Bertine, K. K. (1971). *Nature* **229**, 250.

Turekian, K. K. and Imbrie, J. (1966). *Earth Planet Sci. Letts* **1**, 161.

Turekian, K. K. and Wedephol, K. H. (1961). *Geol. Soc. Am. Bull.* **72**, 175–192.
Udintsev, G. B. *et al.* (1975). "Geological-Geophysical Atlas of the Indian Ocean". Pergamon Press, Oxford.
van Andel, Tj. H., Heath, G. R. and Moore, T. C. (1975). *Geol Soc. Am. Mem.* **143**, 134 pp.
van der Weijen, C. H. and Kruissink, E. C. (1977). *Mar. Chem.* **5**, 93–112.
Veen, J. Van (1936). "Onderzoekingen in de Hoofden". s' Gravenhage.
Veen, J. Van (1938). *Geol. Meere* **2**, 62–86.
Varentsov, I. M. (1970). *Geol. Rud. Mestorozhd* **12**, 93–104.
Varentsov, I. M. (1972). *Acta Mineral. Petrogr. Szeged* **20**, 363–381.
Varnavas, S. (1979). Geochemical investigations on sediments from the eastern Pacific. Unpublished Ph.D. thesis, University of London.
Veeh, H. H., Burnett, W. C. and Soutar, A. (1973). *Science* **181**, 844.
Veeh, H. H., Calvert, S. E. and Price, N. B. (1974). *Mar. Chem.* **2**, 189.
Venkatarathnam, K. and McManus, D. A. (1973). *J. Sediment. Petrol.* **43**, 799–811.
Vincent, E. (1976). "Planktonic Foraminifera, Sediments and Oceanography of the Late Quaternary Southwest Indian Ocean", Alan Hancock Monographs in Marine Biology, 9. Alan Hancock Foundation, University of Southern California.
Vine, F. J. (1966). *Science* **154**, 1405–1415.
Vine, F. J. and Hess, H. H. (1970). *In* "The Sea" (A. E. Maxwell, Ed.), Vol. 4, pp. 587–662. Wiley Interscience, New York.
Vine, F. J. and Matthews, D. H. (1963). *Nature* **199**, 947–949.
Vinogradov, A. P. (1953). The elementary chemical composition of marine organisms. *Mem. Sears. Found. Mar. Res.* **2**, 647 pp.
von der Borch, C. C. and Rex, R. W. (1970). Initial Reports of the Deep Sea Drilling Project **5**, pp. 541–544. U.S. Govt Printing Office, Washington, D.C.
von Herzen, R., Green, K. E. and Williams, D. (1977). *Geol. Soc. Am. Abstr. Progr.* **9**, 1212–1213.
Wadsley, A. D., (1950). *J. Am. Chem. Soc.* **72**, 1781–1784.
Wadsley, A. D. (1953). *Acta Crystallogrophica* **6**, 433–438.
Walker, G. P. L. (1972). Initial Reports of the Deep Sea Drilling Project, 12, pp. 365–366. U.S. Govt Printing Office, Washington D.C.
Wang, F. F. H. and McKelvey, V. E. (1976). *In* "World Mineral Supplies: Assessment and Perspective" (G. J. S. Govett *et al.*, Eds), pp. 221–286. Elsevier, Amsterdam.
Watkins, N. D. and Kennett, J. P. (1971). *Science* **173**, 813–818.
Watkins, N. D. and Kennett, J. P. (1972). *Antarctic Res. Ser.* **19**, 273–293.
Wauschkuhn, A. and Gropper, H. (1975). *N. Jb. Miner. Abh.* **126**, 87–111.
Weiss, R. F. (1977). *Earth Planet. Sci. Letts* **37**, 257–262.
Weiss, R. F., Lonsdale, P., Lupton, J., Bainbridge, A. E. and Craig, H. (1977). *Nature* **267**, 600–603.
Wilcox, S., Mead, W. and Sorensen, P. E. (1972). *Proc. Marine Technol. Soc.* **8**, 499–506.
Willis, J. P. and Ahrens, L. H. (1962). *Geochim. Cosmochim. Acta* **26**, 751–764.
Winterhalter, B. (1966). *Geotels Julk* **69**, 1–77.
Winterhalter, B. (1980). *In* "International Monograph on the Geology and Geochemistry of Manganese" (I. M. Varentsov, Ed.). Publishing House of the Hungarian Academy of Sciences (in press).
Winterhalter, B. and Siivola, J. (1967). *C. R. Soc. Geol. Finlande* **39**, 161–172.
Wiseman, J. D. H. (1937). Basalts from the Carlsberg Ridge, Indian Ocean, Scient. Rep. John Murray Exped. 1933–34, 3, 1–30.

Wyrtki, K. (1971). "Oceanographic Atlas of the International Indian Ocean Expedition". U.S. National Science Foundation, Washington, D.C.

Yeats, R. and Hart, S. (1976). Initial Reports of the Deep Sea Drilling Project, 34. U.S. Govt Printing Office, Washington, D. C.

Yim, W. W. S. (1974). Some aspects of the geochemistry of tin and other elements in sediments off North Cornwall. Unpublished M. Phil. thesis, University of London.

Yim. W. W. S. (1978). *In* Proc. Eleventh Commonwealth Mining and Metallurgical Congress, Hong Kong, 1978. Institute of Mining and Metallurgy, London.

Yoshimura, T. (1934). *J. Fac. Sci. Hokkaido University* **4**, 289–297.

Young, J. A. (1939). *Am. J. Sci.* **237**, 798–810.

Zelenov, K. K. (1964). *Proc. Acad. Sci. U.S.S.R., Earth Sci. Sect.* **155**, 94–96.

Zingg, Th. (1935). *Schweiz. Min. Petrogr. Mitt.* **15**, 39–140.

Appendix

Chemical Analyses of Manganese Nodules from the Indian*, Atlantic* and Pacific† Oceans

Cruise	Vema 15	Vema 15	Vema 15	Vema 15
Sample no.	SBT 82	SBT 80	SBT 77	SBT 79
Type	trawl	trawl	trawl	trawl
Posn	surface	surface	surface	surface
Lat.	23°04'S	12°51'S	08°37'S	11°12'S
Long.	75°09'W	84°28'W	84°41'W	85°48'W
Depth(m)	4406	4640	4367	4460
Mn(%)	27·74	46·90	49·12	42·87
Fe(%)	12·32	1·34	0·73	4·79
Co(p.p.m.)	1050	250	60	650
Ni(p.p.m.)	10640	5290	1720	13130
Cu(p.p.m.)	7440	2530	1330	8710
Zn(p.p.m.)	4150	870	600	9130
Ca(%)	1·46	0·840	1·106	1·162

* Whole sample basis; analyst S. A. Moorby, Imperial College.
† Acid soluble fraction only; D. E. Garrett, University of Ottawa.

Cruise	Conrad 9	Conrad 11	Conrad 11	Conrad 11	Conrad 11
Sample no.	157	3	4	101	102
Type	core	dredge	dredge	core	core
Posn	top	—	—	top	top
Lat.	5°47·3′N	44°04′S	31°17′S	43°04′S	43°42′S
Long.	66°34·7′E	60°00′E	44°16′E	59°50′E	59°50′E
Depth(m)	4111	4713	2040	4806	4709
Mn(%)	17·8	17·1	1·87	0·42	14·8
Fe(%)	20·0	15·6	16·3	9·82	15·4
Co(p.p.m.)	1810	1750	820	125	1660
Ni(p.p.m.)	2710	6000	975	190	5180
Cu(p.p.m.)	760	1630	670	170	1310
Zn(p.p.m.)		840	540		
Pb(p.p.m.)	1070	1190	135	185	955
Ca(%)	2·06	1·96	2·30	1·32	2·28
Al(%)	1·38	1·74	5·66	4·06	1·70
Cd(p.p.m.)	—	—	—	—	—
Cr(p.p.m.)	—	—	—	—	—
Ti(p.p.m.)	—	—	—	—	—

Cruise	Conrad 12	Conrad 14	Conrad 14	Conrad 14	Conrad 14
Sample no.	5	1	2	3	4(a)
Type	dredge	dredge	dredge	dredge	dredge
Posn	—	—	—	—	—
Lat.	0°0′	37°57′S	32°34′S	36°45′S	23°26′S
Long.	75°02′E	26°41′E	36°35′E	44°46′E	50°49′E
Depth(m)	2286	3400	3000	3430	3950
Mn(%)	8·61	13·9	15·0	19·5	9·25
Fe(%)	15·6	18·0	17·4	17·8	14·5
Co(p.p.m.)	2570	4000	4300	6890	2020
Ni(p.p.m.)	1900	2100	2350	3660	1960
Cu(p.p.m.)	250	450	470	840	910
Zn(p.p.m.)	465	600	525	695	485
Pb(p.p.m.)	1060	1850	1710	2160	690
Ca(%)	8·14	1·76	1·97	2·01	1·41
Al(%)	1·91	1·64	1·50	1·31	4·00
Cd(p.p.m.)	—	—	—	—	—
Cr(p.p.m.)	—	—	—	—	—
Ti(p.p.m.)	—	—	—	—	—

Cruise	Conrad 14	Conrad 14	Conrad 14	Conrad 14	Conrad 14
Sample no.	4(b)	5	49	49	55
Type	dredge	dredge	core	core	core
Posn	—	—	top	200 cm	top
Lat.	23°26′S	19°13·9′S	10°38′S	10°38′S	18°12′S
Long.	50°49′E	61°01·3′E	100°52′E	100°52′E	101°10′E
Depth(m)	3950	3180	5273	5273	5991
Mn(%)	14·9	11·8	19·8	17·3	22·2
Fe(%)	18·7	23·8	11·8	13·1	9·70
Co(p.p.m.)	4010	2240	1200	1620	2290
Ni(p.p.m.)	2270	1690	7070	4120	8840
Cu(p.p.m.)	825	1330	5080	3200	6590
Zn(p.p.m.)	500	575			
Pb(p.p.m.)	1330	805	1100	1220	890
Ca(%)	1·66	2·31	1·56	1·32	1·24
Cd(p.p.m.)	—	—	—	—	—
Cr(p.p.m.)	—	—	—	—	—
Ti(p.p.m.)	—	—	—	—	—

Cruise	Conrad 14	Vema 14	Vema 16	Vema 16	Vema 16
Sample no.	59	99	80	80	81
Type	core	core	core	core	core
Posn	445 cm	TW top	70 cm	130 cm	top
Lat.	20°15′S	02°50′N	30°19·5′S	30°19·5′S	30°38′S
Long.	106°20′E	67°31′E	67°16′E	67°16′E	70°06·5′E
Depth(m)	5550	3087	4929	4929	4050
Mn(%)	16·2	12·3	12·9	12·4	11·1
Fe(%)	12·6	17·6	20·5	19·4	17·5
Co(p.p.m.)	2370	1580	2500	2640	1890
Ni(p.p.m.)	3470	2460	1780	1610	2610
Cu(p.p.m.)	1910	705	1330	1370	1140
Zn(p.p.m.)					
Pb(p.p.m.)	935	1110	1220	1210	830
Ca(%)	1·20	4·49	1·07	1·35	1·51
Al(%)	2·04	1·64	2·61	2·34	3·21
Cd(p.p.m.)	—	—	—	—	—
Cr(p.p.m.)	—	—	—	—	—
Ti(p.p.m.)	—	—	—	—	—

Cruise	Vema 24	Vema 28	Vema 28	Vema 29	Vema 29
Sample no.	210	14	15	18	34
Type	core	dredge	dredge	core	core
Posn	top	—	—	10 cm	top
Lat.	31°52′S	11°50′S	17°53′S	03°05′S	05°21′S
Long.	37°13′E	96°58′E	99°06′E	84°52′E	74°24′E
Depth(m)	4960	2925	5290	4435	4762
Mn(%)	12·6	20·3	10·1	17·0	21·4
Fe(%)	16·9	18·1	15·7	13·5	12·4
Co(p.p.m.)	1780	3990	1790	1720	1450
Ni(p.p.m.)	2130	3490	2260	5850	7880
Cu(p.p.m.)	915	445	1070	3870	4910
Zn(p.p.m.)		625	605		
Pb(p.p.m.)	1560	1860	915	1220	1320
Ca(%)	1·44	2·29	1·04	1·57	1·38
Al(%)	2·50	0·76	4·16	2·16	2·04
Cd(p.p.m.)	—	—	—	—	—
Cr(p.p.m.)	—	—	—	—	—
Ti(p.p.m.)	—	—	—	—	—

Cruise	Vema 29	Vema 29	Vema 29	Vema 29	Vema 29
Sample no.	43	54	59	67(a)	67(b)
Type	core	core	core	core	core
Posn	top	TW top	top	top	top
Lat.	12°20′S	22°36′S	19°00′S	32°40′S	32°40′S
Long.	75°05′E	64°59′E	73°08′E	66°23′E	66°23′E
Depth(m)	5150	4329	4954	4810	4810
Mn(%)	26·8	4·6	19·0	13·7	12·9
Fe(%)	5·60	11·9	15·0	15·1	17·5
Co(p.p.m.)	850	375	2140	2170	2120
Ni(p.p.m.)	13200	1960	6290	2950	2630
Cu(p.p.m.)	14400	1480	4150	1910	1760
Zn(p.p.m.)					
Pb(p.p.m.)	500	220	1140	1050	975
Ca(%)	1·40	1·41	1·48	1·91	1·34
Al(%)	2·09	6·41	2·50	3·71	3·26
Cd(p.p.m.)	—	—	—	—	—
Cr(p.p.m.)	—	—	—	—	—
Ti(p.p.m.)	—	—	—	—	—

Cruise	Vema 29	ANTP	ANTP	ANTP	ANTP
Sample no.	92	77D	86D	109D(a)	109D(b)
Type	core	dredge	dredge	dredge	dredge
Posn	top	—	—	—	—
Lat.	36°56′S	18°20′S	17°35′S	27°58′S	27°58′S
Long.	27°22′E	63°38′E	65°39′E	60°47·8′E	60°47·8′E
Depth(m)	4100	3450	2550	5440	5440
Mn(%)	14·0	6·93	14·8	10·5	17·1
Fe(%)	18·7	15·7	22·7	17·5	19·2
Co(p.p.m.)	1710	1020	1840	2510	3900
Ni(p.p.m.)	1670	1210	2080	920	1870
Cu(p.p.m.)	560	1120	900	575	605
Zn(p.p.m.)		365	535	355	385
Pb(p.p.m.)	1640	400	630	970	1500
Ca(%)	1·51	2·22	2·95	1·94	1·85
Al(%)	1·75	4·45	1·09	3·12	1·74
Cd(p.p.m.)	—	—	—	—	—
Cr(p.p.m.)	—	—	—	—	—
Ti(p.p.m.)	—	—	—	—	—

ANTP = Antipode.

Cruise	ANTP	ANTP	ANTP	ANTP	ANTP
Sample no.	113D	114D(a)	114D(b)	117D	136D
Type	dredge	dredge	dredge	dredge	dredge
Posn	—	—	—	—	—
Lat.	29°18′S	29°18′S	29°18′S	30°26′S	10°05′S
Long.	60°38·8′E	60°36′E	60°36′E	60°48′E	66°25′E
Depth(m)	5410	4570	4570	5730	2420
Mn(%)	8·50	13·7	8·76	12·3	1·50
Fe(%)	12·9	19·1	15·8	17·9	9·61
Co(p.p.m.)	1570	3370	2250	2810	335
Ni(p.p.m.)	1680	2140	1470	1380	580
Cu(p.p.m.)	1140	880	560	915	665
Zn(p.p.m.)	340	510	380	435	350
Pb(p.p.m.)	750	1420	900	1370	200
Ca(%)	1·84	1·84	1·66	2·14	1·47
Al(%)	3·04	1·85	2·06	2·55	7·46
Cd(p.p.m.)	—	—	—	—	—
Cr(p.p.m.)	—	—	—	—	—
Ti(p.p.m.)	—	—	—	—	—

Cruise	ANTP	ANTP	CIRCE	CIRCE	MONSOON
Sample no.	145D	153D	115D	116D	47D
Type	dredge	dredge	dredge	dredge	dredge
Posn	—	—	—	—	—
Lat.	7°20′S	2°03′S	25°50′S	23°30′S	17°20′S
Long.	57°56·3′E	53°06·5′E	65°31′E	65°42′E	84°24′E
Depth(m)	2420	4190	4450	4040	5010
Mn(%)	4·50	18·9	13·8	12·6	3·52
Fe(%)	15·7	14·9	19·2	20·6	5·89
Co(p.p.m.)	2840	1770	3020	3110	725
Ni(p.p.m.)	875	6160	2960	2270	750
Cu(p.p.m.)	850	3080	1400	1290	585
Zn(p.p.m.)	435	750	540	565	210
Pb(p.p.m.)	1620	1060	1080	1110	405
Ca(%)	2·50	1·61	1·89	1·89	0·58
Al(%)	4·29	1·68	2·73	2·49	7·60
Cd(p.p.m.)	—	—	—	—	—
Cr(p.p.m.)	—	—	—	—	—
Ti(p.p.m.)	—	—	—	—	—

Cruise	DODO	DODO	DODO	DODO	DODO
Sample no.	75P	110PG	112PG	114D	123D
Type	core	core	core	dredge	dredge
Posn	top	top	top	—	—
Lat.	14°28′S	21°31′S	22°41′S	24°07′S	10°25′S
Long.	93°49′E	78°01′E	76°01′E	72°26′E	63°15′E
Depth(m)	5185	4610	4940	4050	3115
Mn(%)	11·5	16·3	1·80	10·8	11·9
Fe(%)	6·45	12·3	6·36	24·0	22·0
Co(p.p.m.)	1180	2280	370	1550	1720
Ni(p.p.m.)	6010	7880	530	2250	1540
Cu(p.p.m.)	4110	3340	430	1670	860
Zn(p.p.m.)	565	710	275	565	590
Pb(p.p.m.)	465	1130	175	870	670
Ca(%)	1·15	1·27	1·03	1·82	2·05
Al(%)	6·09	2·36	6·94	2·31	1·63
Cd(p.p.m.)	—	—	—	—	—
Cr(p.p.m.)	—	—	—	—	—
Ti(p.p.m.)	—	—	—	—	—

Cruise	DODO	DODO	L/ARGO	L/ARGO	L/HORIZON
Sample no.	129V	143D	123G	155V	42V
Type	core	dredge	core	core	core
Posn	top	—	top	top	top
Lat.	25°20′S	24°47′S	31°27′S	31°04′S	25°42′S
Long.	60°45′E	72°41·5′E	61°49′E	36°43′E	105°22′E
Depth(m)	4940	4130	4200	4535	4840
Mn(%)	9·52	9·66	10·9	3·17	12·0
Fe(%)	15·0	23·3	16·3	14·5	13·5
Co(p.p.m.)	2280	1460	2210	405	2200
Ni(p.p.m.)	1470	2040	1920	645	3670
Cu(p.p.m.)	990	1780	1130	450	920
Zn(p.p.m.)	420	530	895	285	450
Pb(p.p.m.)	930	710	1000	365	980
Ca(%)	1·47	1·56	1·72	4·88	1·74
Al(%)	3·53	2·56	3·10	3·49	2·84
Cd(p.p.m.)	—	—	—	—	—
Cr(p.p.m.)	—	—	—	—	—
Ti(p.p.m.)	—	—	—	—	—

L/ARGO = Lusiad–Argo.
L/HORIZON = Lusiad–Horizon.

Cruise	A. BRUUN	A. BRUUN	A. BRUUN	A. BRUUN	A. BRUUN
Sample no.	367C(a)	367C(b)	368C(a)	368C(b)	369D
Type	trawl	trawl	trawl	trawl	grab
Posn	—	—	—	—	—
Lat.	22°37′S	22°37′S	23°00′S	23°00′S	24°04′S
Long.	41°22′E	41°22′E	38°37′E	38°37′E	36°16′E
Depth(m)	3250	3250	2995	2995	1720
Mn(%)	10·3	15·3	20·3	20·0	0·23
Fe(%)	33·3	19·6	10·6	2·35	47·9
Co(p.p.m.)	920	1160	1830	895	200
Ni(p.p.m.)	6140	8890	9090	7900	755
Cu(p.p.m.)	1360	2180	2690	1920	725
Zn(p.p.m.)	845	1050	945	1650	450
Pb(p.p.m.)	545	630	915	225	140
Ca(%)	1·21	1·75	1·66	7·73	0·54
Al(%)	1·43	2·08	2·58	1·25	1·10
Cd(p.p.m.)	—	—	—	—	—
Cr(p.p.m.)	—	—	—	—	—
Ti(p.p.m.)	—	—	—	—	—

A. BRUUN = Anton Brunn.

Cruise	A. BRUUN	A. BRUUN	A. BRUUN	A. BRUUN	A. BRUUN
Sample no.	369F	375G(a)	375G(b)	384B(a)	384B(b)
Type	dredge	dredge	dredge	core	core
Posn	—	—	—	top	top
Lat.	24°04′S	29°06′S	29°06′S	35°47′S	35°47′S
Long.	36°16′E	36°44′E	36°44′E	36°46′E	36°46′E
Depth(m)	1720	3890	3890	5350	5350
Mn(%)	3·20	12·3	36·5	11·7	7·47
Fe(%)	39·9	17·5	2·46	12·0	8·66
Co(p.p.m.)	460	2140	640	1480	1040
Ni(p.p.m.)	1910	1850	1200	3870	1670
Cu(p.p.m.)	550	695	2300	1810	1620
Zn(p.p.m.)	510	480	250	520	290
Pb(p.p.m.)	180	1540	500	1180	730
Ca(%)	0·73	1·64	0·52	1·21	1·13
Al(%)	1·32	1·74	2·25	2·78	4·17
Cd(p.p.m.)	—	—	—	—	—
Cr(p.p.m.)	—	—	—	—	—
Ti(p.p.m.)	—	—	—	—	—

Cruise	A. BRUUN	A. BRUUN	A. BRUUN	D.S.D.P. XXIV	VAL.
Sample no.	384C	386C	387C	234	13GK(a)
Type	trawl	core	dredge	core	R.core
Posn	—	top	—	3–7 cm	top
Lat.	35°51′S	32°55′S	31°54′S	4°29′N	29°13′S
Long.	36°46′E	35°19′E	34°21′E	51°13·5′E	50°39·5′E
Depth(m)	5450	1265	2700	4721	4877
Mn(%)	14·6	15·0	16·0	11·7	15·2
Fe(%)	13·1	9·69	19·0	9·15	16·0
Co(p.p.m.)	1690	3520	6050	1010	3000
Ni(p.p.m.)	4920	7380	3430	3460	2850
Cu(p.p.m.)	2280	1200	875	1730	1370
Zn(p.p.m.)	670	835	675	535	530
Pb(p.p.m.)	1320	1370	2180	360	1310
Ca(%)	1·40	5·34	1·23	0·92	1·52
Al(%)	2·83	1·74	1·47	3·27	2·45
Cd(p.p.m.)	—	—	—	—	9
Cr(p.p.m.)	—	—	—	—	25
Ti(p.p.m.)	—	—	—	—	9800

VAL. = Valdivia.

Cruise	Shack.	Shack.	Shack.	Shack.
Sample no.	1301D(a)	1301(b)	1303(a)	1303(b)
Type	dredge	dredge	dredge	dredge
Posn	—	—	—	—
Lat.	6°53′N	6°53′N	5°0·5′N	5°0·5′N
Long.	62°53′E	62°53′E	61°33′E	61°33′E
Depth(m)	3960	3960	2940	2940
Mn(%)	17·2	18·1	18·1	13·6
Fe(%)	21·7	18·3	22·3	20·4
Co(p.p.m.)	3740	2060	1830	1630
Ni(p.p.m.)	2450	2680	2270	1890
Cu(p.p.m.)	875	945	255	505
Zn(p.p.m.)	490	550	510	560
Pb(p.p.m.)	1330	1000	1150	980
Ca(%)	1·76	1·68	2·19	2·26
Al(%)	1·14	1·55	0·44	1·56
Cd(p.p.m.)	—	—	—	—
Cr(p.p.m.)	—	—	—	—
Ti(p.p.m.)	—	—	—	—

Shack. = Shackleton

Cruise	Shack.	Shack.	Shack.	Shack.	Shack.
Sample no.	1307D(a)	1307D(b)	1315D	1317D	1317RC
Type	dredge	dredge	dredge	dredge	R.core
Posn	—	—	—	—	—
Lat.	2°35′S	2°35′S	0°16′N	0°12′N	0°11′N
Long.	57°16′E	57°16′E	55°41′E	55°38′E	55°35·5′E
Depth(m)	3440	3940	1200	2320	1550
Mn(%)	16·2	15·5	24·7	18·9	2·23
Fe(%)	20·6	16·2	15·5	19·3	15·2
Co(p.p.m.)	3620	1760	10400	3000	14500
Cu(p.p.m.)	270	4380	4760	3370	4240
Zn(p.p.m.)	770	2580	430	420	170
Pb(p.p.m.)	1370	1050	2530	1810	2410
Ca(%)	2·03	1·71	3·07	2·04	2·20
Al(%)	1·63	2·55	0·58	0·83	0·51
Cd(p.p.m.)	—	—	—	—	—
Cr(p.p.m.)	—	—	—	—	—
Ti(p.p.m.)	—	—	—	—	—

Cruise	Shack.	Shack.	Shack.	Shack.	Shack.
Sample no.	1323GC	1325D	1326D	73:077·18	73:077·33
Type	core	dredge	dredge	dredge	dredge
Posn	top	—	—	—	—
Lat.	1°22′N	0°9′N	1°13·5′S	36°31′N	36°31′N
Long.	5°37′E	55°10′E	5°01·5′E	11°46·5′W	11°46·5′W
Depth(m)	2860	1500	2800	1600	1600
Mn(%)	13·0	16·5	18·3	12·3	10·6
Fe(%)	15·8	18·3	19·4	18·8	18·1
Co(p.p.m.)	1810	5300	5450	5500	1950
Ni(p.p.m.)	1750	3580	2850	2350	4600
Cu(p.p.m.)	1240	375	695	420	3300
Zn(p.p.m.)	400	575	495	580	560
Pb(p.p.m.)	710	1850	1560	2600	1300
Ca(%)	2·37	2·29	1·85	1·70	0·68
Al(%)	3·19	1·73	1·42	1·48	3·45
Cd(p.p.m.)	—	—	—	10	10
Cr(p.p.m.)	—	—	—	150	40
Ti(p.p.m.)	—	—	—	7350	4750

Cruise	Shack.	Shack.	Shack.	Shack.	Shack.
Sample no.	1318D	1320D	1321D	1322GC	1323D
Type	dredge	dredge	dredge	core	dredge
Posn	—	—	—	top	—
Lat.	0°15′N	1°12·5′N	1°19′N	1°17′N	1°21′N
Long.	55°39′E	56°37′E	56°35·5′E	56°34·5′E	56°36·5′E
Depth(m)	1490	860	1890	1700	2800
Mn(%)	17·6	3·72	16·0	16·9	6·23
Fe(%)	16·7	7·94	21·7	30·7	29·0
Co(p.p.m.)	8870	2250	4080	3920	2170
Ni(p.p.m.)	3190	1970	2560	2500	1170
Cu(p.p.m.)	190	265	445	480	380
Zn(p.p.m.)	470	380	580	450	550
Pb(p.p.m.)	2300	1150	2080	1940	1740
Ca(%)	5·98	26·8	1·95	1·79	1·39
Al(%)	0·5	0·54	1·18	0·34	1·66
Cd(p.p.m.)	—	—	—	—	—
Cr(p.p.m.)	—	—	—	—	—
Ti(p.p.m.)	—	—	—	—	—

Cruise	Shack.	Shack.	Shack.	Shack.	Shack.
Sample no.	73:100·2	73:100·3	73:169·1	73:169·3	73:169·6
Type	dredge	dredge	dredge	dredge	dredge
Posn	—	—	—		
Lat.	35°08′N	35°08′N	36°17·5′N	36°17·5′N	36°17·5′N
Long.	12°56′W	12°56′W	12°35′W	12°35′W	12°35′W
Depth(m)	1450	1450	3700	3700	3700
Mn(%)	13·9	13·8	11·8	6·96	11·4
Fe(%)	19·5	18·7	15·5	26·4	13·4
Co(p.p.m.)	7900	7350	1400	1100	1300
Ni(p.p.m.)	2450	2950	1900	2000	2000
Cu(p.p.m.)	425	540	1450	2000	1400
Zn(p.p.m.)	570	520	550	660	490
Pb(p.p.m.)	2550	2650	1100	1250	1050
Ca(%)	3·60	6·70	1·80	0·49	1·50
Al(%)	1·70	1·66	3·18	2·84	3·26
Cd(p.p.m.)	10	10	8	7	14
Cr(p.p.m.)	80	50	38	68	50
Ti(p.p.m.)	8100	9100	4200	4550	4950

Cruise	Shack.	Shack.	Shack.	Shack.	Shack.
Sample no.	73:169·14	73:169·17	73:169·20	73:171·15	73:178·2
Type	dredge	dredge	dredge	dredge	dredge
Posn	—	—	—		
Lat.	36°17·5′N	36°17·5′N	36°17·5′N	36°18·5′N	36°02′N
Long.	12°35′W	12°35′W	12°35′W	12°34·5′W	12°51′W
Depth(m)	3700	3700	3700	3800	4600
Mn(%)	7·0	7·82	8·10	2·60	9·63
Fe(%)	14·3	12·7	17·2	27·9	20·5
Co(p.p.m.)	1750	2150	1850	290	1700
Ni(p.p.m.)	1100	1600	1300	1350	2200
Cu(p.p.m.)	1200	1200	1300	2000	1750
Zn(p.p.m.)	420	420	550	540	560
Pb(p.p.m.)	920	920	1250	1050	1500
Ca(%)	0·82	1·60	0·97	0·31	0·69
Al(%)	3·76	5·09	3·82	3·23	2·97
Cd(p.p.m.)	10	13	12	6	7
Cr(p.p.m.)	55	80	45	65	45
Ti(p.p.m.)	4750	5350	5600	5850	4500

Index